Zionist Israel and Apartheid South Africa

This book is a comparison of two ethnic-national states which have been in conflict – apartheid South Africa and Zionist Israel – and how internal dissent has developed. In particular it examines the evolution of effective white protest in South Africa and explores the reasons why comparably powerful movements have not emerged in Israel.

The book reveals patterns of behaviour shared by groups in both cases. It argues that although the role played by protest groups in peace building may be limited, a tipping point, or 'magic point', can become as significant as other major factors. It highlights the role played by intermediate variables that affect the pathways of protest groups: such as changes in the international system; the visions and strategies of resistance movements and their degree of success; the economic relationship between the dominant and dominated side; and the legitimacy of the ideology in power (apartheid or Zionism).

Although the politics and roles of protest groups in both cases share some similarities, differences remain. Whilst white protest groups moved towards an inclusive peace agenda that adopts the ANC vision of a united non-racial democratic South Africa, the Jewish Israeli protest groups are still, by majority, entrenched in their support for an exclusive Jewish state. And as such, they support separation between the two peoples and a limited division of mandatory Palestine/'Eretz Israel'. This timely book sheds light on a controversial and explosive political issue: Israel being compared to apartheid South Africa.

Amneh Daoud Badran is Lecturer and Head of the Political Science Department, Al-Quds University, Palestine, and Honorary University Fellow, University of Exeter, UK. From 2001–2005, she was the Director of the Jerusalem Centre for Women, actively involved in Israeli–Palestinian peace-building initiatives, and received The Liberty Award by *Dialogue on Diversity* in 2003 in recognition of her work for the cause of conciliation and human rights.

Routledge studies on the Arab–Israeli conflict
Series editor: Mick Dumper
University of Exeter

The Arab–Israeli conflict continues to be the centre of academic and popular attention. This series brings together the best of the cutting edge work now being undertaken by predominantly new and young scholars. Although largely falling within the field of political science the series also includes interdisciplinary and multidisciplinary contributions.

1 **International Assistance to the Palestinians after Oslo**
   Political guilt, wasted money
   Anne Le More

2 **Palestinian Political Prisoners**
   Identity and community
   Esmail Nashif

3 **Understanding the Middle East Peace Process**
   Israeli academia and the struggle for identity
   Asima A. Ghazi-Bouillon

4 **Palestinian Civil Society**
   Foreign donors and the power to promote and exclude
   Benoît Challand

5 **The Jewish-Arab City**
   Spatio-politics in a mixed community
   Haim Yacobi

6 **Zionist Israel and Apartheid South Africa**
   Civil society and peace building in ethnic-national states
   Amneh Daoud Badran

Zionist Israel and Apartheid South Africa

Civil society and peace building in ethnic-national states

Amneh Daoud Badran

LONDON AND NEW YORK

First published 2010
by Routledge
2 Park Square, Milton Park, Abingdon, Oxon OX14 4RN

Simultaneously published in the USA and Canada
by Routledge
270 Madison Ave, New York, NY 10016

Routledge is an imprint of the Taylor & Francis Group, an informa business

© 2010 Amneh Daoud Badran

Typeset in Times by Wearset Ltd, Boldon, Tyne and Wear
Printed and bound in Great Britain by TJI Digital, Padstow, Cornwall

All rights reserved. No part of this book may be reprinted or reproduced or utilized in any form or by any electronic, mechanical, or other means, now known or hereafter invented, including photocopying and recording, or in any information storage or retrieval system, without permission in writing from the publishers.

British Library Cataloguing in Publication Data
A catalogue record for this book is available from the British Library

Library of Congress Cataloging in Publication Data
A catalog record for this book has been requested

ISBN10: 0-415-48981-4 (hbk)
ISBN10: 0-203-87250-9 (ebk)

ISBN13: 978-0-415-48981-2 (hbk)
ISBN13: 978-0-203-87250-5 (ebk)

To my Mother

Contents

	List of illustrations	viii
	Foreword	ix
	Acknowledgements	xi
	List of abbreviations	xii
	Introduction	1
1	Historical backgrounds and political developments in both conflicts: a comparison	25
2	Political systems and civil society in apartheid South Africa and Zionist Israel	52
3	The politics and roles of white protest groups in apartheid South Africa	88
4	The politics and roles of Israeli (Jewish) protest groups	123
5	Conclusion based on comparative analysis	172
	Appendices	198
	Notes	211
	Bibliography	237
	Index	249

Illustrations

Figures

A.1	The ECC's launching declaration	209
A.2	A list of the ECC's supporting member organizations	210

Tables

I.1	Research variables	6
1.1	South Africa and madatory Palestine – area and population	42
3.1	Categorization of white protest groups	94
4.1	Classification of Israeli protest groups	139
A.1	The different categories for South African white protest groups	205
A.2	The different categories of Israeli (Jewish) protest groups	206
A.3	Peace organizations in 1980s South Africa	207
A.4	The leading peace and conflict-resolution organizations in South Africa	208
A.5	The leading anti-apartheid non-governmental organizations in apartheid South Africa	208

Foreword

In recent years, scholars and journalists alike began to consider seriously the benefit of comparing apartheid South Africa to the Israel/Palestine case study. It began with a series of newspaper reports and it proceeded with scholarly articles and one or two monographs. These previous works hitherto validate the need to pursue further this project. The historical background of both case studies is grounded in the age of colonialism and modern nationalism. The practices and ideologies behind the white colonization of South Africa and Palestine were quite similar. The settlers sought to control the land and the native population by variety of means stretching from land control, through segregation, ethnic cleansing and finally modern-day systems of legal discrimination.

The historiographical and sociological comparisons have so far produced a better understanding of the origins of the Zionist project, the failure of the anti-colonialist Palestinian project and illuminated in a new light the current predicament on the ground. As with all comparative studies it has also exposed the significant differences between the two cases, always an inevitable and useful outcome of any comparative exercise.

This book constitutes a very important and valuable contribution to the comparative endeavour. First and foremost as it touches on a component of the two case studies, which was ignored hitherto. The role of the peace movements in both places escaped the attention of those who were already juxtaposing the two cases. As readers of this book will be quick to learn when the comparison focuses on this subject matter, the differences of the case studies become apparent and not only the similarities.

But the attention to the peace movements highlights another aspect of the comparison, which is not entirely academic but nonetheless at the heart of the matter. The impulse for comparing apartheid South Africa and the Israel/Palestine reality was never purely scholarly. The search for a comparison is always pursued by people who are committed to peace and reconciliation in Israel and Palestine. There is no better way of finding out what worked in this respect in the South African case and why it failed to materialize so far in the other case. And much of what is written in this excellent book is food for thought in this direction. It focuses on the role of the NGOs, peace movements and individuals within the greater matrix of international forces, regional actors and governments in bringing about a change to a part of the world that needs it as badly as apartheid South Africa craved for it, in its time.

The book concentrates on protest groups within the general framework of a civil society that as a rule does not question the agenda formulated by the political and military elites. As such it constitutes also a valuable contribution to that well trodden field of civil-society studies. The empirical data and the theoretical framework chosen open new vistas to this somewhat elusive term and concept. This is brought home by the serious effort invested in finding adequate classifications of protest groups; a typology which helps to explain the various dimensions in which human beings try to challenge effectively the dominant ideological consensus, be it apartheid or Zionism. This is also examined against the various models of civil societies that developed in both countries and which also serve as an explanation why in one place, South Africa, protest movements were successful, and in the other, Israel, they are still a failure.

The book leaves one with a mixed feeling, if we would take it as departure point for looking ahead into the future. The book provided me with a very convincing explanation for the failure of the Israeli protest movement to achieve the same impact on their society as their South African counterparts attained. But it also accentuates the possibility of transforming these Israeli movements into a useful tool in confronting the hegemonic ideology of Zionism, with the help of external pressure and intervention. This was my own take from the book, others would find they are energized in other directions, and this is what makes this book such a good read.

Professor Ilan Pappé

Acknowledgements

The process of conducting doctoral research and then developing it into a book is not easy. It is a challenging and demanding course of action, during which support is certainly needed on various levels. The rather lonely process I lived through was eased with the support of a number of persons whom I would like to acknowledge and thank.

I thank Professor Michael Dumper, my PhD supervisor, whose intellectual support has been crucial to the development of this study; the testing process of writing has become more illuminating as result of his guidance. Many thanks are due to my external and internal examiners, Professors Raymond Hinnebusch and Ilan Pappé, who provided additional insights to my study and encouraged me to seek publication.

My sincere thanks are to my family, sisters and brothers who have been there for me whenever I needed their support. Thank you Jameeleh, Muhammad, Itidal, Ismael and Suad for your unconditional love and care!

I would also like to thank my friends in the Palestine Solidarity Campaign (Exeter branch), and my loving friends from the Women to Women for Peace; especially Sylvia Baker, Joy Uglow and Gail Parfitt. In addition, I would like to convey special thanks to my two friends Jannettja Longyear and David Chappel for their kindness during my stay in their house while living in Britain. Also, I would like to thank my two dear friends: Amira Moosa and Amal Ghussein.

My thanks go to all of my interviewees, both South African and Israeli, for sharing their time and knowledge with me. I would also like to thank friends and colleagues who were helpful in providing contacts and material relevant to my research.

I would like to thank the following for permission to reprint material in *Zionist Israel and Apartheid South Africa*: Palgrave Macmillan for permission to reprint Table 7.1 "Peace Organisations in 1980s South Africa", from page 165, *Peace Building in Northern Ireland, Israel and South Africa*, edited by Colin Knox and Padraic Quirk, ISBN HB 978-0-333-68189-3. Oxford University Press Inc. for kind permission to reprint Tables 4.1 and 4.2 from chapter "South Africa and the Role of Peace and Conflict-Resolution Organizations in the Struggle against Apartheid", by Rupert Taylor, pp. 72, 78, from *Mobilizing for Peace: Conflict Resolution in Northern Ireland, Israel/Palestine and South Africa*, edited by Gidron, Katz and Hasefeld (2002). By permission of Oxford University Press, Inc., www.oup.com.

Finally, I also acknowledge the very good work of my proofreader, Mrs Lindy Ayubi. Thank you Lindy!

Abbreviations

AIC	Alternative Information Centre
ANC	The African National Congress
AZASU	Azanian Student Union
BS	Black Sash
B'tselem	The Israeli Information Centre for Human Rights in the Occupied Territories
CCR	The Centre for Conflict Resolution
CD	The Congress of Democrats (white)
CIS	The Centre for Inter-group Studies (later named the Centre for Conflict Resolution)
CISA	The Christian Institute for Southern Africa
COSATU	The Congress of South African Trade Unions
CPC	The Coloured People's Congress
CPS	The Council for Peace and Security
CWP	Coalition of Women for Peace
ECC	The End Conscription Campaign
ECF	Economic Cooperation Foundation
FFF	Five Freedoms Forum
GS	Gush Shalom
IBM	The Inkatha Black Movement
ICAHD	The Israeli Committee Against House Demolishing
IDASA	The Institute for a Democratic Alternative for South Africa
INC	The Indian National Congress
MW	Machsom Watch
NP	The National Party
NPG	New Profile Group
NUSAS	The National Union of South Africa Students
OPT	The Occupied Palestinian Territories
PLO	The Palestine Liberation Organization
PN	Peace Now
PNA	The Palestinian National Authority
PP	The Progressive Party
PPC	The Peres Peace Centre

RHR	Rabbis for Human Rights
SACP	The South African Communist Party
SAIRR	The South African Institute of Race Relations
SANSCO	The South African National Students' Congress
UDF	The United Democratic Front
UP	The United Party
WIB	Women in Black
YG	Yesh Gvul

Introduction

The idea of the book

In April 1964 Nelson Mandela, who was to become one of the world's most iconic figures, spoke at the opening of the Rivonia Trial in Pretoria:

> During my lifetime I have dedicated myself to this struggle of the African people. I have fought against white domination, and I have fought against black domination. I have cherished the ideal of a democratic and free society in which all persons live together in harmony and with equal opportunities. It is an ideal which I hope to live for and to achieve. But if needs be, it is an ideal for which I am prepared to die.[1]

Mandela's ideal was the vision of the dominated side, in which the black majority, including the 'coloureds' and the Indians, would organize themselves in a resistance movement to get rid of oppression and build an inclusive free society. Thirty years later, in 1994, the year that apartheid formally collapsed, his vision had to a significant extent been achieved.

This prompts some valid questions. What was the role of the white dissent or protest groups in building peace? Were their politics, their political platforms and their subsequent roles significant in the quest to reach a settlement that adopted the principles spoken of by Mandela – principles that conform to the universal values of human rights? What shaped the political views of the white groups, and how did they evolve over the years?

These are among the main questions that this book aims to answer as part of a comparative research model. The other case study is that of Israeli Jewish protest groups, where the same questions are raised, examined and answered. The intention is to identify the similarities and the differences in their respective visions, positions and roles. It will also be possible to draw out patterns within each case and across the two cases.

In the realm of protest, the characteristics and functions of protest groups differ from case to case. Existing political settings and subsequent challenges usually shape the politics, priorities and roles of protest groups. In areas of conflict, a high percentage of protest groups become active in different initiatives that seek peace building and/or conflict resolution across the divide. This has been the situation with the two cases chosen for examination here. However, it is not the intention to address peace-building initiatives across the divide between the dominant–dominated sides in both cases, as is more usually done. Instead the study focuses on protest activism in the dominant communities of apartheid South Africa and Zionist Israel – i.e. the white population and the Jews – and compares the politics, political platforms and roles of both.

To do this protest groups in both countries were studied as components of their respective civil societies; therefore the relation between the state political system and civil society serves as the theoretical framework. The author believes that an understanding of the existing political systems of these two ethnic-national states and their effects on their respective civil societies illuminates how, in both cases, the politics, political positions and the subsequent roles of protest groups have been shaped and played out. Details of the research methodology are explained in more detail below.

In both ethnic-national states, protest groups flourished as part of the quest for building peace. While a majority of scholars and activists have in both cases been critical of the role of protest groups from the dominant side, and have claimed that this role has been marginal or even insignificant, this study argues differently. It maintains that their 'marginal' role can, at a critical point, prove to be essential once it has been combined with other factors (as, for example, a shift in the balance of power), that allow for a political settlement to take place. Thus, once other conditions become ready for a political breakthrough, their perceived 'insignificance' over a period of time can be shown to be incorrect, and, as this research will prove, the insignificant can become vital. The argument of this book therefore provides a fresh perspective on the politics and role/s of protest groups as a component of civil society and as contributors to the public space, i.e. where different powers and interests compete for shaping the moral order of society and obtaining the support of the state.

At this point, the author wishes briefly to explain two conceptual issues pertaining to this book and to highlight the existence of meta-conflict in the Israeli–Palestinian conflict, an essential element that explains a major difference between the two case studies.

First, the term used here is 'peace building', rather than 'peace making'. Although some scholars and practitioners use the terms interchangeably, the author accepts that there is a distinction between them. In the field of peace studies and conflict resolution, the term 'peace making' is usually used in association with formal processes at the leadership level, to broker a deal between conflicting parties. With this type of process, power politics usually dictates and produces a win/lose result. On the other hand, the term 'peace building' is associated with a process that aims to build peace at different levels: grassroots, middle-rank leadership and high leadership.

For example, in his model of peace building John Paul Lederach stresses the need to address the complexity of "multiple actors, pursuing a multiplicity of actions and initiatives, at numerous levels of social relationships in an interdependent setting at the same time".[2] His model also emphasizes that peace-building processes pass through three stages: transition, transformation and reconciliation.[3] In such processes, one paradigm of power relations is given up for an alternative paradigm that addresses the needs of both parties as well as the history of the conflict and can therefore move towards structural change. In other words, the process of power politics represents a settlement process, while one that addresses the felt needs and interests of all conflicting parties represents a resolution,[4] or peace-building process. As such, in the context of researching protest groups as units of analysis, the term 'peace building' is more accurate. However, it should be made clear that its use does not imply that all or most protest groups in and across the two cases have abandoned the mindset of power politics, even though they have acted at different societal levels.

The second conceptual issue has to do with the author's use of the term 'protest groups' rather than 'peace groups' or any other. There are two reasons for this. First, in both cases protest groups themselves have not used a common label. The Israeli groups chose to label themselves 'peace groups' while South African white groups referred to themselves as 'anti-apartheid groups'. The second reason, which is no less important, is that 'peace' as a word has many meanings: in the Palestinian–Israeli context, it has been misused and/or overused to such an extent that it is difficult to refer to it in a positive or neutral way. Some would even describe it as a contaminated word. Thus, the author felt that it was important to have a term that was neutral enough and could be used to refer to both cases with ease. The term 'protest' meets this function.

The term 'protest group' is used to refer to groups that developed ideas and ran activities with the aim of building peace in their conflict areas. Some protest groups took the form of opposing the existing ideology in power and its state political system, as in the case of South Africa where, by the mid-1980s, most white protest groups stood against apartheid and for regime change. Others continue/d to associate themselves with their state's exclusive ideology and prevailing consensus, and seek/sought compromise that would be of benefit to the dominant side. This has also been the case with a majority of Israeli protest groups. In the Israeli Zionist/anti-Zionist divide most of them belong to the Zionists.

A third aspect to be highlighted in this book is a major difference that exists between the two case studies. It stems from the existence of meta-conflict, which represents a strong presence in the Israeli–Palestinian conflict. Meta-conflict means differing over what the conflict is all about, i.e. "a conflict about what the conflict is about".[5] This political reality translated itself into the development of different versions of peace, no agreement as to the causes of the conflict and, as such, no agreement on the end result. These disagreements exist among the Israeli protest groups, as well as between them and Palestinian civil-society organizations.

This was not the case in apartheid South Africa. By the mid-1980s, a joint platform had been agreed upon – that of a united, non-racial and democratic South Africa. The South African white protest groups never stood for a separate

4 *Introduction*

historical narrative. They did not legitimize the colonial history of white settlers, and they sought a joint future based on equal political rights. In the case of Israel, most Israeli protest groups stand for a separate historical narrative since they believe in the legitimacy of the Zionist settler project in Palestine and, as such, seek separation and the Palestinians' acceptance of the legitimacy of that narrative.

The following sections explain the methodology used in this book, including the relation between the different variables involved, and discuss a number of principles, values or concepts that have been associated in both instances with peace-building initiatives. These concepts – equality, justice, racism, truth and peace – are examined with reference to their broad literature and their connection to the two case studies. This conceptual background provides initial thoughts about the political orientations and characteristics of white and Jewish protest groups in the two conflict areas. From this it becomes possible to detect how far protest groups have moved from their governments' positions on these concepts, and whether protest groups are primarily pragmatic, principled, selective or practical, or offer a combination of these qualities. The final part of this Introduction includes a brief literature review.

Research methodology

As noted, this is a comparative study of two cases that share many similarities and differences. The cases researched were not selected randomly (the qualitative method used is discussed below), but were chosen on the basis of what the research wished to explain – the dependent variable(s) or outcome variable(s), which are the politics and role(s) of protest groups in peace building in the two settler ethnic-national states. Both states – Zionist Israel and apartheid South Africa – have lived, or live, in conflict. To better understand the Israeli case, where protest groups have mushroomed, it was logical to compare them with the case of apartheid South Africa, which witnessed a similar phenomenon during the quest for peace. The comparison also contributes to a better understanding of the politics and role of white protest groups in South Africa. The dependant variables, i.e. both sets of protest groups or units of analysis, are each studied in relation to an independent (causal) variable that is the political system in both ethnic-national states.

Importantly, with reference to the latter, the book argues that the independent variable, i.e. the two political systems, does not represent democratic systems. The criterion used is that of compatibility with civic nationalism or civic public culture,[6] which is a prerequisite to an inclusive democracy that protects liberties and represents and serves all its citizens equally. Inclusive democracy contrasts with totalitarian and authoritarian systems and other systems that adopt an exclusive ethnic nationalism. Both examined states adopt/ed the latter and consequently developed restricted or exclusive 'democracies' or a 'masters' democracy'[7] for the ethnic group in power. By their nature, they were not able to incorporate the values, laws and procedures of inclusive nationalism, or, in other words, that of civic citizenship of a liberal democracy. The political characteristics of both systems are specified in Chapter 2.

In addition to the book's focal variables – the dependant variables and the independent variable that are discussed in detail in the following chapters – it is important to highlight a number of intermediate or contextual variables: these affect the environment in which the focal variables function and consequently influence their positions and modes of behaviour.[8] To a significant extent, they determine the different pathways taken by the different variables and, as such, produce variations in the outcomes of the two cases. Unlike the dependant and independent variables they are not examined in detail, but will be discussed briefly or referred to as appropriate. They include external factors and 'objective' realities. They can be organized into three groupings: changes at the international level, e.g. the fall of the Berlin Wall; the visions and strategies of the resistance movements in both conflict areas, i.e. the PLO (Palestine Liberation Organization) and the ANC (African National Congress) and their respective successes and failures; and finally a number of internal factors, some of which are products of strategic policies undertaken by both ethnic states as part of shaping their strategic interests and relations with the dominated side.

Among the latter is the demographic balance that both political systems developed vis-à-vis the Other. In the case of apartheid South Africa, the apartheid political system, as its predecessor, ran a 'masters' 'democracy' in which an ethnic minority governed the majority. In the case of Zionist Israel, the Zionist movement aimed for a Jewish ethnic state where the Jews would be the majority. As a result, different schemes were implemented to transfer the indigenous population, the Palestinians, and to a great extent have succeeded in achieving this aim. Since its establishment in 1948, Israel has run a 'masters' democracy' vis-à-vis a minority of Palestinian citizens. After having conquered the rest of mandatory Palestine in 1967, the state of Israel did not grant citizenship status to the Palestinian population there but left them stateless and under its military occupation. In the two cases these different demographic realities affected the political environment of protest, and in both instances influenced the politics and roles of the protest groups.

Another example of the intermediate variable is that of state legitimacy. From an early stage the South African political system lost its claim to be a legitimate democratic system. It was based on racial grounds and exercised extensive discriminatory laws and policies, which more or less doomed it to worldwide condemnation. This has not been the case with Zionist Israel. Israel has managed to promote itself as a Jewish liberal democracy, or even as the only democracy in the backward Middle East. Its ethnically-based nationalist ideology, its exclusive 'democratic' system and subsequently its discriminatory laws and policies towards the Palestinians have received little attention over the decades. Only in the past ten years or so have some critical voices begun to question the notions of exclusivity built into Israel's ethnic political system and that have promoted a 'masters' democracy'. This intermediate variable has also been crucial in determining the pathways followed by certain protest groups.

6 *Introduction*

The economic relations developed by both political systems vis-à-vis the Other, and the support given to the respective resistance movements by neighbouring states, also constitute other intermediate variables. The relationship of economic interdependency in the case of South Africa prepared the ground for a different outcome (an inclusive settlement) from that in the Palestinian–Israeli conflict, where Palestinian economic dependency contributed to a different political discourse of protest. A majority of Israeli protest groups continue to play a significant role in forming opinions in favour of ideas that promote separation, evidence of which is seen in Chapter 4. As to support received from neighbouring states, as briefly noted in Chapters 1 and 5, it too had a different impact in both cases.

As well as changes at the international level, one should remember another intermediate variable, i.e. that compared with the white South Africans, the Zionists have had a substantial advantage through shaping the policies of the hegemonic powers (the United Kingdom and later the United States of America). As to other intermediary variables, they are referred to or discussed briefly throughout the book as appropriate. The research variables are shown in Table I.1.

The research process adopted in the study was that of a wheel model; that is to say, the author did not adopt a linear research model whereby:

1 a theory is specified;
2 a hypothesis is developed;
3 data is specified and collected;
4 data is analysed; and
5 research is written.[9]

Unlike in the linear model, in a wheel process these components are not followed as a set of steps. Instead the research process may take the shape of a circle, where one component leads to another, and changes and repetitions can occur over and over again during the process until all components are illuminated.[10]

Table I.1 Research variables

Types of variables	*Research variables*
Independent variable	The political system (in both cases)
Dependant variables	The politics and roles of protest groups (in both cases)
Intermediate or contextual variables	E.g. visions and strategies of both resistance movements, the ANC and the PLO Changes on the international level, e.g. collapse of the Soviet Union Economic relations between the dominant and dominated side State legitimacy

At the initial empirical level, the author collected and analysed data on protest groups in both apartheid South Africa and Zionist Israel. Investigating the empirical world of the politics, political platforms and roles of the protest groups led eventually to the development of the theoretical approach of the study – the conceptual framework – which was state–civil society relations. This process, whereby the researcher takes the empirical world as the starting point to further develop the chosen problem and dependent variables, and then attempts to build a theoretical explanation, is described by Silbergh as an "inductive research approach".[11] What has been adopted here can thus be described as a comparative qualitative research design with an inductive approach.

This process has sharpened the research question and hypothesis. The research question asks: what are the politics, political platforms and roles of protest groups from the dominant community in settler ethnic-national states that are (or have been) in conflict? When speaking about the politics of protest groups, it should be made clear that this entails specifying whether they are liberal or leftist, and where they stand along a continuum of inclusivity versus exclusivity. Do they promote a (just) inclusive peace or promote a compromise that benefits the dominant group and keeps its structure of exclusivity? As to the political platforms of protest groups, they are based in the first place on the politics adopted by the different protest groups. They manifest their positions in more detail and expose their ideas and activities in more concrete ways. With regard to the roles of protest groups, they are meant to examine whether the political ideas, discourse and activities of groups are effective in altering the overriding consensus among the dominant societies towards a peace-enabling direction that could make a difference when the conditions and balance of power are right; and also in checking how far they alter this direction, i.e. whether they move towards a rights-based inclusive peace or promote compromise that benefits the dominant side.

As such, the research hypothesis examines whether or not protest groups make a difference in peace building, and whether they promote an inclusive (just) peace or a partial settlement that benefits the status quo. It also verifies whether the intermediate variables between the system and outcomes determine the different pathways that can be taken to deal with contradictions and legitimacy problems in both settler-ethnic states; and to deal with the ongoing conflicts that they produce.

Most scholars and activists who have addressed, or been active in, the researched protest groups have argued that their roles in peace building were/have been marginal, minimal or ineffective and that in certain aspects they have perpetuated the status quo of oppression. They argue that this is due to their small size and consequently their small level of influence. Others refer to the politics and political platforms from which, on many occasions, the researched groups have continued to protest, within the confines of the consensus developed by both systems of exclusionary 'democracies' and their exclusionary civil societies.

As the research process evolved, the study developed a somewhat different argument. It contends that in both cases, the role of protest groups in peace-building processes is not as limited and marginal as most scholars and practitioners perceive it to be. In both these ethnic-national states, functioning as components of

8   *Introduction*

a highly exclusivist civil society has restricted their membership size or numbers. Nevertheless, as the research demonstrates, in terms of shaping or preserving the existing moral order and promoting parameters for projected settlement/s, they have played significant roles in developing political discourses and elements of compromise which, at a 'magical moment',[12] become/became crucial. This crucial role is not necessarily inclusive and rights-based. It is argued, in addition, that the intermediate variables are determinable factors in shaping the pathways of such a role and outcome. This contention is thoroughly tested in Chapter 5 where all the findings are analysed in relation to each other.

As qualitative research, the study sought evidence in kind, not in numbers. It used interviews as a major research method and semi-structured interviews were conducted with (former) activists, leaders of protest groups, church leaders and academics in both Israel and South Africa. A number of the interviewees represented an elite[13] in both civil societies,[14] and some even combined an elitist status in both the informal and formal sectors. Before choosing the semi-structured interview method, a few pilot interviews were held, and changes were then made in the structure and questions of the interviews according to the interviewees' experiences and the research needs. Some sections of the interviews were therefore more structured than others. Over forty interviews were conducted with the Israeli side (during the summers of 2004 and 2005), while thirty interviews were conducted during a field visit to South Africa (in February–March 2006). Other interviews relevant to the two cases were conducted in other parts of the world (see Appendix for lists of interviews).

In addition to the interview data, the author reviewed other primary data sources, such as protest groups' own statements, brochures and reports, and checked secondary sources, such as documents written about the subject, including samples of media resources (newspapers, documentaries and films). Through cross-checking of data, a triangulation strategy was adopted. Together, all the data sources contributed to a better understanding of the political issue being examined, where inference was grounded on empirical work and different data sources. In this context, it is also important to note that the author is the former director of the Jerusalem Centre for Women, a Palestinian organization that worked closely with Israeli protest groups on joint Palestinian–Israeli initiatives aimed at promoting peace from below. Though she was not practising the role of an observing researcher at that time, she brings insights from her own experience.

This study was not meant to be an impact evaluation research, and therefore did not employ quantitative research methods such as social surveys or computer-assisted statistical analysis programmes. Consequently, the roles of the researched protest groups were not scrutinized using the four components of comprehensive evaluation,[15] but were examined by assessing how different protest groups view/ed their role and how scholars have referred to them. With this in mind the researcher inferred her conclusions, in both cases, on the roles taken by protest groups.

To ensure the best possible explanation, the research aimed to achieve a balance between the depth and breadth of the variables studied. It also followed the research principles of ethical conduct, validity (where evidence sought is entirely relevant to the problem), reliability (if methods of inquiry are used again, the same or, at the least, very similar results are produced), and representation (variables studied can, by and large, be considered typical).[16] Finally, the research was aware of and took into consideration the problems of value bias (the perspective from which a researcher sees the world and which might affect his/her ability to separate fact from value along the construction of the comparative study),[17] and ecological and individualist fallacies (when inferences drawn about one level of analysis are based on evidence from another level, and information about the aggregate level has been used as evidence at the individual level).[18]

The research had two levels of analysis, macro and micro. The first examined the political systems in both cases at the macro level, while the second, the micro level, examined both civil societies as well as the politics and roles of protest groups as components of their respective civil societies. The influence of the macro level on the micro level was obviously crucial and was also examined. A comparison was sequentially drawn between the two cases on the macro and micro levels, by looking into the similarities and the differences, and at patterns in each case and at shared patterns across the two cases. It is still important to note that, while protest groups can be considered as representatives of a macro level (since, in relation to political systems, they represent a collective of individuals and not individuals per se), by relativity it becomes more appropriate to consider them as part of a micro level.

The research studied the influence of the independent variable on the dependent variables, on the premise that the political system has an upper hand in setting the rules of the game for civil society and its components; this is especially so in ethnic-national states, which set the constraints or the size of space available for protest groups to function in. However, the research was also aware of the role played by intermediate variables and the fact that a change in any variable would affect the other variables. Sometimes this constant dialectical dynamic provides dependant variables – in this case the protest groups – with the ability to cause change in the system itself, as is explained in the concluding chapter.

The period researched in the case of apartheid South Africa was the 1980s and the early 1990s, until the formal dismantling of the apartheid system in 1994. In the case of Zionist Israel, the period researched extended from the beginning of the first Intifada in 1987 up to the signing of the Geneva Initiative in 2003 (during the second Intifada). The following factors influenced the choice of period of study:

- analogies can be made between the two periods of the two cases;
- there was an increase in protest activities (co-operation across the divide, mobilization, provision of services for the oppressed, etc.);
- the number of protest groups also increased;
- these periods were considered as times of transition for political change;

10 Introduction

- secret and open, formal and informal negotiations were held during these periods;
- strife and tension among and across the divided communities reached unprecedented levels;
- these periods were respectively described in the Israeli–Palestinian case as the 'peace industry' and in apartheid South Africa as the 'change industry'.

In the case of the Palestinian–Israeli conflict, the fifteen years from the start of the first Intifada (1987) saw the creation of a so-called 'peace industry', especially after the signing of the Oslo Accords in 1993. During that time, issues such as the fate of the occupied territories and other contested topics were introduced into the debates not only of the Israeli establishment, but also the Israeli public. After the leaders had shaken hands and signed agreements, there was a period of euphoria about an approaching peace, and the later People-to-People and second-track diplomacy programmes flourished. It was also the period of trust building (to different degrees) and trust destruction (almost entirely in the second Intifada), and during this time meetings and joint programmes became both legitimate and public.

Different formal agreements encouraged bi-national encounters, with the declared aim of getting to know the Other, finding common ground, setting up joint ventures, building a culture of peace, overcoming stereotypical images, and paving the way for historical compromise (for some) or territorial compromise (for others) and reconciliation. That is to say, this was what was written in the formal agreements, donors' guidelines, and separate and joint project proposals. Protest organizations and groups were also very active during this period, after years when there had been only a few meetings with those from the other side without the explicit consent of the Israeli governments and the Palestine Liberation Organization (PLO). Furthermore, this was the period when it was believed that final talks would finish (1999) with a final settlement. Although agreements over the end result of the conflict were not reached at either the macro or the micro level, this did not mean that certain parameters for settling the conflict had not developed over the years within the framework of a two-state solution.

In the case of South Africa, the period between the early 1980s and 1994 saw the development of highly organized protest activities against apartheid under the leadership of the United Democratic Front (UDF). These preceded the negotiations and the settlement that led to the first general non-racial democratic elections of 1994. It was also during this period, when the apartheid regime was strongly condemned (morally and politically) throughout the world, and had hard sanctions imposed on it, that the winds of change started to be felt. The leaders of the whites began to realize that their racial project of separate development and ethnic states was no longer practical, profitable or viable, and white liberal voices started to become stronger in criticizing the National Party government and proposing ways to break the stalemate. By the mid-1980s, divisions had occurred within the liberal protest movement, and the majority moved, in different degrees, to embrace the platform of the UDF. As a result, a joint non-racial front was established in support of a united non-racial South Africa.

This period also saw the release of Nelson Mandela and most of the other political prisoners, and the holding of (final) negotiations; and also witnessed the internal clashes that occurred not only between the Africans and the whites but also among the Africans. Preparations were also taking place at this time for the first general elections. Finally, there was the abolition of apartheid, the writing up of the interim constitution, the election of the first black president and the establishment of a government that was to represent all equally.

Through the use of this research design and strategies, the main question and hypothesis of the research are answered with appropriate evidence, as are other relevant sub-questions. The latter include, but are not limited to, the following: what are the political systems in Zionist Israel and apartheid South Africa? What kind of civil society emerged and developed in both states? What are the models, politics, political platforms and role/s of protest groups in both cases? To what extent do protest groups in both cases address core issues in the conflicts, such as equality, respect for the universality of human rights, justice and social justice?

From the point of view of Israeli 'left'/liberal groups, to what extent does addressing these issues threaten the viability of the state of Israel as a dominant Jewish state? How do the politics and role of Israeli leftist groups differ from those of the liberals? What are the categories of protest groups in both cases? Did South African white liberal protest groups advocate a compromise politics that preserved the apartheid system in some way/s? What kind of political platforms did the liberals and leftists adopt and what roles did they play in the struggle against apartheid? Did white protest groups in South Africa hold positions similar to those of the Israelis at a certain point of the conflict, and why and when did a shift occur, if any? What lessons can be drawn from the case of South Africa in relation to the Palestinian–Israeli conflict? What are the political patterns within and across the two cases?

Based on the research design developed here, the book is divided into five chapters as well as this Introduction. The research outline (chapters) does not follow the sequence of how the research process developed, but instead considers how this research can best be presented. The first chapter provides background to the two conflicts and draws a comparison between the two, while the second examines both political systems and civil societies, and provides the theoretical framework of the study, thereby paving the way for understanding the realities in which protests groups emerged and developed.

The third chapter researches the politics, political platforms and role/s of white South African protest groups, and the fourth examines the politics, political platforms and role/s of the Israeli protest groups. Chapter 5 draws out existing similarities and differences at the macro and the micro levels in both cases, and sheds light on existing patterns within each case and the shared patterns across the two cases. It also links the theoretical approach with the empirical side of the research, revisits the hypothesis and tests its validity, and is the concluding chapter in which the overall outcomes are presented.

12 *Introduction*

Equality, justice, racism, truth and peace: a conceptual discussion

This introduction to the research topic cannot be completed without examining the concepts that are/have been associated with peace building in apartheid South Africa and in Zionist Israel. To do this, concepts of equality, justice, racism, truth and peace are addressed in relation to their respective general literature and to their application in the two cases, since, as noted earlier, this helps to show these concepts in broader as well as more specific terms. This conceptual background provides initial thoughts about the political stances and characteristics of protest groups in both conflict areas, and facilitates a sense of whether these groups are pragmatic, principled, selective, practical.

These five concepts and their meanings have been at the heart of the two conflicts. In both conflict areas, the two sides – the dominant and the oppressed – referred differently to these concepts. Each side across the divide (has) provided meanings to fit with its own perspective(s) on the perceived legitimacy of its own cause and how future settlement/s might be envisioned. For example, being open to a plurality of interpretations, the issue of legitimacy contributed to how truth continued to be a highly contested issue, and this has been especially evident in the case of the Palestinian–Israeli conflict. In addition, the conflicting sides across the divide (have) had different views as to the real meaning of 'equality' and 'justice', and the word 'peace' (has) had different meanings even within each side, though to a lesser degree. While in both cases the oppressed side stressed the need for equality and justice as would be demanded by an egalitarian, the dominant side either neglected these concepts or argued that there were different types and different angles from which to look at them. The idea of the impossibility of attaining absolute equality and justice was connected to the need for compromise and was very much argued about. Both sides also claimed to have the higher moral ground. The oppressed highlighted the need to include morality in defining these concepts, while the dominant believed that realpolitik would find a compromise that was morally acceptable to both. The role of morality in defining these concepts was also contested.[19]

In the two cases, the concepts of equality, justice, racism, truth and peace remain(ed) at the forefront of the struggle for power.[20] The dominant side wanted to maintain and maximize its power, while the oppressed wanted to create a shift in the balance of power in order to achieve change in its favour. With regard to 'equality', the South African government argued that equal rights equalled 'national suicide',[21] since in that context, equal rights meant majority rule which the government rejected. It proposed states for ethnic groups in which equal rights would be enjoyed in each designated area, e.g. the Bantustans for the blacks. White protest groups had other views from those of their government. They agreed that the apartheid system was not a democracy. By the mid-1980s, progressive views were dominant among white protest groups that adopted the UDF/ANC vision of a united non-racial democratic South Africa. All white protest groups, both mainstream and progressive liberals,[22] stressed the existence of inequalities and the need to address them. The mainstream groups distanced themselves from the UDF platform and advocated a compromise that both sides could live with, although without providing clear views, especially on the 'one-person-one-vote' issue. Some accepted this principle in exchange for a minority veto power. The progressive groups accepted the grand vision of the UDF/ANC platform but did not discuss equality in detail. It can be argued that it was easier to be against inequality than to be in favour of a specific equality. As to social equality, the social democrats differ/ed from the socialist democrats, and both differed substantively from the liberal democrats.

With regard to Israel, Israeli governments avoided the issue of equality in two ways: first, by ignoring the issue as being irrelevant, and second, by creating the impression that by way of negotiations, a form of two-state settlement would be reached, through which the Palestinian–Israeli conflict would eventually end. The issue of equality was only discussed in the context of the rights of the Palestinian citizens of Israel. As to Israeli protest groups,[23] a majority, even among the critical Zionist groups, not to mention the mainstream Zionist groups, have still not addressed this issue in relation to the Palestinians from the territories occupied in 1967. Both categories view Israel as a democracy or a democracy that can be improved. They separate the struggle for equality inside Israel from the struggle against occupation. The mainstream Zionist group, Peace Now, does not see addressing equality as part of its role; while the Peres Centre for Peace considers that addressing it is not timely because the Israeli public is not yet ready for it.[24]

The task of addressing the issue of equality per se is not taken on board by most critical Zionist groups, even though a number of them mention it in their political writings. For groups such as Ta'aush, Women in Black, Gush Shalom, Yesh Gvul and Bat Shalom, the main focal issues are raising awareness about the atrocities of the occupation, and the call for the ending of occupation. When the issue of the right of return of the Palestinian refugees is broached in the context of the existing Israeli Law of Return (which allows any Jew from any part of the world to come to Israel and become a citizen), the common counter-argument of the Zionist protest groups, whether mainstream or critical, is that equality can be applied in different ways, and that in this instance it is not applicable, since it endangers the existence of Israel as a Jewish state. They would argue for the need to compromise and to be creative in addressing this issue. The tiny anti-Zionist groups that adopt the universal values of human rights and accept international law believe in the applicability of equality.

The fact that the majority of Israeli protest groups choose to avoid addressing the concept of equality, while the white South African groups chose not to discuss it in detail, reflects the difficulty and controversy around commitment to any form of equality. This difficulty stems from competing ideologies, interests and, consequently, justifications for or against one type. In cases of conflict situations, it can be stated that the privileged side usually favours vague answers, along with an argument for political compromise that is contrary to the argument for rights and the law emphasized by the underprivileged side. Thus, both protest groups tend to make proposals that are selective and different in some aspects, and to adopt, partially or fully, theories that promote compromise as a pragmatic choice. The literature on equality addresses the issue from political, socio-economic, and rights and law perspectives.

In political discussions, different types of equality are identified. Plato argued for the principle of treating 'like cases as like', while Aristotle recognized two kinds of equality: numerical, which treats all persons as indistinguishable; and proportional, which believes that reward and punishment, benefits and burdens should be proportional to what a person deserves.[25] The Athenians argued that human beings were unequal by nature. Centuries later, social contract theory laid down the principle of equal dignity and respect, a principle that is accepted as a minimum standard throughout mainstream Western culture.[26] However, it set a moral principle that does not guarantee uniformity of treatment, since it allows rational reasoning objectively to justify any inequality. One such justification can be the consent of the other person or side. While the realists of power politics approve of this type of justification, it is criticized by their opponents, who argue that the level of free will or the options available for one of the sides may undermine the legitimacy of an agreed-upon degree of equality.

In terms of socio-economic rights, liberal Western democracies stress the fairness of the individual's right to equal opportunities. Libertarianism and economic liberalism postulate an original right to freedom and property, and support free market and minimal redistribution and social rights,[27] while utilitarianism argues that the morally proper action is one that maximizes utility through considering all desires. Others focus on equalizing the level of welfare or equality of resources, stressing the need to provide the same initial expectations of basic goods and to empower the disadvantaged.[28]

Equality by law, codified by laws, and practised in legal frameworks, does not claim to provide total equality. By themselves, laws cannot secure full equality in their nature or practice. While their nature reflects interlocking factors, such as social, economic, political, legal and cultural issues, in reality, a verdict usually reflects a balance of arguments in which a simple black and white judgement is not feasible: "Only those considerations which go into the scales are weighted."[29] Inequalities of power, such as wealth, prestige, the power of argument, and so on, are unavoidable. Law, the credibility of judges, and the ideals of a society will eventually play a major role in deciding the acceptable level of inequality. Thus, one can argue that the measure of equality that is produced in a specific place and time depends on a balance being achieved by different powerful factors or forces.

These views on equality, whether political, socio-economic or legal, reflect the difficulty of addressing equality in concrete terms. The difficulties increase when the demand for equality is part of an inter-national struggle. For example, agreement on the acceptable level of equality or inequality as part of a peace deal or a legal contract depends on how the conflicting parties are able to justify their claims and exert their powers. The balance point was reached in South Africa's case when the black majority received political power through 'one-person-one-vote', while the white minority retained economic power. The settlement also included a bill of rights that upheld the equal rights and protected the property of the individual. In the case of the Palestinian–Israeli conflict, the gap between the way the two sides perceive equality remains quite wide, and lags far behind what has been achieved in South Africa. For the Zionist groups, international law is not accepted as the term of reference. Based on the existing balance of power, they advocate different formulas for compromise that will, above all, secure Israel as a Jewish state.

Concerning justice, it is agreed that equality is an intrinsic part of justice, and that justice is associated with pursuing ideals which are not necessarily stressed equally or in the same way. Its related ideals include personal and collective freedoms; defeat of domination and stigmatization; development of human capacities and fulfilment of human potentials; and the achievement of social justice. Like equality, justice is widely considered to be an equally elusive concept, and political theorists, politicians, legal professionals, and even peace and human rights activists differ over its meaning and the best ways to address it. They also differ over its sources. It is thought to be harmony, divine command, natural law or human creation: it might be based on fundamental ethical standards or perhaps be less important than is supposed. Because of the controversy around its meaning, sources and methods of achievement, justice is viewed as the ideal that has never been realized or, as some would wish to show it, simply as a virtue.

In general terms, justice is divided into two broad types, distributive and retributive, which together cover its political, socio-economic and legal dimensions. Distributive justice is concerned with giving all members of society a 'fair share' of the available benefits and resources,[30] which include wealth, power, reward and respect. Retributive justice is concerned with the proper response to past wrongdoings, and proposes various ideas as possible responses. However, many see restorative justice as a better response to a retroactive approach that justifies punishment as a response to past injustice or wrongdoing.[31] Two examples of theories of justice are John Rawls' theory, and utilitarianism. Rawls distinguishes between a total system of equal basic liberties; and social and economic goods, substantial benefits for the disadvantaged, and widespread equality of opportunity.[32] Utilitarianism stresses maximization of welfare, and legitimizes the sacrifice of some for the good of all.

In terms of justice by law, a fair[33] trial in an intra-national court room is supposed to achieve a proper balance between the ability of the defendant to establish innocence and the ability of the prosecution to establish guilt.[34] However, in cases of inter-national conflicts, alongside the procedures, codifications, interpretations, arguments and counter-arguments, a balance of power that includes players beyond a nation has, or can have, a significant role. Depending on the existing balance of powers in the international system, in cases of inter-national conflict, it is the first to agree to address, and then to consent to, ways to address injustices. Agreed-upon or imposed justice can include restoring the balance that existed before a wrong was committed, providing other methods to address the wrong act, and/or maintaining the status quo. A balanced verdict can be considered by one or more sides as a victory for justice, as a miscarriage of justice, or as somewhere in between.

In both case studies, the ideals of justice, i.e. the redistribution of political and social power, along with retributive (including restitutive) justice, represent/ed core elements in the conflict. Contradictory claims, justifications and legitimacy issues were at the heart of discussions on the concept of justice, different elements of which received different degrees of emphasis. In the case of South Africa, the apartheid government argued for its just cause, but by the mid-1980s, white protest groups were claiming that the system was unjust and had to be dismantled. Even so, the mainstream and the progressive groups chose not to address details of the justice that was being spoken about. The mainstream and, to a lesser degree, the progressives, voiced concern over the ANC's expected view of social democracy and retributive justice when the Congress, in attempting to galvanize support for its grand vision of political liberation, failed to stress a socialist agenda, and also sent conciliatory messages to calm the fears of the white population with regard to expected legal follow-ups or black revenge. Eventually, the restorative type of justice adopted by the South African Council of Churches was the one adopted by the new democratic South Africa. Along the same line of thinking, the Truth and Reconciliation Commission did not include justice as a component in its mandate, focusing instead on recognition of responsibility in exchange for amnesty as a means for reconciliation. The state took responsibility for addressing past injustices by employing different policies to help the victims.

In the case of the Palestinian–Israeli conflict, both mainstream and critical Zionist groups argue for the just cause of Zionism. The problem is perceived to be the occupation of 1967. Mainstream Zionist groups do not address the concept of justice in their political discourse, and their members share such views as, 'in reality there is no justice', 'search for justice, get no peace', or 'through compromise an attainable justice for both sides can be found'. In the last few years, several Critical Zionist groups have started to make linkages between the ramifications of the 1948 war and the occupation of 1967, and how they impact on the Palestinian people and thus on the conflict as a whole. Although most still refuse to take up position, they have also begun to mention the issue of the right of return of Palestinian refugees. A few maintain that it is necessary to recognize part of the responsibility (mainly moral), and even to accept this principle (though not its implementation). The argument about the need to compromise on justice is common, not only on the right of return issue but also on other concerns such as settlements, Jerusalem, water, and the sovereignty of the future Palestinian entity. Leftist anti-Zionist groups accept the Palestinian demand for justice in accordance with international law.

A related concept to that of justice and equality is racism, which was/is also at the core of the two conflicts, fuelling, in addition to being rooted in, the quest to control land and resources and to gain power. Racism was considered to be at the forefront in the case of South Africa, where apartheid was openly based on racial categorization and legal discrimination, and the ANC developed an anti-apartheid vision of a new, inclusive South Africa. In the case of Zionist Israel, on the other hand, racism is somewhat covert. The conflict has been portrayed as one between two nationalities fighting for the same land. This depiction of the cause of the conflict has prevailed over the version that sees resources, land and power at its heart. The struggle for control over space meant that racism and discriminatory structures have become entrenched. In other words, the exclusivity of Zionism, and its policies of colonial expansionism before, during and after establishment of the state, continuously fed racist notions along with the quest for controlling more resources and maximizing power. However, fears about accusations of anti-Semitism, the PLO's acceptance of separation as part of a two-state vision, and the fact that there are many definitions of racism, have so far prevented Zionist Israel from being associated with racism by Western mainstream politics and scholars.

While there is no agreed-upon definition for racism, certain major elements are generally used in defining or referring to it, including feelings of superiority, prejudice, exclusivity and the quest for power. Ezekiel argues that racism is prejudice with power which translates itself within policy and institutions, thus enforcing domination by one group over the other.[35] The *Oxford Dictionary of Philosophy* defines racism as: "the inability or refusal to recognize the rights, needs, dignity, or value of people of particular races or geographical origins ... the devaluation of various traits of character or intelligence as 'typical' of particular people".[36] The *Oxford Dictionary of Politics* defines racism as: "the tendency to show hostility or lack of moral respect for members of other races", and defines racialism as: "the doctrine that racial categories are important to in determining human behaviour".[37] The latter notion, 'racialism', had lost all scientific and moral ground by the mid-twentieth century, with the fall of Nazism and the process of decolonization, but racism remains very much alive and has become indistinguishable from ethnic chauvinisms and ethno-nationalisms. The latter is referred to as 'closed nationalism' and is based on race/ethnicity, in contrast to 'open nationalism' which is based on a universalistic conception of the nation.

Both apartheid South Africa and Zionist Israel adopt/ed closed nationalism. It is because of this, and the fact that they developed institutional forms of discrimination, that both were defined as forms of racism according to the 1965 UN International Convention on the Elimination of all Forms of Racial Discrimination. Both systems meet the definition of Article 1 of the Convention, which defines racial discrimination as:

> any distinction, exclusion, restriction or preference based on race, colour, descent, or national or ethnic origin which has the purpose or effect of nullifying or impairing the recognition, enjoyment or exercise, on an equal footing, of human rights and fundamental freedoms in the political, economic, social, cultural or any other field of public life.[38]

It is important to note that Israel managed to cancel the UN decision in this regard after the signing of the Oslo Accords in 1994. Ironically, the same Accords that further institutionalized Israeli racism in Palestine paved the way for repealing the UN resolution that equated Zionism with racism.[39] The Oslo

18 *Introduction*

Accords split the post-1967 war Occupied Territories into A, B and C areas, enhanced a system of checkpoints and sieges around Palestinian-populated areas, and grabbed more land through settlement expansion and the construction of a bypass network of roads to link Jewish settlements, thereby fragmenting Palestinian areas and populations and linking exclusive Jewish settlements by Jewish-only roads.

In the argument about cultural differences, racism also reinvented itself as a method of distinguishing, excluding, retaining and maximizing power. This argument was used by the apartheid system to justify its plan to divide the country along ethnic cultural lines with the aim of having a pure white state that was able to control black 'independent' Bantustans or 'states'. As for Israel, which defined itself in exclusive terms from day one of its establishment, it claims the right to all 'Eretz Israel', but is ready give up part of the occupied territories of 1967 to protect its Jewish majority. The 'cultural difference' argument is stressed by many Israeli politicians and academics as part of their further justification for the formula of a two-state solution.

The position on existing racism adopted by South African white protest groups recognized that apartheid was a racist ideology that produced inequalities and injustices. They therefore rejected racism and defined their struggle as anti-apartheid and anti-racial. The case of Israeli Zionist protest groups is different. Mainstream and critical Zionist groups do not view Zionism as a racist ideology. Some argue that Zionism is not inherently racist, but that the Zionist movement, and later Israel, implemented racist policies. On an individual basis, a few critical Zionists, who prefer to describe themselves as non-Zionists or post-Zionist, would, for example, criticize the component of Zionist exclusivity and its ramifications, such as inequalities, segregation and occupation,[40] whereas others would only criticize the results of exclusivity. Even so, whether mainstream or critical Zionist, they would not question the legitimacy of Zionism or the state. The Zionist movement is regarded as a national liberation movement like any other, which unfortunately made some mistakes during the stage of state formation. Since the existence of racism is not acknowledged, the issue is not discussed by the Zionist protest groups, and thus is absent from their political agendas for peace. The tiny leftist anti-Zionist groups hold an opposite view. They equate Zionism with racism and consider that one of their roles is to raise awareness about it. They view the Israeli society as racist, whether it belongs to the political right or the political 'left'/liberals.

The fourth controversial concept in the quest for understanding peace building is 'truth'. In both case studies, truth has been the issue that dealt with history and narratives across the divide. It is connected with legitimacy, upon which the status of war, violence and peace is based. Literature on truth reflects the plurality of opinions around it. There are many theories of truth and there have been many debates as to what constitutes truth, ways to identify and define it, and the role of already-acquired knowledge in shaping it, as well as questions as to whether it is subjective, objective, relative or absolute. Theories of truth[41] include: coherence theory;[42] pragmatism theory;[43] semantic theory;[44] idealist theory;[45] Heidegger's theory;[46] and functionalism theory.[47] Others are: correspondence theory;[48] constructivist theory;[49] consensus theory;[50] and redundancy theory (also called the 'no truth' or deflationary theory).[51] Religions too, in addressing truth, have proposed different perspectives on truths, and/or claims to being the truth.

All these theories looked at the concept of truth, each from a particular angle, and stressed notions of social coherence and constructivism, pragmatism, and subjectivity, notions that are also central in political arguments on truth by Kierkegaard and Nietzsche. Kierkegaard argued that human beings cannot find truth separate from the subjective experience of their own existence, while Nietzsche stressed that the will for power is the truth because "a living thing seeks above all to discharge its strength".[52] Foucault expresses a similar view, claiming that truth is part of, or embedded within, a given power structure: "Truth is linked in a circular relation with systems of power, which produces and sustains it, and to effects of power which it induces and which extend it. A 'regime' of truth."[53] Based on the above, it could be argued that relations between these different notions in a certain place and time allow many truths to exist simultaneously. Each reflects a balance point between the powers of dominant notions and interests from within available knowledge. Thus, an absolute truth for one side could be seen as a relative or subjective truth for another.

In the case of apartheid South Africa, white protest groups did not argue in favour of a separate truth for whites with regard to historical narratives. This reflected the fact that apartheid ideology lost legitimacy and that the ANC's unity platform progressively overcame the government's Bantustans plan. In the case of Israeli protest groups, Zionist groups, whether mainstream or critical, argue for the need to accept the existence of two narratives. This position reflects their commitment to Zionism as a legitimate ideology that represents the right to a Jewish state in Palestine, as well as to the history of state establishment. Their commitment to Zionism and the state is beyond any recognition of the consequences of establishing an exclusively Jewish state for the indigenous population. In addition, the 'two narratives' approach is part of their commitment to a two-state solution formula. Terry Greenblatt of Bat Shalom, a critical Zionist group, addresses truth saying:

> the Middle East conflict's ultimate resolution is embedded in our ability to envision and create a common truth that is as nuanced and complex, as deep and as profound, as the conflict itself – a truth that encompasses and legitimizes both the Israeli and Palestinian narratives, even when they contradict each other, a truth that permits each side to maintain its dignity and political integrity within its own community.[54]

Finally, after discussing the four major concepts associated with peace building in both conflict situations, this section examines the concept of peace. The literature on peace shows that there are different perspectives on addressing peace. There are different angles from which one can approach the concept, and there is no agreed-upon definition. Philosophers, political theorists, religions, politicians and peace activists differ/ed between and among themselves on the meaning of peace and how to achieve it. The most common perspective looks at peace as the antithesis of war, violence[55] and conflict.[56] International relations holds that a balance point, agreed by the different associated powers, decides what type of peace will prevail, and this balance gives approval to a dominant justified perspective, in a specific context, and at a certain historical time and place.

Once reached, such a balance may produce negative or positive peace. The first is the most common form of peace, which is absence of war or violence. In many cases, it is achieved by the consent of the weaker side and thus can be an unjust peace that gives rise to slavery or capitulations. A positive peace is one that has made justice an intrinsic part of it to allow human beings to realize and fulfil their potential.[57] As such, the notion of positive peace is perceived as the antithesis of both violence and structured violence. Structured violence is one that is built into a structure, translating a situation of unequal power and consequently unequal life chances.[58] In the literature that addresses racism, it is referred to as 'system of oppression' where one group subordinates and maintains control over another racial or national group.

Raymond Aron stipulates three types of peace: equilibrium, hegemony and empire in a given historical space.[59] Peace by equilibrium is achieved where the forces of the political units are symmetrical. Peace by hegemony is when a state practises hegemony over other states who do not seek change to the status quo; nor does the hegemonic power try to absorb them to the extent where their external independence is reduced to impotence.[60] Peace by empire is one "where all units, save one, lose their autonomy and tend to disappear as centres of political decisions. The imperial state, in the end, reserves to itself the monopoly of legitimate violence".[61] Consequently, the order of an empire prevails and, on the surface, imperial peace becomes indistinguishable from civil peace. Civil peace is associated by Hobbes and Locke with the existence of a civil government that adheres to the notion of the Social Contract wherein government secures life and property. It succeeds in this role as long as it manages to maintain a balance between existing powers and meet peoples' expectations, as stipulated in the contract. The concept of peace by social contract stresses principles of justice and equality. It expects government to achieve them as best as it can, given existing interests and capabilities.

In support of the presence of equality and justice, Martin Luther King agreed with Mahatma Gandhi, who argued that a society in which one group is oppressed by another lacks peace, even in the absence of violence. Idealists stress the principle that all nations have an inherent leaning towards independence, freedom and justice, and once they fulfil their duty to choose, live and respect others, peace is achieved. The pacifists, by their commitment to total non-violence under any circumstances, offer another perspective on peace. Others refer to peace as a state of quietness and tranquillity or a state of inner peace: of mind, body and soul. This view contrasts totally with that based on

Plato's long-lived notion of using war to attain peace. The Allied forces used this in their propaganda in the First World War – the 'war to end all wars' that sowed the seeds for a still bloodier conflict, while the Bolsheviks, thinking along the same lines, used 'civil war' against the central power, which resulted in the loss of almost one million people.

Ending wars produces new types of peace that in turn reflect new balances of power. In this context, peace can be defined as a state of power. According to Rummel, war is understood as a dispute about the measurement of international power, while peace marks the rough agreement about the measurement.[62] In the process, the most powerful have the upper hand in deciding the balance point. Martin Wight describes the results of power politics: "in most cases the freedom or rights of one nation or nationality have been purchased only by the oppression of another nation or nationality".[63] Consequently, the international law of peace is perceived by many as subordinate to such a balance. Oppenheim comments that:

> a law of nations can exist only if there be an equilibrium, a balance of power, between the members of the family of nations. If the powers cannot keep one another in check, no rules of law will have any force, since an over-powerful state will naturally try to act according to discretion and disobey the law.[64]

Examining these perspectives on the concept of peace and how it has been used by protest groups in the two case studies suggests that non-identical compromises have been made along the line between the position of the idealist and that of power politics, or that of positive peace in contrast to negative peace. In both cases the protest groups differ in their understanding of peace. The white South African protest groups did not label themselves as peace groups. They called themselves anti-apartheid groups, and addressed the asymmetry of power by supporting the dismantling of the apartheid system. The mainstream and progressive groups differed over the strategies to dismantle apartheid and whether to ally themselves with the Charterist platform of the UDF/ANC. From the mid-1980s a majority of South African white protest groups supported a united non-racial democratic South Africa. This entailed equal rights in voting and, therefore, majority rule in a country that would belong to all. A bill of rights that protected equality, justice and existing individual property ownership before the law was agreed upon. Many disapproved of social justice that entailed nationalization of land and private properties, something that others also found contentious. The balance point achieved in the final settlement allowed political as well as economic power-sharing, and reflected a considerable victory for the values and principles of anti-racism, equality and justice.

In the case of the Palestinian–Israeli conflict, the Zionist protest groups called themselves peace groups and many claimed to be peace movements. They did not name themselves anti-occupation groups. A few associated themselves with certain political principles, while the majority called for the end of occupation and a two-state solution, without commitment to further details (such as, for instance, certain principles of equality, justice and anti-racism). Peace-with-security-by-compromise has been the most common feature in the discourse of both liberal Zionist categories. While critical Zionist groups proposed better deals for the Palestinians, groups in both categories still required the Palestinians to compromise over land, water, the right of return, Jerusalem, and the sovereignty of a future Palestinian 'state' to be established on land occupied in the 1967 war. The conflict has been addressed in a piecemeal fashion. Mainstream and critical Zionist groups have not addressed the asymmetry of power, and both search for a compromise that can be reached from within the existing Zionist power structure. Ron Pundak of the mainstream Peres Centre for Peace argues that it is not necessary to address this asymmetry, and praises the Oslo Accords for accepting the political reality "as it is".[65] A few members of the critical Zionist groups express an unfavourable view of the Israeli peace groups for failing to address the asymmetry of power between the Palestinians and the Israelis in their peace work.

Meanwhile the few anti-Zionists address the existing structure of power, arguing that the ideal and best settlement is a one-state solution because this is the best way to address issues of anti-racism, equality and justice. They argue that Zionism and the existing system are exclusive and racist, and that a state for all citizens on an equal basis is the only formula capable of resolving all the issues in the conflict. However, bearing in mind the existing balance of power, they opt for a two-state solution as a first phase, to be followed by a bi-national or one-state solution in the future. They stress the need for equality and justice and for combating racism, accept the Palestinian historical narrative, and support the right of return. They also accept international law as the term of reference that is either refused or selectively accepted by the Zionist groups, perceiving it not only as a legal base but also as a tool to empower the weaker side, the Palestinians.

Literature review

There is a vast amount of literature on the two conflicts, but this study focuses specifically on comparing protest groups, something that it does not cover in any great depth. In the case of South Africa, available literature addresses the history, causes and nature of the conflict, the rise and fall of apartheid ideology, and the ANC-led resistance to the apartheid system. In the case of the Palestinian–Israeli conflict, many studies similarly focus on the history of Zionism, the establishment of the Jewish state in Palestine, the causes and nature of the conflict, and Palestinian resistance initiatives at different points of history. There are also studies that examine the (formal and informal) processes of negotiation in South Africa and in the Palestinian–Israeli case, along with innumerable reports on separate and joint protest programmes.

Literature on conflict resolution was also briefly reviewed by the author, who looked at the factors guiding parties to move towards a resolution, e.g. both

Introduction 23

parties have been hurt by the conflict, both realize that neither side can win over the other, and both realize that a compromise is possible or that the balance of power allows for imposing a settlement.

As for research that compares and contrasts both conflicts, there has been interest in the topic since the mid-1990s. Analogies made between the two conflicts steered many discussions, and many articles were written by practitioners and activists involved in the Palestinian–Israeli peace-building initiatives. In terms of academic studies, a small number exists that have addressed the issue from different angles, including work by Heribert Adam,[66] Kogila Moodley and Heribert Adam,[67] Marwan Bishara,[68] Thomas Mitchell,[69] Uri Davis,[70] Daryl Glaser,[71] Ran Greenstein,[72] and Muna Younis.[73] Younis looked at the resistance movements of the Palestine Liberation Organization and the African National Congress but while her research is related to the area of this study it is not the focus of it.

The researcher came across only two studies that were relevant to the focus of this study in addressing peace-building initiatives among protest groups, and comparing the Palestinian–Israeli case with that of apartheid South Africa and Northern Ireland. These are: *Mobilizing for Peace: Conflict Resolution in Northern Ireland, Israel/Palestine, and South Africa*, by Benjamin Gidron, Stanley N. Katz and Yeheskel Hasenfeld (2002) and *Peace Building in Northern Ireland, Israel and South Africa: Transition, Transformation and Reconciliation*, by Colin Knox and Padraic Quirk (2000).

These two books are related to the themes of this study but cannot answer the research question: what are the politics, political platforms and roles of protest groups from the dominant community in both ethnic-national states in peace building? This research examines protest groups through focusing on their politics and in connection with the ideology in power prevailing in both states, which was not a consideration in the two publications noted above. Its theoretical framework is also different, being based on state–civil society relations which is illuminating in such cases; however, neither used this methodological approach. Nor did they examine the kind of political system that exist/ed in both cases or the way it affected and contributed to shaping the civil society in which protest groups (whites and Jewish) function. The author believes that examining both variables – political systems and civil society (Chapter 2) – and then analysing the effect of the political system on civil society and subsequently on protest groups, is critical to understanding the latter's political stands, modes of action, and roles. In order to examine the politics of protest groups in the two cases, awareness of the role played by intermediate variables is paramount. Therefore the book examines ethnic-ideologies and their systems and civil society, though it does not focus on dissidence in general.

The added value of the research stems also from the fact that it centres on protest groups in the dominant communities of the two ethnic-national states. By examining them in the realm of state–civil society relations, the book provides a new comparative outlook as to why protest groups adopt/ed certain positions and act/ed according to a certain pattern, and when and why such a pattern might change. It is also possible to explore whether the respective protest groups have been agents of change vis-à-vis the prevailing ideology in power, or have sought to influence state strategies and/or tactics, but from within a framework that protects the ideology in power and benefits the dominant group.

How this research differs in other aspects from the two studies mentioned above is explained in Chapters 3 and 4, which examine protest groups in the two cases and provide critical views and arguments to counter some of those presented by the authors.

A concluding note

This introduction discussed the topic, the research methodology, and some key concepts associated with the work of protest groups for peace building, and provided a methodological framework for presenting the various chapters. Chapter 1, which follows, compares and contrasts the two conflicts. It looks into their histories, relations between the dominant side and the dominated side, and how the two conflicts have been framed in terms of causes and solutions. It also examines the role of religion/s, the legitimacy of the ideology in power, and the size of the areas and population. It thus provides a historical and political background to the two cases.

1 Historical backgrounds and political developments in both conflicts
A comparison

Introduction

In examining political developments in both apartheid South Africa and Zionist Israel, Chapter 1 provides a historical and political background to both conflict situations according to their respective exclusive ideologies and political systems. It focuses on presenting the political realities of both conflicts during the periods studied (the 1980s and early 1990s in South Africa, and the 1990s and the early years of the twenty-first century in Israel), and offers insights into the relations that exist/ed between the dominant and dominated sides. This helps the reader to understand the context from which the two civil societies emerged and developed, and to identify and study protest groups as a component of civil society, as well as their politics and roles in peace building in both cases.

The chapter serves the research aims by showing the contextual limits to the development of a genuinely inclusive civil society based on civic ingredients and enjoying a high level of independence (as will be examined in Chapter 2). It shows the structure of power between the dominant and the oppressed sides in both cases, as well as the similarities and differences, and reveals a number of intermediate variables that contributed significantly to shaping the pathways of the two sets of protest groups. It also indicates the context that allowed protest groups in both civil societies to continue to represent a societal minority made up mainly of liberals. Other elements needed for examining the dependant variables of this research – the politics and the role of protest groups in peace building – are explained in Chapter 2.

The present chapter is intentionally structured to examine the similarities and the differences between the two conflict situations. It is important to look at the political developments of both conflicts from a comparative angle and to identify the existing similarities and differences, since there is much to be learnt from dissimilarity as well as from likeness. Such a comparison will also explain the historical and political background that shaped the politics of different protest groups and their consequent role/s and, as will be seen in Chapter 2, will shed light on many issues that complement the analysis of both political systems and their respective civil societies. These issues are discussed below, and are very much connected to the whole protest discourses in the two cases. For instance, in the political platforms and subsequent activities of both protest cases certain issues have been very much in evidence, including historical narratives; discrimination policies; visions for political settlement; state militarism; indoctrination in ethnic societies; visions and strategies of the liberation movements; economic relations between the dominant and dominated sides; legitimacy of ideologies in power; how the two conflicts have been framed in terms of causes, nature and solution; and the role of religion (see also Chapters 3 and 4).

Initially, each of the similarities is presented under a specific theme and is followed by the differences, again with reference to specific topics. Although each theme discussed could constitute the topic for a whole research project, the chapter gives a brief account only of the issues that shaped the two conflicts. The concluding section sheds light on the results of the comparison and links to Chapter 2. The shared similarities identified by the author are presented in the following section, and the differences in the section that comes after it.

Similarities between the two conflicts

Both conflicts are founded on colonialism and racist notions

In both conflict areas, the settler communities, whether whites or Jews, immigrated and settled on lands populated by indigenous peoples who happened to live in less developed parts of the world. Their main policy for control has been based on power politics, reflected in the different schemes used to dominate the native population and control maximum amounts of land. Both settler communities have been equipped with stronger military forces, and economic and technological advancement. In the case of South Africa, the Dutch started the colonization process in 1652[1] when they sought a refreshment station during their journey to the East and landed in Cape Town. From that moment, the settlers began to take over the land of the indigenous people,[2] and were soon joined by the French, German and English. Africans were not exterminated but were enslaved and later used as workers. Over the following centuries, the Afrikaners (farmers) and the English (owners of mining and industries) excluded the Africans from political power and exploited them as cheap labour.

After the establishment of the Union of South Africa in 1910, when the Afrikaners and the English joined to establish an 'official' white South African nation,[3] various methods were utilized to preserve white domination. 'Nonwhites' were excluded from political power and land control, and the Native Act of 1913 made it illegal for Africans to purchase or lease land outside the designated 'native reserves' that comprised 13 per cent of the territory of South Africa.[4]

Like other colonial enterprises, colonialism in South Africa was driven by racist beliefs of superiority. Besides using the myth of 'a land without a people', the whites believed that they were at the top of the evolutionary scale while blacks were at the bottom, being primitive, less intelligent and idle.[5] The Dutch Reformed Church, the state church, asserted that God was eternal, infinite, wise, and just and the creator of the universe. He was believed to have planned the life and the fate of each individual on earth; the 'chosen' were saved, as long as they adhered to the church's teachings.[6] The victors decided that Calvinism's doctrine of predestination meant that "the natives belong to the damned and the settlers to the saved",[7] and the church adopted this belief. Reference was also made to the biblical story of Ham, who was black and cursed while his people were supposed to serve the whites. Thus, the imposition of the apartheid system in 1948 did not come as a total surprise, but rather was seen as a culmination of a process of racism, discrimination and domination towards absolute and total separation between whites and blacks.

Developments in South Africa in the late nineteenth and early twentieth century coincided with the establishment of the Zionist movement and the subsequent Jewish migration to Palestine. Jewish immigration began with the Zionist movement's quest to create a political entity for the Jews in Palestine, a project that was led by European Jews and was directly supported by Great Britain, one of the greatest colonial powers at that time, even before the League of Nations granted it a mandate over Palestine. The Zionist project built itself by Jewish immigration, land colonization, military force, the revival of Jewish heritage and the building of a new collective Jewish identity and autonomous institutions.

In common with the whites in South Africa, the Zionists held colonial racist notions. Adopting the dominant outlook of European chauvinism, Zionism considered any territory as empty and available if its indigenous population had not yet achieved national independence and recognized statehood.[8] To that end, the first Zionist Congress in Basle in 1897 called for the colonizing of Palestine, paying no attention to the rights of the indigenous population. The Palestinian Arabs were mainly treated as non-existing or ignored and denied collective and individual equal rights. Avineri maintains that Herzel, the founder of Zionism, overlooked the national rights of the Palestinians, the indigenous population.[9] But for Herzel, the notion of providing civil rights for what he called the Arabs, was accepted. Along similar lines, Neuberger argues that only few Zionists regarded the Arab presence as a real obstacle to the fulfilment of Zionism, since at that time Arab nationalism did not exist in any form and the Arab population of Palestine was sparse and apolitical.[10] Such Zionist claims were made (up until the war of 1948) at different periods during which the Jewish population never exceeded the Palestinian population. In 1922, Jews in Palestine constituted 11 per cent, a figure that, through massive immigration, became 31.5 per cent in 1943 (539,000 out of a total population of 1,676,571) and one-third of the population by 1948.[11]

Racist views were also legitimized by religious beliefs, e.g. being the chosen people to be served by other nations, and with the land of Canaan (Palestine) being the land promised by the God of Israel to Abraham, Isaac and Jacob and their descendants.[12] This view of religious supremacy fed the notion of otherness, where the other was referred to as a non-Jew or a *Goy*. In this context, Knox and Quirk refer to Smith's analysis of Ben Gurionism, which stressed the

28 *Background and political development*

distinction between Israel and world Jewry on one hand and the *goyim* or non-Jews on the other:[13] "If the latter did not fulfil their perceived obligations to Israel, they would at best be ignored, at worst fought."[14] Thus the other's religion and/or nationality were looked down on. In this context it is important to note that while the Zionist ideologues were primarily secular, they still mixed Jewish history with religious beliefs to promote a political ideology and its aims. For instance, Ben-Gurion referred to the Bible as the Jewish people's sacrosanct title-deed to Palestine,[15] and "The Bible is our Mandate"[16] became a core notion in claiming legitimacy and even in challenging the British mandate authority when it planned to curtail Jewish migration to Palestine in 1936. Chapter 2's discussion of Zionism shows how a new Jewish national identity – that of an Israeli – was shaped, and also illustrates how religion has been incorporated as a component to justify a claim for legitimacy and exclusivity.

The alliance between the Zionist movement and the colonial power of Great Britain was manifested in 1917 with the Balfour Declaration, which promised the Jews a home in Palestine:

> His Majesty's Government views with favour the establishment in Palestine of a national home for the Jewish people, and will use their best endeavours to facilitate the achievement of this object, it being clearly understood that nothing shall be done which may prejudice the civil and religious rights of existing non–Jewish communities in Palestine or the rights and political status enjoyed by Jews in any other country.[17]

The British declaration denied the Palestinians national collective rights. But for many Zionists, Palestine was seen as "a land without people for a people without land",[18] or 'empty' because the native Palestinians were largely invisible to them.[19] Other Zionist thinkers saw it as occupied by 'strangers', meaning every non-Jewish person who had been living in Palestine since the Roman period.[20] It is worth noting that in 1918, the Jews made up 5 per cent of the population of Palestine.[21]

To achieve an exclusive Jewish state, the leaders of the two major strands of Zionism agreed to use violence and refuse minority status. Contrary to the South African case they did not opt for a minority governing a majority. Jabotinsky, a Zionist revisionist argued for the inevitability of war or violence against the Palestinians, argued: "Has a people ever been known to give up its territory of its own volition? Likewise, the Arabs in Palestine will not renounce their sovereignty without violence."[22] With regard to having minority status, Golda Meir, a Labour Zionist, was asked by an Anglo-American Commission during an interview in 1946, whether she would be satisfied if the Jews, as a minority, had the same privileges as those promised to the Arabs as a minority. She replied: "No, sir, for there must be one place in the world where Jews are not a minority",[23] even though, as noted earlier, the Jews were at that time still a minority. Over twenty years later, in 1969, Golda Meir of the Labour Party reiterated the mainstream Zionist pre- and post-state claim that:

There was no such thing as Palestinians. It was not as though there was a
Palestinian people in Palestine considering itself as a Palestinian people and
we came and threw them out and took their country away from them. They
did not exist.[24]

While the South African case represents a classic case of colonialism (territorial conquest, exploitation of natives, exclusive political power and claim of moral and cultural superiority), the case of Israel includes many of these and other characteristics. At the beginning of Jewish immigration, the Zionist movement started buying lands from the Palestinians to build independent Israeli colonies/ *Yeshuves*. By 1947, Jews owned 6–7 per cent of the land of Palestine,[25] although immigrant Jews at that time did not use or exploit the Palestinian labour force, but were self-reliant. This autonomy of the pre-state colony was part of the preparations for nation and state building. It also reflected Zionism's vision of an exclusive Jewish state. Weizmann had expressed this vision in 1919 saying that Palestine should become as Jewish as England is English.[26] To that end a process of ethnic cleansing was undertaken, primarily during the war of 1948, by the Jewish army and militia who expelled some three-quarters of a million Palestinians (or 54 per cent of the total Palestinian population of mandatory Palestine).[27] This meant the destruction of 412 villages, not to mention urban areas, cities and towns.[28]

Benny Morris, the famous Israeli 'new historian' argues that Ben-Gurion was right:

If he had not done what he did, a state would not have come into being. That has to be clear. It is impossible to evade it. Without uprooting of the Palestinians, a Jewish State would not have arisen here.[29]

Ilan Pappé unfolds the Zionist masterplan for cleansing Palestine through systematic operations around and during the 1948 war, in order to achieve a Jewish state with a Jewish majority.[30] In the case of South Africa, Africans were ethnically cleansed inside the country, with three and a half million being pushed into the native 'homelands'. In the case of Palestine, they were pushed outside mandatory Palestine, being displaced within what has become referred to as 'proper Israel', or expelled to the West Bank and Gaza Strip.

Britain did not support the whites and the Zionists separately, since a tripartite alliance brought all three together at least until 1950. After Israel's establishment and the Afrikaners' seizing of political power in South Africa in 1948, the close connection began to fade, but an interdependent relationship developed from that time. Different leaders at different periods had come together in planning and implementing their colonial schemes; thus, the partners in the first phase, which began in the late 1890s, included Theodor Herzel, Cecil Rhodes and Joseph Chamberlain (British Colonial Secretary),[31] while the second phase (1917–1950) was dominated by figures that included Chaim Weizmann, General Ian Christian Smuts, Lord Balfour and Lloyd George.[32] The third phase (1950–1994) saw a close association of interests between the two colonial outposts, as different prime ministers on both sides developed different areas of cooperation, e.g. in military, economic, trade and media matters. For the colonial planners, a Jewish state in Palestine and a white-controlled South Africa were regarded as strategic assets for the British Empire, especially in terms of controlling trade routes (India, the Cape and Cairo) and Third World resources.[33] In 1918 Weizmann wrote to Balfour from Palestine: "I see that the welfare of Zionism is intimately linked up with the strength of British Policy in the East, and I feel that London, Cairo, Jerusalem and Delhi are very intimately connected."[34]

Discrimination by law and policy

In both cases, structured discrimination was imposed on the indigenous populations by self-tailored laws, i.e. the laws of the dominant side that were shaped in line with existing racist notions and as part of the policy of control. The Native Act of 1913, which allowed the 'non-whites' to own or lease only 13 per cent of the barren land of South Africa, was followed after 1948, as the apartheid system came into force, by many more discriminatory laws, including, for example, the Population Registration Act (1950), the Bantu Authorities Act (1951), the Reservation of Separate Amenities Act (1953), the Public Safety Act and Criminal Law Amendment Acts (1953) and the Group Area Act (1957). As a consequence of such legislation, discrimination could be found in such areas as land allocation, development, provision of services and budget allocations. In the South African case, a policy of separate development was put in place, which ensured that blacks were educated separately and that the educational curriculum for blacks was designed to prepare children solely for menial jobs. It also needed minimal expenditure of government resources – only one-tenth of what was spent on the whites during the 1970s,[35] and almost unaltered in the 1980s. The policy also ensured that economic disparity between privileged whites and underprivileged blacks was protected, since the latter were pushed into the Bantustans, where they were left to provide cheap labour according to the needs of the whites, and with the minimum of resources to survive.

In the case of Israel, land acquisition took a more complicated route. According to Israeli figures, by 1949 the state of Israel and Jewish owners possessed 12 per cent of the entire area of the new state, while the remaining 88 per cent belonged to "the Arab owners who left the country".[36] Through measures enacted by the Knesset, the properties of the 'absentees' were at first transferred to what came to be known as a 'Custodian of Absentee Property'.[37] Next the government set up the Development Authority, an 'independent' body to which the properties were transferred. This body was allowed to do anything, including selling land, although certain restrictions meant that any sale required government consent and could be made to the state, the Jewish National Fund (JNF) or to local authorities if certain criteria were met.[38] Eventually most 'absentee' lands were sold to the state and the JNF and, for many decades since, land controlled by both these agencies has been sold exclusively to Jewish buyers.

Significantly, human rights groups in recent years have been challenging the JNF and the Israel Lands Administration (ILA), a government-owned company, on the basis of their policies of exclusivity.[39] In the Occupied Palestinian Territories (OPT) taken in 1967, the remaining Palestinian areas to the east of the newly-built wall make up 53 per cent of the West Bank.[40] As to the land of the Gaza Strip, the Israeli army deployed from it in 2004, as part of the Israeli unilateral disengagement plan. It evacuated the Jewish settlements, but kept up the siege on Gaza from outside. It should not be forgotten that the OPT represent 22 per cent of mandatory Palestine.

Other examples of legalized discrimination are based on the Law of Return and the Citizenship Law. The 1950 Law of Return allows any Jew from any part of the world to 'return' to Israel and become an Israeli citizen who may live inside the Green Line or in the OPT settlements. However, Palestinian refugees are denied this right since the Israeli government "[made] a bold decision ... fully supported by all the inhabitants of the state that under no circumstances should the Arabs return to Israel".[41] It is important to note that this right is recognized by UNSC Resolution 194. Discrimination is also legalized in the Citizenship Law, which grants automatic citizenship to all Jews by virtue of the Law of Return, but allows it to Palestinians only by birth or naturalization.[42] The latter concession was amended in 2003 in a way that further limits certain types of naturalization. A Palestinian man or a female citizen of Israel can no longer live with his/her spouse inside Israel if the spouse is from the OPT because the latter is denied a permit to enter Israel; nor does the Law any longer allow so-called 'family unification' with Palestinians from the OPT. This violates a citizen's basic civil right according to a security justification that serves the demographic policy of keeping a Jewish majority.[43] For the same reason, inequality under the law also translated itself into family subsidy, where it was linked to serving in an army in which there are very few Palestinian citizens.[44] From 1997, the Knesset revoked differential subsidies because of the pressure exerted by the Palestinian community inside Israel and its Jewish supporters.[45]

In apartheid South Africa, the 'non-whites' were forcefully pushed into the 'homelands'/Bantustans and were subject to different 'legal' policies of division and containment, as is further explained below. In the case of Zionist Israel, most Palestinian citizens of Israel have ended up living in separate enclaves. This has resulted from a policy of control which has been used by successive Israeli governments since 1948. Ian Lustick identifies three strategies used to serve the policy of control: segmentation (isolating and fragmenting the Arab minority); dependence (Arab economic dependency); and cooptation (capture of the Arab elite).[46] Eventually this policy limited the growth of Palestinian villages, towns and cities so that it was possible to control Palestinian citizens at a low cost. This manifested itself in inadequate social services, due to unequal budget allocations and lack of equal opportunities. As such, inequalities have characterized almost every aspect of the social, political and economic life of Palestinian Israelis.[47] As for the Palestinians of the OPT, they were not granted Israeli citizenship and have been under military rule of the Israeli occupation for the last forty years. They live in far worse conditions, even in the presence of a Palestinian Authority.

Because of its discriminatory policies, Israel was recently requested to stand before the UN's Committee on the Elimination of Racial Discrimination, and on 22 and 23 February 2007 was questioned about denying residency rights to Palestinians married to Israelis, failing to indict those responsible for the death of thirteen Palestinians citizens of Israel during demonstrations in October 2000, and other issues with regard to the treatment of both its Palestinian citizens and Palestinians in the OPT.[48] Such issues included land distribution, house demolition, freedom of movement, failure to protect Muslim holy places, treatment of Bedouins, municipal services, equitable funding and racial profiling.[49]

Separation seen as the solution

In both cases, the dominant side preached and sought separation. In South Africa, the Separate Amenities Act no. 49 of 1953 stated that all races should have separate amenities – such as toilets, parks and beaches – that did not need to be of an equivalent quality.[50] A South Africa Bantustan/separation system was put in place to separate and exclude the black majority, and between 1960 and 1984, 3.5 million blacks were forcibly removed from 'white areas' to the Bantustans,[51] from which they needed permission to leave. Since men had to leave the Bantustans to get jobs in white areas, they resided in hotels for most of the year, away from their families who were left to survive with no adequate housing, education or health facilities. The white South African government established ten separate Bantustans/'homelands'; four of these were declared independent and their black citizens stripped of their South African citizenship.[52] The white government hand-picked their leaders but no country in the world recognized these leaders as legitimate governments except Israel, which even formalized a twin cities agreement between the Ciskei Bantustan/'homeland' and the Israeli Ariel settlement in the early 1980s.[53] The intention behind this system was eventually to make the rest of South Africa a totally white country where blacks could claim no political rights at all, while white South Africa would continue to exercise its hegemonic power over the scattered Bantustans. Chapter 3 examines the positions of different white protest groups on this issue.

In the case of the Palestinian–Israeli conflict, the Zionist movement historically had accepted the partition of Palestine, but after the 1948 war and the expulsion of most of the Palestinian population, Israel never marked out its borders. The capture of the rest of the land of mandatory Palestine in 1967 was translated in such a way that Palestinians residing in the newly-occupied land became stateless and lived under Israeli military rule while the land was classified as part of the 'Land of Israel'/'Eretz Israel'. Over the years, Israel tried to find formulas that would allow it to seize and keep the maximum amount of land and dispose of the maximum number of Palestinians, with the aim of separating Jews from Palestinians and Palestinians from Palestinians, in order, as noted earlier, to weaken them.

Inside Israel today, as discussed, most Palestinian citizens live in separate and less developed areas, in overcrowded neighbourhoods, with most of their land having been confiscated. Such a reality is founded on many years of separation under military rule. During the period between 1948 and 1966, Palestinian citizens lived in Israel under rigorous military control; these emergency defence regulations covered all aspects of their lives and controlled freedom of speech, movement, expropriation of property and means of transportation.[54] Populated Palestinian areas were defined as security zones. Under three military governors,

> all the Arab villages and settlements in Galilee, the triangle, and the Negev were divided into small pockets called "closed areas" usually consisting of one or more Arab villages, which no Arab could leave or enter for any reason without first obtaining a written permit from the military governor of the area.[55]

During and after this period, they were allowed to participate in the procedural element of the national Jewish state democracy – voting in the elections. Further, while their standard of living has progressed over the years, they still (mostly) live separately and as second- or third-class citizens.

Since 1967, similar Zionist policies mean that settlement strategies inside 'proper Israel' have come to represent the same government objectives within the OPT. The objectives have included dispossession of the indigenous population and the incorporation of their lands into the Jewish state.[56] Different settlement belts were put in place, to further divide and conquer while simultaneously separating, e.g. the Allon plan and the Sharon plan,[57] according to which it would be possible to give "autonomy for the people, but not the land", since the minority population would find it "difficult to form territorial and political continuity".[58] This was so because Jewish settlements are built and linked through a road system that fragments the Palestinian-populated areas while connecting the Jewish ones. Built on confiscated Palestinian land, Jewish settlements are inhabited solely by Jewish residents: there are 146 settlements with a population of 400,635, of whom 180,144 live in settlements in East Jerusalem.[59] Many commute separately, using bypass roads also built on confiscated Palestinian land. According to a Peace Now report, there are seventeen routes in the West Bank on which Palestinian vehicles are completely prohibited, ten routes on which Palestinian travel is partially prohibited, and fourteen routes on which Palestinian travel is restricted.[60]

The building of the wall started in 2002 and is another step in the direction of further physical separation which reinforces the tearing apart of the Palestinian-populated areas in the West Bank. The wall, the settlements, the bypass roads, the checkpoints, and the closed or restricted areas all produce fragmented Palestinian enclaves that differ in size and are totally cut off from East Jerusalem. As for the Gaza Strip, it is already a big walled area which Israel controls from outside. A similarity could be drawn here between the policy of separate and fragmented 'homelands' in South Africa and the policy of fragmented and separate Palestinian enclaves. In both cases, the dominant side used 'homelands'/enclaves as the way unilaterally to solve the conflict by offering the dominated side self-rule or autonomy in the orbit of the hegemony of the dominant side. In the case of apartheid, a wall was not built but the other strategies were used. However, the system of separation and fragmentation was eventually unsuccessful.

In the case of Zionist Israel, it has so far managed to build and impose a system of separation and fragmentation more advanced than that applied in South Africa. Over the years, the form of separation has moved from expulsion to separation by invisible physical walls, and finally to separation by physical walls in the OPT. The invisible physical walls still exist in East Jerusalem and 'proper Israel'. The positions of Israeli protest groups on the separation issue are highlighted in Chapter 4.

Oppression as the way to keep control

Another similarity is seen in the policies of oppression implemented by both ethnic states. Both practised torture, killing and assassination; curfews, pass laws/permits, and house demolition/Group Areas Act; imprisonment on a large scale; the banning of resistance groups, parties and movements; censorship of critical media, and so on. In both cases, the judicial authorities justified and supported the oppressive measures of the existing regimes, as reflected in court sentences. For example, in 1984, two soldiers from the South West Africa Territorial Force were each fined R50 (about US$35–40) for roasting a sixty-three-year-old African man over an open fire and causing him extensive injuries.[61] This case is similar to an incident in 1956 when Israeli soldiers fired on villagers returning home to Kufur Kassim, unaware that a curfew had been imposed. As a result fifty died, many of them children. The highest penalty was a three-and-a-half-year sentence while the battalion commander was fined only one piaster (the smallest Israeli coin).[62] These verdicts and the different oppressive policies reflect/ed systems and political cultures that viewed the Other as less human, of unequal worth. The Other was labelled as a terrorist and/or a communist in South Africa, and as an Arab, a fundamentalist Muslim, radical leftist and/or terrorist in mandatory Palestine and beyond.

The 1967 Terrorism Act in South Africa allowed the death penalty against the resistance.[63] Special forces, including underground killing squads which continued to function until their discovery in the early 1990s, were active in intimidating, harassing and assassinating apartheid opponents.[64] While the death penalty has not been used in Israeli courts against the Palestinians, the policy of extrajudicial assassinations has been used frequently, especially in the second Intifada. Since 2000, over 500 persons, many of them civilians, have been killed as a result of this policy.[65] In December 2006, the Israeli High Court failed to find this policy unlawful, but held that 'targeted assassinations' might be carried out only as a last resort and within the bounds of proportionality.[66]

Oppression also found its translation in the political economic systems that ensured the domination of one group over the other. In the case of South Africa, the economic side of the system ensured that wealth stayed in the hands of the minority, while poverty prevailed among the majority. Blacks were left to beg for work, knowing that if they did find jobs they would be exploited; and were pushed to live in crowded areas, some of which were without running water. They starved and suffered such economic diseases as cholera and polio. Palestinians in the 1967 Occupied Territories live under similar types of oppression. With 500 checkpoints and roadblocks obstructing the freedom of movement within the West Bank, in addition to the wall and the separation of Jerusalem,[67] economic standards have fallen sharply. In addition, because of the economic sanctions imposed since Hamas won the elections in January 2006, 80 per cent of Gazans[68] and 57 per cent of West Bankers[69] live below the official poverty line.

Both oppressive states became militarized states

Apartheid South Africa and Zionist Israel developed into highly militarized states. White South Africans praised militarism and developed a sophisticated army and military industry, and the white regime and society was characterized by a militarized culture. By the 1980s, according to Frederikse, South Africa had become a kind of military state, with an all-pervasive military presence at school, at work, in cinemas and on TV, and in advertisements and comic books; the military establishment penetrated all social spheres:

> the country is led by a former minister of defence. Parliament is no longer the most influential decision-making body; it has been replaced by the State Security Council, which is dominated by top military personnel ... according to the new rhetoric of the military, South Africa is no longer defending White, Afrikaner supremacy, but rather a free enterprise and economic growth. The alliance between government and big business is reinforced by ever-increasing militarization.[70]

By law all white men were required to do two years' national service, twelve years in the Citizen Force, five years in the reserve and further service in local commandos until the age of fifty-five.[71]

In the case of Israel, the military establishment is also very powerful. It not only produces a "society in uniform – Nation in Arms", but has also developed enough power over the years to influence the political establishment's decision-making.[72] This has often been the case, particularly when those in charge have the personal capacities and charisma to be an influence, e.g. Dayan, Sharon and Rabin.[73] Manna and Bishara refer to Baruch Kimerling, who argues that over time there has been an increase in militarism in Israeli society, and that the high-ranking army generals play a basic role, not only in politics but also in the economy.[74] Their role manifests itself in an alliance with big businesses, especially the military industry. Together they have reinforced an ever-increasing militarization in the political and societal levels. It should be noted that every man in Israel has to do obligatory military service for thirty-two months (non-combatants), thirty-six months (combatants), and two to six weeks of reserve service annually.[75] They are called for specific reserve service periods according to the army's needs, and the reserve service is applied to non-combatants until the age of forty-one and to combatants until the age of fifty-one.[76] Women have to do two years of obligatory service but enjoy a margin of freedom to choose not to do so.

Israeli political culture praises the military apparatus and its policies. Israel admires the underground militias of the pre-state period, and the soldiers who later fought for Israel's 'independence and defence', praising them as symbols of bravery and sacrifice. A Jewish Israeli brought up in a Zionist national education system inevitably regards members of the military and the pioneer Zionists as the heroes of modern times, and to refuse to serve in the army is a big challenge to the rooted ethos of what is termed 'the national consensus'. Chapter 2 discusses the latter aspect, where the connection can be seen between the existing culture of militarism and the kind of civil society that developed in both cases.

Becoming regional superpowers

Both states developed into hegemonic regional powers. Apartheid South Africa interfered politically and militarily in many neighbouring countries, and committed grave violations of human rights, e.g. in Namibia, Mozambique and Angola.[77] Namibia was under apartheid South African occupation for decades, and the Namibian people and their resources were exploited. The army and surrogate forces of apartheid South Africa committed many assaults and invasions in Southern Africa, especially in the 1970s and the 1980s. In the case of Angola, 10,000 were killed and 150,000 were left homeless between 1975 and 1982.[78] The aim was not only to punish those states which supported black resistance, but also to demonstrate that the military could act on a larger scale, even when there was no direct threat from a specific state. The objective was the enforced compliance of the Other, and Pretoria's regional strategy was to keep all its neighbours off-balance and dependant on it economically.[79] Through playing the role of a destabilizing force in the region to undermine the power of the surrounding states, it assumed the role of the policeman of the region.

Israel has also assumed itself to be a regional superpower, and has sought hegemony over the area beyond the opponent Palestinians. Hisham Sharabi stresses that Israel has used power politics as its foreign policy model against the Palestinians and the Arabs.[80] Alarmed by the power of its neighbours, Israel has sought to shape and control the behaviour of other Middle Eastern states, and has implemented different strategies, including direct military intervention, direct threats, coercive demands, indirect personal manoeuvring, verbal persuasion and economic inducement. It has built itself into a strong hegemonic power, and at present it is the fourth largest nuclear power and the fifth largest arms producer in the world.[81]

Examples of Israel's hegemonic policy include the Israeli invasion of Lebanon, the attacks on Palestinian resistance groups in Jordan in the late 1960s, the attack on what was claimed to be Iraq's threatening nuclear reactor in the early 1980s, its participation in the tripartite attack on Egypt in 1956, the Camp David agreement with Egypt in 1978, and the peace agreement with Jordan in 1994. Through these two agreements, Israel was granted legitimacy and achieved normalization of relations according to the existing balance of power, which was in its favour. Consequently, the core of the Arab–Israeli conflict – the conflict with the Palestinians – remained as a hostage to Israel's strategic goals. Other examples of its regional hegemonic role include the 'disproportionate' war on Lebanon in summer 2006, and current threats against Iran over its development of nuclear power (2008). Nor should the severe military operations against neighbouring Palestinians in the OPT be forgotten. According to human rights norms, many cases fall in the category of war crimes.[82]

Israel also perpetuated its hegemony through the political agreements it has signed with the PLO. These are based on a grand containment strategy which has divided the occupied territories into A, B and C areas.[83] Driven by Israel's security agenda and containment strategy, the Oslo Accords and subsequent agreements have aimed to establish another form of occupation, but with Palestinian consent.

Israel has gradually become not only a military and political hegemonic power but also an economic regional power. It is shaping its economic relations with neighbouring states, not only through trade but also through establishing industrial zones supported by preferential agreements with the US; especially in the case of Jordan and Egypt. As time has passed, Israel, which has been considered by many to be the destabilizing state of the region, has started to become a cornerstone in the political economy of the region. It has managed to normalize its connections with many Arab regimes and claims that the route to Washington starts in Jerusalem.

Dominant states develop indoctrinated societies

Both states developed indoctrinated societies. Formal education and the media played major roles in this task. In apartheid South Africa, whites were brought up in a system known as Christian National Education, an educational system that had produced apartheid and supported its existence. It taught schoolchildren that "theirs is a political system with all the trappings of any other western-style democracy – parliaments, opposition parties, an independent judiciary – and that Blacks who demand majority rule already have it in ... Homelands".[84] White children were taught that the whites had brought civilization to the country, and were told to love their own land, raise the flag, sing community songs, learn about the evils of terrorism and communism, make use of their superior knowledge, be spiritually prepared, and to be like David against the Philistine Goliath.[85] A young white South African student said

> we've learned of many battles in our history so I think that from a very young age we are trained to cope with any demand our country may ask us ... we are

38 Background and political development

actually fighting for Christianity, because communism doesn't allow you to practice your own religion ... the terrorists are only instruments that the Russians use to fight Christianity ... it is a Christian war. We are not the aggressors; they are the aggressors. We are defending our property and our people.[86]

Soldiers (boys) who died on the borders were referred to as martyrs of civilization.

The media disseminated establishment propaganda claiming the virtuous nature of the apartheid system. It repeatedly declared that the system was defending Christianity, fighting terrorism, defending whites' land and rights and defending the free world and civilization. According to Pogrund,[87] the whites owned the big newspapers that addressed the whites and showed them in total control; when referring to the blacks they showed only black riots. However, by the 1980s a few voices from an alternative critical media were starting to develop. More than 100 laws were passed against a free press with the aim of controlling independent journalism.[88]

Ben-Gurion's *Mamlachtiut* (statehood) vision of education was the basis of the nationalized educational system that eventually developed in Israel. The Israeli Education Act of 1953 stipulates that: "The goal of statehood education is to establish a basic education in this state upon the values of Israeli culture and scientific achievements, on the love of the homeland and loyalty to the State and Nation of Israel."[89] Pedahzur makes link between this and the pre-state 'education of Zionist citizenship' that represented ethno-national aims through instilling ideological thoughts in different courses, e.g. geography of 'homeland', Bible classes, and even mathematics.[90]

Because state education (policies, system and curriculum) has been developed to serve an ideological political motivation,

> pupils have been exposed to beliefs which served the goals of the Jewish state, mainly to organize and coalesce members of the dominant ethnicity and cultivate their national identity. The intention was to gain their full support, agreement, identification, participation and willingness to make sacrifices for national projects, while the grand design was to build a nation, a nation-state, or defend the ethnic nation from real or imaginary threats.[91]

In terms of the image of the Palestinians given in the Israeli curriculum, it has been negative. If not disregarded, they have been patronized or depicted as backward natives.

As to civic education in Israeli schools, Pedahzur maintains that it has focused on the formal procedural aspect of governmental institutions, and that it displays the "formal 'appearance' of Israeli democracy: declaration of independence, legislative and judiciary proceedings, elections procedures, the Knesset and the government".[92] It marginalizes the more substantial issues of Israeli 'democracy', e.g. Israeli citizenship, the non-existent constitution, the status of religion in relation to the state, and the status of the Palestinian minority,[93] and makes no mention of the status of the Palestinians living in the OPT under Israeli occupation. The conflict is taught as an optional subject from a narrow national perspective. Other subjects such as Bible studies, geography and Jewish history are highly encouraged, in terms of teaching hours and teacher training.

As part of state education, canonic school ceremonies take place. The ceremonies evoke many historic, religious, national and military symbols, e.g. the holocaust (six candles), Yizkor/remembrance prayer, personal items of the fallen, the national anthem etc. Lomsky-Feder and other scholars think that these ceremonies have developed into state cults, being part of national education or a constructed culture of bereavement.[94] A sense of victimization is perpetuated, opening a space for the conviction that Jews are hated only because they are Jews. Any ability to see the Other as also a victim becomes unrealistic:

> by drawing attention to the suffering and sacrifice of individuals, (Jewish) Israelis are conceived of as victims of power and not as the wielders of power who occupy and repress another people. Picturing the self and the collective as victims blinds many Israeli Jews from seeing the "other" and distracts them from moral concerns about the nature and uses of war.[95]

Eventually state education not only stressed the rightness of self ethnic goals but also prioritized security, de-legitimized the opponent, projected a positive self-image and self-perception as a victim. Lomsky-Feder gives an example of how Passover is taught as a national religious ceremony:

> Passover establishes the basic mythical pattern of Jewish history as that of recurring cycles of persecution: riots, pogroms and attempts at annihilation, followed by redemption and salvation. The period between Passover and Independence Day applies the same mythical structure to the modern era. Each year, Israeli society is reminded that persecution is part of the fate of the Jews, and that a Jewish state with a strong army is the only viable answer.[96]

The image of a 'new Jew' is moulded there. He or she learns to perceive himself/herself as the opposite to the weak Jew in Europe before state establishment.[97] The 'new Jew' is strong and capable of defending his country and his people. Thus, another annihilation will never be allowed, and "Never again" becomes the statement of a nation.

The media also contributed to the national education project by serving national ideological aims. In describing relations between the establishment and the media, Yoram Peri of the Hebrew University stresses the fact that a historic relationship was forged over the years, and that the level of the establishment's (political and military) interference and authority have decreased over time. Israel's early years witnessed a situation where the media was a total agent of the state and its parties, mainly dominant Labour. Journalists gained more space after the 1973 war because of public criticism of the government's conduct

40 *Background and political development*

before and during the war, and during the late 1980s and the 1990s, liberal voices among journalists enabled a certain independence, though naturally from within the Zionist framework of the Jewish national state and its ethos.[98]

Both societies developed a number of shared characteristics, of which fear and arrogance are major examples. According to Mitchell, arrogance is usually accompanied by fear among settler societies.

> Arrogance is due to an innate feeling of superiority. This superiority is usually a material/technological superiority which is then transformed in the minds of the settlers into cultural, national, religious, and racial superiority ... where the natives and settlers are of the same race, as in Ireland and Palestine, this assumed superiority becomes more problematic and takes the form of national or religious superiority.[99]

He adds that fear exists because of the settlers' memories of the past suffering of the natives, and of uprisings and massacres committed against them.[100]

In Chapter 2, it is possible to see the connection between having an indoctrinated society and the kind of civil society that develops/ed in both cases. It is an issue that in both cases also leaves/has left its traces on the politics, political platforms and the roles of protest groups (Chapters 3 and 4).

Both settler states enforced their ethnic symbols while undermining that of the natives

The governments of apartheid South Africa and those which preceded apartheid, stressed white sovereignty beyond the use of force. They used many symbols associated with the white history, culture and ideology in power. The English gave their names to different parts of South Africa, e.g. East London, Port Elizabeth, Hyde Park and Kimberly, while the Afrikaners named different areas and streets after their famous leaders. A visitor to South Africa today would be astonished that many of those names are still seen on road signs. In the process, the languages of English and Afrikaans were also enforced, while those of the natives were undermined.

In the case of Israel, Jewish symbols have been extensively used as signs of Jewish sovereignty, e.g. the lion (the symbol of 'Judah' which is used as the emblem of the Jerusalem municipality),[101] the national emblem (the *menorah* –the candelabrum of Chanukah), *Ha Tikva* (the national anthem),[102] and the flag of Israel (inspired by the *tallit* – the shawl with blue stripes worn by Jews during prayer).[103] In order to Juda-ize the geographical space, biblical and historical places, heroes and colours were also used to serve the claims of the ideology in power. Hebrew terms and names prevail, even with reference to areas in the 1967 occupied territories, e.g. Judea, Samaria, Gush Etzion etc. As to street names, even a blunt racist such as Meir Kahane from the extreme right-wing party Kach has a street named after him.[104] In contrast, the history and symbols of the Palestinians were either undermined or denied.

Differences between the two conflicts

Area and population

South Africa and historical Palestine differ in size and demographic distribution. South Africa has an area of 1,224,691 sq km with a population of 41.5 million people (75.7 per cent black, 12.6 per cent white, 8.5 per cent coloured and 2.4 per cent Asian).[105] Israel, which has no official borders, has a population of 6,100,000 of whom 1,200,000 are Palestinians holding Israeli citizenship and 400,000 Jewish settlers.[106] The settlers live in the Palestinian territories occupied in 1967. The Palestinian population of the Occupied Territories captured in 1967 is 3,400,000.[107] If the population of mandatory Palestine is divided according to nationality/ethnicity, the Jews make 4,900,000 while the Palestinians make 4,600,000. In terms of size, the area of mandatory Palestine is 26,995 sq km.[108] Israel (according to the armistice line) has 20,770 sq km (78 per cent) while the occupied territories of 1967 have 6,225 sq km (22 per cent).[109] Table 1.1 organizes these figures.

The statistics show that the demographic gap is very small while the land distribution gap is wide. Given the high rate of fertility among the Palestinians, by 2010 the Palestinian population in mandatory Palestine will exceed the Jewish Israelis.[110] Even so, the ratio gap between the two populations is not as significant as that in South Africa, where the 'non-whites' were citizens of South Africa, except in the four 'independent homelands' that were not recognized by the international community. The Palestinians of the occupied territories have not been granted Israeli citizenship. In addition, the small percentage of whites in the overall population of South Africa represents a significant difference, as does the size of the country in terms of area. With such numbers, it was impossible to control South Africa, especially when the leadership of the resistance decided to make the country ungovernable through well-organized strategies.

Visions and strategies of the two liberation movements

Another difference is the focus of the struggle of both liberation movements. The struggle in South Africa, led by the African National Congress, focused on non-racialism, the unity of South Africa, majority rule, land distribution and economic development for all. In the case of Palestine, the Palestinian struggle, led by the PLO, moved from the aim of regaining the whole of Palestine to a two-state solution. By doing this, the PLO recognized the existence of Israel as a fact and accepted the partition of Palestine. The ANC stood firm against the partition of South Africa (the Bantustans/'homelands' plan). It ran a liberation struggle that aimed to create a shift in power and destroy the apartheid regime altogether, and managed to develop a clear and common political vision for an ideal South Africa.[111] The anti-apartheid movements were able to buy and promote this vision, for example through the church, protest groups, community-based organizations, and unions (students and black labour unions). In the case of Palestine,

Table 1.1 South Africa and mandatory Palestine – area and population

Conflict area	Details	Area	Population	Population details	Jewish and Palestinian population in mandatory Palestine
South Africa		1,224,691 sq km	41.5 million	75.7% black 12.6% white 8.5% coloured 2.4% Asian	
Mandatory Palestine		26,995 sq km			4,900,000 million Jewish Israelis and 4,600,000 million Palestinians
	Israel	20,770 sq km	6,100,000 million	– 1,200,000 Palestinian citizens of Israel	
	The Occupied Palestinian Territories	6,225 sq km	3,400,000 million	+ 400,000 Jewish settlers	

there has been no single clear, common, strategic political vision to which most adhere. The debate on one state or two states is still not closed and the degree of acceptable compromise still varies and fluctuates.

The South African resistance movement adopted many strategies in its struggle: the military-against-state apparatus, the civil society mobilization through the United Democratic Front (UDF), and the mobilization of international sanctions against the apartheid state. The PLO and other factions also used the military strategy but this made no clear distinction between civilians and state apparatus. The PLO, and later the Palestinian National Authority (PNA), also failed to develop any partnership relations with Palestinian civil society in service provision and resistance, especially during the Oslo period; indeed, the PNA took competitive and sometimes oppressive measures against the NGOs because of funding and political differences. In South Africa the UDF managed to lead and mobilize, in terms of providing services, by acting professionally enough to be able to link that to the strategies of the political struggle.[112] It therefore managed to engage, mobilize and maintain credibility.

There were four reasons why, in the Palestinian case, such a supportive grassroots vehicle failed to develop. First, the PNA was established before liberation and has had to function according to the limits of the Oslo Accords, which reflect the asymmetry of power between Israel and the PLO. This left the PNA with a tiny margin with which to run any resistance. Second, civil society has become fragmented over whether or not to support the agenda and policies of the PNA or to run opposition at times when the political parties were/are in crisis. Third, the majority of Palestinian non-governmental organizations are run by professionals, and since the beginning of the Oslo period have, to a great extent, lost their connection with the grassroots level. They have been institutionalized into professional centres, whereas in the case of South Africa, black civic organizations were run by activists who worked, or maintained close relations with, the grassroots level. Finally, the PLO and the PNA never adopted sanctions as a strategy. Some have called for sanctions, but this has never been a formal strategy in the struggle.

In comparing the two liberation movements, Mona Younis concludes that the South African movement was more successful for a number of reasons, including a higher level of democracy within the ANC; the ANC's ability to organize the working class and mobilize it on the economic and political fronts; the questionable agreement signed by the PLO with Israel that intensified the 'Bantustanization' of the West Bank and Gaza Strip; and the PLO's acceptance of a policing role on behalf of Israel.[113] This latter reason undermined its ability to lead any resistance.

Chapters 3 and 4 prove that in the two cases the dependant variables, the politics, political platforms, and roles of protest groups cannot be examined without considering the visions and strategies of 'the other' – both resistance movements. The latter constitute intermediate variables as discussed in the Introduction. Both are inter-connected.

44 *Background and political development*

Support received from neighbouring states

Another difference between the two cases is the level of support each received from neighbouring states. According to Ebrahim Ebrahim, a leading ANC figure,[114] the Arab League does not play a positive role in supporting the Palestinian resistance; this represents a substantive difference from the case of South Africa, where neighbouring states supported the anti-apartheid resistance, including its armed struggle. Many countries opened their territories to the political and military wings of the resistance – and paid a heavy price for their support. Regarding the Palestinian struggle, Edward Said describes the support of the Arab states for the Palestinians in the face of Israeli aggression and oppression as rhetorical, and sometimes less than that: "On the formal level, Palestinians faced explicit hostility or dispassionate support."[115] As the years passed, state national interests won over pan-Arabism, and the Arab League failed to develop an Arab regional system to combat Israel as a superpower within the region. This was not the case in Southern Africa, where neighbouring states supported the black resistance and resisted the hegemony of the apartheid system.

Economic dependency versus interdependency

Palestinian–Israeli economic relations never achieved a level of interdependence that Israel was unable to relinquish, unlike the case of South Africa where interdependence was achieved. The industries and farms of the whites became dependant on cheap black labour which, once it had become organized in the unions, was able to affect the production process. The Congress of South African Trade Unions (COSATU) was instrumental in organizing workers' rights and in political mobilization, and was active and a part of decision-making at both the grassroots and executive levels. Its leadership was transferred into the various leadership positions of the ANC, from where it managed to transform the black working class into an economic and political force.

This contrasts with the case of Israel, which has used different policies and strategies to strangle the Palestinian economy of the Occupied Territories since 1967, achieving this outcome through control policies that forced the OPT to become dependent on the occupying state and its economy. Such policies involved, for example, border controls on imports and exports, exploitation of natural resources, de-development of Palestinian industries and businesses, and violations of the full range of employment/workforce rights, including through closures.[116] From 1967, Palestinians in the OPT had undertaken labouring tasks, and during the first Intifada this was used for the first time as a resistance tool (boycott). The two Israeli economic sectors affected were agriculture and construction. To overcome this weakness, a potential for interdependence, the Israeli government took a strategic political and economic decision in 1990 to import foreign workers.[117] Between 1987 and 1995, the number of Palestinian workers (blue collar) dropped from 110,000 to 50,000,[118] and by 2003 amounted to a few thousand only. It is important to note that the Palestinian economy will face many more challenges in the years to come. By 2020, the Palestinian labour supply will have more than doubled to about 1.5 million (at 4.5 per cent growth annually).[119] At present, the Palestinians are asking to return to their previous jobs inside Israel, but the latter continues to seek separation while maintaining Palestinian economic dependency.

As a result of de-development and dependency, more than a million Palestinians (out of 3.5 million) live below the poverty line.[120] In 2002, the economic gap between the two sides reached a very high level. Israel's GNP was US$102.5 billion, compared with US$4.2 billion in Palestine (OPT),[121] while GNP/per capita in Israel stood at US$15,600 as against US$1,200 in Palestine.[122] The economic development gap is 1:12 in favour of Israel.[123] Compared to neighbouring Arab states, Israel's economy is three times larger than the combined economies of Egypt, Palestine, Jordan, Syria and Lebanon.[124] Among its booming businesses are the security and military industries, both of which, of course, were very powerful in apartheid South Africa. The economic situation of Israel's Palestinian citizens is also inferior in comparison with the rest of the citizens of the Israeli state, and their economic power is marginal. The Ashkenazi Jews have continued to enjoy the highest economic power, both before and since the liberalization process of the economy, and the gap between them and the Sephardim (Jews of Middle Eastern origin) remains wide.

In both struggles, the economic relationship between the conflicting sides (which constitutes another intermediate variable), was/has, in the two cases, been stressed differently in the politics of protest. Chapters 3 and 4 make this difference clear.

Legitimacy: Zionism versus apartheid

Zionism has managed to gain a legitimacy that the apartheid ideology never enjoyed. Zionist Israel is generally perceived as a democracy and, unlike the case of apartheid South Africa, its legitimacy is not questioned. There are a number of reasons for this. Jeff Halper stresses three: the Jewish history of the holocaust and the resulting Christian guilt; the image that Israel has managed to portray of itself as an oasis of Western democracy, facing fanatical Arabs and terrorism; and the unquestioning support it receives from the US.[125] Other factors can be linked to the historic alliance between the European colonial powers and Zionism: the deep-rooted Western civilizational commitment to Israel, which is founded on psychology and myth (religion);[126] and the lack of clear Palestinian political vision and common strategies of resistance. These issues have undermined the image of the Palestinian cause and the degree of support it could have obtained.

This is contrary to the support that the struggle of the black South Africans gained from the international community, which sympathized with the plight of the native population. The ANC succeeded in mobilizing international support and preserving moral superiority while it developed a human rights-based discourse. This was one of the great ethical struggles and captured the world's imagination because it confirmed the common values of humanity. As a result, condemnation of racism, a boycott of South African products, and the imposition of sanctions received worldwide support. This has not been the case with regard to Zionism and its political system.

The issue of the legitimacy of the ethnic ideologies in power – Zionism and apartheid – is very much present in Chapters 3 and 4, which will show the extent to which, in both cases, protest groups had/have either moved away from it or continued to associate with it.

Citizens versus non-citizens

All residents of South Africa were citizens and they acted in that capacity while resisting the apartheid system. The world never recognized the 'homelands'/ Bantustan system, and never accepted the withdrawal of citizenship from the Africans living in the Bantustans that were declared independent. Though Africans were displaced within their own countries they continued to hold citizenship although not, of course, at an equal level. The Palestinians, on the other hand, were demographically and legally fragmented. Most were either expelled or displaced, and ended up outside mandatory Palestine with the legal status of stateless refugees. Others were naturalized, as in the case of those living in Jordan or other non-Arab countries. Another group was granted citizenship inside Israel while the rest became stateless under Israeli military rule in the OPT of 1967. As such, the demographic power of the Palestinians was undermined; and their political power was even further weakened since they ended up fragmented, in different parts of the world ruled by different political regimes.

As noted earlier, this issue also constitutes an intermediate variable which, in both cases, reflects one of the results of the policies of their respective political systems. Both created different demographic conditions and subsequently different political realities, which in turn affected the pathways of protest groups in both cases.

Role of religion

As time passed and political circumstances changed in South Africa, the role of religion changed. Religion gradually became a unifying factor in which the South African Council of Churches played a major role and in effect became part of the liberation discourse.[127] Major churches, including some members of the Dutch Reformed Church, were instrumental in this endeavour. This has not been the Palestinian–Israeli case. Zionism built its legitimacy on the Old Testament. Israel was defined as a Jewish state and not as a state of all its citizens, since Zionism defines Palestine as exclusively Eretz Israel. The growing power of national religious groups (settlers) has further fuelled the conflict and labelled it with increasingly exclusive religious notions, while the voice of Jewish interfaith non-governmental groups is marginal and apolitical.[128]

Over time, the existing political religious notions and the increasing power of religious groups and parties in Israel, the deteriorating situation on the ground on the Palestinian side, and the failure of the PLO to achieve liberation and statehood in even part of Palestine, have given rise to Islamist resistance discourse/s, and Islamist groups are growing among the Palestinians. As such, the religious component of the conflict (Judaism versus Islam) is growing and is moving in a different direction from that taken by mainly Christian South Africa.

Framing the two conflicts and their resolution

The two conflicts have been framed differently, whether in terms of causes or resolution. In the case of South Africa, the causes of the conflict continued to be framed around colonialism, race and class, and in framing their resolution, the history of colonialism, along with racial and class discrimination were not wiped out. Resolution did not legitimize any of them, but on the contrary tried to challenge them. The resistance movement led by the ANC developed values and a rights-based vision. As time passed, this vision overcame that of the separation adopted by the apartheid regime. The latter was unable to hijack the process of framing the causes, or the resolving of the conflict. To achieve its goals, the ANC worked to create a shift in power that would allow for serious negotiations to take place. Eventually, and despite all the power it enjoyed, the apartheid regime was forced to compromise and a formula of power sharing was reached as both sides realized that neither side could triumph over the other. Thus, the politics of non-racial democracy won over white supremacy and exclusivity, and the politics of separation and division of land failed and was replaced by the politics of inclusiveness. The resistance movement compromised on the economic side, leaving the racial class divide almost unanswered. Whites kept control of more than 80 per cent of the land and wealth.

In the Palestinian–Israeli conflict, the process of framing the causes and resolution of the conflict has been very much outlined by the Israeli side. The Israeli side has succeeded in shifting the debate on the causes of the conflict from being a debate about the legitimacy of Zionism and a Jewish state in Palestine and the fact that the Palestinians, as the indigenous population, were denied their national rights. Instead it has become one of dispute between two national groups over the same piece of land. In terms of resolution, the two-state resolution has become the internationally acceptable formula. Liberal Israelis have been instrumental in propagating this framing, arguing that the two sides have rights and, as such, need to compromise. For the benefit of Israel, this framing has also been security based. The Palestinian Liberation Movement has failed to impose an alternative frame both for the causes and their resolution, and its political positions have become reactionary ones. As such, there are at present only a few scholars and scarcely any politicians who question the legitimacy of Zionism and the colonial history of Israel, not to mention Israel's responsibility for the Palestinian *nakba*.

In terms of resolution, the PLO accepted the two-state formula but has so far failed to make a shift in power that would allow for serious negotiations to take place. Such binding negotiations would allow for a Palestinian state to emerge in 22 per cent of mandatory Palestine and would also discuss other disputed issues, but are not expected in the short or medium terms. The idea that neither side can succeed over the other is not yet ripe to the extent of making the two-state formula feasible. In the meantime, Israel has been recognized as being a Jewish state, and its exclusivity has been accepted; this is the opposite situation from the case of South Africa, where it was refused at the level of framing the resolution and in practice.

The issue of framing the two conflicts is also evident in Chapters 3 and 4, which show how in both cases different categories of protest groups (have) framed, or accepted certain frames, for the two conflicts and their resolution.

Conclusion

This comparison shows that the foundations of the two conflicts are the same. Both have had settler colonial foundations in which racist notions were incorporated. As they proceeded, they developed similar characteristics – those of settler societies – as well as many similar forms of relationship with the indigenous population. Even so, the two conflicts have also developed differences over the years. The Palestinian–Israeli conflict has become more complicated, and the balance of power is still very much on the side of Israel. An examination of the differences indicates, in particular, that a number of factors or intermediate variables existed in the case of apartheid South Africa which led to the fall of the apartheid ideology and system. It could be argued that their absence in the case of Zionist Israel has hindered the possibilities for enabling a shift of power to occur and for an agreement to be reached.

The structure of power which was implanted and maintained by the dominant side translated itself in many ways: e.g. as structured discrimination under the law; religion being used as a means of justifying discrimination and oppression; policies of separation (physical and invisible); brutal forms of oppression; the development of militarized states on the oppressor's side; the oppressed being labelled as terrorists, inhuman and uncivilized; and the societies of the dominant side being indoctrinated by their own governments, media and education. Furthermore, the military establishment has had high levels of influence on the policies of both governments. Such power relations left the Africans and the Palestinians in inferior positions, politically, economically and socially. The Ashkenazim in Israel and the Afrikaners in South Africa respectively, enjoyed the highest level of power vis-à-vis the rest of the Israelis and the South African whites.

The two dominant sides adopted a policy of fait accompli, but (have) achieved different outcomes. The Israeli side has succeeded in continuing with it, and building 'new facts on the ground', while holding onto the old ones has, for decades, been an unchallenged Israeli policy. Israel also continues to expand geographically in the OPT. In discussing possible settlement/s, it argues for the need to be innovative and to find 'practical' solutions that will not undo what has become the 'reality' on the ground. Apartheid South Africa was forced to relinquish (partly) this policy, as part of an agreement on power sharing through which economic power was maintained in the hands of the white minority.

The South African resistance movement, led by the ANC, reversed many of the ramifications of the policy of fait accompli, managing to undermine the ideology of apartheid and weaken its system. It did so by winning the higher moral ground, mobilizing the masses, and making the country ungovernable. It used religion as a unifying factor, benefited from the political and military support received from neighbouring states, and applied the relation of economic interdependency in its favour. The ANC also managed to enhance its vision of inclusivity and its framing for the resolution. Its vision eventually overcame that of the separation proposed by the apartheid government. This has not been the case in the Palestinian–Israel conflict. The PLO did not succeed in undermining Zionism, and did not capture world opinion as the South Africans had done. It did not use mass mobilization as effectively as the ANC did; nor did it manage to develop a relation of economic interdependency. Additionally, the PLO did not enjoy the sort of support from which the ANC had benefited at the regional level.

Based on this comparison, does Israel represent another example of apartheid? While it is recognized by international law and the international community as a legal state, though with reservations over the issue of Jerusalem, Israel is also recognized as an occupying power. For some, elements of this occupation constitute forms of colonialism and of apartheid that are contrary to international law.[129] For a second group, Israel itself is considered a colonial apartheid state similar to apartheid South Africa.[130] For a third group, Israel is neither a colonial nor an apartheid political entity: it is a democracy that can be improved.[131]

The first group looks at the Israeli violations of Palestinian human rights and at Israeli policies on the ground which have forcibly fragmented the Palestinian people and separated them from the Jewish on ethnic/national grounds. It also refers to the policies of discrimination and domination used by Israel, which fall short in terms of respecting the 1966 International Convention on the Elimination of all Forms of Racial Discrimination, and the 1973 International Convention on the Suppression and Punishment of the Crime of Apartheid.[132] The second group questions the colonial history, colonization and nature of the state of Israel and its legitimacy, and also questions Israel's policies of transfer, expulsion, exclusion, expansion and domination. It considers all these as illegitimate and, as such, sees policies of separation and domination inside Israel and in the OPT as equal to apartheid. The third group includes sub-groups that would admit violations of Palestinian human rights, but which do not question the legality of the state and the history of its establishment. Nor does this group challenge the policies of separation that are combined with Israeli domination, since these have to do with demographic and security concerns.

Based on this chapter's comparisons, and in light of these three viewpoints, the researcher believes that Israel has developed a more sophisticated form of apartheid. At first, Israel used expulsion, and for many decades denied the existence of the other national group, the Palestinians. Later, the state of Israel became ready to recognize the Palestinians as a nation, but only after it had been guaranteed recognition within the 1948 borders. This means that future negotiations will only address the conflict in relation to the land occupied in 1967. Thus, Israel has (almost) managed to wipe out a historical period that witnessed war crimes against the Palestinians.

The apartheid system discriminated against the Africans on racial grounds in severe ways, but it did not expel them from the country or deny their existence. Apartheid South Africa based its policies of exclusion, discrimination, separation and domination on clear racial grounds. Israel did this on national grounds but in more subtle ways than those of the South Africans. It also managed to escape being labelled as racist, as happened in apartheid South Africa. There are only a few explicitly discriminatory Israeli laws, although in practice discrimination is implemented on a wide scale. In the case of South Africa, discriminatory laws were the norm. Since Israel practises racism on national but not on racial grounds, it has argued that racism does not apply to it and that discrimination exists everywhere. Israel did not grant citizenship to the Palestinians living in the OPT of 1967, nor was it questioned about their citizenship rights. Those living inside Israel were granted citizenship status, but were obliged by law and force to act within the confines of 'Israel being Jewish and democratic'. While the Palestinians ended up being granted different legal status inside mandatory Palestine and beyond, the land of Palestine has been claimed as Eretz Israel exclusively. So far, this convention, in addition to power politics, has been the starting point in defining Israel's relations with the Palestinians. To give back any of the Palestinian land under any conditions is considered a painful compromise for which Israel deserves to be rewarded.

Bearing in mind the isolation in which Palestinians live in their different enclaves in the West Bank and in the big prison of Gaza, an analogy with the Bantustan system of self-rule can easily be made. The three pillars of apartheid – separation, discrimination and domination – are applicable to the case of Zionist Israel. While the three have always been there, they have become more visible since the signing of the Oslo Accords and the building of the Wall. A system of 'bantustanization' is being built in the OPT of 1967 but without any overt declaration of this. Another subtle system has always existed inside Israel vis-à-vis the Palestinian citizens. Further, the issue of five million Palestinian refugees, who constitute more than 50 per cent of the Palestinian people combined, has no equivalent in apartheid South Africa.

This chapter has shown political developments in both conflict areas, and the kind of relations that existed between the dominant group in power and the excluded indigenous population. This background helps in showing the political realities in which both political systems function, and from which civil societies, in both cases among the dominant groups, have emerged and developed. This helps to locate protest groups – the dependant variable – and to examine their politics and roles. Many of the issues discussed here will also be discussed further or referred to throughout the coming chapters. They provide the basic realities and political notions that have shaped the political landscape in both cases.

Chapter 2 examines the two political systems of apartheid South Africa and Zionist Israel and their relationship with their respective civil societies. Thereafter, it will be possible to detect the political culture and parameters which have shaped the politics and political platforms, as well as the roles of the protest groups, a component in both civil societies.

2 Political systems and civil society in apartheid South Africa and Zionist Israel

Introduction

The preceding chapter compared political development in both conflict areas, particularly during the periods covered by the research. In looking at the relationship between the dominant and dominated sides, it clarified existing political realities and the way the two conflicts emerged, developed and were framed in terms of causes and resolution. It also provided a brief account of the context in which the respective political systems and civil societies act/ed. Chapter 2 moves further towards studying protest groups in both apartheid South Africa and Zionist Israel by examining the theoretical framework of the study, i.e. the relationship of the two political systems that exist, or existed, in both these ethnic-national states with their respective civil societies. The first is the independent variable, while the second encompasses the dependant variables: the politics[1] and roles of protest groups. In both cases, civil society's relation with the state or the political system[2] is/was fundamental in shaping the space that protest groups enjoy/ed and in which they function/ed.

Before examining the state political system and civil society in the two cases, it is important in this introductory section briefly to highlight some issues and/or notions relevant to their study. First, this chapter does not examine the concepts of 'political system' in general terms, since a broad study of the 'political system' and the different kinds of political system would overload the book and would not serve the specific focus of the research. However, a more limited and restricted examination of the kinds of political system that exist/ed in the two case studies is essential in arriving at an understanding of the respective ideologies that are/were in power, the existing political culture, and the kinds of relationships that were built between the political system and other societal spheres; particularly civil society.

These three aspects help in inferring where both political systems and their respective civil societies stand in the political spectrum of exclusivity versus inclusivity, i.e. whether they represent closed nationalism, open nationalism or a point somewhere in between. In the study of ethnic-national states, an awareness of this spectrum is important, as is the ability to deduce where each political system is located. The details of this spectrum provide the basis for defining the kind of system that exists in terms of being democratic, non-democratic (totalitarian or authoritarian), or representative of a restricted exclusive 'democracy' for the master race/group in power. In addition, this study is well aware that both political systems under study (have) developed a hegemonic and corporatist structure towards other spheres of society, and particularly civil society, that left its marks on the latter's position in the inclusivity–exclusivity spectrum. This is discussed later in the chapter.

Second, the chapter does not address the concept of civil society in general terms; however, before examining civil society in the two case studies, it is important to remind the reader of a number of relevant ideas. It should be noted that the concept of civil society is an elusive one that has travelled over time, and that its meaning has developed many dimensions, according to the existing context. There are no definite answers about its functions,[3] components[4] and its relation to other spheres of society.[5] The study therefore adopts a broad definition of civil society.

Civil society is the space between the individual and the state, and is a product of socio-economic and political developments in a certain place at a certain point in time. It has a dialectical relationship with the other spheres of society – the state, political society and the market – and the dynamics of this relationship affect its behaviour, its capacity to influence, and its modes of action. The blurring of the lines between these four spheres (state, market, political society and civil society) contributes to a continuous process of shaping the political culture, moral order, and the legitimacy of the political system. In principle, this space is open for free associational life and for freedom of expression. Within it, organized groups and active individuals take steps to raise awareness on specific or general issues, advocate certain (sometimes conflicting) values, exert pressure to protect or defend certain interests, and lobby for social, economic and/or political change.

The size and nature of this space varies with regard to degrees of independence and of inclusivity (being liberal or ethnic, and so on). In cases where a corporatist system is put in place by a state's political system, civil society finds itself co-opted.[6] Under an authoritarian regime, civil society is most likely to be limited, and its members are either co-opted or, in different degrees, are in a confrontational relationship with the political system. As the system moves towards (participatory) democracy, the size of civil society expands and its roles are (supposedly) expected to develop further and become more influential. Based on this, there can be many types of civil society, each with its distinct context, characteristics and roles. But alongside the distinctions there can be many similarities.

It is important to note that, if one chooses to associate civil society with specific universal pluralistic values in order to exclude from the realm of civil society those with racist, separatist, caste, tribal, violent[7] and/or militaristic leanings, then care must be taken. While the author believes that universal civic values are core components in defining a civil society, she is also aware that she might be accused of bias, or of artificially restricting the civil society space that in reality is not restricted. It is open to all, both with and without universal civic

54 Political systems and civil society

values, to compete for interests and to shape public opinion. In such cases, civil society would incorporate uncivil values such as militarism or exclusive, racist notions. These values contradict those of the liberal democratic system that, at least legally and procedurally, stresses values of pluralism, deregulation, egalitarianism and tolerance.

It can be argued that issues of independency, inclusivity, citizenship and equality are, or can be, controversial in examining civil society. Independency is difficult to assess, given the overlapping and blurring lines between the different spheres and especially in cases of ethnic-national states that developed corporatist structures. Inclusivity, citizenship and equality are very much connected. If the model of a political system that adopts liberal democracy of equal citizenship is applied as a criterion, many civil societies will fall below the standard. If a scholar labels such models as having no civil society at all, he/she runs the risk of not relating to the whole picture of organized popular initiatives. This means that each case can represent a different level of inclusivity, a degree of citizenship rights, and a degree of legal and practical equality, and will thus represent a different degree of democratization. In the two case studies examined here, it will be seen how civil society has not been inclusive, but has instead been divided along ethnic and religious lines in both ethnic-national states. It was also to a certain extent split, in the case of apartheid South Africa, along ideological[8] divisions within the white community; but this was not so in Zionist Israel.

Enjoying part of the space that forms societal values (such as tolerance, pluralism, communitarianism, universalism, closed nationalism or open nationalism), civil society can be a key contributor to processes that shape the moral order of a society and a state. The weakness or strength of the state decides the margins and the influence of civil society. Strong democratic states are more able to create a balance between the two, where independence and freedom of association and expression are guaranteed for civil society, and law and order are preserved by the state. In such a case, it would be assumed that both the state and civil society would adhere to principles of equality, equal citizenship and inclusivity, and that both would agree on the rules for preserving the legitimacy of the system.

In exclusive 'democracies' and/or non-democratic states, respect for these principles varies. As noted earlier, there would be degrees of civil society independency, degrees of freedom for association and expression, and degrees of citizenship and, subsequently, of inclusivity. This chapter applies the definition above and checks the values of both civil societies vis-à-vis the values of a liberal democratic system. It also shows how a centralized system, i.e. a 'strong' state, can have a substantial effect on the nature of civil society. Both states adopt/ed exclusive ideologies that promoted ideas of case uniqueness and peculiarities, and justified discrimination against part of the population. And, as will be explained, both systems developed hegemonic relations vis-à-vis the different spheres of society.

The chapter also reveals how the nature of both political systems, while producing a consensus and having a corporatist structure, were able to limit deviance and space for an autonomous civil society. It displays the nature and the limits of civil society, and explains the nature of the space enjoy/ed by civil society in the two cases. Consequently, it serves the aim of this study, which is to examine the politics, political platforms and roles of both protest groups, and to ascertain whether, in the quest for peace building, their roles were substantive or insignificant. Did such roles promote an inclusive, just peace or a partial settlement that benefited the status quo?

The chapter has four sections. Following this introduction, it looks at the political system and its underlying ideology in apartheid South Africa, and at the kind of civil society that existed there. It does this by addressing three topics:

1. the organized civil initiatives of the Afrikaners in a historical perspective;
2. civil society under the ethnic centralized political system of South Africa; and
3. a definition of South Africa's civil society.

Similarly, the third section examines the political system and civil society in Zionist Israel, and scrutinizes three analogous topics:

1. organized Zionist civil initiatives in a historical perspective;
2. civil society under the ethnic centralized political system of Zionist Israel; and
3. a definition of Israel's civil society.

The final section considers the similarities and differences between the two cases, on the basis of which the main ideas discussed throughout the chapter are reviewed. It also provides a link to Chapters 3 and 4.

It is important to reiterate at this point that while this research focuses on the relation between the state political system and civil society, it does not ignore the fact that other societal spheres also influence civil society. However, because of the need to adopt a specific and focused methodology, the relationship between civil society and the market and political society spheres was not examined here, and in order to maintain the focus of the study, these two spheres or variables were neutralized. While both are mentioned and/or briefly discussed as necessary, they are neither studied nor examined in depth. Thus the two following sections discuss respectively the political system in apartheid South Africa (the independent variable), and its civil society (in which the dependent variables are located), and that in Zionist Israel.

The political system and civil society in apartheid South Africa

The political system in apartheid South Africa

The most common description for South Africa's political system before 1994 was: 'an apartheid system'. While the National Party governments of South Africa claimed to be representative of a Western civilized democracy, their claim was widely refuted on fundamental grounds. The apartheid system negated many components of a democracy, since it was ethnically based and divided the South Africans into four races: white, black, coloureds and Indians. It excluded most of the population from political participation so that they lacked representatives who could be held accountable. The system also denied basic human rights to the majority, as citizens of the state, since there were different degrees of citizenship (white versus coloureds, Indians and black), and because the black majority enjoyed the lowest degree of citizenship. In the proposed tri-cameral reform system of the 1980s, the Indians and the coloureds were granted a higher degree of citizenship compared with the blacks.

According to Guelke, the political system of the Union of South Africa had been modelled since 1910 on the Westminster system, representing the legacy of British rule over the elements that had made up the Union, as stipulated in the South Africa Act of 1909. This act established a constitution for the Union of South Africa that enshrined white minority rule.[9] For eighty years South Africa was governed according the doctrine of parliamentary sovereignty, which meant that any government with a white ethnic majority in the House of Assembly could enact laws in the confident expectation that they would be enforced by the courts and not rejected on the grounds that they conflicted with any basic constitutional principle.[10] Consequently, the most far-reaching restrictions on the lives of the population could be fully imposed by constitutional means.[11]

On the same basis, the apartheid system developed its path and implemented its policies. Barrister John Lloyd of Exeter University describes the apartheid parliamentarian system of 1948 as one that turned the old and rather covert classical colonial system into an overt one.[12] The apartheid system put previous social policies that had been practised for decades into the form of written laws,[13] and further legalized discrimination and exclusion. Shortly after 1948, many discriminatory laws were put in place and coloured voters were removed from the common electoral roll.

The basic tenets of the constitution of the Union of South Africa were protected during the periods before and after 1948 when the apartheid era came into existence. But during the 1970s and the 1980s, when the idea of a 'nation of minorities'[14] and a policy of separate freedoms in the 'homelands' finally reached deadlock, a 'reformed' constitution was put in place in the republic. Based on a 1983 constitutional act, a tri-cameral system of government was adopted. This gave coloureds and Indians the right to elect representatives to separate councils; however, because both were given little authority, most power remained in the hands of the whites. The majority of Africans (blacks, coloureds and Indians) regarded this system as cosmetic, while those on the right of the ruling Afrikaner National party (NP) saw it as a betrayal of Afrikaner nationalism and its ethos. The majority refused it because it neglected the black Africans and kept political power, privilege and security in the hands of the dominant minority. Many saw it as a more advanced policy of co-optation to other 'ethnicities' (the coloureds and the Indians), and as a tool to divide the 'non-whites'. Substantive and genuine political change in the system occurred only in the early

1990s, with the interim constitution. This was the result of negotiations between the National Party and the African National Congress coalition, and led to the first free, non-racial parliamentarian elections.

The political system of apartheid South Africa has been described as totalitarian and/or authoritarian. It was considered a totalitarian system in the sense that its racial policies affected all aspects of the lives of its citizens from the cradle to the grave. Those who reject this description believe that the apartheid system did leave a margin for civil society to oppose state policies and lobby for group interests, and prefer to describe it as an authoritarian system. In this context, reference is made to the severe and oppressive measures that were imposed in order to implement the state's racial policies. Omond refers to the government's security laws (which claimed to defend the whites from 'total onslaught') and its racially-based legislation as being part of a highly authoritarian state system,[15] while Kiloh speaks of a model of an external colonial system that developed into an internal one. The external colonial system existed before the union of 1910, while the internal colonial system was put in place after that date.[16] She differentiates between the two, arguing that the main role of the external colonial state system was the provision of a legal framework for the capitalist development of the settlers, backed up by military force and a legitimizing ideology of European culture and civilization.[17] In the internal colonial system, the expatriate ruling class became a substantive settler minority that considered itself indigenous.[18] To maintain the exclusivity of its internal colonial system, South Africa became increasingly authoritarian, ending with an apartheid system that for decades used detailed legislation to create separate, racially-based regulations in every sphere of public and private life.

The ideology of Afrikaner nationalism (Afrikanerdom) was the leading force behind the apartheid system. It provided beliefs, justifications, and a vision for a white-ruled South Africa – 'the grand separation'. Many scholars believe that the apartheid ideology was the natural outcome of the existing historical and political culture and systems prevailing at the time. Others believe that it was not an inevitable development. Prominent writers, such as Giliomee and Schlemmer, argue that apartheid was merely an instrument of Afrikaner and a broader white nationalism,[19] while Waddy maintains that if the politics of the United Party (UP) had succeeded in the 1948 elections, apartheid would not have been inevitable.[20]

The politics of the United Party, which ruled before the 1948 elections, represented a classical set of English colonial notions that were reflected in a political culture of policies of domination. Its main ideological pillars were: white control and white supremacy (politically and economically), and a mission on the part of the white man to spread civilization. Segregation was promulgated in the context of living separately from blacks but having trusteeship over them. The UP's political platform during the 1948 elections, compared with the apartheid system, was reflected in a gradualist reform policy. Its agenda included support for the old policy of 'segregation', for the continued presence of coloureds on the common voters' roll, and for modest concessions to the Africans in the form of new social programmes, economic rights, and political opportunities in the Natives' Representative Council.[21] The UP also campaigned against the concept of territorial apartheid, and in favour of continuing the process of black urbanization in a controlled fashion.[22]

Afrikanerdom developed during the 1920s and 1930s and was based on individual membership of the Volk (nation), claiming rights to the land, a common history, solidarity and biological superiority (for a few decades), and being God's chosen people. The attitude of the Calvinist church towards the English and the Africans was fundamental in constructing Afrikaner nationalism, as was its role in legitimizing it. Many leading Afrikaner ideologues were prominent church members in the 1920s and 1930s, and were driven by a number of concerns, including demography (majority versus minority), fear, insecurity, material interest, social status vis-à-vis the English speakers, language, culture, and self-image and identity (in light of the trauma they had suffered during the wars with the English and being cut off from the metropolis). All this contributed to their strong feelings about the need to have power and control over their own destinies. To be a member of the Volk meant being white, being affiliated with the Dutch Reformed Church, sharing the same history, being of European descent, speaking Afrikaans, and supporting the national party.[23]

Afrikaner nationalist ideology represented a quest for nation-building in terms of identity, unity and holding power,[24] in pursuit of which Afrikaner nationalism combined crude colonial principles with an exclusive white Afrikaner-run project. To that end, when it came to power in 1948, the National Party put separation rather than segregation into practice as a new policy milestone, arguing that separate nations would achieve equality in a 'nation of minorities'. Thus, equality based on 'equal' nations and not on 'equal' individuals was adopted because the latter was perceived as impractical and suicidal. Here one sees a similarity with the case of the Palestinian–Israeli conflict, where the European Zionist Jews sought a united identity and a Jewish national state in Palestine. The Zionist parties rejected the notion of a 'one state' solution, but from the 1990s, and after decades of denying Palestinian national existence, a number of them adopted the formula of a 'two separate states' solution. As in the Afrikaner case, equality of citizenship in a single inclusive state is seen as suicidal for the Jewish state.

Based on the above, one might infer that, with regard to perceptions of the Other, i.e. the indigenous population, there were no ideological differences between Afrikaner apartheid (separateness) and English segregation, since the latter differed only in the strategies it used and/or advocated. Compared with Afrikaner nationalism, the UP adopted gradualist, liberal strategies of exclusive control, but after 1948 and as power moved into the hands of the Afrikaners, the severity of legalized discrimination mounted, so that by the 1960s, apartheid as a notion and as an action-oriented system had assumed a hegemonic position over other white agendas. The apartheid system became extreme in prescribing public behaviour and private intercourse, and in regulating the position of blacks in society.[25] Its operational ability gave it prominence and led many scholars to treat apartheid as a distinctive period, but without paying sufficient attention to its evolution from the previous colonial system.

As well as the components of apartheid ideology noted above, additional complementary elements for understanding this ideology have been highlighted by other scholars. Cohen, for example, described the ideology of apartheid as a 'civil religion'. In this context, this was indicative of the religious dimension of the state, where it was invariably associated with the exercise of power and with the constant regeneration of a social order that provided a transcendent referent for sovereignty within a given territory. He also noted that "the ultimate nature and destiny of political power is thus connoted in the symbols of the civil faith and re-enacted by civic ritual".[26] Similarly, Giliomee and Schlemmer argue that the four tenets of apartheid ideology stemmed from a conviction that the individual had no rights while the Volk had a God-given right to exist, and that whatever rights the individual enjoyed were derived from this collectivity.[27] Thus the four tenets were that the basic unit of society was not the individual but the 'God-given' Volk; and that individuals could realize their human potential only through identifying with, and in the service of, the Volk. The best means of avoiding political friction was apartheid, which also ensured the survival of whites and facilitated the highest measure of development for each ethnic group; additionally, apartheid granted others what one group (Afrikaner) demanded for itself.[28]

Cornevin stressed the ideological communitarian component, arguing that there was a tribal element connected with the ideology of apartheid, the white South African society and the state. She saw this as similar to that of Israel: "Africa's unique white tribe of Afrikaners ... see themselves as a sort of Israel in Africa."[29] The communitarian aspect in the case of Zionist Jewish Israel is discussed later in this chapter, where Azmi Bishara and others who have highlighted this element are referred to in relation to how Israeli Jewish society is socialized into Zionism from cradle to grave.

To maintain power in the hands of the whites, the NP developed a centralized system that continued for decades to be able to regenerate the ideology in power and to consolidate the social order (the latter point is discussed in the following section). Nor should some of the characteristics of the system that developed over time be forgotten; e.g. the way it became highly militarized, oppressive, hegemonic and indoctrinating (as discussed in Chapter 1). It developed an extensive policy network and an extensive welfare apparatus that promoted state legitimacy and its centralized nature. The state was involved in almost all facets of people's lives, and used ideology, symbols, rewards and a consolidated social order to unite people around it. At the same time it used sanctions to punish those who opposed these communitarian beliefs, and also utilized the hostility directed towards the system from the deprived majority inside South Africa and from neighbouring countries to feed the idea of the need for a strong state that could unite the people against external enemies. In that sense, it created a corporatist system. These elements are similar to those seen in the case of Israel, as the chapter discusses below (pp. 70–80).

60 *Political systems and civil society*

In conclusion, it is argued that before the non-racial elections of 1994 South Africa had an exclusive parliamentarian system, rooted in historical colonial ideas and Afrikaner ideology, that developed over the years into a grand, racially based system and then became an ethno-nationalist system in which everything was geared to association with membership of the Volk, and which was also unambiguously authoritarian towards the 'non-whites'. At its core was the communitarian nature of the white society, in which a majority was socialized into Afrikaner nationalism as part of a quest to achieve 'self-determination' and seize power. The initiatives taken to consolidate the social order prior to, and after the 1948 elections, contributed to the development of a highly centralized system that reflected a strong ethnic-national state in relation to its society. Over the years, the colonial political culture, along with the high sense of communitarian membership, especially among the Afrikaners, constantly reproduced the same ideas of exclusivity, feelings of superiority, and a determination to preserve its power and keep its existing privileges. This leads to a discussion of civil society in South Africa during apartheid.

Civil society in apartheid South Africa

Literature on South Africa's civil society is mostly associated with the black African civil society that developed as part of the struggle against apartheid,[30] whereas different researchers have looked at white civil society from different angles, three of which, in particular, were identified by the present study. First, Heribert Adam, Hermann Giliomee, Lawrence Schlemmer, Frederik van Zyl Slabbert and Marianne Cornevin focused on white civil associations, used by the Afrikaners before and after the 1948 elections as part of nation-building and consolidation of the social order. Second, Frene Ginwala, Luckyboy Loyd Pipswane and Howard Wiarda focused on the interest groups, exclusive to whites, that reflected a discriminatory civil society. The third angle is that of Professor John Dugard who compared white civil society with Israeli civil society, seeing the former as much bigger and further ahead of the latter. In South African civil society, reference is made primarily to English protest groups.

These angles do not negate each other; rather, in the case of apartheid South Africa, they complement the picture of civil society. Since the focus of this research is protest groups in the dominant side, this section addresses civil society among the white population only. It looks at three specific aspects: Afrikaners' organized civil initiatives in a historical perspective; civil society in the ethnic centralized system of apartheid South Africa; and a definition for white civil society.

It is important to note here how the South African society was/is constituted. It is made up of many groups, divided along race, ethnicity and class. In terms of class, there are upper, middle and lower classes. In terms of race, it is divided between the white and the African, who are in turn divided into black, coloured and Indians. The blacks, who constitute the majority, are composed of many tribes and the coloureds vary in their origins. The whites are made up of the Afrikaners, who are the majority, the English, the Jewish and other European immigrants. Along and across these divisions, there are class and ideological groupings.

Afrikaners' organized civil initiatives in a historical perspective

When examining white civil organization in South Africa before 1994, it is necessary to look at the civil groups that were organized before the 1948 elections and that later continued to function in the realm of the apartheid system. The various civil society organizations developed by the white society did not differ greatly from those of other European societies, except in their adoption of the value of exclusivity since, for the most part, they were discriminatory and limited to the white population.[31] This had to do with the existing political culture and a long history of exclusivity and segregation.

In this regard the most famous civil group was the Broederbond (Band of Brothers). It was established in 1918 as a secret organization that aimed to promote Afrikaner political and economic interests and the Afrikaans language at times when the English were in power, and it recruited among those who strove for the ideal of an everlasting and separate Afrikaner nation. By the 1930s and 1940s, its members included key figures among the Afrikaner political, cultural and economic elite, and in 1952, it had 3,500 members (including 2,039 teachers, 905 farmers and 357 clergymen).[32] By the 1970s, members included the prime minister, the entire Cabinet, three-quarters of the NP membership, most university rectors, the chairman of the National Educational Advisory Council, 171 university professors, sixteen managers of newspaper groups and all the nationalist editors, and 40 per cent of white Dutch Reformed Church ministers.[33] Its membership also included pensioners, businessmen, public servants, lawyers and policemen. The educators had the biggest ratio. The Broederbond also included thousands of junior affiliates, including 800 branches and the FAK,[34] a public arm that had 200 cultural, religious and youth bodies.[35]

The second prominent organization was the Dutch Reformed Church (NGK – the Afrikaans abbreviation). It provided religious justification for the Christian nationalist programme of the NP during the nation-building period and for the Afrikaner leadership when the NP later seized power.[36] In support of Afrikaner Christian nationalism and in cooperation with the FAK, NGK ministers had the task of working with school children of Afrikaner origin to foster "a sense of pride in belonging to God's chosen people and to organize separate lower-level education for non-whites".[37] The NGK stood firm in support of apartheid ideology, not only fostering a religious discourse, education and religious leaders, but also producing political leaders, for example, when ex-church ministers (such as Malan[38]) became state leaders. The religious element in this political project was recognized by the constitution of the Republic of 1960 which referred to God's support: "The People of the Republic of South Africa acknowledge the sovereignty and help of Almighty God."[39]

There were other smaller organizations, such as associations and interest groups that were on many occasions divided along issue and English–Afrikaner lines. They included clubs, other churches (e.g. Anglican and Catholic), sports teams, and many kinds of professional and business societies and fellowships. Some of these, along with new associations that were formed later on, held agendas opposed to that of the state, and ran their anti-apartheid agendas from within the 'legal' system, as was evident during the 1970s and to a greater extent in the 1980s. While the majority continued to adopt exclusivity of membership and worked on empowering the Afrikaners and pressuring government for the benefit of the whites, many of the protest groups welcomed non-whites as part of their staff and/or membership, and held liberal views to varying degrees. This, as is seen in Chapters 3 and 4, was in line with the vision of inclusive democracy, non-racialism, and unity of the country that the ANC and the progressive whites had agreed upon by the mid-1980s.

Civil society under the ethnic centralized political system of apartheid South Africa

Because the pre-apartheid process of consolidating social order and power continued for several further decades, South Africa's strongly centralized system of apartheid was evident through an intensely interlocking relationship between white civil society and other societal spheres, the market, and the political society. The Broederbond, the Dutch Reformed Church, the trade unions, and such National Party branches as women, youth and businessmen, all acted in support of the ideology in power, and through close connections with the political establishment headed by the National Party. For the white society, they created a top-down, corporatist system that fixed the social structure in place and prevented change.[40] The framework in which white civil society functioned was designed to produce an extensive, separate and corporatist political community, and to a great extent succeeded in its aim of controlling all areas of social life. Political society, represented mainly by the National Party, was instrumental in this process and was quite effective among the Afrikaners.

As for the main representatives of the English-speaking community, the views held by both the United Party (UP) and the Progressive Party (PP), which remained out of power for over forty years, were liberal compared with the NP. Increasingly over time, English civil society associations became the source of dissenting views and action against apartheid among the liberal (mainstream and progressive) minority, and it is important to note that, with the UP having lost most of its constituency by the early 1980s, the PP became the formal oppositional party. The best turnout the latter managed to achieve among its supporters was 5 per cent of Afrikaners[41] and 19.4 per cent of the overall white vote in 1981.[42]

The market sphere had close connections with, and benefited from, the apartheid system. While the state invited input from leading powers in the market sphere, it held the upper hand in generating, formulating, deciding and implementing public policy,[43] and only in the mid-1980s, when political crises began to have an adverse effect on the economy, were a few voices critical of apartheid heard from the market sphere. These coincided with the formation of new associations that aimed to defend the interests of the business sector during the predicted transition phase by using the civil society sphere to discuss the principles and parameters proposed for solving the conflict. Among such organizations were the Urban Foundation and the Consultative Business Movement.[44]

The interlocking relationship between the existing centralized political system and civil society in particular (along with the other two societal spheres), was evident through overlapping memberships and functions. For instance, it became impossible, especially under the leadership of Prime Minister Verwoerd, to separate the ruling party (the NP) from the Broederbond and the Dutch Reformed Church, where clear convergence happened.[45] A striking example in 1960 was Verwoerd's interference in the Dutch Reformed Church's decision to accept a World Council of Churches resolution opposing apartheid. As a result of his rescinding of the decision, the NGK adopted a position in line with the government's political stand, stating that the only way of obeying divine law was "to let each nation express its own identity within the framework of separate development, since each nation is a distinct entity resulting from a specific command by God, who planned its particular inner structure".[46]

The three main pillars of Afrikaner nationalist consolidation – the NP, the Broederbond and the NGK[47]– became inseparable and, led by the NP, served the state system. To a great extent, too, although tensions did exist with the English community, the four white societal spheres fed into each other; and being interlinked in terms of aims, roles and overlapping membership, managed to consolidate an exclusively Afrikaner nationalism,[48] a closed form of nationalism. Political socialization throughout the bureaucracies of the different spheres made the linkages unclear. Instead the lines became blurred between the political elite in the state system, the political society, and the majority of the civil society elite, and this produced a sophisticated system of political socialization whereby the society voluntarily accepted state hegemony. This case fits with Gramsci's argument on state–society and state–civil society relations in Western elite democracies, where a state political system gains the consent of society/civil society through an elaborate form of cultural hegemony.[49]

This interlocking relationship between the state political system and white civil society delayed the oppositional functions of civil society actors. Only in the late 1970s and early 1980s did protest groups became visible in terms of their numbers and clearer anti-apartheid views. Since the Broederbond and its public arm, the FAK, as well as the NGK, and many other such groups, had served the government for many decades and had prevailed as powerful actors across the different spheres and levels of society, the role they played, like that of the government, was oppressive towards these civil society actors. For instance, the Broederbond used the civil society sphere to disseminate the ideology of separate development and to provide a forum for debating a rational reflection on the best interests of the Afrikaner people. As well as providing counter-arguments to the voices of dissent that marginalized the dissidents, it also worked on shaping the national consensus. It circulated its members' points of view internally to imbue them with a sense of ethnic discipline, channelled views and ideas between the government and the Afrikaner elite, and nominated young leaders and important staff, thereby contributing to the process of shaping the national consensus.[50]

With their extensive apparatus, the Broederbond and the other groups had close connections with the elite circles on the one hand, and managed on the other to reach the public at the grassroots level. They provided a political socialization process that addressed members of the Volk and its ethos by cutting across class interests and producing a common identity, unity and solidarity.[51] As a result, state and society ended up feeding off and empowering each other.[52] Such relationships and roles resemble those taken by organizations that were associated with the Mapai Party, e.g. the Histadrut, before and after the establishment of the Israeli state.

The Afrikaner political socialization process produced communitarianism and consensus politics. It encompassed a bureaucratization of ethos that manifested itself in the Afrikaner's life, e.g. unions, banks, student groups, parties, cultural organizations and so on, to such an extent that an Afrikaner became an "organization man".[53] According to Slabbert, this process produced four effects.[54] First, it integrated leadership at the top of Afrikaner organizations by tracking top personnel, e.g. Malan, who went from minister to professor to editor to prime minister, and Verwoerd, from teacher to party organizer to cabinet minister. Second, it introduced a great deal of organization into everyday Afrikaner life; thus a child born into an Afrikans family could move from cradle to grave within the framework of Afrikaner organization. Third, it facilitated the formulation of collective goals and introduced a unity of purpose into corporate Afrikaner action, e.g. the church supported the government, the universities supported the church, and vice versa. Finally, the average Afrikaner was presented with his own establishment. Thus, the Volk notion became in effect one of the highest values, if not the highest. Around it, the *laager* mentality[55] was constantly reproduced, and the politics of consensus became the norm. As such, it was impossible to achieve a civil society "protected by the state and open to use by equal citizens".[56] The whites retained full citizen status while the Africans retained a lesser or a sham citizen status.

As a result of the politics of consensus, even universities were faced with tension between their universalistic commitments and communal ethnic interests. Like the vast majority of civil-society actors they adhered to the Volk ethos and interests. Afrikaans-speaking universities, in particular, stood firm by the Volk ethos. In this context, H.B. Thom, a former rector of Stellenbosch University speaking of that tension, said: "[It is] the duty of a university to resolve this by performing in such a way that it wins the trust of the Volk", while the rector of Rand Afrikaans University argued that "we have to take into account the reasonable norms and prejudices of the community without becoming slavishly conformist".[57] A 1978 survey at Stellenbosch University showed that such political attitudes were also reflected in the position adopted by the majority of Afrikaner students, who uncritically accepted the status quo, while the few who were critical tried to influence the limits of the prevailing political consensus from within.[58] As to research institutions, some were complicit. For example, the South African Bureau of Racial Affairs became a subservient intellectual arm of the NP. As a result of Afrikaner academic institutions in particular adopting such stands, dissident voices in the late 1970s commented on the need to have academics who would work to break down the system which previous academics had contributed to building up.[59]

Counter to the exclusive civil society of the whites, black African civil society developed extensively during the 1970s and 1980s, and responded to the apartheid system by establishing NGOs and community-based organizations (CBOs), churches, and trade unions. In terms of activities, this response involved provision of services and political mobilization around the principles and values of a non-racial democracy.[60] As for the mainly English-speaking white liberal organizations, they constituted a third segment, and by the mid-1980s most had moved very close to the civil-society agenda of the UDF, which had adopted universalistic values based on the inclusive vision of the ANC. The politics, political platforms, and roles of white protest groups are discussed in Chapter 3, which also looks in detail at how the white liberals worked from within a Western tradition of dissent, i.e. from within the law of the state.[61] Nevertheless, they represented progressively independent views, compared with the views of the communitarian Volk, since they were more autonomous vis-à-vis the state, the political society and the ideology in power. Eventually the progressive white liberal organizations and the UDF mainstream black-run organizations came together to find a third way. For Robert Fine, this 'third road' was neither utopian socialism nor utopian capitalism but was an alternative way; where the emphasis was on

> social movements of civil society retaining or obtaining autonomy from whatever political party is in power, pushing the state from below for beneficial social changes and nurturing the seeds of democracy, civil rights and tolerance in their own sphere of activity.[62]

Definition of white civil society in apartheid South Africa

Based on the above discussion, which looked at the kind of political system that existed in apartheid South Africa, the historical development of Afrikaner civil society and the relationship between the state political system and civil society, this section offers a definition for white civil society. Such a definition is also based on the general definition stipulated in the Introduction above. To do this, a number of related observations should first be highlighted.

1   Specific historical developments shaped the role of South African civil society. In the process of nation-building that preceded the coming to power of the Afrikaners, civil organizations moulded the political ideas of Afrikaner

nationalism. After achieving power they continued this role as believers and supporters of the governing party. The National Party, as noted, ran the state for more than four decades. The state retained an interlocking relation with civil society, especially Afrikaner society, but exercised a hegemonic role towards it by elaborating a sophisticated form of hegemony that used all the machinery of the state – military, education, media – and by maintaining a tight relationship with all spheres of society to preserve the dominance of a set of ideas that supported the state's ideology and form of governance. The voluntary consent of the white society was achieved and maintained through a socialized set of core values, supported and disseminated by a majority of civil society associations. This example fits with Gramsci's argument about hegemony in Western elite democracies.

2   The apartheid system was an ethnic authoritarian regime where the majority, the black population, was denied all political rights. But as the whites enjoyed elements of a liberal democracy, a space for an ethnic civil society was preserved for them in particular. With constraints, the whites-based exclusive 'democracy' provided a tiny margin for opposition. This was used by the English liberals and individual Afrikaners, and later by many organizations such as the UDF and its affiliates.[63]

3   As membership in society was not based on equal citizenship, civil-society institutions in apartheid South Africa were divided along ethnic lines, both white and African. The whites were in turn divided into English-speaking and Afrikaans-speaking groups, the majority of which were (pro) establishment organizations while a minority saw themselves as alternative organizations.[64] The famous Helen Suzman[65] divided white civil-society organizations into three categories: those with liberal values; those wanting to save their own privileges; and those that were apolitical such as the Red Cross, and sports associations.[66]

4   Civil-society organizations can be instruments of oppression. Afrikaans-speaking organizations were instrumental in a process of political socialization in favour of the National Party, both before and after coming to power. They preserved an exclusive Volk communitarian culture and privileges. Over the years, by action or silence, Afrikaner and many English-speaking groups contributed to, and protected, the siege mentality and the politics of consensus, thereby prolonging the life of the prevailing culture of exclusivity and domination. Opposition continued to be minimal for decades, and even at its peak represented a minority in the white society.

5   Civil society can become a mirror for political polarization. During the transition period of the 1980s, liberal organizations flourished and, to differing degrees, moved away from the political system and its ethos towards a middle point in the direction of the political platform of the UDF – the public branch of the ANC. In the same period, other white groups opposed the system for totally different reasons. For example, a number of Afrikaner groups developed into an uncivil militia, opposing a compromise settlement with the Africans. Uncivil civil society initiatives are not unique to this case.

Based on the above discussions, and in defining white civil society, it can be argued that the apartheid system, which is not democratic but represents an exclusive 'democracy' that is strong, ethnically based and centralized, led to the development of *an ethnically based, mainly exclusive, limited and weak civil society*. It is ethnically based because the state is defined on ethnic bases. The state's political system enhanced the exclusivity of the group in power through adherence to its exclusive ideology. It was exclusive because it was ethnically based and because it continued to represent the Volk and its ethos, which undermined the rights of the majority. It continued to reproduce communitarian, 'tribal', culture that was removed from civil universal values, but was limited because the state continued to maintain strong influence on civil society and other societal spheres. It developed an interlocking relation with all spheres, and practised hegemony over them, using different means. It was weak because of the other reasons and/or characteristics mentioned, and because of the fact that it was divided along ethnic, ideological and class lines.

As a result, most of the white civil-society organizations continued to be exclusive and conformed with the exclusive racist ideology that was in power. The space provided for white civil society brought together different interest groups and NGOs, mainly to defend the interests of the whites. It contributed to the shaping and reproduction of an ethnically based culture where inclusivity, equal citizenship and independence from the party in power and/or the state and the ideology in power were ignored. The state continued to maintain an interlocking relationship with civil society, and a majority of civil-society actors continued to provide legitimacy to the state, by playing the integrative and legitimizing roles noted earlier. By the late 1970s and during the 1980s, liberal groups (mainstream and progressive) that represented a small proportion within the civil-society space, challenged state ideology and, as such, its legitimacy. The progressive groups accepted notions of equal citizenship and inclusivity, but continued to be a small minority representing a minority. In general terms, it can be concluded that white civil society continued to reflect the development of the political system at that time. It was far from being a genuine civil society of a liberal democracy.

The political system and civil society in Zionist Israel

The political system in Zionist Israel

This section examines the political system and civil society in Zionist Israel. By doing so, it disaggregates and aggregates the theoretical framework of this comparative research and prepares the ground for examining the two case studies in Chapters 3 and 4.

With regard to the political system in Zionist Israel, there are many scholarly views on the type of system found in Israel. On the procedural level, it is a parliamentarian representative system. However, compared with Western liberal democracies Israel has, with some reservations about its treatment of its Palestinian citizens and religion–state relations, been described as liberal (Mick Dumper);[67]

as a consociational democracy (Ian Lustick);[68] an ethnocracy or ethno-national democracy (Peled and Smooha);[69] an ethnic state and not a democracy (As'ad Ghanem);[70] a non-liberal democracy (Yael Yishai[71] and Ami Pedahzur);[72] a tribal democracy (Azmi Bishara);[73] and a settlers' colonial state (Edward Said,[74] Michael Warschawski[75] and Maxime Rodinson[76]).

Each of the above viewpoints has tried to address the paradoxes and dilemmas of being simultaneously a Jewish state and a democratic state. Some have chosen to analyse the state political system from a historical perspective, and have looked critically into how the state was established and its legitimacy. Others have chosen to analyse it on the basis of how Israel defines itself and how it runs its type of ethno-democracy. Consequently, while all have agreed that being Jewish and democratic necessarily undermines the value of equality – a cornerstone in Western liberal democracies – they still differ over how much stress this point has been given, and the angle through which the whole issue is seen. Consequently, they have reached different conclusions.

As'ad Ghanem argues that Israel is a not a democracy by challenging three scholarly points of view. He rejects the notion that Israel is a consociational democracy because that would imply "recognition of the two or more groups as equal in practice: they would participate equally in deciding the common good of the state and their members would all enjoy the same measure of civil rights";[77] and this is not the case. As to being liberal, it is not, because a truly liberal regime "would privatize ethnic affiliation and base the relations between citizens and the state on civil rather on any ethnic affiliation. All citizens by virtue of their being citizens, would receive the same treatment by and benefits from the state."[78] This is not the case either, as the state prefers to favour the Jews against the Palestinian citizens. Ghanem also rejects ethnic democracy because it is not a democracy. There are two reasons for this: as the basic foundation of a deeply divided society, its two concepts are logically, practically and historically contradictory; nor does Israel preserve the fundamental principles of democracy, such as equality.[79]

Smooha defends ethnic democracy, describing it as a democratic system of government that is imperfect: "Rights are granted to all citizens while at the same time, a favoured status is conferred upon the majority. It is predicated on two conflicting principles: democracy for all and the majority's structural subordination of the minority."[80] While Ghanem searches for a democracy based on the principles of universal values, in particular equality, Smooha approaches it from a relative angle. It is a system based on the idea of the uniqueness of each case, not on the principle of equal citizenship in a liberal democracy.

Based on the foregoing, Ghanem holds the view that Israel is an ethnic state and not a democracy. However, he refers to Israel as being more tolerant towards the rights of the minority: "Israel conducts sophisticated policies of exclusion allied with limited inclusion in all spheres of life."[81] Ghanem and others, such as Kimmerling and Shafir, link Israel's policies of exclusion to the pre-state political ideology and culture that aimed to establish, and later on to keep, a Jewish state. Ghanem refers to Jewish society before state establishment as a 'settler society', as do others like Edward Said and Maxime Rodinson.

Ami Pedahzur, who adopts the view that Israel is a non-liberal democracy, also believes that it represents an ethnic democracy, arguing that it has the minimum requirements of a democratic polity: free elections and separation of governmental authorities.[82] But while Israel adheres to the formal procedural aspect of governmental institutions, it fails to adhere to the basic values of democracy, e.g. equality and liberties. This is why, for Pedahzur, an ethnic democracy, because of its nature, cannot guarantee the same liberties for all of its citizens.[83] It is a nature that has left the state of Israel without a constitution or clear lines between religion and state, and without an answer to the nature of Israeli citizenship. As such, for him it is not a liberal democracy; nor is it a democracy for Ghanem.

For Azmi Bishara, Israel is a tribal democracy. He argues that Israel:

> is the most fanatically "communitarian" democracy – it is a democracy with very definite borders to the community.... The community is Jewish, the limits of the community are Jewish and democracy only functions inside these limits.... It is a tribal democracy where your rights are deduced from the fact that you are a member of the tribe.[84]

Because of this nature of Israeli democracy, liberalism in Israel is perceived as being on the (radical) left. As such, those liberals/'radicals' who struggle for the rights of the individual, for free access to information, for changing Israel from a Jewish state to a state for all its citizens, for peace with neighbours, and for nuclear disarmament find themselves cast out of the community/tribe.[85]

For Rodinson, Said and Warschawski, Israeli society is a settler society that is part of a colonial project that developed into a state and was recognized by international powers. Its goal has been the building and preserving of a national Jewish state, and in this context, the two main issues have been land and control. Zionist settlers used different methods to grab land, including expulsion of the native Palestinians, as well as to control the remaining population. Different policies and strategies have also been used to dissolve the national identity of the native Palestinians and subsequently to impose submission and control over them. Such policies were directed towards both the Palestinian citizens of Israel and those in the OPT of 1967 and beyond.

With reference to the Palestinians citizens of Israel, one of the most alarming examples of formalized secondary citizenship against them was articulated in the amendment to the Election Law in 1985. While this amendment was aimed at limiting the participation of a racist Jewish party, Meir Kahane's ultra-nationalist Kach Party,[86] and stopping it from standing for the Knesset, it explicitly disregarded the national identity and rights of the Palestinian citizens, whether as individuals or group. The amendment stated:

> A list of candidates shall not participate in elections to the Knesset if its goals, explicitly or implicitly, or its actions include one of the following: 1. Negation of the existence of the State of Israel as the state of the Jewish people; 2. negation of the democratic character of the state; 3. incitement of racism.[87]

70 *Political systems and civil society*

As such, this author concludes that Israel's political system encompasses more than one characteristic; this has led a number of scholars to describe it as a non-liberal democracy, a description that is quite benign in explaining such a system. Portraying Israel as a non-liberal democracy encompasses recognition that it is a democracy, but with a lesser status in comparison with a liberal democracy. The fact that it adheres to the minimum procedural requirements of a democracy, such as free elections and allowing Palestinian citizens of Israel to participate in them, has, in the eyes of many, qualified it for this definition. Other facts, such as being an occupying power and practising nuances of discriminatory policies against the 'non-Jewish' citizens do not receive equivalent attention.

The Israeli political system is based on Jewish ethnicity with limited inclusivity for the Other, as long as the latter does not endanger the Jewish nature of the state. This puts it on the political spectrum of democracy as a 'non-democracy', compared to Western liberal inclusive democracies, and as an 'ethnic democracy' or a 'restricted democracy' when compared with totalitarian states. It is also a settler colonial state, because of its colonial history prior to establishment of the state, and its colonial and colonization schemes since 1967. It is also a 'tribal democracy' because, first and foremost, it is based on, and shaped to serve, the Jewish community of the Jewish state. A citizen's rights stem from being a member of the dominant ethnic group, Jewish tribe, or community. As such 'the masters' democracy' of the Herrenvolk regime, as discussed in the Introduction,[88] is also applicable here, since it is democratic for the master group, but authoritarian for the subordinate Other.

In this regard, it is very similar to the case of apartheid South Africa where belonging to the Volk community was the basis for inclusion and state definition. The South African system was an ethnic-national system that discriminated against the others on a racial basis, but in the case of Israel, discrimination is based on ethnic-religious grounds.[89] Thus, despite some similarity, the two systems have been differently perceived. As noted in Chapter 1, the South African system lost its claim to be a democratic system at an early stage. And while the Israeli system has won world recognition as a 'democracy', it too has been losing this claim during the last decade or so, in different degrees and in different locations.

The kind of political system that Israel has developed has to do with the nature of Zionism, the political ideology that underlies it. Zionism is an ideology based on the conviction that Jews, like any other nation, have the right to a national state and that this state is to be in 'Eretz Israel',[90] i.e. Palestine. Political Zionism is very much linked to its founder Theodor Herzl, who saw the Jewish problem in Europe as a political one that needed a political solution. In the first Zionist conference in Basel, Switzerland, the Zionist aims were stipulated clearly as being: "a *secure* haven, *under public law*, for the Jewish people in the *land of Israel*".[91] Zionism had defined two goals for itself: liberation from oppression, and unity through gathering Jewish exiles from the four corners of the world to the 'Jewish homeland'.[92] While it declares itself to be a secular ideology and movement, religion has been at the core of its claim to legitimacy, its claims to rights to the land of Palestine have been based on biblical texts, Jewish history in

Palestine and religious rituals. Continuous references have been made to religious prayers or stories: "By the waters of Babylon, there we sat down and wept when we remembered Zion" (Psalms 137:1)[93] and the Passover prayer: "next year in Jerusalem".

In line with such biblical references, the statement "The Bible is our Mandate", was made by the secular leader Ben-Gurion when challenging the British authorities in 1936.[94] As mentioned in Chapter 1, the slogan was used in response to fears that Britain had changed its policy towards the political aspirations of the Zionists in Palestine. Unlike the case of South Africa, there was no equivalent to the Dutch Reformed Church as a religious institution that served the ideology of Afrikanerdom. In the case of Zionism, the secular leaders used the Old Testament and Jewish history for constructing a national identity and a collective cause. They also used religion to consolidate support and legitimacy for the new Zionist state. As part of this quest, the Jewish Agency made an agreement on 19 December 1947 with the leadership of the religious party Agudat Israel, through which the nature of the anticipated state was agreed upon.[95] To include and obtain the support of religious groups, concessions were made and a status quo agreement that specified further Jewish features of the state was stipulated; it stressed certain Jewish traditions, such as respect for the Sabbath and the autonomy of ultra-orthodox education, and left family law in the hands of the religious courts.[96]

Zionism is the ideology (idea) that transformed a group of the faithful (Jews) into a nation. It constructed a collective national identity based on Judaism and beyond and lifted its connections to Palestine beyond those of history, religion and ritual. After the first Zionist Congress in 1897, the Zionists stressed that Jews looked at Palestine or, as they called it, 'Eretz Israel', as a territory associated with both their past and their present and because of which they were a minority in exile.[97] From that time the issue of linkage to the land was brought to the fore.

According to Shlomo Avineri, Jewish nationalism in nineteenth-century Europe was a response to the challenges of liberalism and nationalism far more than it was to anti-Semitism, and thus could not have happened earlier.[98] The challenges referred to concerned the fact that the universal values of a secular national state opened the eyes of Jews to new notions (e.g. those of the French Revolution) that did not guarantee them equal citizenship. Herzel used the case of Dreyfus to stress that European nationalism was steeped in racism against the Jews, and as such, argued for the need for a national Jewish state outside Europe. Concerning the kind of state to be established, Herzl envisioned a socialist state where social justice and tolerance would be the guiding principles. However, he overlooked the national rights of the indigenous population, the Palestinians,[99] even though he accepted the notion of providing 'the Arabs', as he called them, with civil rights. Eventually, as religious collectivism was transformed into a nationality for the Jews, Zionism fostered itself as an exclusive nationalistic ideology. Zionism was criticized for this and for setting up an exclusionary and semi-theocratic Jewish society, when Jewish survival everywhere else counted on the maintenance of secular and pluralistic societies.[100]

72 *Political systems and civil society*

Other aspects of constructing the new national identity were put in place. The Hebrew language was revived as a modern language to be used by Jewish immigrants in Palestine. Additionally, as part of organizing the Jews into a social force that strove to achieve the goals of Zionism, labour on the land was encouraged and elevated to being part of redeeming the Jewish people and 'their' land. A new ethos for a new self-image of a Jew in his 'homeland' was also envisioned and put forward for implementation. The holocaust was converted to heroism, death to new life, diaspora to homeland, weakness to power, and passivity to activism.[101] In this way, the so-called 'second exodus' from slavery to freedom and the call for controlling one's own fate became cornerstones in shaping the new Zionist collective identity. As discussed earlier, similar notions were raised by Afrikaner nationalists in South Africa.

The ideologues of Zionism realized that to achieve a Jewish nation-state in Palestine, they needed to take the issue to the top levels of world politics and to work on the ground. Herzl was the leading force on this front and was followed by Chaim Weizmann. Alliance with the colonial superpower, which at the time was Britain, facilitated this ideological project. Mutual interests that were agreed upon included addressing anti-Semitism for the benefit of both sides, and establishing a colonial outpost in the Levant, as "a wall of defence for Europe in Asia, an outpost of civilization against barbarism".[102] The historic Christian–Judaic civilizational connection played a supportive role in this endeavour. As for Ben-Gurion, while giving weight to international support for his cause, he insisted on building a strong social force on the ground and linking it to the land.[103] For him this was necessary so that social revolution could take place, thereby transforming the immigrants' class structure through turning the nation into a melting pot with roots in the land. Eventually, Ben-Gurion's Labour Party developed a hegemonic social, economic and political status in the Yishuv through its branches and its strong institutions, particularly the General Labour Federation, the Histadrut.[104] It was a status that deeply affected the kind of civil society developed by Israel in the post-state period. A similarity can be drawn here, since the hegemonic role played at that time by the Labour Party is similar to that of the National Party in the case of South Africa before and after the elections of 1948.

Zionism has, in addition to exclusivity, had a maximalist nature. The maximalist value has been based on the belief that the area of mandatory Palestine has to be the minimum for fulfilling the purpose of Zionism.[105] While Ben-Gurion stressed the need for flexibility in terms of setting the boundaries of the state, he argued that they should never be fixed.[106] Thus, the mainstream labour Zionists, the revisionists, and other supporters of Greater Israel found a common ground that encompassed all their ideological convictions and strategic reasons, and their different maps. Some of the maps extend to the Litani River in Lebanon, the Euphrates in Iraq, the Nile in Egypt and the other bank of the River Jordan, and it is this common ground that kept the door open for later territorial expansion and imperial domination in the region.[107] Both values consciously left Israel without a constitution since, if one was to be stipulated, it would have to define state borders and set clear principles for citizenship rights. The latter is very controversial because of the exclusive nature of the state's ideology.

Israel replaced a constitution with a declaration of 'independence' and subsequently with basic laws. While these stressed the sovereignty of the Jewish people in 'Eretz Israel' and preached equality, justice and freedom,[108] they wiped Palestine and the Palestinians off the map of the area. Comparing this case with apartheid South Africa, it can be seen that the constitution of the Union (1910) declared a state for the whites who, through an elected council, could 'legally' discriminate against the majority. In the case of Israel, its legislative body, the People's Council and later the Knesset, declared – and have constantly stressed – the principle of state Jewishness. Minority rights have been tolerated, provided this principle and the security of the Jewish state are guaranteed through its ethnic-national political system. As such, the increase in the Palestinian population inside Israel is perceived as a threat to the state system and ideology, since it would eventually change the demographic balance in the state. At a recent conference of the Herzliya group (January 2007), many participants regarded such an increase as more dangerous than the threat of a nuclear Iran.[109]

While Zionism has core notions or beliefs, members of Israeli Jewish society do not adhere to one perspective in defining Zionism, even though there are certain basic principles that are common among the majority of that society. Thus, for most people, Zionism was a movement for Jewish national self-determination that eventually led to the establishment of Israel; the Jews have a connection with, and a right to, 'Eretz Israel' beyond the religious link; and therefore Israel is a legitimate state. The same vast majority have additional perspectives on understanding and further defining Zionism. Hence, an Israeli Jew can be a liberal Zionist, a communist Zionist, a religious-nationalist Zionist, a revisionist Zionist and a labour Zionist. On the margins, a small minority that is critical of Zionism is divided into groups that describe themselves, or have been described, as non-Zionist (can also be communist), anti-Zionist or post-Zionist. Their respective politics are briefly described in Chapter 4.

Civil associations that bring together members from liberal Zionism and those on their left, as well as active individuals and intellectuals, have produced what, in the 1990s, came to be known as the Israeli (Jewish) civil society. They compete with groups in the political centre and on the right for the formation of public opinion, but only a handful challenge the societal consensus concerning collective identity and the collective meaning of Zionism. As with the earlier examination of civil society in apartheid South Africa, the following sub-section discusses civil society in Zionist Israel along with several relevant factors.

Civil society in Zionist Israel

The literature on civil society in Israel is recent and is mainly traced to, and associated with, the processes of liberalization through which Israel passed following the 1977 elections. It was then connected with the cultural, economic and political processes that ensued after this political turning point, and that reached their

74 *Political systems and civil society*

peak in the 1990s. Many scholars who addressed the topic in the 1990s claim to have been the first to study it. Some have concluded that there are two civil societies in Israel, one Jewish and the other Palestinian, while others argue that in a 'tribal' society like that of Jewish Israel, the notion of civil society is not valid. A third group referred to the existence of an Israeli civil society without reservation; a fourth spoke of an emerging civil society that has been moving away from the status of being a state-dominated and highly mobilized frontier society; and a fifth consciously prefers to use the term 'third sector', instead of the term 'civil society', in describing Israeli civil associations. A sixth group maintains that the Israeli society is a strong military one that leaves little room for a civil society to emerge.

To discuss the kind of civil society that exists in Zionist Israel, this section is divided into three parts that follow the outline used above in examining the South African case. These are: Zionist organized civil initiatives in a historical perspective; civil society in the ethnic centralized political system of Zionist Israel; and a definition of Israeli civil society. Since this research is examining the politics of protest groups in the dominant side, it will not discuss civil society initiatives among the Palestinian minority inside Israel or Palestinian civil society in the occupied territories of 1967.

It is important here to underline the composition of the Israeli society, which comprises two major groups, the Jewish Israelis (majority) and the Palestinian Israelis (minority). It is divided along ethnicity (religion and nationality), religiosity, origin and class lines. The Jewish group is divided along ethnic lines: Ashkenazi (of European origin), Mizrahi (Middle Eastern origin), Russians and Ethiopians. The Jewish group is also divided along religiosity lines: secular Jews, Haredi Jews (ultra-orthodox) and fanatic national religious Jews, the settlers. The Palestinian minority consists of a majority of Muslims and a minority of Christians. In terms of class divisions, the Ashkenazi Jews have historically constituted the majority of the elite and the middle classes.

Israeli (Jewish) civil organized initiatives in a historical perspective

As in the case of apartheid South Africa, civil organized initiatives started during the nation-building period. In the case of Zionist Israel, it was the Yishuv pre-state period. As part of the Labour Zionist movement to build a social force that could carry the national project to achieve the goals of Zionism, organized civil initiatives flourished in the 1920s and 1930s. Different forces were involved at that time, but the most powerful was the Labour movement, which managed to organize different sectors and connect them to the Mapai Party,[110] and its branches and institutions. Eventually, under the leadership of Mapai, the Labour movement exercised hegemony that was to last from the early 1930s until 1977.[111] It managed to organize the labour force in the form of one big union, the Histadrut; this did not function as a federation of unions but developed a centralized structure and a one-member (not one trade union), one-vote system to deprive trade unions of their autonomy.[112] The Histadrut also developed an expanded system of social services, providing its members with medical care, a complete system of primary and secondary schools, theatres, sport associations, newspapers, a publishing house, insurance schemes, loan funds, workers kitchens, and so on.[113] By doing this, it served its members but also created bonds of dependency with a large part of the Jewish population in Palestine. By 1926, 70 per cent of Jewish workers were members of the Histadrut.[114]

At its height, the Histadrut possessed an economic empire which encompassed agricultural, manufacturing, construction, marketing, transportation and financial bodies, and until the 1990s it controlled about 25 per cent of the economy and employed about 25 per cent of the labour force.[115] A roughly equal share of the economy and almost all land was directly owned by the state.[116] This enabled Histadrut's members to enjoy subsidized services, obtain jobs and be part-and-parcel of the collective national Zionist project that for decades was led by Mapai. As a prominent ideological and strategist force, Mapai managed thereby to develop cultural hegemony or a moral order, similar to that analysed by Gramsci earlier. By consolidating of different powers, Mapai became the most powerful political, social, economic and cultural force.

Prior to the establishment of the state, other Zionist parties or factions were involved, alongside the Labour movement, in the organizing of civil life. Committed to the Zionist project of a Jewish state in Palestine, they were active participants in different civil initiatives. Kaminer describes the political parties and their roles as being:

> more than instruments for registering mass sentiment in the electoral process ... most combined deep ideological conviction with day to day activity on behalf of the party and readiness to defend the party and its interests ... as a rule, the social institutions which offered such services were managed and controlled by party members who saw their work as part of their party duty and mission.[117]

Angelika Timm argues that during the first two decades of the state's history, non-governmental organizations were linked with political parties which mobilized people in correspondence with the dominant ideology serving the goals of the state; in other words, "civil society was part and parcel of the national effort".[118] In the process, Israel developed one of the largest public sectors in the world. In addition, decisions (about prices, salaries, reserve duty, and war) were made by a highly centralized governmental system, and market relations were dominated by the large state enterprises.[119] The state or political parties regarded their role as being to lead the society on every issue of importance from health issues to charity drives – they set the agenda and defined the extent and mode of public participation.[120]

Over the years, Israel witnessed many socio-economic and political developments. The various wars, the defeat of Labour in 1977, economic growth, the forming of a new middle class and the strengthening of liberal tendencies among the Ashkenazi segment of society, promoted the establishment of non-profit organizations. While the vast majority took on the role of providing services that different governments were unable to offer because of the privatization policies they had adopted since the late 1970s, a small number of liberals who were interested in downsizing the state and wished to open up a space for civil society and to integrate it into the international economy, were considering new issues.[121] They sought political and social change, but did not give up their connection with, and roots in, the Zionist labour movement. Referring to this connection, Kaminer notes that the new middle class that formed many of the liberal associations in the 1980s and the 1990s had, in one form or another, personal, social and psychological links with the leaders and the cadre of the deposed labour Zionist movement.[122] Such closeness continued to affect the autonomy of such associations.

Such scholars as Yishai,[123] Gershon Shafir, Yoav Peled[124] and others have examined the liberalization process through which the Israeli society has passed since the 1970s. Some have focused on the economic side while others concentrate on the internal politics of the different political actors. The author believes that the political and the economic sides have been very much interconnected. Both have been linked to the perception and results of the Arab/Palestinian–Israeli conflict and the internal rivalries between the various Jewish ethnic and religious sectors in the society. Changes in the attitudes of the Israeli (Jewish) society have been linked to numerous major wars and peace agreements: e.g. the 1967 war; the 1973 war; the invasion of Lebanon in 1982; the first Intifada and the second Intifada; the Camp David peace agreement with Egypt; the Oslo Accords; and the failure of the Camp David talks between the Palestinians and the Israelis in the year 2000.

In addition, the 1977 elections (in which the right-wing became a strong competitor to the dominant Labour Party), the moves towards privatizing the economy, the weakening of the Histadrut, the increased power of religious groups, and the mass communications revolution have all represented influencing factors and/or results. Yishai and Shafir and Peled conclude that the widening divisions, whether political, religious or class within Israeli (Jewish) society have produced a new middle class along with the priorities of a new generation. Some, though not all, of these priorities are regarded as liberal in comparison with the views of the rest of the society and of older generations of Zionists. They stress individualism, not collectivism, a free market rather than a centralized one, equal rights for the individual as long as this does not threaten perceived state security, a political compromise with the Palestinians over territory as part of a two-state formula, subject to certain conditions, and more secular policies. These are 'liberal' Zionist priorities.

Civil society under the ethnic centralized political system of Zionist Israel

As noted above, the role and hegemony of the Labour movement during the pre-state period and until 1977 produced a highly centralized system whose legacy continued to persist for many years. A strong state was put in place and developed an interlocking relationship between and among the political society (the Labour Party, previously Mapai), civil initiatives (led mainly by Labour members), the government (led by Labour), and the economy (mainly led by the Histadrut, an arm of Labour, and state enterprises). The military establishment, too, was a very influential actor, through its strong influence on the policies of subsequent governments and its outstanding ability to develop a 'nation in uniform'. As in the case of apartheid South Africa, Israel's history of nation- and state-building produced similar interlocked relations between the different societal spheres. As a result, civil social networks became tied to the government in a number of ways: e.g. through law (the 1980 Law of Association) and the space made available for freedom of thought and expression vis-à-vis the national consensus, whether ideological or political,[125] and through financial support and connection to the political society (mainly Labour).

The Israeli government passed the Law of Association in 1980 to regulate interest groups and the space available for them. It was articulated to serve two objectives. According to Yishai (quoted by Migdal), by enacting this law, the state tried "to grasp the rope at each end"; in other words, it attempted "to ensure the freedom of association and to control the group arena. The absence of a similar law in many other democracies, however, highlights the prominence of the state in the Israeli context".[126] Yishai also argued that the development of this law was connected with the establishment of Al Ard, a Palestinian campaigning group which demanded the setting up of a Palestinian state as part of restoring political will.[127] The law requires registration which may be denied if the objectives of an association are contrary to law or public morale, and if they endanger the security of the state or public order.[128] It also gives the state the right to supervise the internal affairs of associations. Given that no single inspection has been carried out since this law came into force, Yishai points out that the law seeks cooptation of those defined as subversive and that this is done through registration: "upon receiving their credentials, interest groups become 'insiders' whose activity is co-opted by the political establishment ... it makes little difference whom it attempts to influence".[129]

It should be noted that the Law of Association was passed almost unanimously and was supported by Knesset member Sholamit Aloni, leader of the civil rights party that has been a leading force for liberalization. The law is committed to the Zionist ethos, and has been seen as a national interest issue and as a technical financial matter that does not endanger the democracy of the Jewish state. In line with statism,[130] it has been part of a corporatist regime put in place by the state of Israel, through which it has defined the patterns of institutional practices and cultural norms for membership of individuals or groups in the society, and for which it has allocated entitlements, obligations and domination.[131] According to Shafir and Peled, it has also created

> concentric circles, in which the boundaries become more rigid as one moves towards the periphery: inclusion in internal circles is based on force of habit

or custom, whereas in the outer ones it is based on force and the sanction of law. Movement towards the centre indicates social mobility, since it implies more rights and greater access to resources.[132]

In other words, the Israeli political system has built the parameters for inclusion in the society, and these have developed what has become commonly known as the national consensus. It is an essential part of the Israeli political culture, which legitimizes certain political discourses and disregards or de-legitimizes oppositional ones. The inclusion parameters of the national consensus have provided societal consent, similar to what Gramsci highlighted as a sophisticated system of cultural hegemony used in elite democracies. In this context, one is reminded of the Israeli policy of indoctrination discussed in Chapter 1.

A discussion on civil society cannot avoid examining the issue of citizenship. By the 1990s, three discourses of citizenship had become acceptable in the Israeli society, all fitting within the basic Zionist aims and ethos as well as representing the ideological stands of major political parties across the political spectrum. Peled and Shafir[133] describe these discourses as the republican, the 'ethno-national' and the liberal. The republican discourse is associated with the 'pioneer Zionists' who have been committed to the moral purpose of state formation through colonization, and are connected mainly to historical Mapai. The ethno-national discourse is an expression of citizenship that is based not on individual rights but on membership of a homogenous descent group. Its main affiliates are the Likud, settler groups, and Mizrahim, although Labour also overlaps with it. The liberal discourse of citizenship, however, is based on the individual who is the bearer of universal, equal and publicly affirmed rights. Its advocates are the newly formed elite (the historical Ashkenazi state-building bourgeoisie) who ceded from Labour parties during the late 1970s and early 1980s (today's Meretz and Yahad). They demand liberalization of the economy and society, and separation from the Palestinian non-citizens.

The republicans enjoy a 'new wave' representing the ultra-nationalists who have been supported by the Likud, which is a supporter of liberal economic policies. The notions held by Labour, which holds the centre ground, overlap in different degrees with the three discourses (or what Uri Ram calls 'corporatist regimes'[134]), a fact that leaves the discourses representative and legitimate. However, because the contradiction between the ethnic and the liberal regimes is based on ethnic grounds, it continues to be unsettled because of the state's definition, which leaves the non-Jews, i.e. the Palestinians, unable to enjoy equal citizenship status since it is not a state for all its citizens. In terms of representation among the liberals, Meretz has the lowest level of popular support among the major political party actors. Meretz won six seats in the 2003 election, representing 5.2 per cent of the population,[135] but only five seats in the 2006 elections,[136] results that show a decline in its popularity, since it won twelve seats in 1992, nine in 1996 and ten in 1999.[137]

The three citizenship discourses are derived from exclusive Zionism, which produced ethnic Israel. Israel primarily represents, and derives its legitimacy from, its ethnic society, the Jews. In this context, Warschawski describes Israeli society as tribal and lacking a culture of opposition since it conceded to a culture of consensus – i.e. national consensus. He argues that this stems from strong beliefs in the unity of the nation, as a single family and not as a society with differences over issues like the nature of the state or citizenship, or issues that address the right of the Other to equal treatment.[138] Bhabha Muhammed[139] finds that this set of communitarian notions is what the Jewish Israeli society and the Afrikaner society have in common, and what links them to a besieged mentality. He notes that they both formed invisible circles around themselves as a defence against the Other, and that as a result they became tribes ranged against all the others for fear of total onslaught.[140] This mentality made it difficult for oppositional voices from within the tribe to move away from the politics of consensus. Therefore, those who wanted to develop political initiatives independent of the monopoly of the parties or the government and at a distance from the consensus either failed, or achieved only limited success, or were cast aside as irrelevant.

The exclusive nature of Zionism and the communitarian nature of the Israeli Jewish society prompted Jeff Halper, another veteran activist and scholar, to propose a similar argument. He also believes that the Israeli society is tribal, seeing Israel as a Jewish state for the Jewish tribe, which excludes non-Jews (the goys) and discriminates against them by law.[141] He maintains that there is a complementary relationship between the state and the tribe, in which the tribe leads, by conviction and mindset, and the state controls, according to the framework designed by the tribe's convictions. The latter are derived from the ideology in power and from the elite that guards the interests of ideological Israel. As such, those who get outside 'the box' or the structure of the tribe become marginalized and/or ostracized. Until the second Intifada, only a handful of persons (around twenty) had ever challenged the consensual stand on the notion of an exclusive Jewish state.[142]

Both corporatism and communitarianism have fed the notion of national consensus, and since the establishment of the state, the *concept of national consensus* has been a strong feature in Israeli political culture. It is assumed that a good political decision is as good as its agreement with the national consensus, and that it is 'the box' or the limit that defines the parameters for a secure and Jewish Israel.[143] As already noted, anyone who crosses this limit becomes marginal and on the fringe of society and politics, and will often be described as radical, lunatic, heretical, or even irrelevant. This is related to the fact that the Israeli leadership, Israeli society, and Zionist ideology feed into each other in developing a political *laager* around themselves.[144] Historically, the major actors who have shaped the political *laager* and consequently the *laager* mindset have been the political and military elites, the media, the intellectuals (apart from a handful), the educational system, the unions, and the religious leaders. In a culture of national consensus, opposition is accepted only from within it and preferably away from its edges. This feature is highlighted empirically in Chapter 4 where the politics, political platforms and roles of Israeli protest groups are discussed.

It is important to emphasize that there are two levels of national consensus in Israel – the ideological and the political. The ideological is the primary level and is based on the Zionist ethos of the right of the Jewish people (from everywhere) to a national secure home in 'Eretz Israel', or Palestine, and this is manifested in a democratic Jewish state that holds the values envisioned by the prophets of Israel. This is the common premise that unites the right, the centre and the 'liberal'. Zionism is what binds the 'peace' people with the ultra-nationalists.[145]

Based on this ideological level of the national consensus, the political consensus then evolves. It has clear principles, stands and viewpoints. However, it is not static and can sometimes be momentary. For example, after decades of a consensus of denial with regard to the existence of a Palestinian nation, the consensus has changed and the Palestinian people have now become recognized as a nation. Another example is the principle of a two-state solution. Whereas it was a very marginal notion twenty years ago, it has since become part of the present Israeli political lexicon.

Looking at the Israeli national consensus from other angles reveals other components. Warchawski describes the national political consensus as a network of principles, "a Jewish state that is part of the free world, represented by the US, where both stand behind the same slogans and symbols, the army, national security and the national interests".[146] Another Israeli activist defines it as the "acceptance of state-determined values such as 'security' and the 'survival of the Jewish people', even the 'Jewish character' of the state, as superseding more universal values such as peace, justice and the like".[147] As for the security ethos, it is at the heart of the politics of national consensus. With regard to the Palestinian–Israeli conflict, it is defined as part of power politics and as an existential struggle. The Palestinian–Israeli struggle is seen as a zero-sum struggle, and Israel's struggle with its neighbouring states is viewed as part of a pattern of persecutions and catastrophes that has recurred throughout Jewish history; thus the Israeli army is glorified, and to serve in it is regarded as a primary obligation.[148] Furthermore, control of the historical 'land of Israel' and maintenance of the state's Jewish character are seen as connected and indispensable to the nation's existence, while any significant territorial compromises would affect Israel's national character and jeopardize its very *raison d'être*.[149]

A final important point to note on this issue concerns the type of changes that occurred in the national political consensus with regard to the conflict with the Palestinians. Changes in Israeli public opinion have been directed by debates on the best ways of protecting the long-term interests of the Jewish state. In the process, a number of older consensual issues were broken. By a majority, these issues were about the Other (the Palestinians) and had nothing to do with the security ethos or the national ideological consensus. The national consensus has changed with regard to the Palestinians and how to find a settlement to the 'Palestinian problem', but it has not changed with regard to state security or the belief of Israel being Jewish and democratic, of being victim, and moral.

Keeping in mind the context discussed above, a brief examination follows of the numbers, nature and functions of registered civil-society organizations. In

1982 there were only 3,000 registered organizations,[150] but by 1998 the number of Jewish organizations (Amutot) had reached 25,029, while those of the Palestinians (inside Israel) numbered 1,009.[151] Active organizations in the area of religion represented 23.4 per cent, those active in education and research were 32 per cent, while registered organizations engaged in advocacy accounted for 4.7 per cent.[152] By 2001, Israel had 34,291 registered organizations, three-quarters of which were engaged in service provision, primarily in religion, education and research, welfare, and culture and recreation.[153] In 1997, 64 per cent of the income of the organizations came from public funding,[154] and in terms of employment, they contributed roughly 10 per cent to Israel's economic activity in 1995.[155]

Different organizations have been established along ethnic and religious lines. This is because the 'melting pot' strategy was replaced by a cultural preservation and pluralism approach.[156] Different organizations also emerged along party politics and religiosity lines. Religious associations affiliated with the Shas, Agudat Yisrael and Mifdal parties represented ultra-orthodox and national religious views and countered (liberal) secular associations. Others were established to provide such services as advocacy for the rights of (new) immigrants, e.g. the Russians and Ethiopians or the Mizrahim, the historical underdogs.

Migdal classifies existing civil organizations into six categories, according to their functions and their relations with the state and/or the political society. First are the fellow travellers, who are nominally independent of the government, but were originally organized by political parties and government agencies, e.g. Histadrut, immigrant associations, associations on behalf of the soldiers, council for beautiful Israel, etc. Second are the patriots, who have not been organized into associations, but even so have participated in a civic life that is quite supportive of the state. They attend memorial services, and help forge a public space, with deeply shared values, for Jews coming from seventy different countries. Their role is complementary to that of the state, and they have excluded the Arab population inside and outside the Green Line. Third are the do-gooders who have intersected with issues of public policy by acting like interest or lobby groups, e.g. the society for the prevention of smoking, the heart society, cancer society. While their role is complementary to that of the state, they have been co-opted by the state or the political parties.

Fourth are the complainers, who have sought the greater accountability of public institutions, e.g. ombudsmen and consumer organizations. The individualistic nature of complaints and the kinship and friendship ties that have been extensively used throughout this sphere of work, have limited the scope of its voice and this category has continued to be exclusive rather than civic. The fifth, the protestors, represent a collective form that became visible in the 1970s by protesting, for example, against poverty, the government welfare system, government practices in the 1973 war, Land Day – when Palestinian citizens of Israel protest about land confiscation, the 1982 war, and government policies against the first Intifada. While these protest groups opened the space for the public to be heard in relation to the political process, their actions have nevertheless been sporadic in nature, and they have not managed to create long-lasting ties in civil society as a kind of permanent space outside the realm of the state. Sixth are the interest brokers, of which the prototype is the manufacturers' association. They aimed to represent employers and promote the interests of the industrialists, and maintained close connections with the Zionist parties; later, however, they found themselves either co-opted or smothered by the state.[157]

In their study of the Israeli third sector, Gidron et al. formulate another classification for Israeli civil organizations, when they distinguish between civil-society organizations and what they call the 'Integrated within the Welfare State System' organizations.[158] They define the third sector as "the sum total of formal non profit organizations in a given country – an absolute and quantifiable definition",[159] while civil society is defined as "a sphere of activity that, in addition to formal organizations, includes social networks, informal organizations, and the unrecognized activities of individuals".[160] Accordingly, they differ in two elements. The 'Integrated within the Welfare State System' organizations (IWSS), function as executive arms of the government, and receive significant public funding, but the civil-society organizations (CSOs) do not receive government money and have developed independent funding sources.[161]

As mentioned earlier, the 1990s witnessed a growth in the number of registered organizations. The vast majority, as shown above, continued to be tightly connected to the state, being supportive groups or sub-contractors who addressed the needs of the society that emerged as a result of economic liberalization policies. While the liberal organizations were fewer in number, though less dependent vis-à-vis the state and the political society, they continued, even so, to act within the limits of the ideological national consensus. However, they differed in the degree of adoption of the national political consensus. They were supported by Jewish Diaspora donors who adopted liberal Zionist views, e.g. the New Israel Fund and the Abraham Fund, as well as by international donors. Grants were mainly channelled towards co-existence and human rights initiatives.[162] Many of the organizations became involved in advocacy activities, and only then was it possible for the Palestinian Israeli citizen population to develop its own civil organizations. Some refer to them as the Arab or the Palestinian civil society in Israel.

Liberal groups increased, especially after the signing of the Oslo Accords, hoping to improve Israeli democracy and to contribute to peace-making efforts. In relation to their increasing numbers, many Israeli scholars began to refer to the emergence of an Israeli civil society, and to the possible transition of Israeli society from a colonizing military society into a globalized capitalist one.[163] Nor did liberal organizations start from an antagonistic position towards the state; rather they continued to be a loyal 'opposition' that disagreed with many of the state's strategies and tactics. The space available to them, along with other factors, opened the door to the emergence of a new phenomenon, that of post-Zionism. Some of the post-Zionists challenged core values of the national consensus.

The post-Zionists comprise a very few new historians and critical sociologists, and a number of activists. Through academic research, the new historians have questioned the Zionist discourse regarding state establishment and challenged the collective identity, narrative, state history and Zionism,[164] while the critical sociologists have questioned the dominant representations of Israeli society and culture formulated by leading Israeli social scientists in the first thirty years of the state.[165] By doing so, both contested the power relations developed by the state of Israel that conventional studies of Zionism, written by Israelis, either neglected or minimized.

The third group consists of those who embraced the post-Zionist label but turned a blind eye to the component of power relations. They argue that the era of Zionism belongs to the past,[166] having ended with the war of 'independence' and the consolidation of a Jewish state. Critics of this latter group argue that this view ignores the continuing effects of the Zionist discourse in shaping the basic mechanisms and structures of Israeli society, politics and culture.[167]

In light of the politics of consensus, the post-Zionists were heavily criticized. Their critics were of two types. First were the Zionists who fought back to defend Israeli cultural space from what they perceived as a threat to the Zionist hegemony, jeopardizing Israel's ideological foundations and thus calling into question its *raison d'être* as a state.[168] For them, daring to challenge the Zionist 'truths' disseminated through schools, universities, scholarly texts, the military, the media, state documents, laws, geographical sites, memorials, the official calendar and others, represented a danger to the historically exclusive Zionist control over Israeli culture.[169] The post-Zionists were therefore intensely criticized, and many were accused of anti-Semitism and self-hating. The second type of criticism came from anti-Zionists, non-Zionists and other academics who accused the post-Zionists of exaggerating their numbers and their power in terms of affecting the cultural space. They were also criticized for not defining the exact meaning of post-Zionism and for not adopting a position on the existing political structures.[170]

The discussions above address the history of Israeli civil organizations before and after state establishment, and the relations between civil society and the state's political system. In this context, the relation of civil society with other societal spheres, especially the political society, was briefly mentioned where appropriate, and there was also discussion of the different components that shaped the political culture in which civil-society organizations functioned, and the number and nature of existing civil-society organizations. Based on this and on the study's own designation of civil society, the following section offers a definition of Israeli civil society that reflects its broad characteristics, as well as a brief discussion of a few themes that are linked to the concluding definition vis-à-vis this book's own definition.

A definition of Israeli civil society

Bearing in mind the above discussions and the general definition adopted here for civil society, it is possible to define Israeli civil society. Since a civil society is the space between the individual and the state that is produced by socio-economic and political development at a certain time and place, the author reaches the following conclusion with regard to the Israeli case. Israeli civil society is ethnically based, mainly exclusive, limited and weak. It is defined as ethnic because it has been formed in line with the definition of the state of Israel as being a Jewish one. It is exclusive because the state was defined on the basis of ethnicity and promoted a communitarian, 'tribal' culture for the group in power, which civil society did not question. On the contrary, the majority of its actors continued to feed and support this culture. Consequently, it has failed to promote universal civic rights of equal citizenship, and particularism has continued to overcome universalism.

It is limited because the state developed a strong centralized system where relations between the different societal spheres were interlocked under its hegemony. This stemmed from the history of the state, and the processes of nation- and state-building through which it passed under the leadership of the Zionist socialist Labour party, pre- and post-1948. It was left with a very limited space in which its parameters, including certain structures for inclusion and exclusion, were designed and put in place by the state through its corporatist system. It is weak because of the three characteristics mentioned above and because of the fact that the state continuously regenerated the culture of national consensus, which is Jewish and Zionist.

The values of independency, plurality, equality and citizenship are problematic in the case of Israeli civil society. Because of the interlocking relations between the different spheres – state (including the military), political society, the market and civil society – and because the majority of organizations are state-funded and have their agendas shaped by the prevailing and continuously regenerated Zionist discourse, it is quite difficult to argue for an independent Israeli civil society. The ability to use the space of civil society to debate freely and without being ostracized if challenging the national ideological consensus or sometimes the political consensus, is almost non-existent. Being pluralist instead of Zionist is not an acceptable norm vis-à-vis the Jews. Plurality is accepted only from within Zionism, and Palestinian citizens are expected to understand and accept this as fact.

With regard to equality and citizenship, which are interconnected, they again fall short because of the non-inclusivity of the state by definition. Consequently, the calls of liberal associations for equality for the Palestinian citizens of Israel continue to fall short in the face of the ideology in power and security considerations. Thus, if the criteria of a liberal democracy for a civil society are to be applied to the case of Israel, the latter is not compatible. This is why a number of activists and scholars, including Azmi Bishara, Judy Blanc, Jeff Halper and Michael Warschawski, would argue that the term 'civil society' should not be used to describe Israeli civil initiatives.

If we are to apply a less value-charged and restrictive approach to Israeli civil society, we can speak about a space that brings together groups that vary in their dependence on the state and political society. They can be secular (rightist, centrist or liberal), religious, racist[171] and militant, or can see no contradiction in militarism being part of a civil society. This space is divided along two major ethnicities, Israeli Jewish and Palestinian. The Jewish one is divided along many lines but shares a collective Zionist identity and narrative. By a vast majority, the Jewish part struggles for the good of the Jews in the Jewish state. The Palestinians are still perceived as the Other. They struggle for full equality and (some) for recognition as a national group. Jewish voices which challenge the national consensus from within are perceived as legitimate. The liberals are a minority among them. Those who challenge the Zionist discourse, such as some of the post-Zionists and the anti-Zionists, are very few in number (a tiny minority of the minority) and are not yet a legitimate voice in this space, which is still a space dictated by the ideology in power.

To conclude, Israel, which represents an exclusive 'democracy' or a 'masters' democracy' on the political continuum of democracy versus no democracy, takes the role of the guardian of the Zionist ideology and the Jewish state. Consequently, it has undermined possibilities for establishing a free space and universality among civil associations. Most associations continue to feed into particularism and exclusivity, since the state continues to define society on narrowly religious and ethnic criteria rather than on broadly civic ones. The small numbers which seek social and political change do so from a position of loyal 'opposition'. They have not sought a radical model motivated by ideal interests, with an alternative discourse that contains a meta-political critique of the existing social order.[172] While they have forged elements of public life outside the direct control of the state, they have continued to accept the state as the proper address to which to direct their protests. Rather than creating arenas – public spaces – where the state is largely absent, or at least negligible, in the struggles over the establishment of the norms and patterns of daily behaviour, they (liberal associations) have further emphasized the centrality of the state and underscored the exclusive particularism within the population.[173] The existing structure of power has not been challenged. The elements of public life outside direct state control remain very limited. As such, what some refer to as the nucleus of Israeli civil society can be seen as a mirror to the political maturity of Israeli 'democracy'. It is still far from being a genuine liberal civil society that could make a transition towards equality and inclusivity.

A comparative conclusion: similarities and differences between the two cases

This conclusion summarizes the main ideas discussed in this chapter in the form of a comparison in which similarities and differences between the two cases are specified. This helps to reorganize the main ideas of the theoretical framework of this comparative research, and will also provide a linkage to the following chapters.

Based on the above examination of the two cases, a number of similarities can be drawn. Both states are based on colonial history and both developed exclusive ethno-national political systems. Compared to liberal inclusive political systems, neither are democracies. They represent exclusive 'democracies' that benefit the dominant group, and fit the category of 'masters' democracies', where both developed authoritarian systems vis-à-vis the indigenous populations. 'Legal' discrimination was based on racial grounds in apartheid South Africa while it has been based on national religious grounds in the Palestinian–Israeli case. Concerning their ideologies, Afrikaner nationalism and Zionism share basic tenets: membership is based on belonging to an exclusive ethnicity, the Volk, or on being a Jew; claiming rights to land by settlement, biblical text and historical connection; strong feelings of having power and controlling their own destiny; both developed national identities in light of past traumas; and both are charged with convictions and feelings of superiority, e.g. being God's chosen people, and being culturally superior.

Both also had/have centralized political systems in which the state built an interlocking relationship with the different societal spheres. The state exercise/d hegemony over the different spheres and both states continue/d, to a great extent, to control the moral order through corporatist regimes that manifest/ed themselves in the politics of national consensus. Consequently, both developed ethnically based, mainly exclusive, limited and weak civil societies. It is important to note that both civil societies were part-and-parcel of the national effort towards nation- and state-building, and later of state protection. In the case of Israel, the majority of civil organizations still represent arms for the government or subcontractors to the state. As such, it could be argued that most actors in both civil societies have contributed to the oppression of the Other or have prolonged the status quo of oppression, since neither questioned the existing ethnic-based structures of power. Hence, for both civil societies, issues of inclusivity, independency, equality and citizenship constitute/d challenges.

Both civil societies have had a minority of liberal organizations and groups who sought change from within the national consensus. Only a very few adopted views that broke away from the national consensus. As was discussed, they were mainly leftists with radical agendas. The way the politics of the liberals and the leftists evolved over the period researched and across the two cases, is not altogether similar, a point that is discussed in detail in Chapters 3 and 4.

In terms of differences, the two cases differ on two main issues. First, the two systems have been differently perceived. The apartheid system failed to project itself as a democracy and from an early stage was condemned as immoral and illegitimate. Zionist Israel managed to project and to promote itself as a democracy, or even as the only democracy in the Middle East. Only in the last decade or so have voices challenging Israel's claim to democracy become acceptable. Second, while Afrikaner nationalism was supported formally by the Dutch Reformed Church, Zionism had no similar supporting religious institution. The Zionist ideologues were secular but used biblical texts to make connections to Palestine and claim legitimacy. Shortly before the state was established, an agreement was made with the religious leaders to secure their support for the new state that was to be born.

Finally, this chapter examined the theoretical framework of the study, including both political systems and the relations between them and their respective civil societies. It examined the kind of civil societies that emerged and developed under both ethnic-national political systems, and also made a comparison between the two cases. Thus, it paved the way for examining the dependant variables of this research, in both cases the politics and roles of protest groups. These are studied in the two following chapters. Chapter 3 examines the politics and roles of white protest groups in apartheid South Africa.

3 The politics and roles of white protest groups in apartheid South Africa

Introduction

Following the discussion in Chapter 2 of the political systems and civil societies that exist/ed in both apartheid South Africa and Zionist Israel and of the theoretical approach of this research, Chapter 3 presents and analyses the different politics, political platforms and roles[1] of a sample that represents South African white protest groups. The sample was chosen to reflect the whole spectrum of the politics of protest groups (and sometimes individuals). Given constraints of time and resources, this study cannot claim to have collected all information and examined all groups, but it does include most, if not all, veteran and influential groups, which are categorized according to their politics, not their functions, aims or strategies. This choice is intentional since it fits with the main question of this research: i.e. what are the politics and roles of protest groups in the dominant community of settler ethnic-national states that are (have been) in conflict?

The author differs with the few scholars who have examined peace-building processes in apartheid South Africa and Zionist Israel, with regard to the theoretical framework used for analysis. In both cases this research has examined state–civil society relations, which were not used by others as a theoretical framework. This research has also developed a new categorization for the different protest groups, as is examined later in the chapter.

This chapter and Chapter 4 follow a similar outline to enable appropriate comparisons and patterns to be drawn across the two case studies while linking them to the theoretical framework. Chapter 3 includes six sections. Following this introduction, a second section addresses issues relevant to the study of white protest groups, and explains the context with regard to what is right, left and liberal in apartheid South African politics; the transition period studied; white membership; why people joined dissent/protest groups; and the model of 'protest work' used by whites. The author's new categorization for white protest groups is presented, along with a description and a critique as to how other studies have categorized them. The politics and roles of liberal protest groups (mainstream and progressive) are analysed, and participation of whites in black-run mainstream and radical leftist groups is examined. The last section summarizes the main ideas and links to Chapter 4's survey of Israeli protest groups.

Primary data is used as a main source of information. More than forty semi-structured interviews were held with respondents who included (former) activists, leaders of protest groups, party leaders, church leaders and academics. Some were part of the pre- and post-apartheid South African elite,[2] in the sense that they were/are part of what the Centre for Inter-Group Studies refers to as the influential opinion-leaders or opinion formers.[3] They contribute/d to the debate on public needs, interests, values and the ends and means in a (liberal versus social/socialist) democracy, and most represented organized groups in a system of white democracy. To a certain extent, they managed to intervene and influence the competitive circle[4] of political elites – those responsible for what is called 'elite consensus'.[5] This was done at times when the system was under attack on different fronts and they pushed for a political change. Elite circles usually include persons in leading positions in large corporations, trade unions, churches, political parties, and professional and veteran organizations, as well as the leaders of political and military establishments.[6]

Another primary data source included reports, statements and brochures of the white protest groups. Here the author had some difficulty in identifying exact dates of some of the original material on the various protest groups contained in the files that are archived at the University of the Witwatersrand, since internal reports or minutes of discussions are sometimes undated. However, they are organized with reference numbers, so that where a date is missing, an approximate timing (based on the context of the material) is provided, and the reference number of the file from which the material was taken is mentioned. The chapter also used secondary sources.

In terms of its argument, Chapter 3 contributes to the overall study in showing the limitations of the protest groups in relation to their size and influence on the structure of power; this fits with the kind of political system and civil society (mainly co-opted by the system) that existed. It also shows how a shift in the politics of protest groups contributed substantively to the debate on the wrongs of apartheid and the fact that it had no future, and thereby helped to set the parameters for a resolution that envisioned a new South Africa. The part that a few thousand individuals, led by prominent figures, played in challenging the apartheid ideology proved fruitful in the anti-apartheid struggle when conditions were right and when the balance of power had shifted sufficiently to allow for change, i.e. when both sides had reached the conclusion that neither could overcome the other. This also occurred because of intermediate/contextual factors (as discussed in the Introduction) and resulted in a compromise that the protest groups helped to shape and that took into consideration the concerns of the whites and the political aspirations of the blacks. This point is looked at in more detail below.

By the end of this chapter, it will possible to check whether the political ideas and activities of white protest groups were effective in altering the dominant national consensus towards peace, and how far they altered it. To what degree did they move it towards a just/inclusive peace?

Protest groups in context

To better understand the politics and role/s of the protest groups, it is important to look at what was right, left and liberal in apartheid South Africa's politics. It is also important to note that the distinctions between them were not entirely clear-cut, and that not all liberals or progressive liberals, for example, held identical points of view. They could be fluid.[7] Within each of the political orientations there were different political stands to the right or left of the centre.

The politics of the right was associated with the National Party (NP), which came to power in 1948, and the more rightist party, the Conservative Party (CP), which was established in the 1980s in defiance of the reform policies that the NP had started to implement. Liberal politics was historically associated with the United Party (UP) and later with the Progressive Party (PP), which held more liberal views. The latter renamed itself the Progressive Federal Party (PFP) in 1977. The left was associated with the politics of the resistance, e.g. the African National Congress (ANC) and the South African Communist Party (SACP), and with those on the left of these two.

The National Party represented Afrikaner nationalism. It stood for apartheid as an ideology (discussed in Chapter 2), and for the policy of separate 'homelands' or Bantustans. It aimed to build a white South Africa that would retain the political and economic privileges of the whites, and allow for state domination over the 'independent homelands'. It stratified the population along racial and ethnic lines, and developed a 'legal' system that decided the degree of rights allowed for each, classifying the black majority at the lowest level. Its wide range of legalized discrimination was justified by the ethos of Afrikanerdom, a historical legacy of colonialism, and the support of the Dutch Reformed Church, as discussed in Chapters 1 and 2.

The United Party (UP) opposed the extreme politics and policies of Afrikaner apartheid, and for reasons of pragmatism and a commitment to a gradual approach, advocated segregation and trusteeship instead of strict separation. Compared with the National Party, it was distinguished by these two characteristics as a liberal party, but its paternalistic attitude towards the indigenous population, and its fear that separation would lead to loss of parts of the land of South Africa, made its political positions ambivalent. On the one hand, the UP continued to fit with the historical colonial system of privileges and domination, as set out in the 1910 political system of the Union, and on the other it propagated gradual reform, advocating a federal policy as part of the latter, although it did not specify its details. According to Lemon, the UP suffered

> from the inherent difficulties of a white party appealing to the interests of white electors, but attempting to do so in more liberal and usually less tangible and more ambivalent ways than its principal opponent.... The party ... was forced on the defensive in relation to controversial racial issues, where its stance was popularly described as "me too, only not so loud".... The UP manifesto concentrated on relatively safe economic issues, and lacked the evocative appeal of the "tribal drum".[8]

In comparison with the Israeli case, its political characteristics and tendencies are similar to those of the Labour Party in Israel.

On the left of the UP was the PP/PFP, whose politics were the closest to those of most white liberal protest groups. The PP/PFP adopted clear liberal policies and ideals, i.e. it was non-racial, supportive of free enterprise, sympathetic to individualism, and unenthusiastic about welfare policies. Representing liberal capital, it did not recognize the linkage between the system and the wealth in the hands of the whites,[9] and advocated a multi-racial democracy with a system of checks and balances to prevent discrimination or group tyranny.[10] In 1981 it envisaged that a constitution would be based on proportional representation and consensus government, with a system of checks and balances including a minority veto,[11] and it also stressed other issues, such as the cost of apartheid and its effect on white incomes, the importance of not losing time (which would eventually lead to violent confrontation), and the fact that most blacks preferred negotiations.[12]

It is also important to note that until 1978, the PP advocated a qualified franchise, where qualifications would be based on educational and property criteria;[13] while playing the role of a loyal opposition, it also sought change from within the system. Helen Suzman,[14] who represented the PP, criticized and shamed apartheid, but at the same time argued that the system would evolve gradually through persuasion and that order had to be maintained. Similarities can be drawn between the PP and the Meretz Party in Israel.

The resistance parties and/or movements, such as the ANC and the SACP, stood on the left of the PP. The ANC, which represented the majority of blacks and was black-led, adopted an inclusive political vision. Its politics, along with those of the UDF platform, are discussed briefly later in the chapter. The politics of the SACP represented socialist politics. The party renounced the entire system of capitalist apartheid and joined the struggle alongside the ANC. It had a military wing and was banned in 1960, at the same time as the ANC. A multi-racial party, initiated by mainly Jewish whites, it stood for majority rule and rejected the apartheid system as being colonial and illegal.[15]

Those on the left of the Communist Party were/are the 'uncompromising' Marxist–Leninists and the Trotskyites. Having refused the apartheid system altogether and being committed to the struggle for a socialist revolution, they were therefore critical of the settlement reached in 1994. They accused both the SACP and ANC of accepting a bourgeois democracy, and attacked the multi-racial leadership of the ANC/SACP for "pulling the strings in direct service of their masters, social imperialists".[16] They argued that it was an elitist-brokered settlement of blacks and whites, which had failed to develop a popular democracy with vibrant public participation and a social agenda that would bridge the gap between the rich and the poor.[17]

As to the period researched, many scholars and activists refer to it as a 'transition period'. Some refer to the late 1970s and the 1980s as the transition period, while others refer to the period between 1990 and 1994 either as *the* transition period or as another transition period. As discussed earlier, the present study considers both periods as part of the transition period. The fact that formal negotiations started in 1990 and finished in 1994 does not change the fact that before and after 1990, the system of apartheid was in a process of transition, and that it ended officially only with the 1994 elections. However, it is important to note that many of the legacies of apartheid still exist.

Historically, with regard to membership of white protest groups, most members of the different white protest groups were (partly) politically close to the PP/PFP. Lemon described them as the enlightened, the better educated, or the better off, whose jobs and lifestyles were not under threat.[18] They were mainly English speakers from the urban middle class, with a few affluent Afrikaners. Sheena Dunkan, former president of Black Sash, described members of this veteran group as mostly white, educated, from the middle class and with the time and resources to invest in activism.[19] Benjamin Gidron, Stanley N. Katz and Yeheskel Hasenfeld differentiated between the leaders and the constituency of the white protest groups, arguing that the leaders shared a set of socio-economic characteristics: they were predominantly university educated, white and male, with many of them holding, or having held, faculty posts at leading South African universities and with many of the Afrikaans-speaking among them having a background in theology.[20] The constituency below the leadership was composed largely of white liberal middle-class English speakers, often with professional training in service provision.[21] Only a few blacks joined these organizations, and the overall number of active supporters during the 1980s did not exceed 10,000,[22] a figure close to that estimated by Roland Hunter of 8,000 activists in all-white organizations.[23]

Having briefly described the characteristics of white protesters and their numbers, it is logical to ask why they joined the different protest groups. It is not an easy question to answer, although the above description of members and the answer that follows does give a sense of who was able and/or ready to join the anti-apartheid struggle and why. As a result of the interviews conducted by the author as to why whites joined protest groups, it was possible to arrive at four answers, each associated with different reasons and/or motives. Some people were motivated by national or pragmatic white collective interests, while others were motivated by personal interest, since they felt that change was coming and wished to plant seeds for their future careers. Both realized that a shift in power was occurring, and wanted to influence the outcome or take advantage of the anticipated change. Others, motivated by conscience and a sense of moral obligation, chose activism. The fourth group was motivated by ideological commitment, e.g. the communists. It should not be forgotten that change in perceptions of the Other also encouraged them to move forward. In this context, supportive international opinion and the non-racial inclusive discourse adopted by the ANC proved helpful.

The model of protest work that was developed by white protest groups during the transition period could be described as objective-driven to fit with an agreed-upon grand goal. By the early 1980s, the grand goal of the majority had shifted from opposing apartheid (anti-apartheid) per se to opposing apartheid and struggling for a united non-racial democratic South Africa. In this context, Colin Knox and Padraic Quirk refer to the shift in the NGO network from being an anti-apartheid force to becoming partners in a new dispensation.[24] The struggle was not addressed piecemeal away from the grand goal, since most of the organizations, including many human rights and research centres, saw their work as part of the overall struggle to undermine apartheid and promote the inclusive platform of the United Democratic Front (UDF). As the next chapter shows, this is the reverse of the case of the Palestinian–Israeli conflict. For instance, most Israeli protest groups continue to address the conflict in a piecemeal way, many refuse to take a position on how the final settlement should look, and there is no agreed upon (inclusive) vision towards which everyone is focusing their efforts.

Within South Africa's model of protest, human rights organizations were part-and-parcel of the protest effort. They did not claim to be apolitical or to be active only as professionals, but took their position/s from apartheid, with many condemning the whole political system and challenging existing laws. They saw their work as part of the anti-apartheid struggle. Through their legal services, they joined with the protest organizations to defend the rights of the majority, and by working at the grassroots level, they gathered and disseminated information that shamed the apartheid ideology and raised awareness about the plight of the black majority and the brutality of the system. Apartheid as an ideology and system was attacked and condemned. This has not been the case in Israel. Israeli human rights groups claim to be apolitical and therefore do not adopt positions; nor do they see themselves as part of the peace groups. The Zionist ideology has not been condemned by the majority of protest groups but has, on the contrary, been protected by them. There are in fact only a few who, in addition to condemning Zionism, will criticize its exclusivity.

In South Africa, many white activists were involved in more than one organization, including the black-led UDF. This had to do with the inclusive vision agreed upon for the resolution of the conflict, and again is the opposite of the Palestinian–Israeli case, where the vision for conflict resolution, being based on separation, i.e. a two-state solution, did not promote a UDF-type umbrella. A majority of Israeli protest efforts have continued to take place in the loop of a zero-sum equation as will be seen in the next chapter.

Categorizing white protest groups and individual activism

For the purposes of the research, protest groups were classified into categories; this helped to unfold the details of the different components of the protest arena and assisted in revealing the political strands within this milieu, so as to see how each contributed to the anti-apartheid struggle. The white protest groups are classified in two major categories, each of which is further divided into two sub-categories.

The first major category is what the author describes as white liberal protest organizations/groups, and its sub-categories are mainstream liberal groups and progressive liberal groups. The second major category is that of whites in black-run leftist resistance groups, and its sub-categories are mainstream left and radical left groups. This categorization reflects their politics during the 1980s when major shifts occurred, especially towards a political centre where UDF non-racial inclusive politics became dominant. Table 3.1 illustrates this categorization, while the Appendix includes lists of groups/organizations that belonged to each category.

This classification shows the political spectrum in which white protest groups and individuals[25] worked. Lines between categories and sub-categories were not clear-cut and were sometimes blurred, but there were certain beliefs, principles and values that characterized each category. This classification is the result of intensive research that led the author to differ from the two books that made comparisons in examining mobilization for peace building in both South Africa and Israel. These are: *Mobilizing for Peace: Conflict Resolution in Northern Ireland, Israel/Palestine and South Africa*, edited by Benjamin Gidron, Stanley N. Katz and Yeheskel Hasenfeld (2002), and *Peace Building in Northern Ireland, Israel and South Africa: Transition, Transformation and Reconciliation*, by Colin Knox and Padraic Quirk (2000).

Gidron *et al.* classified[26] white protest groups into two categories: peace and conflict resolution organizations, and anti-apartheid non-governmental organizations.[27] Through the research interviews and the reviews of organizations mentioned in the lists of the two categories, it is obvious that the naming of the first category is not correct. All the organizations mentioned defined themselves as anti-apartheid groups. They did not define themselves otherwise, and certainly not as 'peace and conflict resolution organizations' as the authors chose to name them for the sake of differentiation. Being anti-apartheid did not mean having a collective position over all details of the political solution to the conflict; rather, it was the general objective decided upon by the organizations mentioned in both lists/categories. All agreed that apartheid should end, and referred to themselves as anti-apartheid groups.[28] Based on this misconception another error was made, which put together a number of organizations that were actually different in their politics, strategies, focal issue/s and subsequent specific objectives. This mixing-up reveals itself in the artificial naming of the objective-oriented category that is presented under the title of 'peace and conflict-resolution work'.[29]

An example of a clear error is the classifying of Black Sash as part of the peace and conflict resolution category, alongside the South African Institute of Race Relations (SAIRR). Both, in fact, defined themselves as anti-apartheid organizations, and not as mentioned above. In addition, Black Sash was vocal in terms of its political stand with regard to the future of South Africa, and was

Table 3.1 Categorization of white protest groups

Liberal white protest groups	1 Mainstream groups
	2 Progressive groups
Whites in (black-run) leftist groups	1 Mainstream left
	2 Radical left

close to the politics of the UDF. The SAIRR chose 'neutrality' and objective research as a means to undermine apartheid – at least, this was their declared position. They differed over political details, strategies, and understanding of liberalism, as will be discussed later in the chapter. Even so, both were put together under a misrepresentative name.

In addition, it is inaccurate to claim that all those listed as peace and conflict-resolution organizations were politically neutral and impartial.[30] Organizations like Black Sash and the End Conscription Campaign (ECC) took clear stands in objecting to militarism and supporting an end to conscription. They stood against the war launched against neighbouring countries, and against the police and army presence in the townships. Black Sash was present at the launching of both the UDF and the ECC, and the latter worked closely with the UDF. In a few cases, ANC members worked in white organizations, e.g. Black Sash, ECC and IDASA (Institute for a Democratic Alternative for South Africa).[31] Working in proximity together and having overlapping membership is hardly an indication of impartiality. These organizations and others took stands. Nor, as claimed by Gidron *et al.*, were they located between the ideological extremes of Afrikaner nationalism and the Africans.[32]

This book also differs from the second study, by Knox and Quirk, on the basis that it mixes the white progressive liberal organizations with the mainstream leftist ones, which were mainly black and were led by the ANC/UDF (and are discussed in detail later on). While both groups of organizations were brought together by positions that they held in common, such as the struggle against apartheid policies and for non-racial democracy, they did differ over some of the ANC's principles and strategies. For example, the economic dimension of a settlement in a predicted new South Africa remained a contentious issue between some of those mentioned in the category of 'Peace with Justice' (one of the three categories presented by Knox and Quirk, the other two being peace as 'absence of war' and 'exposing facts').[33] Thus, it is difficult to envision what (social) justice actually meant for all those groups mentioned in the 'peace and justice' category.

In addition, using specific terms like 'peace' and 'peace with justice' as underlying criteria is difficult to understand, since these terms are loaded with meaning. The authors do not define or explain to the reader how these terms were used or referred to by white protest groups/activists, or by the black resistance in contrast to the white. It is important to reiterate that the struggle was not shaped as a struggle for peace but was an anti-apartheid struggle. White anti-apartheid groups/activists were associated with liberalism or the left. Some among the liberals were more progressive in challenging the system than others. Some were active at the grassroots level, while others chose to challenge apartheid through research, dissemination of information, and provision of training. By the 1980s, most did not see themselves as neutral, nor did they define themselves as white peace groups or movements. Rather, they were part of the anti-apartheid struggle for a non-racial South Africa. Sheena Dunkan was astonished when asked if there was a white peace movement: "We didn't want a white movement in the 1980s. We wanted to promote non-racialism and interfaith co-operation."[34] Makgane Thobejane, a black member of the ANC and the SACP who worked actively in the struggle also emphasized the point made by Sheena Dunkan that there was no separate white peace movement.[35]

In Knox and Quirk's second category, only the South African Institute of Race Relations (SAIRR) was mentioned. But the SAIRR was not the only organization which exposed facts – this was also done by the Centre for Conflict Resolution (CCR) and other activist groups. Having reviewed the material of both research centres and met a representative of the SAIRR, the author wonders how the SAIRR can be presented as neutral and alone in the 'exposing facts' category while the CCR is classified in the 'peace as absence of war' category? The latter, if not neutral, was surely more progressive than the SAIRR which was headed by John Kane-Berman: in July 1985 he called on the apartheid government to take the initiative from the hands of the revolutionaries and begin negotiations on the principle of power sharing. As a loyal opposition, Kane-Berman's version of power sharing was based on gradualism and no commitment to majority rule democracy. In his ten-point peace package, he argued that,

> Once the principle of power sharing was accepted, the precise form it would take, and detailed formula for the make up of the country and of Parliament, would all be matters for negotiation, along with appropriate measures to protect cultural and language rights, religious freedoms, the rule of law, civil liberties and so on.[36]

It was a discourse similar to that of the people who advocated the ending of apartheid through multi-racialism and consequently federalism. In addition, the Institute's position on 'political violence' was veering towards that of the government in the way it argued about how to make the state security forces' presence in the townships accepted there "as protectors of the peace and guardians of legitimate authority",[37] at a time when it was no secret that the South African police did not have clean hands with regard to violence. (The politics of the CCR, which started life in 1968 as the Centre for Inter-group Studies, are discussed later in the chapter.)

Another and final example of disagreement concerns the placing of the Quaker Peace Centre under the category of 'peace as absence of war'. While this NGO did not take a position on the kind of political system suited to a new South Africa, it still held a clear position in opposing apartheid, in believing in a non-racial society, and in supporting consciousness objection.[38] Some of its members chose to take a neutral role by focusing on peace education and development activities, but others sought a positive peace that addressed injustice and sided with the oppressed.[39] There was no uniformity. The Quaker Society endorsed the ECC's declaration, and a number of members of the Quaker Peace Centre were active in the ECC in their personal capacities, while others participated in the SAIRR or the UDF and the ANC.[40] Therefore, the author does not think that in this case such a clear-cut classification is suitable. Fluidity would be more appropriate here. As such, the Quaker Peace Centre could be placed between mainstream liberals and progressive liberals.

Finally, taking into consideration the research question, analysis and critique of other studies, this book, as mentioned earlier, has developed another and more flexible categorization. In this book the categories are based on analysing the politics held by the different white protest organizations, and they help in clarifying the political positions and roles of different protest groups/organizations by showing the various political spectrums they represented. It is therefore important to note that categories are classified for research purposes and should not be seen as rigid boxes. They are constructed to assist with answering the research question that concerns the nature of the politics and roles of protest groups among the dominant side in peace building.

As mentioned above, this study divides white protest groups into two main categories, each of which has two sub-categories. The following sections look at their political stands, activities and roles, and examples of relevant protest groups are given to explain each category under discussion. The Appendix includes an illustration of the categorization established in this study.

Liberal protest organizations/groups

This section looks at the category of liberal organizations, which are divided into mainstream liberal organizations and progressive liberal organizations. It is important to clarify here what is meant by 'liberal', 'mainstream' and 'progressive'. In the context of South Africa, the liberal organizations are those that historically held political views similar or close to those of the Progressive Party/ Progressive Federal Party. They were gradualists who sought change by process, and adopted policies and strategies that fitted within the legal framework of the political system. They usually did not commit themselves to a clear end result, were skilful in marketing their positions at the international level (since they were well connected with the free market business community), and supported a decentralized system where government intervention was limited. While certain values were important for the liberals, they still argued for 'case uniqueness', e.g. the uniqueness of the case of South Africa. They were also keen to address cultural differences which could be used as a justification for (some sort of) separation.

The Helen Suzman Foundation, which is a landmark of liberalism in South Africa, states that it supports and promotes liberal democratic policies and ideals. These goals are very similar to those held by liberals in Europe and certain countries in the East, where liberals are non-racial in their views, support free enterprise and are generally sympathetic to individualism, although their views on, and support for, welfare policies vary both within countries and between countries.[41] In the case of South Africa, they stress individual empowerment and self-reliance instead of persistent government intervention and state transfers for the poor, which they believe disempower the poor and leave them dependent.[42]

Jill Wentzel, a solid believer in liberalism, an activist in Black Sash (BS) during the 1980s who opposed the shift in BS positions, and a close friend of the SAIRR, defined the liberals as pragmatists who believed in parliamentary democracy, free speech, individual rights and liberties, non-racialism, rule of law and non-violent change.[43] She argued that liberalism in South Africa had witnessed a slide by the mid-1980s, an obvious indicator of which was the resignation of Drs Slabbert and Boraine from the Progressive Party, and their publicly stated position that opposition from within the parliament had no further role to play in effecting change within South Africa.[44] Instead they found refuge in the civil-society sphere, by establishing the Institute for a Democratic Alternative for South Africa (IDASA) and opening direct contact with the ANC.

The shift in the views of many liberals and liberal organizations is what led to a chasm among the liberals, and is recognized and reflected by the author in the categories presented in this chapter. The liberal organizations are divided into two sub-categories: the mainstream and the progressive. The mainstream organizations are those which retained the old points of view, positions and strategies. According to Wentzel, a meeting in 1985 that brought together those who had not changed their liberal principles, re-established such values and stated four key roles for the liberals:

1. *oppositional*, which involved saying 'No' to what the government was doing, criticizing it and organizing against it in such fields as trade unions and forced removals;
2. *defensive*, against violence and the violent overthrow of the state;
3. *exploratory* and co-operative with the reform initiatives of the government; and
4. *innovative*, putting forward new policies, especially in the fields of unemployment, housing and education.[45]

The progressives are those who challenged some of the old views, positions and strategies, and who either adopted or came closer (in different degrees) to the platform of the Freedom Charter. They moved towards support of majority rule (e.g. Black Sash,[46] IDASA,[47] FFF,[48] ECC[49] and NUSAS[50]), and a form of social democracy instead of liberal democracy, thereby opening the door for talks about talks and a compromise on South Africa's economic policies. Voices that did not support violent means of resistance, but understood why blacks had resorted to it, also appeared among them. Many became affiliated with the UDF or worked closely with it. Thus, progressiveness in this context was associated with coming closer to the politics of the oppressed (mainstream left), and with finding common ground to enable them to work together in the struggle against apartheid and for a non-racial democracy of one-person-one-vote. The mainstream groups continued to be associated with the historical views, stands and strategies of the liberals; such as the Progressive Party, the SAIRR and the Urban Foundation.[51] The latter was a business group that opposed apartheid but stood firm in protecting free market policies and the business interests of the whites.

Based on this introduction to the politics of liberalism in South Africa, a discussion of the political positions, activities and roles of a sample of white protest organizations follows. It should be noted here that this book does not refer to all the organizations mentioned in the two comparative studies on peace building referred to earlier. Those studies did not mention identical sets of organizations, nor does this work mention the same set of organizations. It mentions those that the researcher, as a result of the interview findings and reviewing the relevant material, perceives as the major influential bodies. It is also important to emphasize that it was impossible to obtain sufficient material on all the organizations that the author came across: there were also constraints in terms of time and resources available. Even so, the author believes that this research presents a sample that adequately reflects organized white protest work.

Mainstream liberal organizations

By the mid-1980s, the number of mainstream liberal organizations had, as noted above, decreased due to the shift in the politics of many groupings. Among the organizations that continued to represent the old liberal mainstream was the South African Institute of Race Relations (SAIRR). Through a review of their publications (including their famous annual survey of race relations), and by reading articles by director John Kane-Berman and interviewing a research staff member, Frans Cronje, the author concludes that the institute continued to hold the old liberal ethos. It had been a liberal multi-racial organization in which whites always played a dominant role, and being multi-racial gave it significance, compared with others who saw themselves as non-racial or anti-racial. Multi-racialism gives significant weight to racial differences, non-racialism recognizes the four races in South Africa but seeks unity, while anti-racism does not accept the concept of race.[52] Even though the institute managed to develop a well-researched survey on the political, economic, educational and other aspects of South African life, among the liberals it still continued to hold 'right wing' political views. While it claimed to play the role of the neutral academic think tank, given earlier discussions about SAIRR, the author is not able to regard it as apolitical or neutral.

The goal of the SAIRR, according to Frans Cronje, was to find truth, and to make truth known through factual research to show the impact of apartheid. A review of their annual surveys does not identify propaganda for the apartheid government; rather, a reader will discover relatively neutral language, see both views (from formal and informal sources) referred to, and find reference to results from many other research organizations/centres. In the mid-1980s, a lot was invested in documenting political violence with a focus on intra-black violence, whereas the system of structured violence inflicted by apartheid policies was not referred to directly. This imbalance does not undermine the fact that the survey used factual data.

From the surveys by the SAIRR that were examined, it was clear that the Institute played a major role in disseminating information about the situation in South Africa. The detailed annual survey was regarded by many, nationally and internationally, as a document of great importance in terms of factual data, and in understanding what was happening in apartheid South Africa. The survey, along with others, sensitized international bodies and challenged government reports and analyses of the situation. At some point, even ministers in the apartheid government came to the Institute to discover facts about the real situation on the ground. As well as this role, the SAIRR ran a humanitarian aid programme called Operation Hunger at some point in the early 1980s, which addressed the needs of the poor, but this was fairly soon given up since the Institute, not wishing to plunge into a new business, decided to retain its principal mission which was research. The Operation Hunger programme coincided with the crises witnessed by the liberals and the intensifying of the UDF-led struggle while the strategy to make the country ungovernable was taking place. While most liberal organizations moved towards more progressive political stands, a few, like the SAIRR, tried to relate to the crises in other ways, such as through humanitarian types of activities.

Another organization that held similar views to those of the SAIRR was the Urban Foundation, which retained the old mainstream liberal principles of a free market, opposition to 'violence' as a means of changing the political situation, and support of gradualist policies. It was a business-driven initiative that studied business relations and recommended policies in this field with the aim of defending the interests of and promoting the commercial sector.[53] It opposed apartheid but at the same time sought to defend the interests of the whites, including a free market policy in the new dispensation. Other organizations belonging to this sub-category were Assocom, the South Africa Foundation, and the Steel and Engineering Industries Federation of South Africa.[54] They were created and/or supported by the business sector to represent its special or general interests.[55]

Although relations between these organizations and the PP/PFP were not official, informally they were close[56] in terms of politics and of political socializing. For example, Helen Suzman, former leader of the PP, was a board member of the SAIRR, and was also a close friend of Harry Oppenheimer, the director of the Anglo-American Company, probably the biggest capitalist corporation in South Africa. Oppenheimer was one of the closest allies of the PP and one of its sponsors. In line with the principles of economic liberalism, Helen Suzman and the other mainstream liberal organizations opposed economic sanctions, arguing that they badly affected all South Africans.

Progressive liberal organizations

This sub-category includes the largest number of white protest groups according to their politics in the 1980s. Of course, their politics were not identical and different views existed even within each group/organization. Even so, they shared certain political stands and ideas, and represented degrees of closeness to the UDF Charterist politics.[57] Among the main groups who fitted this category were the National Union of South African Students (NUSAS), Black Sash (BS), the End Conscription Campaign (ECC), the Five Freedom Forum (FFF), the Institute of Democratic Alternative for South Africa (IDASA), the Christian Institute for Southern Africa (CISA), the Centre for Inter-group Studies/Centre for Conflict Resolution (CCR), the Cape Town Democrats, the Christian Youth Workers (Christian socialists), and the Civil Rights League.

They were not alone in their protests, and received support from a number of sympathetic universities and active academics (in their individual capacities) who also stood against apartheid beyond the old liberal political discourse. Among the sympathetic universities that voiced their rejection of apartheid were the University of Natal in Durban, Cape Town University, and the University of the Witwatersrand in Johannesburg.[58] Sympathizers and protesters also existed in the cultural sphere, e.g. the Market Theatre in Johannesburg, which expressed very strong messages against apartheid,[59] and many writers who challenged apartheid strongly, such as Nadine Gordimer and Alan Paton. It is worth noting that the writings of Nobel Laureate Nadine Gordimer are not to be compared to those of famous Israeli liberal writers such as Amos Oz and David Grossman. Hers are much more challenging to the system, and are more progressive in terms of associating with, and reflecting the plight of the oppressed under the existing system. Importantly too, Nadine Gordimer's novel *The Burger's Daughter* was banned by the government because of this. Finally, one must not forget the role played by a number of newspapers in disseminating the information gathered by some of the above-mentioned organizations, e.g. the *Rand Daily Mail*.

In order to sum up their shared political stands and vision, one must recall the principles of the Freedom Charter of 1955, which provided the broad political platform that brought these organizations into or closer to the non-racial democracy platform of the UDF/ANC. Such closeness or affiliation was possible after the UDF, in order to create a wide front against the government,[60] had softened its position on certain articles in the Charter at a time when the apartheid government's plan for reform through the tri-cameral system was seen by many white activist groups as a means of building another form of apartheid rather than getting rid of it. The claimed reform was analysed as a way for the government to retain white control, while fragmenting the opposing side by containing the Indians and coloureds through separate Houses of Delegates. In 1985 the black Africans were promised a say in the second tier of administration, the local authority, and were assured that ways to incorporate them in the President's Council would be considered.[61]

In the political circumstances of the 1980s, the Freedom Charter became the middle ground. It had been agreed upon in 1955 by the four Congresses – the African National Congress, the Congress of Democrats (white), the Indian National Congress, and the Coloured People's Congress, in addition to the South African Communist Party. It was presented by the UDF in a broad and vague manner that allowed each side to stress the article/s to which it gave priority. The UDF described its goals as a "united, democratic South Africa based on the will of the people ... and an end to economic and other forms of exploitation".[62] It was possible for the majority of blacks and progressive whites, who received a mild message from the UDF, to mobilize around the Freedom Charter, which included the following in its 1955 policy declaration:

- The people shall govern
- All national groups shall have equal rights
- The people shall share in the country's wealth
- The land shall be shared among those who work it
- All shall be equal before the law
- All shall enjoy equal human rights
- There shall be work and security
- The doors of learning and culture shall be opened
- There shall be houses, security and comfort
- There shall be peace and friendship.[63]

The UDF, claiming two million adherents belonging to 680 affiliated organizations,[64] made it clear that they did not need to worry the whites, but would include those who were ready to adopt its goals, which were based on the Freedom Charter. To achieve this, the UDF considered that one of its responsibilities was not to leave the white sector for the white UDF affiliates, but to involve all UDF members. Its strategy was to organize and mobilize different white sectors, e.g. Afrikaners, academics, youth, soldiers, schools, academics, women, and business, cultural and religious organizations.[65] Blacks were also encouraged to join whites in their activities in the white areas. With regard to the economic agenda, there was not much emphasis on the nature of the ANC's economic policy, nor did the ANC take hard positions or prioritize its social agenda during (elite) informal encounters.[66] As such, the ANC/UDF led the national mass movement that brought together liberals, Marxists, communists, nationalists and religious groups. It took into consideration not only the concerns of the whites about the ANC's historic socialist agenda, but also the concerns of the Christian groups which did not want to associate themselves with communism. In the process, the SACP, the major ally of the ANC, compromised over its socialist agenda. This issue will be discussed further when second-track diplomacy meetings organized by IDASA and FFF, e.g. the famous Dakar and Lusaka meetings, are addressed.

Thus, the main principles that connected the above-mentioned white organizations belonging to this category included: being anti-apartheid, support for non-racialism, acceptance of one-person-one-vote (majority rule), the rule of law and the need for a bill of rights to protect citizens' civil and political rights, the belief that whites had a place in a new South Africa run by the ANC, opposition to imposition of emergency law, no commitment to capitalism per se, but a commitment to non-violent protest and to a negotiated settlement. Some organizations stressed some of these principles more than others. Some supported sanctions while others chose not to take a position. Most did not support violent resistance but showed an understanding of why it had been turned to by the black majority. Sheena Dunkan of BS said: "I don't approve of violence but I understand why people resort to it."[67] Some were more vocal than others, but even so they became the Charterists compared to the rest of the liberals, and were also referred to as progressive liberals.

A sample from the organizations mentioned above is looked at here and their specific political stands, principles, aims and activities are discussed. The veteran organizations in this category are Black Sash (BS) and the National Union of South African Students (NUSAS). Black Sash was established in 1955 by a group of liberal women, and is an example of an organization that moved from the cradle of mainstream liberalism to 'militant' or 'radical' political positions (in the view of the 'old' liberals), or to progressive liberalism (as seen by those on the left). It moved from silent protest about violations of human rights (pass laws, forced removals, detention without trial, inequality, repression, etc.) in the 1950s and 1960s, to the provision of legal services through its countrywide advice offices. BS was also involved in monitoring and recording protests, and kept lists of those banned, banished, or who died in detention or disappeared into lengthy periods of imprisonment without trial. It linked its research and political statements to its fieldwork, and managed to build a credible voice as an anti-apartheid protest group and as one that was struggling for social democracy.[68] In his first speech after being released in 1990, Nelson Mandela referred to Black Sash as "the conscience of white South Africa".[69]

During the 1980s, Black Sash worked closely with the UDF. Its political stands and principles were reflected in the statements it made and in the kind of activities in which it was involved, together with other groups, as part of their concerted efforts to exert pressure for change. Black Sash's principles included a commitment to justice (refusal to accept apartheid and its policies), respect for human rights and the rule of law, and political as well as other freedoms. Sheena Dunkan also stressed commitment to the five freedoms identified by the Five Freedom Forum: "freedom from want, freedom from fear, freedom of speech and association, freedom of conscience, and freedom from discrimination".[70] Equality for Black Sash meant equal rights, not income, which was what the rule of law was about.[71]

The political stands of Black Sash were clear on a number of issues. They were reflected in its declared statements, which challenged the apartheid government. For example: "South Africans must remember that their fellow South Africans have been driven to armed struggle by the institutionalized violence of apartheid. The only way to end violence is to establish justice and the rule of law."[72] In the same press release, Black Sash stressed that the government's military raids beyond the country's borders violated international law. Concerning internal political violence, Black Sash stated:

> it has become clear that Smith's troops ... were involved in many ugly incidents ... this was a matter of military strategy, designed to undermine the internal political influence of the guerrillas and to discredit them internationally ... political violence is escalating as black aspirations are blocked by white intransigence.[73]

Another statement in 1987 equated the apartheid government's policies with those of Nazi Germany:

> Nursery schools, creches, clinics, vegetable gardens, sport, hunger relief, rural development, Christian crusade, are all used by the state through the security forces to control the populace and to prevent the expression and organization of civilian opposition to S.A. government policies, leadership training in schools, community education programmes which are compulsory for civil servants, evangelical outreach, all redolent of Nazi Germany in the 1930s, of the 20th century Russia ... [These] are the weapons of the South African state in its attempt to destroy the image of the enemy – communism – which it created in the first place. There is no enemy. There are only people who want freedom to decide their own future.[74]

With such clear political stands in support of the oppressed, combined with the resistance discourse of the UDF/ANC, it is no wonder that the number of members of Black Sash dropped from 10,000 in 1955 to 1,500 by the 1980s.[75] Most whites at that time saw such positions as counterproductive since they encouraged violence, endangered white safety and undermined white power in future negotiations. If these positions are compared to those of Women in Black or of Bat Shalom, two leading Israeli women's organizations, there is no doubt that those of the Black Sash were more daring and challenging to the system, as will be seen in the next chapter.

Black Sash played a significant role in raising public awareness of the suffering of the majority, both locally and internationally. It provided factual information and services and, as mentioned above, presented political stands that challenged those of the government and the mainstream liberals. It was actively present in the networks among white groups and the white–black network. This contributed to the provision of a space to be bridged between whites and blacks and strengthened co-operative efforts in the framework of the UDF political platform. In choosing that path, Black Sash, with others, created a chasm within the old liberal cluster and weakened it. Finally, it is important to mention that Black Sash was involved in second-track diplomacy meetings, which were considered by many as talks about talks to prepare the ground for official negotiations. As such, Erika Wessels' argument that Black Sash contributed positively towards a constitutional government that reflected the real South Africa – not of white dominance but of majority rule[76] – could well be valid.

Unlike the Black Sash women's group, the second veteran white protest group, The National Union of South African Students, NUSAS, was affiliated to the UDF. NUSAS was established in 1924 as a white student union, but when the first black campus was admitted as a member of NUSAS in 1945, the Afrikaner campuses walked out of it.[77] Then in the 1970s, the black minority walked out of NUSAS, headed by Steve Biko, who was leader of the Black Consciousness Movement, and formed the Azanian Student Union, AZASU. The split occurred because the black students felt that they needed to empower themselves, lead their struggle, and decide their priorities on the basis of their own experience of repression. Referring to that split, Pascal P. Moloi of the black student movement commented: "There can't be assimilation of normality in an abnormal society."[78] It is important to highlight that this split did not stop co-operation on specific programmes between the two unions.

NUSAS stood against apartheid and racism, and for justice, freedom for all, and equalities, including equal citizenship.[79] On the value level these positions were not translated into more detailed stands. For example, the Union did not take specific positions on issues like land control or the displaced, but organized visits to the homeland as part of its awareness-raising efforts.[80] On university campuses, NUSAS sought freedom of speech and academic freedom, in addition to being against state-imposed conditions and intervention, e.g. the government's plan to impose a racist quota system in 1983, and government threats in 1987 to cut off state subsidies as a punitive measure.[81] NUSAS ran political debates, provided white students with information and critical views, and organized demonstrations. Its members saw themselves as a power for change, in which the university campus had a role to play. They wrote: "we reaffirm ... the right of students and staff to debate their social and academic concerns about the future openly. The university's concerns cannot be separated from the broader society."[82] On the educational level, NUSAS highlighted issues of inequality of education and the role of a university in addressing this issue in a progressive fashion: it also focused on the structure and administration of universities in terms of the composition of the student body, and decision-making.[83] No such challenging and powerful student protest group exists in Israel.

NUSAS became a hub for young dissidents. By the mid-1980s, all English campuses were affiliated to it, as were three other groups established among Afrikaans-speaking universities.[84] Many of its members had overlapping memberships in other groups, including the End Conscription Campaign, and the UDF. Through its close ties with the ECC, NUSAS wanted to challenge the level of militarism in South Africa and deepen the divisions over conscription in the white community. Via the UDF, it wanted to contribute to the struggle for democracy through commitment to the principles of non-racialism and one-person-one-vote, and therefore chose to take a political role that went beyond defending the daily needs of students. NUSAS had a history of mobilizing opposition against apartheid – i.e. a history of political resistance.[85]

During the 1980s in particular, the government tried to limit its actions, publications and funds. NUSAS was intimidated, provoked and brutally treated by the apartheid government and by its police forces on campuses, but stood firm against government intimidation and intervention. For example, it opened communication with the ANC, while the latter was still banned. NUSAS also remained committed to the mandate it had received from 10,000 members who agreed to continue to co-operate with the South African National Students Congress (SANSCO), which was mainly black and black-led.[86] SANSCO adopted the Freedom Charter and was associated with the UDF and the ANC, moving away from its political origins in the Black Consciousness movement and AZASU.

Being perceived as daring and radical by the white community, NUSAS was then blamed for the loss, in the 1987 elections, of the PP/PFP, which had the status of the official opposition, and was accused of calling on students not to take part. NUSAS's declared position at that time was that "voting was not the most important issue in the White elections and ... students should decide whether to vote or not according to their conscience".[87] Such a stand reflected the distance NUSAS had moved during the 1980s from mainstream liberalism, and the gap that had occurred among the liberals.

The NUSAS was not alone. It was supported by many prominent figures who held principled positions against apartheid, and had left behind the *laager* mentality of the ethnic 'tribe'. A number of staff members in universities joined the NUSAS in its progressive agenda, and contributed to making several universities into islands of dissent and protest as well as venues for popularizing the UDF platform. One of the public figures who supported the NUSAS was the Afrikaner religious leader, Beyers Naude, who left the Dutch Reformed Church and established the Christian Organization for Southern Africa, an NGO that supported the black struggle. He was the honorary president while Helen Joseph (English-speaking) was known as its Grandmother. Joseph was a member of the national executive committee of the South African Congress of Democrats, one of the speakers in the Congress of the People that had produced the Freedom Charter in 1955, and an honorary patron of the UDF.[88]

Finally, it is important to note that the NUSAS merged with the non-racial students' organization, the South African National Students Congress (SANSCO) in September 1991, thereby forming a united non-racial student congress, the South African Student Congress (SASCO), as a reflection of a new and dawning political dispensation.[89]

Among the visible and powerful organizations of the 1980s was the End Conscription Campaign (ECC), which shared similarities with the two previous groups described. The idea of establishing this campaign began with a call to end conscription made by Black Sash in 1983.[90] Since Black Sash could not call for refusal to serve in the army, since it was illegal to do so, it called for an end to conscription as a way of circumventing the law. From the beginning the idea found many supporters, such as the NUSAS, Black Sash, the UDF, the South African Council of Churches, and the Conscientious Objector Support Groups (COSG). While the COSG objective was to provide personal support for the objectors (sometimes helping them to escape and go into exile), the underlying aim of establishing the ECC was to give a high profile to its opposition to militarism (which intensified structured violence), to its challenge to the apartheid state and the government's discourse of total onslaught, and to its aim of bringing in more whites, if not closer to the UDF platform, then at least away from that of the government. The latter was part of an ANC strategy – to win more whites to its side while dividing the white consensus.[91]

The ECC was a 'one issue' campaign which targeted the white community. Its aims were to make people aware of the consequences of the apartheid system and it did this in cooperation with other organizations. It wished white families to see the evils of apartheid and how men were brutalized by conscription, and by doing so, it hoped to undermine the army.[92] The ECC brought together activists, from religious to communist, across the political spectrum, including church, women, students, and civil rights and political organizations. Though not affiliated with the UDF, it worked with it closely, and funds were channelled to it through the South African Council of Churches.[93] The latter was a close but unaffiliated ally of the UDF, in which many of its members were leaders.[94] Many of the ECC affiliate organizations were also affiliated with the UDF and the UDF was directly represented on the ECC committee in Cape Town. By 1987, the ECC had branches in four university campuses and it worked closely with NUSAS to popularize the UDF as an alternative to the existing reality in which society was seen as divided and disordered by conflict and inequality.

The ECC's politics were in line with the mild version of the Freedom Charter presented by the UDF. The objective was democracy by full citizenship, and while it stood for the principles of peace and justice through building a non-racial, democratic and peaceful alternative,[95] it did not move any further towards debating the meanings of equality and justice in the future South Africa.[96]

Though only a few hundred individuals joined it, its influence was much greater than its numbers, and it persuaded thousands.[97] In 1984, a survey conducted in all the English-speaking universities indicated that 70 per cent supported the call to end conscription.[98] According to Sue Britton, a founding member, the ECC played a role in making whites see morality and self-interest differently, and added a dimension to the political debate, that of anti-militarism. She added that the ECC's influence enabled it to receive assurances from the ANC that it would end compulsory conscription when it came to power, a promise that was kept.[99] The ECC also claimed that the shift in the PFP's policy in November 1984, when it called for an end to compulsory conscription, resulted from ECC pressure.[100]

Endorsement and support for the ECC was received from familiar names like Sheena Dunkan, Helen Joseph, the Reverend Allan Boesak (coloured), the Reverend Beyers Naude, and the Reverend Wesley Mabuza, beside other prominent religious and academic white figures. At the launching, forty white organizations endorsed the ECC declaration, while another fifteen became members.[101] The declaration was entitled "Towards a Just Peace in Our Land"; it stressed the existing injustices and inequalities and the right to exercise freedom of conscience, while emphasizing its refusal to condone the illegal occupation of Namibia, and refusal to fight a brother.[102] Such positions were countered by the government, which imposed restrictions on the ECC's work under the mid-1980s emergency regulations. It was banned in 1988. If the political stands and influence of the ECC are compared with those of Israeli organizations, which call for different forms of refusal to serve in the army, those of the ECC were without doubt more supportive towards the oppressed, more daring in challenging the system and its ideology, and more influential.

Other young organizations emerged in the 1980s along the same political lines as the UDF (non-racialism of a united rainbow nation), and played different or overlapping roles. The special role of two of these will be discussed here – the Five Freedoms Forum (FFF) and the Institute for a Democratic Alternative for South Africa (IDASA). Both were associated with talks about talks (second-track diplomacy), and played a significant role in sensitizing the white community towards the ANC and its political platform.[103] According to many scholars and activists, the two famous meetings at Dakar and Lusaka were instrumental in debating a more detailed vision for a new South Africa, as well as in discussing how the well-being of the white community would be safeguarded and the kind of role the whites could play in the struggle.[104]

These meetings were among more than seventy that had been held between ANC exiles and whites from inside South Africa by June 1989, when the Lusaka meeting took place.[105] Secret meetings were also held, including those with Mandela in prison, but are excluded from this number. The noticeable growth of these meetings was such that it was referred to as the "industry of meetings".[106] Among the first to take such initiatives, during the 1984–1986 flare-up of resistance among the blacks, was a significant portion of the business sector who did this by visiting the ANC abroad and holding talks with key ANC leaders.[107] The Lusaka meeting was described as a major step forward in the tortuous matter of starting a real process of negotiation between whites 'at home' and the major liberation movements outside the country.[108] The earlier Dakar meeting in July 1987 was also considered highly significant because it legitimized talks with the banned ANC and opened space for future dialogue initiatives: such matters were regarded as acts of civil disobedience,[109] and as well as having substance, were also strongly symbolic.

The experience of IDASA as a facilitation institute that believed in the broad principles of non-racialism, democracy that encompassed one-person-one-vote, and negotiations by process without commitment to an ideological content, was put into practice in Dakar. Dakar was a high-profile forum where white political activists and members of the academic, religious, cultural, professional and business fields met publicly with members of the ANC: among the white participants, sixty-one were Afrikaners (majority) in addition to a seventeen-person delegation from the ANC.[110] They participated in their personal capacities but shared a common commitment to rejecting both the ideology and the practice of the apartheid system.[111] Makgane Thobejane, an ANC member, argued that the Dakar meeting was organized in response to an initiative proposed to IDASA by the ANC, and believes that negotiations were anticipated, desired and driven by the ANC which by then had adopted the two-stage theory.[112] Brett Davidson of IDASA assumed that the Dakar meeting was IDASA's initiative since it aimed to get both sides to talk,[113] while David Schmidt, also of IDASA, believed that Dakar represented the mutual interests of both sides,[114] arguing that IDASA's commitment to a negotiated settlement coincided with a shift in ANC's policy towards recognizing the importance of engagement.

The four-day meeting in Dakar in 1987 had four principal topics: "strategies about building for fundamental change in South Africa, the building of a national unity, perspectives with regard to the structures of the government of a free

South Africa, the economy of a liberated South Africa".[115] All participants shared a unity of purpose – the building of a united, democratic and non-racial South Africa. (The same phrase had had 'non-sexist' added to it when it was heard eight years later at Nelson Mandela's presidential inauguration speech in 1994.) By the end of the conference, the participants had not only stressed their preference for a negotiated settlement but had also blamed the apartheid government for putting obstacles in its way: they also agreed that the release of all political prisoners and the un-banning of organizations was a fundamental prerequisite for such negotiations to take place.[116] These conditions were met in the following three to four years.

Two years later, in June 1989, 182 delegates came together in Lusaka, of whom 115 were white delegates from inside South Africa.[117] This time the delegation was much bigger; the English-speaking attendants were the majority, while only twenty-eight were Afrikaans-speaking. The diversity among the white delegates was significant, in terms of reaching out to many sectors and their form of representation. The delegation included twenty-three academics (eight professors), twenty businessmen, sixteen journalists and authors (six editors), nine school principals/teachers, six lawyers, twenty-three politicians/political party workers, four ministers/church workers, three farmers, three doctors, two trade unionists and two architects.[118] There were also members and representatives of at least twenty-two white or white-led NGOs. While some delegates participated in their personal capacities, many participated as representatives of their organizations, differently from the case in Dakar. It is thought that they represented scores of thousands of whites, since many delegates held positions of influence in their communities.[119]

During the four-day Lusaka meeting, white concerns and black aspirations which shaped the final settlement were stipulated in a more detailed programme. Because of this, the proceedings of this meeting are examined here at length. The parameters of the envisioned solution were drawn according to a more specific agenda by ANC leaders and (progressive) white delegates, in addition to representatives from the white business sector. Reading the Lusaka proceedings, it is evident that the ANC's two-stage theory of political democracy followed by economic revolution prevailed over the socialist agenda that it had held decades earlier, while the essence of creative ambiguity[120] that allowed for a compromise on economic policy was also laid down. For instance, with regard to one of the major contentious issues, an ANC member would send contradictory messages to appeal to both blacks and whites concerning the structure of the political economy of a post-apartheid South Africa. On this issue, an ANC presenter said:

> the balance between social and private property will be guided by a number of imperatives – ultimate control by the post-apartheid state over economic resources in the interests of the people as a whole; and this will be effected by direct control over key sectors such as mining, banking and certain monopoly industries; indirect state regulation to ensure the well-being of all

sectors of the population; and a land reform program which will end restrictions on ownership and occupation but will meet the aspirations of people who have been dispossessed of their land – the exact forms and mechanisms of state control are left open in our programmatic perspectives. The element of private participation in state enterprise is occurring more and more in socialist countries, both in relation to management and capital input, and has not been addressed.... Those whites who are genuinely prepared to contribute their talents and skills will have a place and their rewards will have to be commensurate with their contribution. We will need those skills badly and will have to bear in mind that incentives will be needed to keep them. [121]

The positions of white participants on this issue reflected white business concerns about what socialist policy the ANC might adopt. Brian Pottinger and Peter Hugo[122] both stressed that the purpose of uplifting the livelihood of the majority of blacks would not be served by the creation of a social welfare public sector and an interventionist role by the government in the economy.[123] Peter Hugo argued that there was a need for economic growth above 5 per cent in order to provide sufficient jobs and to create the wealth to improve the quality of life for all: "we need to build a strong economy to generate confidence among the business community to invest in the manufacturing process and so to create more jobs and more importantly inspire overseas investors to put money into South Africa."[124] A third speaker, Ronnie Bethlehem,[125] claimed that most whites supported at least a partly socialist state and put forward four ways to address existing economic inequalities without making preferences. These were economic empowerment through growth-driven processes; programmes involving ownership for increasing numbers of people, thus bringing more people into the process of wealth generation and access to wealth; some form of government intervention; and finally confiscation and redistribution of wealth by the state.[126] The last was never implemented but the first three were adopted by the ANC after it came to power.

On the political side, one-person-one-vote for majority rule was not a contentious issue and thus was not put forward for discussion by the delegates. This fulfilled a major element in black aspirations, on the basis of which it became possible to put more specific issues on the agenda, e.g. negotiations (who, how and when), violence (causes and effects), sanctions (facilitating or impeding change), models for South Africa's constitutional dispensation, the role of parliament and the parliamentary opposition, role of extra-parliamentary politics, role of local government, education (planning for the future), role of the media, and women's role in shaping the future.[127] It was possible to go so far because many delegates were either members of the influential elite, or members of 'intermediate groups' that flourished as the crises mounted. This fits with Kornhauser's argument on the development of intermediate groups during times of crisis.[128] Knox and Quirk, adopting Lederach's peace-building model, refer to the intermediate groups as significant Middle-Range Leaders.[129] The participants in these groups play/ed a more powerful intermediary role between the top leadership and the masses than usual, since, with their loss of faith in the central government's politics and ability to deliver, they began to take more commanding positions.

The conference, in itself, was viewed as very significant, since it helped

> to legitimize the participation of many people inside and outside South Africa in the process of planning the future [that is] facing South Africa in its transition to a democratic and non-racial society.... Contact cannot be left only in the hands of the government, for there is no real progress there ... we seize the opportunity to promote this climate further by encouraging all white people to see how important it is that the basic obstacles to negotiations are removed ... that the ball is in the government's court.[130]

One could conclude that the ANC's elite who adopted the People's Power policy to empower and mobilize the black masses had intentionally joined hands with white middle-range leaders to influence the white government and white masses to create change. Eventually, the Declaration of Lusaka became the framework for formal negotiations.[131] Thus the parameters of the compromise were (almost) set.

In discussing the talks about talks, we should focus on two issues; the whites' demand for a bill of rights in a future constitutional South Africa; and how the issue of security would be addressed. Whites stressed the need for a bill of rights (or 'a bill of whites' as some blacks called it).[132] "Whites wanted assurances that the ANC would not take the economy",[133] and a bill of rights was seen as a guarantee protecting individual property rights. Alternatively it can be argued that majority rule was exchanged for free enterprise and individual property rights, instead of the minority veto that had been suggested earlier by mainstream liberals when they gave up the idea of a qualified franchise in the late 1970s. The idea of a bill of rights was accepted at Lusaka and later in the formal negotiations, and the 1996 constitution of South Africa incorporated a bill of rights. The section on property stipulates that

> a person or community dispossessed of property after 19 June 1913 as a result of past racially-discriminatory laws or practices is entitled, to the extent provided by an Act of Parliament, either to restitution of that property or to equitable redress.[134]

However, this did not nullify the confiscation in 1913 of 87 per cent of the land of South Africa; and a process that allowed the government to expropriate property for public purpose was put in place in the same section of the constitution which addressed the issue of property:

> Property may be expropriated only in terms of the law of general application ... subject to compensation, the amount of which and the time and manner of payment of which have either been agreed to by those affected or decided or approved by a court.[135]

Consequently, twelve years after the fall of apartheid the white community still owned over 80 per cent of the land.

Concerning the security issue, it was not addressed as a separate issue or as a condition as in the case of Israel. Mike Oliver, chair of the FFF, referred to it as part-and-parcel of the settlement. In a paper presented in Lusaka on the role of whites in a changing society, he said: "I believe security comes from being part of the process and from knowing that you are part of building the future; it does not come from assurances sought second hand nor from sitting on the fence."[136] This position fits with the discourse of the UDF/ANC. An ANC member expressed a similar view during an interview with the author, stressing that there was no discourse on security: "the country belongs to all of us and once the regime is over, there is no need to care about security".[137] It is obvious that by then agreement over the grand vision for a new South Africa had been achieved, and that the UDF's platform appealed to most of the black resistance groups and white progressive protest groups.

Another organization that belongs to this category and that had been involved in mediation at different levels and across sectors and races is the Centre for Inter-group Studies (CIS), which, as noted above, was established in 1968. In the early 1990s it was named the Centre for Conflict Resolution (CRR), since it had played this role in its capacity as a research centre. While the CIS is associated with the University of Cape Town it is not part of the university, and it has also been made clear that it did not receive any government subsidy.[138] The work of the CIS included not only research and training in negotiation, facilitation and mediation but also provided a forum for contacts and discussions between representatives of the different conflicting groups. On many occasions it took the role of mediator as a third party, which was part of what it called "constructive involvement".[139] The Centre's director at the time was Professor H.W. van der Merwe, who, being a devout Quaker committed to non-violent conflict resolution, played an instrumental role in that quest. He had initiated personal contacts with the ANC in exile, ongoing since the 1960s, and in 1984 this led to a meeting in Lusaka between him, the assistant editor of an Afrikaans pro-government newspaper, and ANC leaders. This meeting was perceived as historic, and received worldwide publicity; it was also claimed that it promoted other dialogue initiatives,[140] an assertion made by other white groups during that period. A year later, van der Merwe was invited to intervene in the conflict between the UDF and the Inkatha black movement. These personal roles of the director fed into the Centre's mission. David Schmidt and Dr Caroline White reflected on the work of the Centre by associating it with initiatives to legitimize dialogue with the ANC, and with the way it played an overlapping role with IDASA, Black Sash, FFF and ECC.

Although the CIS claimed neutrality, it still opened its forums and training workshops to those who were perceived by other liberals as extremists. In the 1970s, for example, at times when the Black Consciousness Movement was demonized by the government, CIS provided a forum for Steve Biko (the black nationalist on the left of the ANC), along with a representative of NUSAS and another from the Afrikaner Studentbond, to discuss the role of students in South Africa.[141] At a time of political upheaval in 1984, the Centre brought together leaders from the NP, PFP, UDF, the Soweto Civic Association and Inkatha to meet on the same platform at an international conference on Conflict Accommodation and Management.[142] In 1993, Nelson Mandela and Professor Carel Boshof, of the right-wing Afrikaner Freedom Foundation, were brought together for talks while formal negotiations were taking place.[143]

This role intertwined with another two tasks with which the Centre was engaged. The first was research that aimed to examine the requirements for fundamental change in South Africa. This contributed to the provision of new perspectives on peace and security. As such, during negotiations over the reconstruction process between 1990 and 1994, the Centre was involved in shaping and implementing the National Peace Accord, along with other participants from civil society who were invited to participate. The Centre's expertise was recognized by the ANC, the Democratic Party, Umkhonto we Sizwe (the military wing of the ANC), the SACC, and the Consultative Business Movement during their discussions about the new philosophical base and the reconstruction process of the police and the army. They even appointed Laurie Nathan, the Centre's co-ordinator of the project on peace and security, as a consultant on military matters.

The second task was the Centre's outreach activities, through which it managed to disseminate information, provide skills to different levels of leaders, especially black, and gather information from those active on different levels and across different sectors. Both research and outreach fed into each other in terms of gathering and disseminating information, which undoubtedly contributed to the development of dialogue initiatives and the growth of new white and black perspective/s on the process for democracy in South Africa. Here, the role played by an academic elite that managed to link with other elite groups in addition to being a middle range leader, is obvious. The CIS was responsible for developing and disseminating perspectives/opinions, as well as taking the part of a facilitator and/or mediator between the antagonists. The task was made possible by progressively building up research that was not rejected by the underdog, and by keeping channels of communication open. As gradual acquaintance and trust was developed with the exiled ANC, it became possible to implement these roles more widely.

A final example of a body that fitted within the progressive liberal category is a religious organization, the famous Christian Institute for Southern Africa (CISA), which adopted the politics of non-racialism. It was established in reaction to the racist and rigid views of the state church, the Dutch Reformed Church (NGK), some of whose members dissociated themselves from it in the 1960s and 1970s. The most prominent of these was the Reverend Beyers Naude who established the CISA. The role played by the Christian Institute (1963–1977) was of substantial significance. In religious terms, it countered mainstream theology by challenging it publicly from a religious point of view. It also supported the goals of the black political movement led by the ANC, by standing for peaceful resistance including economic sanctions. Such stands were politically significant in terms of developing joint white–black resistance on common grounds and initiatives. The Institute even went as far as providing financial support to black community programmes or channelling money to them.[144] These positions were costly both for the Institute, and for Beyers Naude who was branded as traitor to his people and his church.[145] The Institute was banned by the government in 1977.[146] It is important to note that there is no equivalent to it in the Israeli case, as the next chapter will show.

One might also wonder where the famous South African Council of Churches (SACC) would be placed in this study. Given that the focus is on the politics and role/s of white protest groups, the fact that the SACC did not represent a membership where whites were the majority, and that the different political stands of white churchmen along the hierarchy were not consistent, the author believes that it cannot be located under this category. A possible alternative might have been in the next category, where the role of whites in black-led organizations is examined, but this is not the right option either, due to the fact that the role played by whites at the top leadership level was not consistent with those along the hierarchy. In addition, leadership positions were mainly held by whites.

The SACC was established in 1968, as a religious umbrella outside the realm of the Dutch Reformed Church. At that time, it was comprised of thirteen million members, twelve million of whom were blacks. Bishop Tutu was the first black to be elected as the general secretary in 1978.[147] The Council has had a complicated history in terms of maintaining consistent stands along the lines of the hierarchy in white congregations.[148] For example, the Council leadership would agree on a statement or position that reflected the desire of the majority of members (the blacks), and pass it down to the priests who, in many cases, would not adhere to it in their local white congregations.[149] In that sense, the positions and roles of white clergies became contradictory. It is difficult to answer the question as to who or what to examine – the role of the white leaders who had progressive views, or the middle-rank white priests who refused majority demands and the positions of the church leaders? It would in fact be quite simplistic to locate the SACC in either category. Furthermore, a thorough study of the role of whites (leaders and middle-rank priests) in the SACC would be a very demanding task that is neither the focus nor the aim of this book.

However, it should not be forgotten that the SACC was instrumental in supporting the struggle of the majority, not only by providing services and channelling money to the UDF affiliates[150] who mobilized the public, but also by challenging formal church theology, doing so on religious moral grounds. Through its membership as the South African national committee in the World Council of Churches, the SACC managed to galvanize international support for its views, discourse, and the struggle of the oppressed. It further publicized the struggle and legitimized its moral stand. It managed as a result to obtain grants from supportive organizations and governments at times when many European civil-society organizations, particularly in Scandinavian states, were becoming keen to support progressive liberal groups and the UDF members and affiliates. The SACC had another significant role during the negotiations, in terms of taking a mediatory role and providing an alternative discourse in the discussions.[151] Again, there is no equivalent to the SACC in the Israeli case.

Whites in leftist (black-run) resistance groups

This study focuses on the protest work of groups in the dominant communities, but does not in any way neglect the role of white individuals who chose to join black resistance parties/movements in their personal capacities. The number of whites who chose this path is limited but certainly amounts to more than a handful. In many cases, too, prominent figures chose this path, revoking the communitarian 'tribal' consensus, and even joined the military wings of the ANC and the SACP. The role/s of whites in the struggle for non-racialism, inclusivity and democracy in South Africa cannot be reflected totally or to the highest possible degree without addressing this category, which has not been examined by other studies.

This category is divided into two sub-categories. In the first, the author looks briefly at the role of whites who joined the mainstream left, represented by the ANC, the UDF and the SACP, and as described by a number of white members and black members (including coloureds and Indians) of the three groups, or as mentioned in the UDF papers. The second sub-category involves looking very briefly into the politics of the radical left or the ultra left, to see how a handful of whites consistently stood firm for a clear socialist agenda, or what they called a 'socialist democracy'. While the majority of whites who chose to attach themselves to the struggle of the dominated side joined the mainstream left, a small group joined the radical left, and despite their very limited number and influence, the author believes that to show the spectrum of white protest in the most comprehensive way, the politics and role of the radical leftists should not be ignored or treated as irrelevant.

Before examining the two categories, this section briefly highlights the politics of the ANC, the UDF and the SACP for a better understanding of what was adopted and fought for by white individuals alongside the black South Africans who belonged to the mainstream left.

The ANC and its public branch, the UDF, stood for a milder version of the principles of the Freedom Charter, discussed earlier. It struggled for the unity of South Africa and for an inclusive vision embracing all races and ethnic groups. The ANC ran a strategy of resistance based on four pillars: armed struggle; mass mobilization (to make the country ungovernable); galvanizing international pressure (which manifested itself in different forms of sanctions); and openness to negotiations.[152] Over time, their stands on the form that the new South African economy would take softened and shifted from a socialist-oriented to a mixed economy, and finally to a liberal-oriented one. The national liberation agenda won over the socialist revolution.

It is important to note that whites were accepted as members of the ANC in 1969 and that only in 1985 were they welcomed onto the National Executive Committee.[153] The ANC saw itself as one of the four Congresses (white, black, coloured and Indian) and at the same time was keen that the blacks would lead the struggle. As it became the dominant movement in the struggle, it gradually opened its membership to whites. The UDF from the start opened its doors to white membership, participation and affiliation, and stressed the notions of the rainbow nation and people's power and their ability to build alternatives. As part of its working strategy it linked provision of services to political mobilization for change.

The SACP was established in 1921, as a mainly white party, to organize trade unions. It later connected the struggle for the rights of the working class to the national struggle, since both were seen as inseparable. It established the roots of today's South Africa since from an early stage it was the party that stressed non-racialism by stipulating that South Africa belonged to all who lived in it.[154] It was banned by the apartheid government in 1960, and later went underground for thirty years. It accepted the ANC as the leader of the national struggle, and represented a socialist agenda within the ANC coalition. By 1990 it had 7,000 members, the majority of whom were black, but afterwards continued to lose membership.[155] It can be argued that this was due to the collapse of the Soviet Union and to the fact that the SACP and the ANC were criticized by many for compromising over the socialist agenda in the negotiations. As a member of both groups remarked: "We negotiated ourselves into an economic defeat."[156] Other members rejected this criticism, arguing that pragmatism was essential since the ANC was not capable of toppling the government by force. The latter fits with the point of view that both leaderships reached the conclusion that neither could win over, and they needed to find a compromise.

By 1986 a stalemate had been reached that made it impossible to solve the conflict without negotiation and compromise. It was clear that the choice was either to take a country in ruins or to compromise, and that compromises could be made in negotiations. This point is made clear in a display at the apartheid museum in Johannesburg,[157] where a statement argues that the 1980s produced a stalemate in which bloodshed was seriously expected. The ANC then chose not to take what was left of the country in ruins, but to save what was possible. The deal reached by negotiation prepared the ground for building an inclusive political system, which fell short of redressing many past injustices.

Whites in mainstream leftist resistance groups

By the 1980s, the mainstream left had evolved into being pragmatic and accommodating as it tried to broaden its political platform in a way that could include as many white liberals as possible while dividing them; and this would also appeal to international concerns. In the process it compromised over a number of issues; especially the economy and ways to address issues relevant to justice, such as restitution for the displaced, and distribution of land and resources.[158]

As a legal organization, the UDF managed to join forces with white protest organizations, and had white affiliates that included groups such as the Cape Democrats, NUSAS, JODAC (Johannesburg Democratic Action Committee) and the Youth Congresses.[159] It also had white members, most of whom were members of the banned ANC. The UDF included people from the whole political spectrum who agreed with its general political platform, and it offered an inclusive platform that enabled members, affiliates and close partners to use the phrase 'our country South Africa', as can be found in the writings of the UDF, IDASA, FFF, ECC, Black Sash, NUSAS and the Cape Democrats who used peaceful and 'legal' means of protest. As discussed earlier, different organizations had different degrees of closeness with the ANC, and eventually the lines between progressive liberals and mainstream leftist groups, in terms of political views, objectives and strategies, often became blurred.[160] Coordinated work became the norm of the day. As they came closer to the politics of the UDF/ANC, white members and affiliates played an important role in dividing the broad white consensus and fracturing the white community, leaving it without one voice.[161] As a result, a new and powerful voice of non-racialism developed, that was inclusive of whites but against racism and the system. In terms of numbers, the presence of the whites was also disproportionate, but it had an important symbolic role – to show the rainbow nation.[162] In addition, many helped by hiding black activists, and providing transportation and printing facilities etc.[163]

Others who joined the banned ANC and the SACC walked a dangerous path that cost some of them their lives, such as Ruth First, or permanent injury, as in the case of Judge Albie Sachs. Those individuals were driven mainly by moral and/or ideological beliefs, and by joining the ANC they exercised different forms of resistance. On moral grounds, Roland Hunter spied for the ANC, informing it about the plans of the South African Defence Forces to destabilize neighbouring Mozambique.[164] He was jailed for five years (1983–1989), and during the period of his incarceration, a further fifteen white prisoners were imprisoned for joining the ANC.[165] Hunter estimates the number of whites who had direct connection with the ANC at 5,000 countrywide, while those who were active in all white organizations numbered some 8,000.[166] These are impressive numbers compared to the case of Israel.

Stephen Boshoff, an Afrikaner, also joined the ANC in the 1980s. As a socialist planner, he was involved in what he called professional resistance planning with conscience. "I refused to be an instrument of the system while doing my job."[167] He believes that he belonged to the new generation of educated Afrikaners who saw Afrikaner nationalism losing esteem and who could no longer listen to the patriarchal system. He claims that they were on the fringe, even though the opposition inside the Afrikaner community was substantial.[168] Another example is Mark Sweet, a communist who was recruited by the ANC in 1977. He joined the underground structures and was engaged for some time in sabotage activities. He was involved for seven years in the trade unions movement in exile, focusing on trade unions education and promoting progressive and non-racial notions of the Congress of South African Trade Unions (COSATU).[169] The COSATU developed into a very powerful African organization which challenged the apartheid system and the white business sector, and became a powerful arm in the struggle.

The role and influence of the whites who belong to this category is seen differently by different scholars, activists and freedom fighters. As noted, one's point of view depends on where one is sitting. Scholar Hermann Giliomee, who describes himself as a liberal and cultural nationalist Afrikaner, claims that the famous Joe Slovo of the ANC and the SACP had no influence on the whites, but rather was seen as a threat, except in the eyes of the 1–2 per cent who supported the ANC.[170] White communist Mark Sweet claims the opposite, arguing that white liberals were the unhelpful ones since they did not address class exploitation, racial exploitation and gender exploitation and, as such, were selling false hope by focusing on human rights issues.[171] Roland Hunter of the ANC argued that whites in the ANC or in the white protest organizations had very little effect on the white community because the ground was not fertile; even so, they still contributed the idea of non-racialism.[172]

A black member of the ANC and the SACP viewed the role of the whites who belonged to this category through a positive lens. Makgane Thobejane used the word 'fraternity' in referring to whites who defended blacks and shared in underground activities or who were active in the international arena, whether in the eastern bloc (mainly members of the SACP) or in the West.[173] They therefore played an important role in internationalizing and building a solidarity movement. Phyllis Naidoo, a veteran Indian member of the SACP, stressed that while the number of whites was minimal, their contribution was significant.[174] This point of view complements that of many who stressed that white participation, though small, sent a message to the black majority that there were whites who opposed apartheid and took risks in protesting against it and in supporting the struggle of the oppressed. This message contributed not only to the validity of the notions of non-racialism and inclusivity, on which the final agreement was based, but also to the idea of reconciliation.

Another issue rousing contentious views concerned the role of white members in decision-making. Black members of the ANC, the UDF and the SACP insisted that they, not the whites (liberals in the UDF), led the struggle. Black members of the ANC made it clear that they welcomed the contribution of the whites who supported or joined them but according to their terms that were agreed upon by the ANC-led coalition,[175] which had encompassed the shrinking SACP by the late 1980s. Those who belonged to the radical left believed that the white members (liberals), being better educated, more articulate, confident and connected at the international level, had gradually softened the politics of the ANC.[176] Jeenah adds that such characteristics allowed them to be at the forefront, visible and part of decision-making, and that this allowed for the infiltration of the business sector.[177] The same view is articulated differently by a member of the SACP who introduces the idea of 'syndrome of entitlement', i.e. the entitlement of a (liberal) white to lead, referring in particular to the case of the UDF.[178]

Whites in radical leftist groups

The second sub-category is that of white radical leftists. The radical left or the ultra left continued to be entrenched with the socialist agenda. It was critical of both the mainstream and progressive liberals and the mainstream left. Radical leftists perceived the liberals as a patronizing elite, seeking self-interest and unable to address racial exploitation and class exploitation while perceived the mainstream left as not radical enough and ready to compromise. They did not accept the mainstream left's policy of pragmatism, arguing that it was part of a policy of compromise which would end up in a sell out. They perceived the 'two-stages theory' of national political liberation to be followed by an economic revolution as misleading, and looked at it from a conspiracy theory point of view, arguing that it was possible to defeat the apartheid system totally without any such compromise. The political settlement was viewed as an elitist deal that led to a neo-liberal political system,[179] a democracy that was a product of South Africa's whites ceding political power to the ANC, in return for the ANC accepting that (mainly white-run) capitalism would continue.[180]

Nowadays, they organize themselves under the banner of a socialist movement, challenging the ANC government's policies towards the majority of blacks who are entrenched in poverty with a high rate of unemployment (27 per cent according to official figures,[181] and more than 40 per cent according to figures shared in civil society circles), and among whom 5.2 million are on record as HIV positive).[182] Issues of contention are mainly the degree of state intervention in the economy, land reform, budget allocation, and the means to broaden black empowerment. Their voice is becoming louder, but is not yet influential, because the geography and the inequalities of apartheid are still very much intact twelve years after its formal end. As such, they are trying to organize shanty dwellers into demanding better services, and to change government economic policies, especially on the land issue. During local government elections in March 2006, a group in Durban raised the slogan of 'No land, No vote', calling on the public not to participate in the elections.[183]

Historically, the starting point for the ultra left was negating the apartheid political system on ideological grounds and seeking its total change. They have continued to be consistent in their political analysis, ideals and vision, and are concerned with justice, social justice and redistribution of resources. They have understood apartheid as racial capitalism, not as racism per se, and have recognized the struggle as a class struggle. Thus, they advocate popular democracy rather than liberal democracy since they see the latter as one that does not incorporate social justice and that can develop into an oligarchical system of procedural democracy or an elite democracy. Patrick Bond goes beyond that in arguing that South Africa today is a capitalist sub-imperialist country, and a surrogate state of the US.[184]

These radical leftists are those who have refused the path of the SACP, but could not galvanize sufficient public support for their views. Some associate them with the Trotskyists. They have always been a tiny group with few whites among them, and have historically been considered as marginal and non-influential. At the time of writing, their presence is visible in few NGOs and in universities, e.g. Kwazulu Natal University in Durban.

Conclusion

This chapter examined the right, liberal and left in South Africa during the apartheid era. It discussed the whole political spectrum of the white protest/opposition to apartheid, and explained what was liberal, including mainstream and progressive liberalism during the transition period of the 1980s and up until the first non-racial elections in 1994. It also looked into the left, focusing on its two main strands, the mainstream and the radical/ultra left. It showed how a shift in the politics of many white liberals and protest organizations had occurred by the mid-1980s, and how this had opened the door for new organizations to emerge. They left some of the mainstream liberal political ethos behind, and joined or came closer to, the broad platform of the UDF, a public surrogate of the ANC. Together they met around a centrist political platform that was broad enough to include as many individuals as possible across class and race. This platform was that of a united, non-racial and one-person-one-vote democracy. It should not be forgotten that the number of whites who joined the different groups was limited, amounting to a maximum of 10,000 from the whole white community (which comprised some 4.5 million), but including many prominent figures.

The chapter also showed how the liberals who historically played the role of criticizing the system from within did not mobilize to overthrow the government since they believed in gradualism. Nevertheless, as a number of intermediate variables[185] developed over the years in favour of the dominated side, led by the ANC coalition, changes occurred within the liberal milieu. As they split, the progressive liberals moved towards the inclusive human-rights based political platform of the oppressed, and participated in the mobilization to change the system peacefully. While some of the progressive liberals focused on service provision, e.g. legal and humanitarian, others used different strategies to disseminate information, raise white awareness, and mobilize whites against the ideology of apartheid and of the political and military establishments. Many of these groups or their members were also involved in informal negotiations or second-track diplomacy initiatives, as the 'industry of meetings' that flourished from the mid- to late 1980s, when the ANC and other black organizations were unbanned and formal negotiations started.

These meetings laid the ground for the parameters of the future settlement. This was done without developing different and separate peace plans as happened in the Palestinian–Israeli case (see Chapter 4). While first encounters had symbolic meanings, since they broke the taboo of talking to the ANC, the many that followed did a serious job in terms of discussing how the new dispensation would look, and the role of whites in achieving it. The vision adopted for a new South Africa, a rainbow nation, stressed that whites were an integral part of it. The basis for the historical compromise was discussed: majority rule in exchange for a bill of rights that protected individual property and the free economy, but with a margin of state power for intervention – this was referred to by the ANC at the time as a mixed economy policy. Such a deal was perceived by the progressive liberals as the way to get rid of the apartheid system peacefully, and was regarded by the ANC and its coalition as part of the pragmatic 'two-stages theory', where national liberation was the first stage, to be followed by a socialist revolution.

Second-track diplomacy meetings reflected the role of an elite, that at times of crisis took a role beyond the usual. Since the ideology of apartheid was in crisis and since the government was not able to move forward towards genuine negotiations, a number of politicians, activists, academics, businesses and others used protest groups and organizations – or, in other words, the space of civil society – not only to protest but also to find alternatives. In the process, they contributed to the development and promotion of another discourse, one which was closer to that of the resistance groups of the UDF. This discourse was broad and vague enough and, as such, represented a centrist view that brought the progressive liberals together with mainstream leftists around a sort of liberal democracy that envisioned settlement. It adopted a human rights-based approach that was compatible with a liberal democracy. Those who belonged to the ultra left, where few whites – mainly academics – were active, continued in their consistent rejection of such a vision, considering the giving up of socialism for a liberal democracy as a sell-out by the ANC and the SACP. They perceive/d the role of the progressive liberals with suspicion or even from the angle of conspiracy theory.

The roles played by the different categories of white protest groups and individuals varied, and different people gave different viewpoints as noted throughout the chapter. The researcher believes that even though the mainstream liberals did criticize the policies of the apartheid system and provided some services, their politics of gradualism without commitment to an end result were still not effective in terms of challenging the apartheid system. Also they were sometimes used by the apartheid government to improve its image as a 'democracy'. It could be argued that the mainstream liberals continued to be driven mainly by ethnic (white) interest, and contributed to prolonging the life of the apartheid system.

The progressive liberals managed to read the changes that were occurring, e.g. apartheid ideology losing legitimacy in their eyes and the eyes of many whites, the ANC becoming stronger nationally and internationally, sanctions badly affecting the economy, and the country becoming ungovernable. They moved towards more daring activities and political stands, including the inclusive vision of the ANC. By accepting majority rule and joining efforts with the resistance groups under the umbrella of the UDF/ANC they exerted more pressure on the government and further undermined the ideology of apartheid. They also managed to find common ground or parameters for a future deal with the black elite. As to whites who joined the ANC and the SACP, while they were considered for decades as traitors by their own people, they were highly respected by the blacks as comrades, and as such fed the notion of the rainbow nation free of racialism. The tiny ultra left with its few whites (has) continued to be marginal.

Finally, bearing in mind the limited space available for opposition in the ethnic national state of apartheid South Africa (discussed in Chapters 1 and 2), white protest groups managed to recruit and mobilize a few thousand members. The mainstream liberals and the progressive liberals, through their service provision and human rights work, played the role of awareness raisers internationally, and locally sent messages that not all whites were supporting the apartheid system. The progressive liberals in particular played three major roles. First, they further undermined the ideology of the political system – apartheid – on both the political and moral levels. Second, they created a space that legitimized the white–black encounters that occurred in the framework of the UDF/ANC platform. Third, they also contributed to the fall of the apartheid system by contributing to the development of the political alternative, and reaching out to the elite of the resistance groups, the mainstream left represented by the ANC and the SACP.

Historically, as a component of civil society, they were left with limited space due the constraints of the political system; especially the corporatist structure it imposed. At that time of crisis and as intermediate variables became conducive, they became an influential force and contributed skilfully to the shaping of the new parameters that aim and prepare for an inclusive political system vis-à-vis the old exclusive one. As for those whites who joined the ANC and the SACP, some played a major role in building the strategies of resistance, while others were active in implementing them. They also sent a strong message to the majority in support of non-racialism and inclusivity. Thus, the author concludes that each category played a role/s, but the role of the progressive liberals, in particular, was quite significant.

With these observations at the forefront of providing preliminary conclusions, we now move to the following chapter, which examines the second case study, the politics and role/s of Israeli protest groups.

4 The politics and roles of Israeli (Jewish) protest groups

Introduction

The politics and role/s of Jewish protest groups in Zionist Israel are examined in this chapter, following a similar structure to that of Chapter 3 which investigated the case of apartheid South Africa. It provides a description and an analysis for a sample of Israeli (Jewish) protest groups that represents the wide political spectrum in which they function, and focuses on their politics, political platforms and roles in peace building. The overall comparison between the two cases, on both the macro and micro levels, is made in Chapter 5, which will also infer patterns in each and across the two cases.

The argument of this study is based on the premise that exclusionary political systems in both ethnic national states left very little space for the establishment of a politically independent civil society able to organize political opposition to the state. In both cases, state and society developed interlocking relations based on ideology and political consensus vis-à-vis the Other, the enemy. As such, protest groups, as a component of civil society continue/d, by a majority, to function according to the frameworks designed by the state and in accordance with the national consensus. They also continue/d to be small and rather marginal in size and influence. However, the author believes that when conditions have been/are conducive (e.g. change in the intermediate variables such as balance of power internally and internationally), their influence and its direction, though small, becomes significant. The Israeli protest groups are examined here to see if their protest and role fits with this argument. The two dependent variables discussed here are the politics and role/s of Israeli protest groups, but it must be kept in mind that they depend on an independent variable that is, in this case, the state political system.

Chapter 4 has seven sections. This introductory section also explains the kind of data used here. The second and third sections discuss the context in which Israeli protest groups function, and categorize both group and individual activism. The fourth section examines the two sub-categories of the liberal Zionist protest groups: the mainstream liberals and the critical liberals, and the fifth discusses the leftist (non-Zionist and anti-Zionist) protest groups. Following a brief discussion about Israelis who have joined the PLO factions in their personal capacities, the conclusion sums up the main political features and roles of Israeli protest groups and makes a link to Chapter 5.

The material used in this chapter is based on primary and secondary data. The author held over fifty semi-structured interviews with Israeli activists, heads of NGOs, party members and academics, and the interviewees included men and women representing different age groups and political affiliation (as well as some without, e.g. the anarchists) across the Israeli political spectrum. Some belonged to organized grassroots activism while others belonged to an elite that is close to the circles of policy-making, but retains connections with grassroots level groups.

They are elite in the sense that they are close to, or part of, the 'influentials',[1] especially when the political environment is conducive to this. As opinion formers, this Israeli elite contributes to the debate on state and public needs, interests, values, and the ends and means of a state. It brings pragmatic liberal points of view to the public debate. The Israeli 'liberal' elite works from within the ideological national consensus, and contributes to shaping the political national consensus,[2] since the first feeds the second. It is important to note that, compared with the case of South Africa, this elite has been more confined. It has not managed to galvanize and mobilize similar support for its pragmatic liberal views among major players of the competitive circle of the political elites.[3] The latter includes persons who hold leading positions in big businesses, trade unions, synagogues and professional and community organizations.

Other primary data sources used here were brochures, the webpages of protest groups, and publications of selected protest groups, whose advertisements in Israeli and (sometimes) Palestinian newspapers were also included. The Israeli media were also scrutinized, especially *Ha'aretz*, the main Zionist 'left' newspaper. Secondary data was also well considered and used.

Israeli protest groups in context

This section examines a number of issues that are essential for understanding the context and, consequently, the politics and roles of Israeli protest groups. The issues discussed are similar to those examined in the case of apartheid South Africa, in addition to a few others that are specific to this case: the concept of meta-conflict with relation to the Palestinian–Israeli conflict; what constitutes right, centre, liberal and left in Israeli politics; a description of the period studied; membership of Israeli protest groups and their numbers; motives of protest groups/individuals; the Israeli model of protest, and historical background to the development of protest activism in Israel; and finally, the national consensus and the role of the 'liberals' in shaping it.

As part of the political context, in which Israeli protest groups functions, there is a powerful case of 'meta- conflict'. As noted in the Introduction to the book, the Palestinians and the Israelis differ over what the conflict is all about.[4] This political reality has translated itself into many versions of perceived and/or sought peace. Israeli protest groups work for peace – which has different meanings or, in many cases, has not been defined. To hold vague political stands is useful and has become the norm for many groups. Thus, constructive vagueness or ambiguity has been an acceptable notion for the Israeli 'liberals': since there is no agreement with the Palestinians on the foundations of the conflict (e.g. causes of the conflict or historical narratives, responsibility of the settler society vis-à-vis the indigenous society), there is consequently no agreement over a clear end result. This culture of political vagueness fits with the language and the different interpretations of the Oslo Accords among and across the national divide.

The existence of meta-conflict and the policy of constructive ambiguity left the two-state solution formula open for many interpretations. As noted, the two factors manifested themselves in formal agreements, e.g. the Oslo Accords and its subsequent agreements which have been understood differently by both sides. The nature, size and power of the future Palestinian state continue to be perceived differently, not only by the two leaderships but also among Israeli protest groups. In this context it is important to note that there has been a lack of consensus on agreed-upon terms of reference. The Palestinian side, weakened by the balance of power, has failed to impose the validity of international law as the term of reference. As a result, political processes at the state and civil society levels have continued to be dictated by power politics, a manifestation of the balance of power in which Israel enjoys the upper hand.

The second contextual issue to be discussed in this section asks: in Israeli politics, what is right, centre, liberal and left? The political right in Israel is represented by the politics of the revisionist Zionists and the religious national fundamentalists. On the Israeli political map they are represented by the Likud Party and those to the right of it. They believe that the 'whole land of Israel'/'Eretz Israel Hashlema' is the rightful inheritance of the present-day state of Israel.[5] They do not specify its borders, while there are claims to lands that exceed those of mandatory Palestine. They strongly support Jewish settlement activities in the Occupied Palestinian Territories (OPT) of 1967, and pre-emptive and punitive strikes as a military strategy, and some publicly call for transferring the Palestinians because they endanger the Jewish nature of the state and its security. They stand against any compromise with the Palestinians. Reuven Kaminer gives a descriptive summary of the viewpoints of the right towards Palestine and the Palestinians:

> all historical Palestine belong to the Jewish people. The demand for Jewish sovereignty in all Western Palestine is an ideological article of faith and not negotiable ... [N]ationalist tendencies have designed various solutions ... ranging from extremist position supporting expulsion to more moderate positions which recognise the civil, though not national rights of 'indigenous Arabs'.[6]

The political centre in Israeli politics has, historically, been represented by the Labour Party, which is the descendant of Labour Zionism. The latter has had right and left wings, Mapai and Mapam, which were the leading parties during the pre-state period. Later Mapai/Labour, in particular, dominated state politics, until 1977 when the Likud Party came to power. According to Kaminer, the political centre's policy is based on a conviction that:

> all historical Palestine belongs to the Jewish people. The source of the Arab-Israeli conflict ... is the refusal of the Arab world to recognise any Jewish rights in Palestine and its war on the Zionist project. These have forced Israel to concentrate primarily on security and military preparedness, while building strategic alliances with the major Western powers which dominate the region. Mainstream Zionism insists that its more pragmatic approach is the effective, step by step, method to maximize the gains of the Zionist movement in terms of territory and military security. Thus, the territorial compromise with the Palestinians may be considered, but political benefits and strategic superiority are prerequisites for any compromise designed to end the conflict.[7]

Such a type of compromise is reflected in the interim agreements of the Oslo peace process negotiated with the Labour government. The Oslo agreements, according to Christine Bell: "provide for a change in status of territory but not external self-determination. They provide for Palestinian autonomy but not internal self-determination. They devolve power and remove some Israeli forces, but do not end occupation".[8]

The political centre is no longer a Labour area, especially after the establishment of the Kadima Party. This newly established party, which split from the Likud under the leadership of Sharon, can also claim part of the centre since it holds a policy that is at odds with the Likud political platform. Kadima leads the policy of disengaging from part of the OPT and dismantling some of the Jewish settlement there to preserve state national interests. It formed a joint agenda with the Labour Party based on three common points: no Palestinian partner, crushing the Palestinian resistance, and unilateral disengagement. Eventually, the Labour Party lost much of its political distinction as a sole political centre, and lines between the two blurred. Thus, it could be argued that by 2005, "Sharon represents the mainstream",[9] or the centre.

The liberals are located on the left of the political centre, and in daily Israeli political discourse are referred to as 'the left' or 'the Zionist left'. They are referred to as such for a number of reasons. The first concerns their attitudes towards the Israeli–Palestinian conflict and how to resolve it.[10] For them, territorial compromise is an acceptable notion which serves two goals: preserving the Jewish nature of the state, and keeping the good image of Israel.[11] Second, they strongly support and abide by the principles of human rights unless such rights affect state security.[12] Even though they compromise on equality towards the 'non-Jews' to protect a Jewish state, they see no contradiction in the notion of a Jewish-democratic state, and do not challenge militarism in Israeli society, their focus on human rights issues gave them this label (the issue of human rights is not a popular subject in Israel). The author refers to them as liberals, not leftist, for these two reasons and for a third and distinctive reason which has to do with their views on socio-economic matters. They do not support leftist socialist principles but stand for a free-market policy, while simultaneously challenging the movement towards total privatization.[13] On the party map, they are represented by Meretz/Yahad Party. Like the liberals in apartheid South Africa, they are pragmatic and gradualist.

Their views towards Palestine and the Palestinians vary. Their 'dovish' ex-Labour members bring with them views that are close to the political centre while the more liberal among them hold milder points of view. Kaminer notes that:

> as a result of historical circumstances, Palestine has become the homeland of two peoples, the Palestinians and the Jews in Palestine. Thus, both peoples have the right to national self-determination. Given present-day realities and the decisions of international organisations, a logical and realistic solution of the Israeli–Palestinian conflict, which is at the heart of the Israeli–Arab conflict, would be the establishment of an independent Palestinian state alongside of Israel.... the Zionist left stresses the importance of establishing separate national identities.[14]

As to the left, it is leftist on both political and socio-economic issues. The left is represented by the Israeli Communist Party or Hadash, and those on its left. The latter in comparison with Hadash is referred to as the 'radical left'. The communist party represents the non-Zionist political line, while a few radical grassroots groups and NGOs represent the anti-Zionist political line. Both adopt communist socialist thought where Israel is perceived as an outpost for the Western imperial powers. Even so, it is important to note that in 1948 the communist party obediently followed the twists and turns of the Soviet Union and as such made compromises with Zionism; including the signing of Israel's 'declaration of independence' by Meir Wilner who headed the party at that time.[15] Since then it has become the pragmatic and accommodating leftist voice from within the system. It was the first Israeli party to call for a two-state solution representing its Jewish and Palestinian members, and as such, the Israeli Communist Party's views on the suitable settlement of the conflict are generally in line with those of the liberals – the 'Zionist left' mentioned above. Still, distinctions should be made on some issues, e.g. the Communist Party stresses the principle of equality.

The radical left, representing an anti-Zionist position, holds a point of view on the conflict that is based on the premise that the Zionist project in Palestine is not legitimate and that:

> Palestine is an Arab country and the homeland of the Palestinian Arab people. The rise of the Israel stems from the exploitation of Jewish suffering to launch Zionism which was and remains an essentially colonialist project. Zionism entered the region on the basis of imperialist sponsorship and operates in the region as a foreign body.[16]

For them a just peace is possible only on the basis of building a secular democratic state, a state for all its citizens where no side excludes the other, and where equality will prevail and thus all will find a home in it.[17] It is represented by dozens of individuals who belong to groups like Matzpen or the Alternative Information Centre, who are anarchists, plus a few academics like Dr Ilan Pappé.

The third contextual issue to be discussed in this section is the period under research, which is referred to as a 'transition period' by many scholars and activists. The whole period between 1987 and 2003 has been regarded as one of transition for political change, and as with the case of apartheid South Africa, it was a time of political strife that reached unprecedented levels compared to the previous twenty years. This led to grassroots activism, both secret and open, and enabled formal and informal negotiations to take place. Israeli protest groups were most active in this period compared to previous years, and participated heavily in the so-called 'peace industry', which is discussed below.

The first Intifada in 1987, the signing of the Oslo Accords in 1993, and then the eruption in the year 2000 of the second Intifada were turning points in the history of the conflict and consequently in the work of Israeli protest groups. The author distinguishes between the three political turning points by dividing the period researched into three sub-periods. The first covers the first Intifada period (1987–1993); the second covers the period of the implementation of the Oslo Accords (1993–2000); and the third covers the second Intifada period, finishing with the declaration of the Geneva initiative (2000–2003). Protest groups are examined along the three sub-periods. This arrangement was designed by the author since each period has had a different political environment and subsequently a different political discourse, and different political views and attitudes have developed among the Israeli protest groups. Because of these complexities, this chapter is relatively longer than Chapter 3, which discussed the South African case.

As to membership of the Israeli protest groups, it derives from the left of the political centre, the liberals, and the left. Members have some common characteristics. By a majority, they belong to the middle class, are well educated, Ashkenazi (of European origin) and Anglophone.[18] Mizrahi Jews, who used to live in the Arab states, tend to join right or extreme right groups. Khulood Badawi of Taayush argues, on the one hand, that this is because the Ashkenazi tend not to address the Mizrahi and also because the Mizrahi tend to be anti-Arab; they enjoy being part of a majority compared with the past when they were a minority among the Arabs.[19] Molly Maleker of Bat Shalom argues, on the other hand, that those who are ready to challenge the system do so because they can afford to. They come from a socio-economic background that enables them to go into academia and/or obtain family support and live a comfortable life. She notes that Mizrahim, the newcomers, Russians and Ethiopians are more dependant on the Israeli army and are more motivated to do the job for social as well as for national religious reasons.[20]

It is common to be a member or an activist in different protest groups at the same time. A member of Bat Shalom can be a member of Women in Black,

Machsum Watch and the Coalition of Women for Peace. An activist/member of Ta'aush could be involved in the actions of the Israeli Committee Against House Demolitions (ICAHD), while a member of Gush Shalom might join members of ICAHD, the Refusniks and Ta'aush on a demonstration or an olive-picking activity, along with members of the Alternative Information Centre in the OPT. A supporter/member of Peace Now could be a member of the Geneva Initiative and the Peoples' Peace Campaign. Since Peace Now does not become involved in joint activities with those outside mainstream Zionist politics, it invites the others to its activities but does not formally participate in theirs. As such, dual or multi-memberships happen most of the time, but in most cases within the same political protest category. However, membership of some individuals in organizations that clearly differ in their political platforms, can be explained. For instance, Galia Golan and Naomi Chazan are members of both Peace Now (PN) and Bat Shalom. The latter has more critical views than those of PN, and the two groups belong to different political categories of protest. But, since Bat Shalom is a political coalition, both Golan and Chazan represent the liberal mainstream Zionist views. Other members of Bat Shalom are either liberal critical Zionist or leftist.

With regard to numbers, there are no exact figures to refer to: they fluctuate according to time, place and issue because of the sporadic or seasonal nature of Israeli protest activities. One must also distinguish between those who are active members in different protest groups and others who attend occasional demonstration/s or participate in an activity from time to time. Numbers shared with the author by different interviewees give a sense of the number of active members,[21] and the ability of different protest groups to mobilize around certain issues at a specific point in time. For example, the Women in Black group, which belongs to the critical Zionist sub-category, managed in the first Intifada to mobilize a few hundred women, but was able to mobilize only fifteen women by the end of the Oslo period.[22] These numbers included the committed activists. As to those active in organizations that support refusal to serve in the OPT, approximate numbers during the second Intifada were: New Profile (fifty), Sheministem (fifty), Courage to Refuse (fifty), and Yesh Gvul (eighty).[23] The Ta'aush Group, one of the biggest in the second Intifada, has a turn-out of participants in its activities that reaches between 500 and 1,000.[24] This number includes Palestinian activists who are citizens of Israel. Members of Women in Black and the refuseniks usually participate in the activities of Ta'aush.

Referring to the critical Zionist sub-category of organizations, Yehudith Harel[25] maintains that by 2005 there were between twenty and twenty-five small groups which formed a mosaic of radicals compared to Peace Now. Each had between thirty and forty supporters and together constituted around 800 persons. The biggest among them are Ta'aush (400) and Machsum Watch (500), while the famous Gush Shalom has fifty active members.[26] In terms of ability to mobilize supporters, the biggest number they managed to mobilize against the incursion into Ramallah, during the second Intifada, was 8,000 persons.[27] Again, this number includes activist Palestinian citizens of Israel. It is important to note that these groups managed to mobilize only 200 demonstrators against the war in Lebanon in 2006 when the news of a new Kana massacre became known.[28] At that time, a public consensus prevailed in support of the war.

As to the sub-category of mainstream Zionist organizations, Peace Now, which is not a membership organization, is the most prominent. It is known for its seasonal activities and has no commitment to a clear peace plan. A few leading core activists decide its plan of action. During the first Intifada, it managed to mobilize 100,000 persons calling for the government to negotiate with the PLO.[29] Peace Now claims that in 2003, it managed to mobilize 150,000 supporters using slogans such as 'stop the killing', 'end occupation' and 'Sharon: not in my name'.[30] In 2004 it managed to mobilize 200,000 in support of the withdrawal from Gaza as part of Sharon's unilateral disengagement plan![31] These numbers have been contested by many who believe that PN has lost 50 to 60 per cent of its supporters since the start of the second Intifada, and that nowadays its list of supporters and friends does not exceed a few thousand.[32] Hermann provides another modest estimation, believing that even at the height of their popularity, the largest peace organizations had no more than a few hundred inner-core activists and some 10,000 latent supporters.[33]

As to the left category, their members and supporters are a few dozen. For example Matzpen, the anti-Zionist group, declined from almost 100 members in the late 1960s and 1970s[34] to its present complement of more than ten and less than fifty.[35] Judy Blanc claims that there are around twenty persons who would challenge the fundamentals of the state.[36] With regard to Israelis who joined the PLO factions, the author came across five; Uri Davis, Ilan Halevi and another three who were convicted of joining the Democratic Front for the Liberation of Palestine. They belong to the Shararah (Spark) group. Numbers in this category are very small compared with the case of South Africa where many more joined or worked closely with the ANC. Here it must not be forgotten that the vision for a political solution in South Africa was inclusive, but in the Palestinian–Israeli case is exclusive with the most advocated vision being separation along nationality.

As to the motives of Israelis for joining protest groups, they are similar to those in the case of South Africa. However they focus on only part of the conflict, i.e. the 1967 occupation and its detrimental effects, not on the totality, as in South Africa. Ending the Israeli occupation is the issue for the vast majority, apart from a tiny group (tens) that questions the state history of establishment, structure and ideology and is ideologically motivated, while the rest are motivated by national self-interest and morality. Some, of course, combine several motives at the same time, but the common motive is national interest, which is most often expressed through a discourse of fear of losing the Jewishness of the state and its security, and fear that occupation undermines the morality of Israeli society.[37]

Women activists express this motive differently. They show concern about what occupation is also doing to the Other, the Palestinians: "I can't bear the thought that my country is committing such things to another nation",[38] or "I want to prepare a good place for my children to live in, I don't want to treat people the way I refuse to be treated".[39] They are strongly committed to a two-state solution and hold different views on how the Palestinian state will look in terms of the size and authority given to it. The small group that questions the fundamentals of the Israeli state either adopts Marxism, radical feminism or the Jewish religious orthodoxy that rejects Zionism. They struggle against Zionism (considered a form of racism), and for equality and justice outside the parameters of exclusive nationality.

The Israeli model of protest is, as noted in the previous chapter, quite different from that in South Africa. Israeli protest organizations, focusing on peace and conflict resolution, are distinguished from human rights, co-existence, interfaith and research organizations. A human rights group would not regard itself as a peace group or part of a wider movement standing firmly against an illegal occupation, the way South Africans did against apartheid. For example, organizations like B'tselem (the Israeli Information Centre for Human Rights in the Occupied Territories) and Rabbis for Human Rights (RHR) define themselves as human rights organizations per se, and do not take clear positions on the conflict in terms of causes or resolution, even from a human rights/international law angle. Rabbi Arik Asherman of RHR describes its work as human rights work because it is not affiliated with any political party and not assigned to any peace plan.[40]

In the case of B'tselem, the language used in its publication reflects certain political statements or implied positions beyond human rights neutrality, if there are any. It combines human rights discourse with a set of Zionist notions that fit with the national narrative/discourse. For example, in an article "Documenting the Facts, Fostering Debate", B'tselem[41] describes Palestinian attacks on Jewish settlers in the OPT as war crimes and a grave breach of international humanitarian law.[42] However, no such statement is made anywhere in the same document in referring to Israel's grave violations of Palestinian human rights in the OPT. As to the right of return of Palestinian refugees stipulated in international law through UN resolution 194, it is not an issue for discussion for B'tselem, which criticizes Israeli government policies in the OPT from the position of a loyal national organization. It does not take a role similar to that in South Africa during apartheid. It continues to act as a national (ethnic) human rights organization, not as an organization that aims to help the oppressed by shaming the system and publicly stating its opposition to illegal occupation. It has a sensitizing role that it implements from a loyal national 'liberal' position.

While human rights and other organizations (inter-faith, co-existence) claim to be apolitical, protest groups define themselves by the majority as political. They have not worked under one broad political grand vision or towards a clear end result, as in the case of South Africa, nor have they defined themselves as anti-occupation (aside from anti-Zionist) as white groups did. The latter defined themselves across the political spectrum as anti-apartheid groups. As from the mid-1980s and by a vast majority, differences between most South African groups did not exist in the grand vision (of a united non-racial South Africa), which meant dismantling the apartheid system and the ideology behind it.

132   Israeli (Jewish) protest groups

In the case of the Israeli protest groups, most addressed the Palestinian–Israeli conflict by focusing not on its totality but on part/s of it, as the chapter shows. The conflict was split into pieces and different organizations addressed specific issue/s without agreement over the end result. Though the formula of a two-state solution meant different things for different organizations, the vast majority agreed that this formula would, and should, preserve a Jewish state. Over the years, they have failed to develop a continuous network or front that feeds into a common end result based on certain clearly interpreted principles or terms of reference. In this context, it is important to note that agreements on the macro level (the Oslo Accords and its subsequent agreements) also failed to do so. As mentioned earlier, their design was established on vagueness for two major reasons: the existence of meta-conflict, along with the power of Israel, the 'strong' side, to dictate the negotiation process.

Based on the above discussion and the range of material available for investigation, there is no attempt in this book to examine the role of Israeli human rights groups or other similar groups mentioned above. Wherever relevant, the author briefly mentions groups whose work has been closely connected, since there is no way that strict separation lines can be imposed between protest work, co-existence, human rights, and research work. But it is important that, as the focus of this study, the politics and role/s of Israeli protest groups in building peace are kept clearly in view.

A further issue to be discussed in this section is a historical background to the development of protest activism in Israel. It facilitates an understanding of how the politics and roles of Israeli peace groups were shaped in a historical context, and shows how activist protest for peace with the Palestinians has gradually evolved in Israel through certain decisive political moments. It provides insights into the initial political positions and how they evolved to shape the attitudes and tendencies of protest groups during the period studied.

Opposition to political Zionism and/or its policies was not a feature of the pre- or post-state period, and any initiatives against mainstream political Zionism failed to survive, even on small scale, prior to state establishment and up until 1967. Before 1948, two organizations, the Peace Covenant (Brit Shalom) in the 1920s and the Union (Ihud) in the 1940s,[43] opposed mainstream Zionism by calling for a bi-national state. Both were denounced by the Yeshuv leaders, who described their members as elitist, naïve bourgeois pacifists, and political outsiders,[44] and therefore both failed. Those who addressed issues of state/society militarism or who stood against nuclear armament in the 1950s did not last long either.

Scholars associate protest activities in Israel with the aftermath of the 1967 victory and Israel's capture of the rest of mandatory Palestine. While most Israelis regarded that victory as a great achievement, or even as a sign from God of a fulfilled prophecy for the Jewish people, critical or 'moderate' political Zionist individuals (and later organizations) called for withdrawal from all or most of the post-1967 occupied territories. Such calls were driven by moral and pragmatic political concerns. Among the first to speak out was Yeshaayahu Leibowitz, the prominent Israeli philosopher at the Hebrew University, who viewed the Israeli occupation as a cancer in the body of the Israeli state and society and called for two states for two peoples who had legitimate rights in the 'land of Israel'.[45]

Those who chose this path chose to challenge the national consensus by acknowledging, at times when the leading Zionist political party of the political centre (apart from the right wing), denied the existence of a Palestinian people, that indeed there was a Palestinian nation. Many also chose to provide an alternative view to that of the national religious group, Gush Emunim (Bloc of the Faithful), who advocated the establishment of Jewish dominance and 'purity' in the whole of 'Eretz Israel'.[46] They did this not by challenging Gush Emunim's biblical and ideological claims, but by stressing the negative social-political and moral costs of occupation.[47] Disagreement rested entirely on pragmatic grounds – on how to achieve the 'true Zionist dream' and protect the image of Israel.[48] In proposing the need for dialogue with the Palestinians and for finding a compromise that included giving up land, they wanted to use the outcome of the 1967 war as a means of trading land for peace and security. For the next two decades, their message/s fell outside the national consensus formed by the central government and its many apparatuses since they represented the views of a small secular minority of what was a mainly loyal opposition to the Zionist ethos.

During those twenty or so years, different organizations emerged in connection with different turning points in the history of Israel, e.g. the 1967 war; the 1973 war and Sadat's visit to Jerusalem; and the 1982 invasion of Lebanon. They represented three main political lines, the mainstream Zionist, the critical Zionist and the leftist (non-Zionist and anti-Zionist). The mainstream organizations included the Movement for Peace and Security (1968), Oz ve Shalom (Strength and Peace) in the mid-1970s,[49] and Peace Now (1978). Unlike the other two, Peace Now survived, even though it had similar concerns and a pragmatic political platform: land for peace and negotiations with any Arab leadership, preferably Jordan, which would agree to negotiate an autonomy arrangement for the Palestinians.[50]

Issue-oriented organizations that did not challenge mainstream politics and chose not to take stands on the conflict, such as Parents against Silence, did not last long. Parents against Silence dissolved itself two years after its establishment, when the Israeli army withdrew to the 'security belt' in southern Lebanon in 1984. A similar organization, the Four Mothers, performed the same role in the late 1990s, calling for a full withdrawal from Lebanon; and once this, according to Israeli perceptions, was achieved, it too disbanded.

With regard to anti-Zionist groups, the secular group Matzpen, being very small, marginalized and fractionalized, had no chance to influence and mobilize on its own. The anti-Zionist orthodox community of Neturie Karta was also dismissed by the Israeli public as a fanatical fringe.[51] During the late 1970s and the 1980s, the secular anti-Zionists joined forces with critical Zionists and non-Zionists, e.g. the Communist Party as it defines itself. They set aside their ideological convictions in a quest to mobilize as many voices as possible against the occupation, the government's violations of human rights, and government policies towards the conflict with the Palestinians. As a result, coalitions like the Israeli Committee of Solidarity with Bir Zeit University and the Committee against the War in Lebanon materialized. Incorporating Yesh Gvul and Women against the War, they managed to recruit 2,000–3,000 activists and to mobilize 20,000 against the war in Lebanon in 1982.[52] Their power is much less today. Their political positions labelled them as militants who acted outside the national consensus, compared with the Peace Now mainstream line that acts from within it. The Committees' positions were: unconditional and total withdrawal from the occupied territories, a Palestinian state next to Israel in its 1948 borders, and negotiations with the PLO.[53] They perceived their role as being to act in solidarity with the Palestinian people in the OPT and to articulate more radical positions and initiate tactics that would provide the leadership of the mainstream peace groups with precedents and tests for moving their own constituencies to more radical positions.[54] The same role continues to be practised.

With regard to second-track diplomacy encounters, the two main groups and the many activists from the committees that held meetings with PLO officials inside and outside mandatory Palestine, were East for Peace (early 1980s), and the Israeli Council for Israeli–Palestinian Peace (1975). Again, their action broke another political consensus issue. The committees had earlier demanded talks with the PLO, but later a number of their members actually held talks. Such meetings contributed to legitimizing the PLO as a partner, provided the beginnings of recognition for the Palestinians as a nation, and enabled debate on the idea of a two-state solution. In response, the Knesset passed a law in 1986 forbidding meetings between Israeli citizens and PLO officials.[55] In this context, two relevant issues should be noted. First, a lot of attention was given at that time to legitimizing the PLO, but very little, if any, was given to considering what peace would look like, or to the values and terms of reference to be adhered to in order to achieve a sustainable two-state settlement.[56] Second, some of the Israelis who participated in such meetings had close connections with the establishment.

While such protest work continued on the Israeli occupation front, parallel work on co-existence was happening inside Israel vis-à-vis its Palestinian citizens. Such work sought to find understandings across the divide, while ignoring state structures and the consequent inevitable discriminatory laws. Those responsible claimed that their approach and aims were apolitical, and that they aspired to build relations and co-operation on the human level, where each side would be sensitized to the other's culture and needs. But though the mainstream Zionist organizations, associated mainly with one of the Labour alignment parties,[57] claim/ed that their work enhanced equality and promoted good citizenship, critics regard/ed co-existence programmes as part of a patronizing scheme aimed at pacifying the Palestinian minority in the Jewish state. Reflecting on the educational co-existence programmes Knox and Quirk quote Al-Haj:

> An inherent contradiction … exists between formal curriculum activities and informal curriculum which promote Arab-Jewish relations. Co-existence

within this context is interpreted as mere tampering at the edges, as the system continues to be a "vehicle for nation-building" amongst the Jews whilst for Arabs "it remains an encouragement towards passivity and co-optation".[58]

Exceptional cases were rare.[59]

With the establishment of the New Israel Fund (NIF) in 1979, issues of civil rights and social justice were incorporated into the co-existence initiatives. The liberals gave more attention to these issues, which were further stressed with the establishment in 1989 of another Jewish 'liberal' donor organization, the Abraham Fund Initiatives which supports co-existence, empowerment and human rights programmes. Both Funds, representing degrees of liberal Zionist mainstream politics and initiated by American Jews, assist Jewish Israeli and Palestinian Israeli organizations that run such programmes. Their local members have close historical connections to Mapai institutions,[60] and both give grants for complementary aims. The Abraham Fund is driven by a conviction that

> the enhancement of Jewish/Arab co-existence and equality in Israel is vital to the future of the state of Israel, its security and stability, and the welfare of its Jewish and Arab citizens ... civic equality for Israel's Jewish and Arab citizens [is] a moral and pragmatic imperative, whereby individual rights and the political, cultural and religious character of the Arab minority must be clearly and unambiguously recognised and respected.[61]

The NIF refers to its mandate as being to "strengthen Israel's democracy by supporting programs that safeguard civil and human right, bridge social and economic gaps, foster tolerance for all inhabitants".[62]

Many Palestinians who have been involved in such programmes view them differently. They see the role of aid organizations as being part of a strategic interest, aiming to protect the Jewish state in the long run through addressing socio-economic disparities, enhancing equality and building better relations with the Palestinian minority to co-opt them more successfully.[63] For Jaber 'Asaqleh of Shateel, the two aid organizations see a tension between the Jewishness of the state and being a democracy, while the Palestinians see a contradiction.[64] As such, both seek to ease this tension through improving opportunities towards a more equal society and/or co-optation. Ameer Makhoul of Ittijah goes further by arguing that such Jewish 'liberal' aid organizations are exerting pressure on the Palestinian organizations through their financial support, so that they will accept that the rules of the game set by the state are Zionist, and thus will stop opposing the occupation and limit their struggle to one for individual equal rights.[65]

It is important to examine briefly the co-existence programmes implemented inside Israel, since many Israelis who worked in those programmes joined Israeli protest groups later on, during the first Intifada and particularly during the Oslo period. Their political mindset, experiences and attitudes translated into many activities that took place during the Oslo period, as is discussed below.

The final issue to be glanced at in this section is the national consensus and the role of the 'liberals' in shaping it. As discussed in Chapter 2, the notion of national consensus is a strong feature in Israeli politics, where it sets the ideological framework and the political features for an acceptable political decision or view. The ideological consensus is static while the political consensus is changing, although very slowly. Israeli Zionist protest groups are united under the ideological consensus, as was discussed in Chapter 2, but they hold different views about the political consensus (see Chapter 2, pp. 79–80), and therefore differ in the degree of acceptance of both the consensus and the security ethos.

Some chose to act from within the national political consensus while others chose to move to the edge of it. A few went outside of it on some issues, e.g. the refuseniks. In other words, they differed over what were the best ways to make changes in the national political consensus for the sake of perceived peace, different versions, and security. The non-Zionists challenge the consensus by adopting positions on the edge of it and in some cases outside it, whereas the anti-Zionist groups challenge the whole state ideology and structure and, as such, act outside the national ideological and political consensuses.

Over the years many issues of consensus have changed. For example, the consensus moved from a denial of the existence of the Palestinians to a denial of the Palestinians as a people. Then it moved to accepting the Palestinians as a nation, and consequently to a need to find a settlement to the conflict. The consensus about resolving the conflict moved from a vision of providing autonomy to the Palestinians to that of a two-state formula that would provide peace and security for Israel. When the first Intifada imposed itself on the Israeli national consensus, the consensus moved from denial of the existence of occupation to recognizing that it exists and that negotiations with the PLO, if it recognizes Israel, are not impossible. The consensus on Jerusalem has also moved. The consensus has changed from the city being the eternal united capital of Israel, to a possibility for compromise where areas populated by the Palestinians could be administered by the Palestinian Authority. The consensus about the availability of a partner has also shifted, from Jordan as the acceptable partner, to a local leadership that could be a partner, to the PLO as a partner, and finally to there being no partner.

At the beginning of the second Intifada, Barak and later the Likud–Labour unity government, managed to develop a consensus with the following components: lack of a Palestinian partner, Palestinians to be blamed for rejecting a generous offer, and force is the only answer. Later, another consensus was built around Sharon's strategy of unilateralism, which is the right strategy to mark the borders of Israel, the Green Line with Gaza, and the Wall in the West Bank.[66] Sharon managed to build a momentary consensus around the disengagement plan from Gaza, but after the war in Lebanon in 2006 unilateralism was not able to live for long because the convergence plan was critically questioned. Finally, it is important to note that, aside from the issue of Jerusalem, the other issue that touches the heart of the ideological and political consensuses is the Palestinian right of return. Only very limited changes, mostly of a rather cosmetic nature, have occurred regarding this matter.

Some argue that the Palestinian resistance, rather than the Israeli protest groups, has had the upper hand in breaking part of the political consensus,[67] or that the Israeli protest groups have had a (significant) complementary role. Others argue that the Zionist 'liberals' have always contributed to the formation and modification, but not the changing, of the national consensus, and that they have done so by developing the assumption that peace is possible while keeping the ideological consensus 'box' intact and making superficial modifications to the substance of the political consensus. The 'liberal' Zionists, directed by prominent intellectuals (many of whom are close to the establishment and well connected at the international level), have pushed for minor or cosmetic modifications to the political consensus, and by doing so have managed to help the government market a false peace. Tanya Reinhart of Tel Aviv University describes such a role and such peace:

> Israel has managed so far to sell its policy as a big compromise for peace ... aided by a battalion of co-operating "peace camp" intellectuals, they managed to convince the world that it is possible to have a Palestinian state without land reserves, without water, without a glimpse of economic independence, in isolated ghettos surrounded by fences, settlements, bypass road ... a virtual state which serves one purpose: separation (apartheid).[68]

Categorizing Israeli protest groups and individual activism

For the purpose of analysing Israeli protest groups in accordance with their politics and political platform, it has been necessary to classify them into categories. Rather than a single voice or strategy they represent many, although the politics and political platforms are closer among some groups than they are to others. After having disaggregated the Israeli protest 'movement' into its components, the author decided to rebuild them in categories according to their politics and political platforms. This is the focus of this study, and paves the way to understanding their political stands and the roles played by each category. This is parallel to the analytical process that was undertaken in the case of the white protest groups in apartheid South Africa (Chapter 3).

Before presenting the categories of this research, it is necessary to investigate how a number of scholars and practitioners have categorized Israeli protest groups when addressing this subject (if indeed they have done). This will provide a number of views and angles on how this topic might be addressed. The two books that compared the case of apartheid South Africa and the Palestinian–Israeli conflict, *Mobilising for Peace* (edited by Benjamin Gidron, Stanley Katz and Yeheskel Hasenfeld) and *Peace Building in Northern Ireland, Israel and South Africa* (Colin Knox and Padraic Quirk) did *not* classify the Israeli protest groups into clear categories; *nor* did they name lists in which groups were included as they did in the case of South African protest groups.

Tamar Hermann's contribution in *Mobilising for Peace* used the expression 'peace movement' to refer to the Zionist mainstream groups, and briefly mentioned the existence of small and marginal non- and anti-Zionist groups.[69] Knox and Quirk distinguished between peace activism during the first Intifada and that after Oslo. Concerning the first, they referred to Peace Now as the representative of the mainstream and those on their left, e.g. Yesh Gvul and Dai Lakibush, as the militant peace groups.[70] They also mentioned the professional groups that sought to extend their activity to similarly placed groups and individuals in the Occupied Territories, and the human rights groups, e.g. B'tselem.[71] During the Oslo period, they distinguished between the 'self interest' school (dominant), and those motivated by moral considerations, compassion and solidarity with the Palestinians, while noting that human rights and professional groups re-focused or downgraded their activities.[72]

Naomi Chazan argues that division across the Israeli 'left' has polarized since 2001, leaving the 'peace camp' divided into two distinct segments: the human rights organizations, and the moderates which are primarily politically oriented.[73] She considers Gush Shalom, ICAHD, Rabbis for Human Rights, Ta'aush, Women in Black, Machsom Watch, Bat Shalom and Coalition of Women for Peace as human rights groups because they are increasingly engaged in assertive protests against the Israeli violations of Palestinian rights.[74] The political category of the 'peace camp' includes Peace Now, ECF, the Council for Peace and Security, Meretz Party and the Peres Peace Centre.[75]

Ilan Pappé categorizes Israeli protest groups according to their relations with the establishment.[76] First is the reform movement, represented, though not exclusively, by Peace Now. It reflects the Zionist parties, and does not have any fundamental argument with the government. Members question tactics, but not strategy or ideology. Second are the revisionists who accept the ideology but question the strategy, e.g. Bat Shalom. They represent Hadash Party politics. Third are the radicals who see the problem not in the strategy or tactics, but as about ideology. They represent those who support the Arab parties.

Finally, Jeff Halper, an anthropologist and practitioner, also classifies them into three categories.[77] First are the mainstream liberals among whom PN, Meretz and left of labour are active and some of whom were the architects of Oslo. Second are the critical 'left' or radicals, where anti-Zionists, post-Zionists and non-Zionists are active. Those who fit into this category are the AIC and ICAHD. Third are those in between the critical 'left' and the mainstream 'left' (liberals), e.g. Gush Shalom, Bat Shalom and Ta'aush.

The present book diverges in its categorization of Israeli protest groups from those mentioned above. The author, learning from, but differing in one or more aspects from each of them, aims to provide a more comprehensive and clearer picture, giving examples from the work of a number of organizations that belong to each category. The categorization developed in this study throws light on the political stands and roles of Israeli protest groups across the political spectrum during the period studied, and it is deep enough to look into the details and broad enough to see the bigger picture. It distinguishes between two protest strands within liberal Zionism, and between an accommodating left and an anti-Zionist left. It gives a brief account of individual activism in the factions of the

PLO, and also looks at the details of their politics and where the lines between them become blurred. It is not totally different from the other classifications and at the same time is not identical to any; it best answers the question raised in this book.

This study classifies Israeli protest groups into three major categories. First is the liberal Zionist protest category which is divided into two sub-categories: the mainstream Zionist groups and the critical Zionist groups. Second are the leftist protest groups which include the non-Zionist and the anti-Zionist strands. The third category includes the Israelis who have joined the PLO in their personal capacities. An illustration for this categorization is shown in Table 4.1. Lists of organizations/groups that belong to each category or sub-category are presented in the Appendix.

Each category is examined in terms of politics, political platform/positions, activities and roles. Examples of groups are given in an extended form in some cases and briefly in others, taking in consideration the size of this chapter, and to avoid repetition. Words and expressions like 'left', 'liberal', 'peace camp', 'peace movement', 'moderate', 'radical' and 'far left' are used carefully. For example, the study does not use the word 'left' as it is normally used in Israeli politics, but as it is usually used in political terminology. Considerable care is taken in using the expression 'peace movement', since this has been over-used without its exact meaning being defined.

Liberal Zionist protest groups

As mentioned above, this category is divided into two sub-categories, the mainstream Zionist groups and the critical Zionist groups, which are often referred to as the left, and less often as the liberal groups. Groups belonging to this category are certainly not leftist and are not liberals in the full meaning of the word, since they do not adopt socialist/communist doctrines; nor do they unconditionally adopt human rights principles. They are also referred to as left because of their location on the political map compared with the right and centre. However, they are referred to in this book as liberals because they support the free market economy, focus on human rights, and because there is a left that holds a leftist political and socio-economic agenda (as discussed in the next section).

Table 4.1 Classification of Israeli protest groups

Liberal Zionist protest groups	1 Mainstream Zionist groups
	2 Critical Zionist groups
Leftist protest groups	1 Non-Zionist groups
	2 Anti-Zionist groups
Israelis who joined PLO	A dozen

140 *Israeli (Jewish) protest groups*

Mainstream Zionist protest groups

Members belonging to this sub-category share the following viewpoints: Israel is a legitimate entity; "The war of 1948 was a fair one. It was either me or you";[78] the 1967 war was a just war of defence, the subsequent occupation in 1967 was the problem; peace is possible through a territorial compromise; Israel has to negotiate from a position of strength; a two-states solution with adequate security arrangements is the answer to protecting state national interests and making peace (only in the 1990s); we are on opposite sides to the Palestinians, "us and them, my interest versus your interest";[79] the two historical narratives are irreconcilable; Palestinians need to show good intentions towards Israel – to prove that they want peace; Israel's image is of concern and they defend it; they are close to the Labour Party's politics and thus it is difficult for them to protest against a Labour government; they refuse calls not to serve in the army; strategic ambiguity in their positions is the norm; finally, they consider the national consensus to be the limit that, if crossed, loses them both credibility and their constituency – therefore they act from within that consensus.

They also share a number of characteristics. First, they suffer from the 'First Day Syndrome'.[80] In case of a military episode, e.g. war, transfer, attack, "on the first day, Israeli progressives line up behind their government, believe its excuses, support and defend its actions. Only after some time ... weeks or months ... [do] they begin to recover and to return to a position of opposition",[81] but only on a tactical level. Among the different protest groups, they are the closest to the security ethos, and many of their leading members are ex-security, army personnel, members or ex-members of the Knesset, or have served in governmental positions or held positions in Zionist parties. Most are Ashkenazim, middle class, and well educated.

Many groups belong to this sub-category, among whose members are supporters of Meretz Party and the left of Labour, along with a few members of the Shinui Party. They differ in their political focus and strategies. Some developed (specific) joint peace plans, as in the case of the Geneva Initiative and the Ayalon-Nusseibeh plan, while others chose not to, or adopted broad political parameters for a future settlement. While most organize joint projects with the Palestinians, they stop short of addressing the existing structure of power between the occupied and the occupier. Groups belonging to this sub-category are: Peace Now, the Economic Co-operation Foundation, the Peres Peace Centre, the Israeli side of the Geneva Initiative, the Four Mothers, the Council for Peace and Security, Arik Institute, the Israeli side of the Ayalon-Nesseibeh plan, the Israeli side of the People's Peace Campaign, and so on. Peace Now, the oldest among them, is the most recognized nationally and internationally, the most capable of mobilizing, and thus the most visible. Peace Now is taken as a major example for examination, and a few others will also be looked at briefly.

The politics, political positions, activities and roles of Peace Now (PN) are examined along the three turning points. The political ideology of Peace Now, as the national Israeli-Jewish peace movement, is liberal Zionism, and its political platform/positions, which have slowly but surely become clearer (or less vague), stem from this ideological basis. Peace Now, which has never had any Palestinian member(s) in its core group, was founded in 1978 during the Israeli–Egyptian negotiations. Its foundation is associated with a famous letter from reserve officers and soldiers to the then Prime Minister, Menachem Begin. The letter from the perceived defenders of the 'borders of Israel' appeared credible since it assured the justice of the cause of Zionism and Israel while choosing the path of peace. It reflected the same concerns, as well as the same political pillars as Peace Now does today. It was a voice of loyal opposition to a first-time Likud government while dominant Labour found itself for the first time out of government. The language of that letter was more challenging and daring than the carefully shaped language developed by PN as it became the broad-based centre protest group. Two versions of the letter exist (both are given in the Appendix). The one on Peace Now's website (2005) fits more with its well-established political wording of mildness and vagueness. Such a style is similar to the principle of creative ambiguity used by mainstream liberals in apartheid South Africa.

After the protest activities that followed the 1982 invasion of Lebanon had faded away, Peace Now went through a period of inactivity. This reflects a Peace Now approach in which its leadership would wait until something happened and then respond. Tsali Reshef, a spokesperson, explained why this approach was adopted by describing Peace Now as "a mood and not a movement".[82] Galia Golan speaks about reading the public's mood and asking "what is the mood today?"[83] Its leadership decides what the public is ready for at a certain point in time. Thus, moving forward or backwards, close to or away from the government's position, is decided by a core group that has given itself the mandate to lead the way to peace which, as PN sees it, preserves the national interest and fits with the national consensus. Until 1988, a year after the first Intifada had broken out, Peace Now's political positions were perpetuated by the prevailing Zionist tendencies to denigrate or deny the existence and rights of the Palestinians as a nation; therefore autonomy in co-operation with Jordan was the acceptable option proposed.[84] The language of international law and universal principles has been absent.

The eruption of the first Intifada in 1987 changed the political scene. For the first time the Palestinians in the Occupied Territories of 1967 took the initiative in running an organized public uprising against the Israeli occupation. As a result, Jordan severed its legal and administrative ties with the West Bank. Occupation as a word and a meaning was brought strongly to the Israeli public and establishment, and to the debates of the international community. During the first year of the Intifada, Peace Now proposed a plan to hold municipal elections. These would allow for an elected leadership to join a Jordanian delegation that would negotiate a settlement on the basis of mutual recognition, a stance close to that of the Labour Party. PN had to relinquish this plan since it raised no echo on the Palestinian side. Concern was also expressed that Israel might find itself ostracized as result of its policies in the territories, which would also destroy its image. And if PN wanted to blame anyone for the political impasse, it would be either Shamir (who represented the Likud Party in a unity government with Labour), or the two leaderships, the Israeli and the Palestinian!

Peace Now made cosmetic changes to its previous positions on the Palestinian question only after the PLO had publicly accepted UN resolution 242 (which indirectly recognized Israel, and limited Palestinian land rights to the areas occupied in 1967 – i.e. 22 per cent of mandatory Palestine), and after Arafat had renounced terrorism. The new position adopted leftist called-for negotiations with the PLO, but according to leftist perceptions fell short in terms of political substance. It was far from advocating a two-state solution based on the principle of equality between sovereign nations; used earlier phrases such as 'Palestinian national existence' instead of 'Palestinian national self-determination', and referred to Jerusalem as the undivided capital of Israel where expression would be given to the Islamic and Christian holy places and to the national affinities of the Arab inhabitants.[85] The Palestinian right to self-determination was later accepted by Peace Now within the framework of the right of both sides to self-determination in 'Eretz Israel', and of guarantees for Israeli security.

Thus Peace Now's aim became to push for recognition and negotiations with the PLO. By raising this as a demand, it took the initiative from the leftists who, as 'militants', distinguished themselves from 'the moderates' by making such demands and through their ideology and clear political positions. Consequently, Peace Now managed to expand its outreach with active Palestinian organizations, especially those affiliated with the mainstream Fateh movement. In late 1988 it also managed to mobilize tens of thousands of individuals to call for negotiations with the PLO.[86] Recognizing the PLO as a partner took precedence over discussing the content of the peace to which Peace Now was ready to commit itself. The perceived huge shift in Peace Now's position was related to the fact that such a demand then shattered an inflated element in the political national consensus that had prevailed for two decades, i.e. that the PLO was a terrorist organization and could not be a partner. It caused a tremendous row, although a few people were sceptical, arguing that Peace Now's stand had only changed on the procedural level, and that their voices were not loud enough.

It took Peace Now a few weeks to react to the Intifada and take a central role alongside the leftists like Dai La Kibush, for example, which had responded within days. During the first Intifada, Peace Now organized demonstrations, held vigils, convened public political meetings at which they hosted Palestinian speakers such as Faisal Husseini and Hanan Ashrawi, and also organized solidarity visits into the Occupied Territories. Some of its members were also involved in informal encounters/second-track diplomacy meetings with PLO members abroad, mainly in academic settings to avoid legal persecution since Israeli law at the time prohibited such meetings. As is discussed later, these meetings in fact contributed to clearing the road to Madrid and Oslo. They legitimized the PLO, the other side, by preparing the Israeli public to accept it as a partner, and also by obtaining concessions from the PLO.[87] Peace Now's representatives, standing for an informal sector, met with the (formal) representatives of the PLO. However, while the latter made many concessions to become accepted as a partner, Peace Now did not commit itself to any specific end result: "We didn't want to make positions."[88] Eventually, compromise, 'realism' and 'politics, the art of what is possible' became integral parts of the political discourse that has prevailed since.

The role played by Peace Now during the first Intifada was multi-faceted. It managed, after a year of the Intifada, to hijack the 'peace' show from the leftists without giving up its political stands, apart from replacing the Jordan option with the PLO option. It managed to convey a message of pragmatism, reflecting a version of the national interest opposed to the 'Greater Israel' version of the right wing. It contributed to changes in public opinion, and by late 1988, polls on the subject showed 54 per cent in favour of negotiations with the PLO.[89] Peace Now also managed to project the impression that there was no contradiction between allying itself with the missions and proposals of the US administration (despite the latter's policies and interests in the region), and working for peace. PN and its members represented the peace of the 'liberals' who associated themselves with America as a strategic ally and partner, as well as the mainstream which, in addition to others, had contributed to setting the political parameters for a settlement with the PLO through second-track diplomacy meetings (see pp. 164–167). Their 'constructive patriotism' approach, i.e. fulfilling their duty to the state by seeking influence from within,[90] and their creative vagueness, paid off politically and enabled them to continue to be the prominent and leading, broad-based and centre protest group.

Before moving to the Oslo period, it is important briefly to highlight how Peace Now reacted to Iraq's invasion of Kuwait in 1990. The part of the PLO that called for Iraq's withdrawal from Kuwait was overshadowed by Arafat's visit to Saddam and by the Palestinian stand against an American-led coalition that was at war with Iraq. On the Israeli side, not only did the government side with America, but so also did virtually all the liberal groups/activists. Tsali Reshef of Peace Now supported an active US military intervention, since Saddam was cast as a threat to regional security.[91] As a result, days after the invasion of Kuwait a crisis occurred in the joint Palestinian–Israeli 'peace' work, the most famous manifestation of which was an article attacking the Palestinians and their position by Yossi Sarid, who accused them of being unworthy of having a state:

> If I supported a Palestinian state only because the Palestinians are worthy of a state – I would today rescind my support. However, I continue to support their right to self-determination and their own state, because I have a right to be rid of the occupation and its ugly effects. Maybe they deserve occupation, but we do not ... until further notice, they can, as far as I am concerned, look for me.[92]

As far as the Oslo period (1993–2000) is concerned, Peace Now supported the Oslo accords uncritically. One can argue that this was for two reasons:

144 *Israeli (Jewish) protest groups*

1 because PN had contributed to shaping Oslo; and
2 because one of its principles was to support *any* agreement with which the Israeli and Palestinian leaderships concurred.

Based on the second principle, with the signing of the Oslo Accords, voices were heard calling for 'closing the shop'. It was argued that the group had accomplished its mission because both sides had been brought to the negotiation table and were doing their job: "Once Oslo happened most of the people of Peace Now quite simply said that their activity was superfluous. The government is making peace anyway. Who needs to demonstrate? What are they going to demonstrate about?"[93] Peace Now perceived negotiations as fair game: who can do better obtains a better result. There was no argument about certain principles that needed to be adhered to in order to achieve peace, e.g. international legality, or universal principles. The notion of "support our government and get the most of it"[94] was the norm. As human rights violations in the OPT increased, Yossi Sarid (Meretz leader and frequent speaker in PN rallies) argued that: "if we have to cut some corners of human rights to get a settlement, let it be, a necessary evil that we will fix later".[95] During negotiations at the time of Rabin, Avnery quoted Sarid as saying, in the same vein: "we must twist the arm of Arafat, but without breaking it".[96]

During the Oslo period, Peace Now took a low profile as a mobilization activist group, redirecting its attention to new types of activities that were seen as suitable during a peace process; first in watching and reporting settlement expansion and 'outposts', and then in organizing small demonstrations against such developments in the Occupied Territories and running dialogue programmes through 'people-to-people' programmes. Time passed without Peace Now publicly confronting the government over its policies and mobilizing against them. It did not link the way that negotiations were dictated by the Israeli side to how policies were implemented on the ground in the OPT, nor did it bring them to public attention. Meetings did take place with ministers and with Rabin himself to discuss the expansion of settlements, but there was no confrontation, especially as Labour was in government.

Nor did much change later, during the Likud government. Peace Now argues that the Israeli public was frightened by the clashes over the opening of the tunnel under Al-Aqsa mosque[97] and by cases of suicide bombing,[98] and that since violence could not be tolerated under any circumstances, it was unable to speak out any louder or to mobilize the masses. This position is similar to that of mainstream liberals in South Africa who refused to acknowledge the reasons why the blacks resorted to 'violence' in their resistance. However, it contrasts with the position of white progressive liberals, who blamed the apartheid government for pushing the Africans to resort to violence.

Because it was not challenging the government's policies, Peace Now was accused by its critics of "going to sleep"[99] or of 'not doing enough'. Michael Warschawski of the Alternative Information Centre explains this by quoting Janet Aviad from Peace Now who said: "we will not convince the Israelis of dismantling of settlements, but [will] find the Palestinian who will accept".[100] As such, 'not challenging' should not be understood as 'not doing enough' or as 'sleeping'. The author argues the opposite. Peace Now was enthusiastic about Oslo and wanted the maximum that Israel could get from it. In addition, as supporters of any arrangement agreed upon by the two leaderships, as well as being advocates of a process rather than a set of peace principles or a clear end result, Peace Now provided ample time for the Israeli side to benefit from a long process of negotiation with a weak side. It also provided its local and international partners with misleading assumptions or false hopes of a coming peace.[101]

As noted earlier, the Oslo Accords did not specify the end result, did not take international law as a term of reference, and did not address the root causes of the conflict. The status of the land occupied in 1967 was changed from 'occupied' to 'disputed' territories, and separation along ethnic/national lines was legalized. During the Oslo period, 'occupation' as a word that had filled the protest discourse during the first Intifada became absent in the discourse of the liberals. Notions like "my security is beyond your sovereignty"[102] and "international law is not interesting to anybody"[103] prevailed. Solidarity work with Palestinians affected by the Oslo measures eventually took on a low profile, and dialogue programmes came to the forefront of Peace Now's work. 'Apolitical' encounters were adopted as the best way to humanize relations, being, of course, away from discussions of the existing political realities or power structures. These were similar to earlier co-existence programmes that had been carried out between Israeli Jews and Palestinian citizens of Israel. Again, while preserving the existing power structure, "another form of occupation with Palestinian consent",[104] or a cheap peace, was perceived as possible.[105]

Some of Peace Now's people would argue that they did what they could; "we couldn't do more, we've been critical enough"[106] or, "we've been a bit ahead of government",[107] or else "We stood against settlements and pushed for implementation of agreements".[108] It is commonly said that Peace Now kept the issue of 'outposts' alive, as if other settlements were legal but these were not; and also that its creation of an organization called Ir Shalem (a biblical name for Jerusalem) was an important step in dealing with the issue of Jerusalem. Even so, others admit that between 1994 and 2000, PN fell into the trap of not speaking up, and they also admit that their work was based on tactics, and not on a strategic plan. The author argues that this is part of a political pattern that stems from being a mood-oriented protest group.

As mentioned earlier, the leadership of PN reads the public mood and decides what positions it is ready to adopt. Choosing to be mood-oriented led to a lack of strategizing out of choice. And in line with the old, traditional approach of the mainstream 'liberals' – of pragmatism, opportunism and gradualism – Peace Now continued to adopt stands and slogans that were very general or vague, and that fitted with its 'constructive ambiguity' approach, where ambiguity was viewed as useful for manoeuvring. Eventually, its talk of a goal to make peace lost its credibility because it was difficult to understand what 'peace' was being spoken about. Finally, it is important to note that up until the end of the Oslo period, Peace Now chose not to deal with the past, i.e. history prior to 1967, which therefore meant that the issue of the Palestinian right of return was left unaddressed. A review of Peace Now's political positions on the final status issues up until 2003 is presented briefly below.

As the second Intifada got under way in 2000, Peace Now once again suffered from the 'first day' syndrome, but this was a long 'first day'. As a mobilization protest group it disappeared, and in fact it was almost two years before the organization took any visible action, and organized a mass demonstration. It adopted Prime Minister Barak's assertions that the Palestinian leadership had rejected Israel's generous offer at Camp David, that the Palestinians did not want peace, that Arafat had orchestrated the second Intifada, that there was no longer a partner for peace, and that heavy-handed force was the means to address the Palestinian Intifada/'violence'. These components developed a new national political consensus that Peace Now then accepted, some of its membership vocally and others in silence.

Along with other mainstream Zionist groups/individuals, Peace Now blamed the Palestinians for the Intifada, and later moved to support 'Oslo minus',[109] because the Palestinians could not be trusted.[110] As a result, relations with Palestinian groups faced a long period without contacts. Ghassan Adoni of the Beit Sahour Rapprochement Centre, which had connections with Peace Now, recalls that after fifteen years of joint work, nobody contacted him at times when harsh military measures were imposed in the OPT.[111] Even after two years of self-criticism into PN's politics and role, such matters as how the Israeli governments had negotiated the Oslo Accords, the fact that Palestinians' lives had worsened since the start of the Oslo peace process, and why Palestinians would resort to a second Intifada, were not put forward for public debate: "Peace Now's people refused to recognize what they know about the situation."[112]

During the second Intifada, Peace Now ceased its earlier but now declining solidarity activities; as Galia Golan commented in 2005: "We don't see ourselves as a solidarity movement."[113] Instead it continued actively with its settlement watch programme, called for the halting of targeted assassinations (extra-judicial killings) of Palestinian activists, and held vigils, e.g. in front of the prime minister's office. After a few years, it also organized a small number of demonstrations, raising such slogans as, 'stop the killing', 'end occupation',[114] 'Sharon not in my name'[115] and 'get out of the territories'. In addition, it became heavily involved in two joint Israeli–Palestinian initiatives, the People's Peace Campaign, which was later replaced by the Ayalon–Nusseibeh Peace plan, and the Geneva Initiative which produced the Palestinian–Israeli peace coalition. Both aimed to find a partner across the divide with whom there was either a certain agreement on general principles, as in the case of the Ayalon–Nusseibeh plan, or for the first time, proposals for a detailed agreement to be put in place, as in the case of the Geneva Initiative.

It was as if the Palestinian side, through semi-formal groups, had once again to prove its eligibility, on the basis of which Peace Now would campaign that a partner did exist. This had happened in the first Intifada, where the PLO had to accept certain conditions in order to be approved as a valid partner. Both initiatives come within the level of second-track diplomacy negotiations, and both also bring in mostly mainstream Fateh members with mainstream 'liberal' Zionists. This is contrary to the case of South Africa, where the UDF was partnered with the progressive liberals, not the mainstream liberals. The UDF worked with those who were ready to work with it on the dismantling of apartheid as an ideology and a political system, and who accepted international law as a term of reference. This has not been the case with the two initiatives/plans identified above. Their main political pillars are discussed in the section on second-track diplomacy (pp. 164–167).

In terms of political position, Peace Now does not oppose the (separation/apartheid) Wall, but argues that another route along the Green Line is preferable. The idea of building a wall has not been refuted on a principled basis. The disengagement plan was supported, even though Peace Now calls for agreement by negotiation, not by unilateralism, and continues to support the following: a two-state solution based on 1967 borders; a Palestinian capital in East Jerusalem;[116] no right of return and no recognition of responsibility, since "the Israeli public is not ready for it";[117] security as a pre-condition and a result; and the evacuation of most settlements, excluding those of Jerusalem (according to the point of view that says "what you kept is yours and what we took is ours"),[118] in addition to the big settlement blocks. Peace Now does not support refusal to serve in the OPT, but has recently taken the position that it should be left to the individual to decide.

To conclude, political pragmatism, gradualism and opportunism, justified by a mood-oriented approach, produced a lack of clear aims and a long-term strategy of having no strategy. This allowed Peace Now to support "any and all steps promising to promote resolution of the conflict"[119] considered appropriate by its leadership. This also enabled PN to continue to stay centrist and close to the politics of Meretz as well as 'left' of Labour. As it adopted Barak's message of no Israeli responsibility for the failure of Camp David, it became weaker and the right-wing parties became stronger. It can be argued that Peace Now, as Israel's leading mainstream protest group, caused damage to itself and to other protest groups by siding with Barak's government. Along with its ability to mobilize them, it lost a significant percentage of its supporters, who had begun to become disillusioned and to move to the right. It also lost many of its Palestinian partners, except those who had been involved with the Ayalon–Nusseibeh plan and the Geneva Initiative.

Furthermore, PN's political independence was increasingly called into question, among other things because of the way it avoided confronting Labour governments and gave uncritical support to Barak's conclusions, and because of the way many of its leading members associated with the Labour and Meretz parties. Non-Zionists and some of the critical Zionists argue that PN acts as an arm for the Zionist 'leftist' parties.[120] Uri Davis says the fact that Yuli Tamir, a founding member of Peace Now, and Amir Peretz, a prominent member, became leading members of the Labour Party and ministers in the 2006 Kadima unity government may constitute 'circumstantial evidence'[121] of a lack of independence from the establishment. The role of both individuals in the war against Lebanon in 2006 prompted commentators to suggest that it was "the first war run by Peace Now",[122] and caused 'leftist' Yossi Sarid to question the role of the 'left' in the war: "with such a left, who needs a right?"[123] Both also contributed to shaping the consensus justifying the war, and were partners in leading the war, a war that Peace Now could also justify.

As to other organizations belonging to this sub-category, two of its prominent bodies are at present led by two of the architects of the Oslo Accords – the Peres Centre for Peace is headed by Dr Ron Pundak, and the Economic Co-operation Foundation is headed by Dr Yaer Hirschfeld. Others, such as the Council for Peace and Security and the Israeli side of the Ayalon-Nusseibeh group are led by ex-military, security generals and ex-government officials. The retired head of the Shin Bet security service, Ami Ayalon, was serving in the Knesset for the Labour Party in 2006. The Israeli side of the People's Peace Campaign, which was replaced by the Ayalon-Nussibeh group, was led mainly by Peace Now members, while the Arik Institute is directed by an orthodox religious Zionist patriot,[124] and the peace it stands for is based on notions that are the same as those of Peace Now. However, each organization approaches its work from a different angle, to serve the specific role or mission that it prioritizes.

The Oslo Accords can be read as having four dimensions: political, security, economic and 'people-to-people'. The Peres Centre for Peace was established in 1996 with its focus on economic and the people-to-people dimensions. It claims to be non-political, "very much not political".[125] However, its stated aims are to realize the vision of Shimon Peres of a "New Middle East" in which people of the region work together to build peace through socio-economic co-operation and people-to-people relations.[126] As much as it possibly can, this vision brings civil societies and governments to join forces on the basis of identified economic and social interests. The idea is to co-operate and not to wait until a settlement is reached. In this regard, Ron Pundak argues: "I don't think we have to address the asymmetry of power. This is terrible and idiotic, eventually we will become equal."[127] How equality will be achieved is the difficult question to answer. But it is important to recall how Ron Pundak evaluates the Oslo Accords. He emphasizes two successes: mutual recognition of the legitimacy of both national movements in the territory, and presentation of a practical solution based on the imbalance of power.[128]

It is assumed that such co-operation will steer a process that has civil society at its core, and will change mindsets, thereby building foundations of peace.[129] As part of that quest, the Peres Centre for Peace runs four programmes to achieve its aims: people-to-people, capacity building, humanitarian assistance, and education for peace. The people-to-people programme[130] involves running dialogue encounters, joint sports activities, youth programmes and joint business initiatives. The capacity building involves providing training programmes for Palestinians, and joint research and joint initiatives to address environmental issues. Humanitarian assistance involves, for instance, caring for Palestinian children for whom treatment is not available in Palestinian hospitals. The education for peace programme involves addressing values of tolerance, reconciliation and acceptance of one another. Regarding justice, equality and combating racism, Pundak claims that given current limitations on addressing these values, the focus is on very basic principles that give thought to how the other side lives under occupation, and the differences and needs of both.

One can say that the Peres Centre for Peace is running co-existence programmes that aim for co-operation within the framework of the existing reality of power relations. In the process, partnerships based on limited interests are built and can produce certain benefits here and there, but the biggest achievement is in getting Israel accepted as it is. The mindset of those involved will accept the existing situation as the only reality, and their aim will be to get the most from it. It is a similar approach to the co-existence programmes inside Israel that have been implemented for decades vis-à-vis Israel's Palestinian citizens. The author argues therefore that the Peres Centre is part of a process that aims to contain and pacify the Other, i.e. the occupied, and that because this is done without addressing the asymmetry of power, it is selling false hopes that peace will eventually come and equality will be achieved. Finally, as a liberal Zionist organization and an advocate for regional economic co-operation, the Peres Centre for Peace stands totally against calls to boycott Israel. Ron Pundak assumes that the situation is remote from apartheid, and for a small problem one does not use an atomic bomb.[131]

The Arik Institute functions along the same line of thought as the Peres Centre for Peace. It is the home of Yitzhak Frankintile, who established the Parents Circle after his son Arik had been killed by Palestinian militants in 1994. The aim of the Parents Circle was to bring together families from both sides who had lost their children, to show how occupation inflicted such losses on the two societies, and to send a message that: "we don't think of revenge but reconciliation".[132] Following the same path, the Arik Institute aims for reconciliation, tolerance and peace. It claims to be non-political since it does not offer political resolutions for the Israeli–Palestinian conflict.[133] However, it supports any agreement that the two leaderships might adopt, based on certain principles: end of occupation; two states for two people; agreed and permanent borders; an agreed solution to the refugee problem; and Jerusalem as the capital of both states.[134] The principles are similar to those of Peace Now, and are broad enough to be open to many interpretations. They offer nothing that questions the existing asymmetry of power, historical injustice or the exclusivity of Zionism, or that stresses the importance of abiding by international law.

The Arik Institute perceives the core of the conflict to be the occupation: the only way to change the situation is for "Palestinians [to] address the Israelis as peace people" and not to look for justice: "go to history … lose future. Justice will not bring peace".[135] As such, reconciliation is seen to include: acceptance of 'the Other'; willingness to admit one's mistakes; mutual requests for forgiveness and compensation for wrongdoings; and "willingness not to set any preconditions and to compromise on our dreams".[136] The Institute seeks a 'wise peace' through activities that include demonstrations (e.g. the Palestinians go inside the Green Line to demonstrate), publication of informative material about the conditions of Palestinians in the OPT, running people-to-people programmes, and lecturing for peace in schools. The values of the peace that it emphasizes include acceptance of the Other, pragmatism and compromise.

Some would argue that such activities give hope to the participants and to those around them that peace is possible; however, others would argue that because such activities do not address justice and equality in connection with the existing power structure, they fail to address the root causes of the conflict. Thus it could be argued that they are a loss of time and are selling a false hope. Also, they can be part of a containment strategy similar to what has already been discussed. The closeness of the Arik Institute to the security ethos is reflected in its position against refusing to serve in the army: "We need to have a strong army, we don't want another Holocaust, to be a defence force."[137] It is also against boycott as a tool with which to pressure the Israeli government.

A final example, which comes from the realm of research, is the Economic Co-operation Foundation (ECF) which focuses on conflict resolution. While it was not a protest group per se, it has nevertheless been quite active and influential in the realm of conflict resolution, having initiated and disseminated ideas that were put forward for discussion in the second-track diplomacy meetings which involved many protest groups. The Economic Co-operation Foundation (ECF) is a 'track two' think tank, and was the initiator of the Oslo process that led, through secret informal negotiations, to the signing of the declaration of principles. It also developed the Beilin-Abu Mazen Understanding, which was central to the drafting of the Geneva Accords, and it played a noticeable role in preparing the plans for the disengagement from Gaza and northern parts of the West Bank.[138] It was founded by Dr Yair Hirschfeld and Dr Yossi Beilin in 1990, and its main objectives were "to build, maintain and support Israeli–Palestinian and Israeli Arab co-operation in the political, economic, and civil society spheres in support of creating a sustainable permanent status based on a two-state solution".[139] It works to achieve these objectives through providing ideas and creative solutions, testing them at the civil-society level and building structures that are then offered to policy-makers locally, regionally and internationally. It plays this role from a point of close relations with the establishment and, of course, from within the parameters of the mainstream liberal Zionist politics that are manifested in the Oslo accords.

Compared with South African research centres and think tanks like the IDASA and the Inter-group Research Centre, the ECF works from the conviction that a settlement can be found while preserving Zionism and the existing structure of the exclusive political system. The South African centres researched possible scenarios, but on the premise that apartheid's ideology and state system had to be dismantled; they produced alternative perceptions of an inclusive political system, values and security. Here it should not be forgotten that the two resolutions were differently framed. The ANC's inclusivity vision won in South Africa, while the exclusivity of Israel has won so far.

Critical liberal Zionist groups

This sub-category examines the second half of the liberal Zionist protest groups. Groups in this category are distinguished from the mainstream liberal ones by the fact that they are Zionists, but critical Zionists compared with the mainstream ones. The critical Zionist groups are keen to preserve the ideological consensus, but they do challenge the political consensus to the extent that they were labelled by the mainstream groups as radical 'leftists'. They represent an array of political positions on the left of the mainstream liberals. Those on their left are the non-Zionists and the anti-Zionists. Compared to the mainstream groups, their political positions are clearer; e.g. Gush Shalom. Some of them bluntly challenge part of the security ethos; e.g. Yesh Gvul and New Profile. Others focus on solidarity and human rights-oriented activities; e.g. Ta'aush, Bat Shalom, Coalition of Women for Peace, Machsom Watch. They are, by a majority, issue-oriented. Those that choose to make political stands propose a better deal for the Palestinians as part of the two-state formula. Even so, the 'constructive ambiguity' approach is adopted, albeit in different degrees; e.g. Bat Shalom. Many reject a boycott of Israel, while some support a selective boycott.

They share some concerns and characteristics. They are concerned about the soul of the Jewish people, since occupation is perceived as 'killing both sides'. They are concerned about democracy and Israel's long-term security. They advocate a compromise but are ready to move further in recognizing Palestinian rights and demands. The gap between the historical narrative they adopt and that of the Palestinian side is narrower compared with that of the mainstream Zionists. Even though some disappear during crises because of the 'first day syndrome', they come back to activism more quickly than mainstream groups. Some lose faith that they can effect change through working inside Israel and therefore put more into advocacy work at the international level. Many challenge state strategies such as the Wall, unilateralism, disengagement plans, assassination of Palestinian activists, the siege of Gaza, and lastly the war on Lebanon in 2006. Few make links between the occupation of 1967 and the war, and the eviction of the majority of Palestinians in 1948. The problem is occupation, but some are ready to acknowledge some mistakes by the state before that, though without questioning state legitimacy. The latter touches the ideological consensus and this they do not challenge. Some believe that their role is to prepare the ground for Peace Now to take new issues to the public: "a small wheel that could move a bigger wheel".[140] Most members and supporters of these groups are supporters of the political platform of Hadash, the Israeli Communist Party. In varying degrees, they are ahead of mainstream liberals in the direction of universal principles of equality and justice.

There are many protest groups belonging to this sub-category, including Gush Shalom, Bat Shalom, Women in Black, New Profile, Yesh Gvul, Refusniks, the Israeli side of the Palestinian-Israeli Joint Action Committee, the Israeli Committee Against House Demolition (ICAHD),[141] Ta'aush, Coalition of Women for Peace, Courage to Refuse, Machsom Watch, the Committee for Israeli–Palestinian dialogue,[142] Campus LoShotek[143] and so on. One of these, Gush Shalom, is examined

152 *Israeli (Jewish) protest groups*

along the three defined political turning points, if applicable, and a number of examples are briefly addressed. It should be noted that this sub-category is home to the largest number of active Israeli protest groups.

Gush Shalom (GS) is one of the oldest and most visible groups. Its political stands are in the middle on the continuum of those that belong to this sub-category, where some choose to take position/s and others do not. For instance, Bat Shalom stands on its right and ICAHD on its left. Thus, Gush Shalom provides a feeling for the political middle ground across the organizations of this sub-category. It was established in 1993 by a group of protesters who had spent forty-five days in late 1992 opposite the Israeli prime minister's office, protesting about the expulsion of 415 Islamist activists. "During the debates in the tents, and in view of the silence of other peace groups, some of the protestors decided that a new Israeli peace movement was needed. They defined themselves as 'more peace-oriented than Peace Now'."[144]

Gush Shalom neither rejected nor fully supported the Oslo Accords, but maintained an ambivalent position. While it read the mutual recognition of Israel and the PLO as a great step towards influencing the Israeli public, it concluded on reflection that Oslo represented a bad agreement, criticized it for not mentioning the ultimate aim, and claimed that this would make the interim stages lose their meaning.[145] Being vocal about Oslo's tragic flaws did not stop GS from requesting Israeli activists, shortly after the signing of the Accords, to support Oslo and concentrate on lobbying within Israeli society and the Israeli government to ensure that the minimum obligations already agreed to by Israel were carried out.[146] Later in the Oslo period, Gush Shalom became very critical of the government's policies in the OPT and the way it had handled the negotiations. In 1995, Uri Avnery accused Rabin of not negotiating in good faith, and argued that by delaying the implementation of the Declaration of Principles, the Israeli government was building facts on the ground, e.g. by expanding settlements, especially in Jerusalem, and by closure and other measures paving the way for an envisioned solution of an archipelago of enclaves.[147]

Gush Shalom was among the first groups in this sub-category to raise the slogan of sharing Jerusalem, and in 1998 it organized a campaign under the slogan of 'Our Jerusalem'. Avnery sees one of its roles as taking an issue that is taboo for the Israeli public and helping to make people see it as acceptable.[148] During the Oslo period, Gush Shalom also highlighted the issue of Palestinian political prisoners in Israeli prisons and called for their release. Other groups in the same sub-category either hesitated to address this issue, or else supported release of prisoners on a selective basis. GS also organized many demonstrations in protest at Israeli policies, in co-operation with Orient House. Compared with the positions and activities of Peace Now, they were ahead, and on some issues far ahead, for instance in criticizing the Israeli government's policies and in acknowledging more Palestinian rights. Even so, GS fell short of unequivocally adopting universal human rights and principles.

During the second Intifada, Gush Shalom criticized Barak for the failure of the Camp David negotiations, and Avnery blamed Barak for delivering a devastating blow to the Israeli 'peace movement', describing him as a 'peace criminal'.[149] GS refutes Barak's 'generous offer' through maps and other analytical material that it disseminates in various ways. Its forms of action include media, solidarity, human rights and advocacy work. It publishes weekly advertisements in *Ha'aretz* newspaper, participates in demonstrations across the Green Line, joins in olive-picking field work in the OPT and shares in rebuilding demolished Palestinian houses. It has also been active against the Wall, was part of a human shield to protect Arafat during the 2003 incursion into Ramallah, and called on the air-force pilots to refuse to implement actions that caused civilian casualties. It usually carries out its field activities in co-operation with other protest groups belonging to this sub-category and the leftists; such as Ta'aush, the Anarchists, the AIC etc. While groups in this sub-category and those on their left work together on specific issues it is important to note they are quite fragmented, according to political differences and personal rivalries.[150]

Gush Shalom's positions during both the periods discussed stem from its goal to influence the Israeli public and lead it towards a peace that is not based on ideology but on a practical political programme for solving the conflict.[151] This programme adopts a two-state solution based, as claimed, on equality and mutual respect, and strives for maximum co-operation.[152] In this programme, perceived equality is conceded through commitment to a Jewish state and dictating the balance of power. Nor does it allow for respect for international law, which is not considered as a useful basis: "It has a very low standing in Israel ... no one takes UN resolutions seriously ... we accept international law if we make a separation between the conventions and the resolution."[153] While compromise and practicality are thus essential components in Gush Shalom's political discourse, the deal it proposes to the Palestinians is better than that of the mainstream liberal groups. The Palestinian 'historical compromise'[154] is acceptable to Gush Shalom, in contrast to the territorial compromise proposed by the mainstream Zionists as a basis from which to negotiate. However, for GS the historical compromise requires a number of compromises on such issues as the right of return, Jerusalem, and the sovereignty of a future state which it says must be demilitarized. Its proposed compromises are milder than those requested by Peace Now.

Gush Shalom supports recognition of the right of return in principle, as well as recognition of the moral responsibility for Israel's part in the creation of the problem,[155] and has lately referred to UN Resolution 194. On Jerusalem, while it stands for evacuation of all the settlements, it does not emphasize this principle with regard to Jerusalem's settlements, which provide residences for around half (200,000) the Jewish settlers. This means that as a result of settlement building and land confiscation, the Palestinians would be left with fragmented neighbourhoods if Jerusalem was a capital for the two states. Gush Shalom's position on security is less demanding and nearer than Peace Now's to the language of equality. It speaks about mutual security but nevertheless, and similarly to PN, stands for a demilitarized Palestinian state. Concerning a boycott of Israel, Gush Shalom stands for boycotting settlement goods only, and distinguishes between boycotting a product of occupation and of the state that occupies. Gila Svirsky of Women in Black adopts a similar position,[156] as does Bat Shalom. GS supports refusal to serve in the Occupied Territories, and Adam Keller, one of its leading members, is a refusenik.

Though its positions are clearer and provide a better 'peace deal' for the Palestinians compared with Peace Now, after reviewing Gush Shalom's publications, the author traces a number of inconsistencies in its positions and language. For example, Rabin was sometimes referred to as 'the man who knew the road to peace'[157] and on other occasions was criticized for negotiating Oslo in bad faith.[158] Gush Shalom proposes more liberal political principles than do mainstream groups; even so, it supports the Geneva Initiative[159] which represents the politics of Meretz, left of Labour, and Peace Now, the ones that GS was set up to challenge for their less peaceful agendas. Inconsistency also occurs in the kind of terms used. For instance, even though each has a specific underlying political meaning, words like 'fence', 'wall', 'barrier', 'separation wall' and 'apartheid wall' are used to refer to the Wall that continues to be established.

Such inconsistency over political positions is found among many groups and supporters of this sub-category, who tend to be selective in adopting the views of the mainstream liberal Zionist groups. For example, a member or supporter of Bat Shalom and Women in Black can also be a member of Peace Now and support the Geneva Initiative. Such multi-memberships or inclinations mean that the individual(s) concerned will have different positions on the same issue at the same time. Selective adherence to the political consensus allows flexibility, so that Gush Shalom's supporters include Zionists, non-Zionists and post-Zionists. Its leader, Uri Avnery describes himself as a post-Zionist,[160] and also defines himself as an Israeli patriot. He has a military history as well as a vision for peace. In 1948, he was a member of the Irgun militia group. As a journalist during the 1967 war, he published a daily newspaper, one issue of which carried the headline "Forward to Damascus",[161] and shortly after the 1967 war, as a member of the Knesset, he voted for Israel's annexation of East Jerusalem.[162] A year after the 1973 war, Avnery secretly started a dialogue with PLO officials, and in 1982 he met Arafat publicly in Beirut, remaining in contact with him until his death, since he considered Arafat the legitimate partner for peace. With such shifts in its leader's position, Gush Shalom regards itself as the true 'peace movement' compared with Peace Now, and the pragmatic one compared to the anti-Zionists. During the Oslo period and the second Intifada, it continued to challenge government policies and in 2006 stood from the very first against the war on Lebanon.

Critics of Gush Shalom describe it as a chauvinist group. They claim that its voice is louder than its actual size and influence, since although it is a voice that echoes very strongly in the international arena, it is actually a tiny faction of around fifty persons.[163] Those on its right label Gush Shalom as being avowedly leftist or radical, while those on its left accuse it of undermining the values of equality and justice. Yehudith Harel, a former member of GS, argues that equality has been treated on the level of slogans, and justice has been limited to support for the two-state solution.[164] Uri Davis, while praising its work with the

1967 occupation and settlements,[165] accuses Gush Shalom, and Avnery in particular because of his role in the 1948 war, of perpetuating the *Nakba* by failing to engage in self-critical analysis of the war crimes committed then, and later betraying the rights of the refugees and their descendants.[166] It should be remembered that the Oslo Accords provide neither agreement over the causes of the conflict, nor recognition of the right of return, and, as such, Avnery argues that he has never tried to be more Palestinian than the Palestinian leadership.[167]

Unlike Peace Now, Gush Shalom played a role in developing a more challenging political discourse vis-à-vis the government's peace negotiation policies and policies implemented on the ground in the OPT. As well as engaging in solidarity actions and advocacy work in the international arena, GS has shared this role with other organizations that belong in this sub-category. The repetition of old and similar strategies and formations has been a feature of the different organizations in this sub-category, and is reflected in the way the tradition of sporadic or seasonal activism was maintained. Established at the beginning of the second Intifada, the Ta'aush group[168] took on a role and strategies similar to those of Dai Lakibush[169] during the first Intifada. Another example is Yesh Gvul, which re-energized itself after years of low key work during the Oslo period. The phenomenon of refusing to serve in the army picked up again in response to the eruption of the second Intifada, a dramatic political event that shook the Oslo political scene, reviving old organizations and giving birth to new ones that repeated many previous political approaches, formations and strategies.

The Ta'aush group, established in autumn 2000 by Arab[170] and Jewish citizens of Israel, was among these new organizations.[171] Khulood Badawi, a leading Palestinian activist and member of Ta'aush describes it as a movement that brings together the widest grassroots group of Israelis and Palestinians with the aim of comprehending the nature of occupation, and making members decide for themselves on such issues as ending occupation, activism for peace and combating discrimination.[172] Ta'aush has no political ideology, but the political vision of the ICP/Hadash is the most prevalent within it. Nor does it see any part of its mandate or role being to debate core issues of the conflict: therefore such issues as Zionism, militarism, equality, justice, colonialism and racism are not discussed in formal meetings. Its major role is to organize protest activities against occupation and discrimination inside Israel.[173] The group recruits many Israelis who are not keen to discuss political views and take stands but are ready to take action in solidarity for/with the Palestinians. This reflects a tendency that political organizations have faced in, and since, the second Intifada, where, after years of silence or undemanding positions, supporters/members have chosen to go to Ta'aush and/or Machsom Watch to engage in practical, tangible actions. Molly Maleker of Bat Shalom shares her personal experience with Israeli women who are not attracted to politically charged initiatives: "Young activists will go to Ta'ayush, not Bat Shalom, to sit and discuss statements and make positions ... lots of women in Bat Shalom don't understand why we insist on political papers."[174]

The activities of Ta'aush highlight human rights violations, such as the Wall and its effects, both locally within its circle and internationally, and also contribute to breaking the national consensus with regard to the absence of a Palestinian partner by being able to bring Palestinians and Israelis together in joint activism on the ground.[175] In this case, the consensus is broken in the mindset of the participants who meet welcoming Palestinian hosts/partners appreciative of what Ta'aush is doing. Ta'aush sends a message to victims of Israeli policies that not all Israelis support their government's policies. A similar role is played, though to a lesser degree, by Machsom Watch,[176] a group that started with three women in January 2001 and has developed into a membership of 400 women. Its goals are: to monitor the behaviour of soldiers and police at checkpoints; to ensure that the human rights and civil rights of Palestinians attempting to enter Israel are protected; and to record and report the results of their observations to the widest possible audience, from the decision-making level to that of the general public.[177]

The one-issue, human rights-oriented work of Machsom Watch has attracted the attention of many who are involved in protest activism. Some see their presence positively, giving credit to their reports, their presence (which embarrasses soldiers), and the fact their companionship at checkpoints makes Palestinians feel a little more secure. Others are critical, arguing that the struggle should be against having checkpoints at all, and not about how to make them benign. Amira Hass refers in *Ha'aretz* to military officers praising the work of this group by questioning "those who delude themselves that, if there is correct education, it will be possible to make the checkpoints humane".[178] While Machsom Watch reports reveal many of the violations and hardships faced by Palestinians at the checkpoints, the language it uses is nevertheless controversial in terms of referring to borders and rights. It fails to address the rights issue in its political context, the existing power structure.

Among the single issue-oriented and long-lived organizations that have managed to survive is Women in Black (WIB). Established in 1988, a month after the eruption of the first Intifada, it adopted one political stand: the end of occupation and, for the last nineteen years, its politics have not gone beyond this aim and slogan. Its strategies consisted of weekly vigils along with sporadic demonstrations when the conflict became highly volatile on the ground, but levels of activism have diminished, from forty vigils per week in 1989, to one vigil (at which fifteen women showed up) in the year 2000.[179] Many had dropped out after the signing of the Declaration of Principles (Oslo Accords), feeling that there was no longer any need for WIB.[180] This position is similar to that of some members of Peace Now at that time, who believed that their role ended when negotiations started, not when an agreed-upon (just) settlement would be reached.

Members of WIB are (mainly) made up of Zionists, non-Zionists or post-Zionists,[181] and are similar in their political orientation to the membership of Gush Shalom. However, they refuse to take positions beyond the ending of occupation. For WIB, there is no clear meaning associated with the meaning of 'end of occupation'. One of its prominent members describes WIB's feminist politics as: "sharing and being flexible that there is a compromise that both sides can live with".[182] The slogans it upholds include: 'Occupation is Killing Us All' and 'We

Refuse to be Enemies',[183] which are similar to those that were used by Peace Now in the first Intifada. WIB advocates non-violence and would move more quickly than Peace Now in criticizing government policies in the OPT. WIB spoke out clearly against the war on Lebanon in 2006. Even so, there is still a contradiction within the group: while it calls for non-violence and supports those who refuse to serve in the army, at the same time "most members have children in the army",[184] and some of their members live in settlements.

WIB has no consensus on the boycott issue, but its most prevalent position is similar to that of Gush Shalom in its support for boycotting settlements' products only. By doing this they separate the occupation from the state behind it. Comparing WIB with Black Sash in South Africa, its positions are seen to be similar to those of Black Sash in the 1950s and 1960s. Black Sash's positions and activities witnessed dramatic change over the years. By the 1980s, as discussed in Chapter 3, it had joined hands with the UDF/ANC in the struggle against the apartheid ideology and system.

In terms of its role, even though WIB has shrunk locally, it has managed to empower and encourage many members to be active against the occupation in different settings. It also manages to play a role that is focused mainly on the international level as part of the WIB network, fulfilling a global function whereby Israeli policies are criticized by Israelis. Critics of this role would go so far as to regard such peace work as co-operating with the various Israeli governments. They see it as contributing to improving Israel's image as a democracy, thus giving Israeli governments more time to implement their plans.[185] For critics, such work gives the impression that there are strong peace movements in Israel and that they can push for change. In fact this is not the case, given that WIB and similar groups do not have any clear vision or strategies for the change they seek, they are not keen to challenge core issues in the national consensus, nor do they have the power to influence decision-makers. WIB chooses to have a broad membership, fearing marginalization if it takes clearer political stands, even though it has failed over decades to recruit more members and, on the contrary, has shrunk. It can therefore be argued that WIB, by fearing to go out of the political national consensus, has instead protected it and has thus failed to be a voice and/or a power for change.

A final example to be glanced at is Yesh Gvul and the phenomenon of the Refusniks. While Gush Shalom advocates a political programme based on a two-state solution negotiated in good faith, Ta'aush focuses on solidarity activities in combat, to violations of human rights, Machsom Watch highlights closure as a violation of civil rights, and WIB keeps the word 'occupation' alive by calling for its end, Yesh Gvul and others working in the same area, challenge a fundamental pillar of the Israeli national political consensus by giving up part/s of the state security ethos.

Yesh Gvul (literally 'there is a limit') is similar to other groups that become inactive during quiet times. It has had three active periods: the 1982 invasion of Lebanon, and the first and second Intifadas. It supports soldiers who refuse duties of a repressive and aggressive nature,[186] stands for a two-state settlement, and contributes to the struggle against occupation by encouraging conscript and reserve soldiers to disobey immoral and illegal orders; once they have done so, Yesh Gvul provides them with counselling and with financial support for their families if they are imprisoned, and organizes vigils in their support. It also reminds soldiers of their obligations under the Fourth Geneva Convention. Yesh Gvul defines itself as a movement that differs from other 'peace movements' by rejecting the 'shoot and cry syndrome': "we don't cry and we don't serve in the Occupied Territories".[187]

Refuseniks come together in other organizations such as Courage to Refuse, Sheministem and New Profile. Courage to Refuse includes the pilots and reserve officers who published letters stressing their patriotism along with their refusal to serve in the OPT during the second Intifada because they considered occupation immoral and bad for Israel; they were 'refusing for Israel'. They run activities to raise awareness of the army's brutal and inhuman activities in the OPT, under the title 'Breaking the Silence'. The Sheministem is a group of high school students who organize awareness-raising activities to encourage other students to refuse the army draft.[188] New Profile, the fourth group, is a feminist anti-militaristic group that was established in 1998. It describes itself as the "movement for the Civil-ization of Israeli Society", since it seeks to change Israeli society "from a militarized to a civil society, from a discriminating and oppressive society to an egalitarian one, from an occupying nation to a respectful neighbour".[189] Besides supporting refuseniks, New Profile runs activities that address militarism in Israeli culture, media and law, tries to encourage forms of education that promote views critical of militarism, and seeks non-violent conflict resolution. It takes the issue of refusal further than the other groups since it addresses the context that perpetuates the occupation. However, it does not go further into addressing the conflict beyond the occupation of 1967.

The refuseniks differ in their reasons for refusal. Most refuse to serve in the Occupied Territories only, some refuse to serve until the occupation is over, while the rest are pacifists and refuse to serve at all. Most are Zionist while some are non-Zionist or anti-Zionist. The minority who choose to make a case for their refusal are usually active in one of the four groups, and participate in solidarity activities, e.g. in Ta'aush. This active minority includes around 200 individuals, while those who have refused had risen to 1,666 by September 2006.[190] During the first Intifada the number of refuseniks reached 1,000.[191] Compared with the End Conscription Campaign in South Africa, these numbers are approximate, but the backing of other organizations is different. The ECC received unconditional support from forty white organizations, many of them prominent, and was reinforced by high-profile white and coloured figures. In this way it influenced thousands, and by 1984, 70 per cent of the students in English-speaking schools were supporting the ECC's call. In terms of its political platform, the ECC also differed immensely in calling for an end to conscription all together, and stressed the injustices, inequalities and immorality of apartheid and the army it protected. It also had a clear position on the final settlement, and sided with the UDF/ANC in supporting a united non-racial democratic South Africa. It is obvious from this example that the two cases were at different political stages, an issue discussed in Chapter 5.

On the far left of this sub-category stands the Israeli Committee against House Demolition. ICAHD started as a one-issue organization in 1997 to oppose and resist Israeli demolition of Palestinian houses in the OPT. Its stands for

> a just and sustainable peace ... that enables the Palestinians to establish what we have, a viable and truly sovereign state of their own ... [and] provide all the peoples of our region with the security, dignity, freedom and economic opportunities they deserve.[192]

In this context, ICAHD does not exclude the idea of a possible regional confederation. Its members include post-Zionists, non-Zionists, anti-Zionists and some Zionists, but it describes itself in general terms as a non-Zionist group.[193] Bearing in mind the prevailing political culture of Israeli society and the existing balance of power, the ICAHD invests around 50 per cent of it capacity in international advocacy and the rest on the Palestinian and Israeli sides. It believes that there will be no meaningful change from inside Israeli society because it is tribal, and because Israeli society is like the whites of South Africa, the Afrikaners who defended apartheid.[194] In 2005 ICAHD supported selective sanctions targeting Israel's occupation rather than Israel itself.[195] Such sanctions are wider than those supported by Gush Shalom and WIB, and include arms sales or transfers that are to be used to perpetuate occupation; selective divestment; trade sanctions due to violation of the 'association agreement' with the EU; boycott of settlements products; holding individuals, including policy-makers, accountable for human rights violations; and banning Israeli sports teams from competing in international tournaments.[196]

The ICAHD fills a space between this sub-category and the second category, the leftists. It challenges parts of the ideological consensus since it criticizes the exclusivity of Israel and stresses the concept of equality. Also, it steps out of the political consensus by calling for such types of sanctions, standing in support of international law,[197] and developing a critical discourse that provides a counter-analysis to that of the government and the 'liberals'. For example, it explains the 'matrix of control'[198] that Israel is trying to impose by military power and negotiations in order to produce another form of occupation with Palestinian consent. In addition, the ICAHD protest is based on a holistic approach that does not see sides but "all in a common mess ... it is our problem". By doing this, ICAHD makes a link with the leftists as is discussed below (pp. 159–163).

Leftist protest organizations/groups

Groups which belong to this category are described as leftists because they share some or all of the following political characteristics. Some oppose Zionism and the state's consequent policies from a Marxist ideological conviction or because they refute all ideologies. Others are ready to dig into the state's responsibility for the eviction of Palestinian refugees, the *Nakba*, by which they challenge the essence of the ideological consensus of the state. Groups that belong to this category are the Alternative Information Centre, Matzpen, Shararah,[199] the Anarchists, Zochrot, Neturei Karta,[200] and Movement Against Apartheid in Palestine.[201] Several academics, journalists and writers are also active in this subcategory. These groups represent and can mobilize smaller numbers than the critical Zionists, which in turn represent and can mobilize smaller numbers than the mainstream Zionists. The activists among this category are numbered in tens. They are labelled as self-hating Jews, lunatics, marginal, ineffective or irrelevant. As an act of protest, some of the anti-Zionists have chosen to leave Israel and live abroad, e.g. the late Shimon Tzabar, who died in London in March 2007.

Over the years, the leftists did not cross the national divide to the extent of joining the Palestinian resistance, including the armed struggle, in the way white members, especially from the South African Communist Party, did in the South African case. Thus, a joint front failed to develop for an inclusive struggle and solution. One can argue that there were several reasons for this. First, it was due to the position of the Israeli Communist Party (Hadash), which did not question Israel's legitimacy and was among the first to advocate a two-state solution. From the 1950s it gave weight to a discourse of compromise and pragmatism as the correct approach, one that the 'liberals' adopted some decades later. Second, the framework of a two-state solution along national lines eventually won over the united secular state framework that the PLO had adopted at some point. Third, there has been little readiness among the leftists to cross national lines and join the struggle of the Other, which would entail a much higher price than that of being ostracized. They continued to work from within the law and there have been very few exceptional cases. Fourth is the historical context in which Israel has managed to cast away the existence of the Palestinians and the Palestinian cause. It took the PLO decades to bring the Palestinian question back to life. Finally, Israeli denial of Palestinian existence and their rights over a long period, divisions along nationality and culture between Jews and Palestinians, and the asymmetry of power have contributed to producing an environment that favours separate work. Hence, Moshe Mochover refers to Azmi Bishara's comment that: "you work with your public and I work on mine".[202]

While values of equality and justice, issues of colonialism, Zionism, racism, and the *Nakba* and the validity of international law have been absent, marginal or discussed only on a limited scale by the different 'liberal' groups, they have also been a strong focal point in the political discourse and vision for peace of the leftists, who stand for universal values and a human rights-based approach to solving the conflict. A major example of this category is the Alternative Information Centre (AIC), because of its long history and the fact that it is a mixed Palestinian–Israeli organization. This makes it a rare case in Palestinian–Israeli peace work. Established in 1984, the Centre is an NGO that brought together former members of Matzpen and Palestinian members of the Popular Front and the Democratic Front. During the first Intifada, it was very active in providing information about the situation on the ground, and in its involvement in solidarity activities and the provision of an alternative political analysis. It also provided a space for joint encounters, sometimes initiating contacts.[203] Later, the Oslo Accords created a political split within the AIC. While all concurred that it was a bad agreement, some saw their role as being to denounce it because nothing good would come out of it. Others, however, saw that Oslo might open up a dynamic that could lead to the end of occupation, so that it was their role to push it further.[204] Later, as Oslo was dominated by the powerful side, the AIC insisted on a rights-based approach in contrast to the compromise approach of the 'liberal' Zionists. The AIC became very critical of the Oslo Accords and the dynamics of the Zionist 'liberal' protest groups, its position being similar to that of Gush Shalom towards the Oslo Accords and the role played by mainstream 'liberals'. The AIC considered the second Intifada as an inevitable result of the failure of the Oslo Accords.

The AIC sees itself as an anti-Zionist organization that is part of the anti-globalization and the anti-capitalist/imperialist movements.[205] It rejects Zionism because it encompasses a negation of the Other, the Palestinians, which, sooner or later, necessarily means ethnic cleansing.[206] Thus, it regards Israel as a racist colonial state, and seeks to develop a joint Palestinian–Israeli agenda in the struggle for justice, freedom and equality. It supports a two-state solution as phasal, but one which adheres to the right of return. The second phase is a secular state for all its citizens, a long-term joint project.[207] This secular democratic solution gives up socialism until the appropriate conditions emerge. Compared to the South African case, the Israeli leftists have a three-stage plan, the first stage of which starts with the division of historical Palestine; this position differs from that of the leftists in South Africa.

At present, the AIC goals are to offer a critical discussion of the political realities "which have been created since the Oslo accords and their implementation, with special attention given to radical democratic struggles, critical perspectives on the colonial nature of the State of Israel, and the authoritarian features emerging in the Palestinian Authority".[208] To achieve this, the AIC disseminates information, provides research and political analysis on Palestinian and Israeli societies, and the Palestinian–Israeli conflict. It also promotes co-operation between the two sides, based on values of equality, social justice, belief in a common struggle, solidarity and community involvement. It claims that it represents a growing minority.[209] In terms of role, it succeeded in reaching and galvanizing support among like-minded groups in the international arena, preserving a space for both sides to meet and search for a possible future. It continues to represent a political perspective of the anti-Zionist Israeli activists.

Zochrot and the Anarchists are the other examples that are examined briefly in this category. Zochrot (feminine Hebrew word for 'those who remember') was established in the second Intifada and aims to "commemorate, witness, and acknowledge and repair the Nakba".[210] By this it challenges the very essence of Zionism, and in a way is anti-Zionist.[211] It seeks to change Israeli society from within by challenging the story of the creation of the state, to transform Zionism, to bring the *Nakba* story to the Israeli public, and to teach part of the history of Israel that was wiped out. It argues for the need to accept the right of return and that there is a place for everyone,[212] and does so by providing alternative information, giving lectures, presenting alternative values, and organizing visits to evicted Palestinian villages where signs are posted using the original Palestinian names. Its strategies include teaching the history and geography of the *Nakba* in Hebrew and maintaining a Hebrew-language database of maps and other information about the *Nakba*.

Zochrot does not believe it is worth lobbying the government. "It is more important to have a clear position, to act on the grassroots in a very radical and creative way."[213] Thus, in comparison with other groups, Zochrot engages in original protest work. Its role of bringing the *Nakba* to the Israeli public also challenges the basic ethos of Zionism from within, and opens doors for Palestinian–Israeli co-operation. This role is similar to that of some of the South African progressive liberal organizations which undermined apartheid and sought joint work with the blacks on the basis of equality and justice.

As for the Anarchists, an earlier group existed during the war on Lebanon in 1982, and another group appeared during the second Intifada. Anarchists Against The Wall is a group of anti-Zionists that considers Zionism as racist and illegitimate.[214] It believes that equality is where all are equal, Palestinians and Israelis, Mizrahi and Ashkenazi, women and men, and considers that justice includes equal freedoms, recognition of the *Nakba* and acceptance of the right of return because a state cannot be democratic and Jewish.[215] It does not believe in hierarchies, so some believe in no state but in independent communities in groups of 100 or 200 persons, while others advocate a one-state solution similar to modern South Africa.[216]

The Anarchists' objectives are: to tear down the Wall, end the occupation and then struggle for one state or no state. Their activities include weekly demonstrations against the Wall and other direct, non-violent actions. Joint demonstrations bring them together with Palestinians and international activists, as well as members of Gush Shalom, Ta'aush, AIC etc. The persistence of the Anarchists and international activists and their support for the Palestinian activists and villagers along the Wall did not stop the Wall but managed in a few places to change its route, e.g. at the Budrus and Beit Suriek villages. They also managed to send a message in action to the Palestinians that there is an Israeli group which is ready to fight with them for their rights and take the risk. Many see glimmers of hope in the work of these new groups, Zochrot and the Anarchists.

Concerning the other groups that belong to this category, it should be noted that Matzpen is no longer active, having suffered from an internal split as well as government harassment. However, Matzpen members are active as individuals in various contexts, including critical Zionist and leftist organizations. Neturei Karta is a very low-profile religious group, but despite its long existence, has failed to develop clear objectives and associated working strategies. As to non-affiliated academics and individual activists, they use different means through which to express their political views, visions and protest voices; e.g. Dr Ilan Pappé (the

Emil Touma Institute),[217] Yehudith Harel (the Internet-based *Occupation Magazine*),[218] Dr Tanya Reinhart (website of the Movement against Israeli Apartheid in Palestine), and Israel Shamir (his personal website).[219]

Compared to the liberal Zionist groups, the leftists are more uncompromising,[220] and the balance of power does not often deter them. Still, while principled and/or ideological about the past and the future, they are pragmatic in addressing the moment. They work with the non-Zionists and the critical Zionists in addressing violations of human rights and in running solidarity activities. It is important to note that the joint work currently implemented with Ta'aush and Gush Shalom is similar to that of the Committees in the early 1980s and of Dai Lakibush in the first Intifada (as discussed earlier). The metaphor of the small wheel that moves a bigger wheel is still used. In general, the leftists support a boycott of Israel. Some support the issue in principle but do not take a public stand on it, e.g. Zochrot. Their numbers are small – indeed, some call them a handful of groups that could be accommodated in one telephone booth. Based on interviews with them the author believes they include between 100 and 200 individuals.

Israeli individuals who joined the PLO

This section is quite small compared with the others, but the author nevertheless finds it worth including because of the need to be thorough in researching parallel issues across the two cases. In addition, the fact that there were many white South Africans who joined the ANC and the SACP, while only a handful of Israelis joined the PLO, does not justify ignoring the latter.

There are two individuals who publicly joined the Fateh movement, while almost a dozen were charged with, or accused of, membership in PLO factions, e.g. the Democratic Front for the Liberation of Palestine and the Popular Front for the Liberation of Palestine. The two who joined and still belong to Fateh are Uri Davis and Ilan Halavi. Uri Davis has been a member of Fateh and the Palestine National Council (PNC) since 1984. He is anti-Zionist and critical of the Oslo Accords. He believes that the weakness of the PNC, the PLO and Fateh stems from the fact that they projected themselves internally and externally as representatives of the Palestinians, not as an anti-Zionist democratic alternative to Zionism.[221] He argues that he did not revoke his membership because he believes that it is easier to correct the PLO/PNC than an apartheid Israeli regime. Ilan Halavi states that, out of realism, he has been a member of Fateh since 1973.[222] He is active in Fateh but critical of it and the PLO because they did not address the values of democracy and instead emphasized the masses rather than the political programme.[223] Prior to that, as an anti-Zionist and a communist, he was active in Matzpen. Halavi argues that Israel is not an apartheid state like South Africa.[224] At present he works at the Palestinian Ministry of Foreign Affairs and he supports the Geneva Initiative. It can be argued that he represents a case where his convictions in the platform of the Israeli communist party (ICP) have prevailed over his anti-Zionist convictions. In this regard, it is worth noting that the ICP supports the Geneva Initiative.

164 Israeli (Jewish) protest groups

Before concluding this chapter it is important to highlight the role/s of different Israeli protest groups in second-track diplomacy, an issue that has occasionally been referred to during the chapter, but is now dealt with here, since it is also at the core of the overall argument of this study. The political efforts of protest groups in this area are shown to be parallel to those discussed in the case of apartheid South Africa in Chapter 3. In both case studies, the parameters for the future settlement were, to a great extent, set in second-track diplomacy meetings and, as such, they provide/d a significant contribution when conditions become/became ripe for reaching a settlement. (The overall argument will be revisited and examined in the concluding Chapter 5.)

Members of the four categories have been involved over the years with informal talks or informal diplomacy which is also known as 'second-track diplomacy'. The term is used to describe encounters that bring together the 'influentials',[225] those who can exert influence on officials and on public opinion.[226] Most of them represent the middle cadre between the individual or unorganized masses, and the state. They can contribute to the public debate on state and society needs, interests, values, means and aims.

The anti-Zionists and the non-Zionists, e.g. members of the Communist Party, started contacts and dialogue with Palestinian counterparts after the 1967 war, brought together by common ideological convictions, and thus paved the way for other initiatives that brought the Zionists into such encounters. By the mid-1970s, as the Palestine National Congress adopted the phasal policy, the PLO became interested in political dialogue with Zionists who were ready to recognize the existence of the Palestinian nation and its national rights.[227] Since then, some Israeli anti-Zionists have found themselves more radical than the PLO, mainly the Fateh movement, because they refused Zionism while the latter accepted Israel as a Zionist state.

Among the first Zionists to hold secret talks with prominent Palestinian leaders in different parts of Europe were three widely acknowledged political and military experts from the Israeli Council for Israeli-Palestinian Peace, established in 1976.[228] They were Uri Avnery, Matti Peled, a general in the reserves, and Ya'acov Arnon, a former director-general of the Treasury. Since most prominent decision-makers at that time, including Rabin, were apprised of these meetings, there was therefore implicit acknowledgement that communication with the PLO was valuable.[229] In Uri Avnery's case, he started meeting PLO officials from 1974. After he and Arafat met in Beirut in 1982, they developed continuous contacts, with Avnery going to 'the Old Man', Arafat, to propose 'practical proposals for joint actions'.[230]

Such political dialogue meetings[231] also took place inside the 1967 Occupied Territories and in the United States. Encounters that took place locally brought the local Palestinian elite leadership and leading grassroots activists (who were known to be affiliated with the PLO but did not admit this publicly, fearing persecution), together with Israeli academics, members of the Israeli Communist Party and members of the solidarity committees that consisted of anti-Zionists, non-Zionists and critical Zionists. Such encounters adopted the 'two states' political vision. The Palestinians wanted to legitimize the PLO as representing the Palestinian people at times when they were not yet considered a nation by the Israeli public (aside from government). Such a quest took precedence over discussing the content of a peace to be.

The Israelis wanted to know the Palestinian leaders and their limits to and positions on reaching a settlement.[232] They also wanted to break the Israeli consensus that there was no Palestinian nation, no occupation and as such no need to talk with the Palestinians. Eventually, with the increasing involvement of mainstream 'liberal' Zionists who managed to label those on their left as radical and marginal, and as the PLO leadership invested more in making contact with the mainstream, the latter undermined and marginalized the leftists. Moshe Machover believes that not only did the mainstream do that but that it also 'rubbished' the PLO later on.[233]

Mainstream Zionists met the PLO affiliates in their individual capacity long before Peace Now's call for talks with the PLO in 1988. Such meetings produced concepts like 'attainable or pragmatic justice', and slogans like 'politics: the art of the possible'. A long-lasting initiative that brought together many who later became negotiators of Oslo or ministers on both sides was organized by Harvard University, whose Interactive Problem Solving programme, which started in the early 1970s, aimed to share different perspectives, reframe issues, explore options in a non-committal way, and engage in a process of joint thinking about solutions that met the needs of both parties.[234] It was to be used in formal processes to help create an environment for negotiations.[235] Its organizer claims that the efforts invested in this programme, along with other activities, contributed to the development and diffusion of ideas which ultimately became the building blocks of the Oslo agreement.[236] After the signing of the Oslo Accords, the Harvard programme sought to write joint papers on final status issues. It is important to note that at some point the role of a third party became less necessary. For instance, as stated earlier, the ECF took the initiative and organized the direct informal talks of Oslo which then became formal.

Activists and academics differ in their points of view about second-track diplomacy initiatives. While some see them as positive and necessary (e.g. Ron Pundak, Ilan Halavi) or powerless (e.g. Debby Lerman), others view them as bad for the weaker side, the Palestinians (e.g. Jeff Halper, Michael Warshawski, Ghassan Andoni, Mahmoud Muhareb). Those who support these initiatives argue that such meetings enabled a compromise to emerge and laid the grounds for Oslo. Those who reject them consider that these meetings provide/d settings that the Israeli side used to soften positions among the Palestinians, to convince the Palestinians to give up, and to understand the limit of the concessions they were ready to make. Further, these informal meetings enabled the Israelis to sense Palestinian priorities.[237] This meant that the PLO people showed a readiness to concede to or to accept certain positions from the informal interlocutors, and then had to make additional concessions when they negotiated later at the formal Israeli level. Those who view them as impotent believe that such meetings brought people who lacked power to play a game without tools, one that would make them feel like doing something while in reality they were contained and maintained.[238]

Second-track diplomacy certainly reflects a battle of ideas that has occurred during the last four decades. Communication allowed each side to obtain information about the other, in terms of positions, leadership and internal dynamics, as well as in building personal contacts. In the process Zionism remained intact; whereas the PLO negotiated informally with liberal mainstream Zionists long before it formally accepted the two-state solution in 1988. By doing so it gave an implicit acceptance of Zionism at an early stage. During the process, the Palestinian participants/side always had to prove that they were a partner, and this partnership meant that the Palestinian side had to compromise over equality and justice as stipulated in international law: at a later stage the PLO was requested to make changes on its National Covenant and did so. The process also led to compromises on the right of return, Jerusalem, illegal Jewish settlements and sovereignty of the future state, in exchange for recognition of the Palestinian people and its rights (but not full rights), whereby Israel would give up parts of 'Eretz Israel', mainly areas occupied in 1967, for the Palestinians to have some kind of a state. Further concessions were made in the two-track two-diplomacy initiatives that developed after the failure of the Camp David talks in 2000.

As the Oslo process failed and the second Intifada erupted, two second-track diplomacy initiatives developed, with an old but nonetheless major aim which was to prove that there was a Palestinian partner. These were the Geneva Initiative and the Ayalon–Nusseibeh plan. Both developed locally, without third party facilitation, and this time ambiguity was less used, especially with the detailed Geneva Initiative. Members of Peace Now were at the core of both, and both were based on the same political principles as Oslo, being security driven and reflecting the existing power relations. Both moved further in giving up the right of return. Publicly they also gave up UN resolution 194, minimizing the issue to a programme of compensation.

According to both initiatives, Israel does not have to recognize the right of return, nor take responsibility for the plight of the Palestinian refugees. Both recognize Israel as a Jewish state, thereby undermining the status of Palestinian citizens of Israel while accepting the exclusivity of the state that is at the core of the conflict. Both stipulate that the future Palestinian state is to be demilitarized and Geneva stresses the issue of security without defining terrorism. Both agree that Jerusalem will be the capital for the two states, but fail to address the issue of Jewish settlements that have swallowed up two-thirds of the land in East Jerusalem, leaving the Palestinian-populated areas as fragmented neighbourhoods. Both stress that their initiatives serve as final agreements for ending the conflict; thus no one has the right to any claim afterwards. The approach of the co-existence programmes (see pp. 134–135) in providing space for dialogue to understand the Other and accept its narrative while avoiding recognition of responsibility or apology by the dominant side, is adopted as the way to reconciliation as stipulated in the Geneva accords.[239] Normalization between the two states is stressed in almost all areas, from security to sport, agriculture, culture, health and so on. However, issues of water, economic relations and legal cooperation are not addressed. The Geneva Initiative is viewed by its drafters as reflecting a historical reconciliation that will pave the way for reconciliation between Israel and the Arab world.

A supporter of the Oslo process would definitely support second-track diplomacy initiatives and the role they played. A rejecter of Oslo would definitely criticize the role of second-track diplomacy initiatives, since they failed to address the asymmetry of power. They therefore failed to empower the weaker side and to pave the way for negotiations with clear and legally recognized terms of reference (international law), nor did they include measures of enforcement with the existing balance of power in mind, and that would have clear end results.

Even though the Oslo process failed, the liberal mainstream Zionist groups still believe that it is the basis for any negotiations and that the Geneva Initiative is the only offer on the table at the moment. Geneva is viewed as helpful because it kept the negotiation option alive, and shocked the Israeli political system which came up with the disengagement plan.[240] Critical Zionists, on the other hand, criticize the Oslo process and want to modify it so that it can be more just toward the Palestinians and be negotiated in good faith to allow for future reconciliation between the two sides. Both are still committed to a two-state solution at times when the reality on the ground does not allow for more than a one-and-a-half, or a one-and-a-quarter state, where the Palestinian 'state' is made out of four isolated enclaves/bantustans. The anti-Zionists believe that there cannot be peace with Zionism and thus there is a need for a structural change in the political system of the state of Israel; one that will give up exclusivity for inclusivity is an absolute necessity.

Conclusion

Due to the complexity of the Israeli case, this chapter has become quite large compared with other chapters. It has examined in detail the politics and the evolved political platforms of different Israeli protest groups that represent the whole political spectrum of protest. It has also highlighted the roles taken by different protest groups across the categories and sub-categories. A whole section discussed the context in which protest groups emerged, developed and have functioned, and addressed a number of issues, including the fact that there is meta-conflict, and a right, centre, liberal and left in Israeli politics. It also specified the period studied as one of transition; highlighted the membership, numbers and motives of activists who join/ed Israeli protest groups; explained the Israeli model of protest; gave a historical background to the development of Israeli protest activism; and finally referred to the concept of national consensus and the role of the liberals in shaping it.

Analytical reasons meant moving further in answering the research question (the politics and roles of protest groups in peace building in both ethnic national

168 Israeli (Jewish) protest groups

states). The author therefore classified the Israeli protest groups, on the basis of their politics, into three categories:

1. the liberal Zionist category, which is divided into two sub-categories, the mainstream Zionist and the critical Zionist: the two sub-categories include most of the Israeli protest groups;
2. the leftist category, which includes organizations and activists who are non-Zionist or anti-Zionist; and
3. the handful of Israeli individuals who joined the PLO constitute the third category.

The discussion showed that liberal mainstream Zionist groups are committed to the ideological consensus and act from within the political consensus, a fact that has to do the corporatist structure that the state's political system developed over the years vis-à-vis civil society. These groups are pragmatic, gradualists and opportunists. They do not commit themselves to clear end results and they act in the framework of a zero-sum equation. They seek a settlement based on compromise, where power politics rather than international law dictates. They support a territorial compromise with the Palestinians out of national interest: i.e. fear of losing the Jewishness of the state in the long run, and fear of losing the image of Israel as being Jewish and democratic. There are a few hundred committed activists in the organizations that belong to this sub-category but through its leading organization, Peace Now, it can mobilize tens of thousands more on a seasonal basis. The political climate and the issue/s raised decide its ability to mobilize. In line with its political approach, Peace Now raises very broad calls or slogans that can sometimes be in support of a right wing plan, e.g. unilateral disengagement.

The liberal critical Zionist groups are also concerned with the image of Israel and its nature being Jewish. They are committed to the ideological consensus but are ready to challenge the political consensus. Some make a linkage between the war of 1967 and that of 1948 and are ready to recognize some of what they refer to as 'state mistakes'. They support a two-state solution, but are ready to propose a better deal to/for the Palestinians. Also, their main approach is a 'peace by compromise' approach, not a human rights-based approach. They have been more vocal in criticizing the policies of Israeli governments with regard to the negotiations and in the occupied territories, and few of them blame/d Barak for the failure of the Camp David talks and the weakening afterwards of the Israeli 'left'. Unlike Peace Now, many groups that belong to this category have stood from the first day against the war against Lebanon (2006). The many organizations that belong to this category (between twenty and twenty-five), include almost 1,000 activists and can mobilize several thousand more on an appealing political occasion.

The leftists, anti-Zionist, view Israel as an illegitimate state, as an outpost of the imperial West in the Middle East, and support a human rights-based approach to solving the conflict. As part of a phasal plan, they would support a two-state solution to be followed by a non-violent struggle to establish a single state, a state for all its citizens equally. For some, the latter will be followed by another struggle for socialism. This category stresses the validity of international law as a term of reference and the values of equality and justice. It includes a small number of activists, no more than a couple of hundred individuals derived from the AIC, what is left of Matzpen, Zochrot and the Anarchists. As to the handful of individuals who joined the PLO, only two are still active in the Fateh faction. In the eyes of the majority they are non-existent as a category.

The Israeli protest groups are divided by and fragmented along different politics and political platforms, and the author cannot describe them as a movement. The Peace Now organization can be described as a separate movement in terms of its ability to mobilize around issues/slogans that fit within the national political consensus, but it is not a movement in terms of leading for change. It has no commitment to a clear set of peace principles or end results, and it has no defined strategies. It also has a problem with organization. As it is not a membership organization it lacks democratic processes of decision-making. A small unelected core group decides the direction of Peace Now according to its reading of the public mood at a specific point in time. Its closeness to the Labour and Meretz parties has led to questions about its independence, and it could be further argued that it serves the ideology in power. The critical liberals can be described as a fragmented network that comes together on sporadic occasions. They act as a network only when they are able to agree on momentous common grounds, but given existing political differences and personal rivalries this is not an easy task. The critical Zionists raise issues that, in various degrees, challenge the national political consensus and they can mobilize much less than Peace Now. The leftists usually join the critical liberals in their activities, or else they organize activities jointly according to broad political aims that can be vague enough to bring them together.

Addressing the conflict and its resolution differently and in pieces was influenced by the different political positions and consequently the strategies used by different organizations. Such strategies included human-rights types of work and the advocacy surrounding it; political education through raising awareness, and advocacy for different political platforms which differ in their degree of ambiguity, dialogue, and co-existence work through creating a space for bi-national encounters and informal negotiations; and disseminating alternative information, research and analysis about the conflict and its resolution. Each group has stressed those strategies that fitted with the role/s it regarded as appropriate at a certain point of time.

The mainstream groups represented by Peace Now claim that they played a role in changing public opinion and they give the example of calling for negotiations with the PLO in 1988. The author believes that it is a valid claim, but it should not be forgotten that it was the PLO that changed its political platform, not Peace Now and those who belong to its political line. Later, committed to mainstream politics and to supporting the government while negotiating, rather than supporting, a clear peace plan, Peace Now did not lead the public during the

Oslo period. During the second Intifada, they[241] worked with Palestinian semi-officials and members, mainly of the Fateh faction, on two initiatives, the Geneva Initiative and the Ayalon–Nusseibeh plan. Both extracted more concessions from the Palestinian participants in order to prove, again, that there was a Palestinian partner. Both repeated the same tactics used with the PLO members before and during the first Intifada.

While Peace Now is sporadic in its actions it has, for the last few years, focused on its Settlements Watch programme. It tries to sensitize the public to the expansion of settlements and their effects. Still, as a loyal opposition protest group, Peace Now has not addressed the illegality of Jewish settlements as such. Like others in this sub-category, Peace Now seeks change by a political compromise that preserves the dominant consensus and existing power structure, and as such it is perpetuating the status quo. By doing this, it can be argued that Peace Now buys time for the Israeli government to continue with its politics and policies.

As for the critical Zionist groups, they claim to play the role of a small wheel that prepares the ground for the bigger wheel to move. They do so by taking more daring political positions compared to mainstream groups, and by challenging the political consensus in different degrees. Labelled as radicals by the mainstream liberals, and bearing in mind the existing political culture, it could be argued that their ability to recruit supporters and change public opinion is limited. Their human rights and advocacy-oriented work is well credited, especially at the international level. In addition, they continue to send a message of solidarity to the Palestinians by being active against the Wall and helping farmers to pick their olives. However, they are not ready to challenge the exclusive nature of the political system and consequently the existing power structure, and continue to have ambivalent and inconsistent political positions. Nor, because they are fragmented, have they managed to develop into one bloc, as an organized network or a movement. They give the impression that there is a thriving peace movement in Israel but, in reality, they have addressed the conflict piecemeal.

The leftist groups, limited in size and outreach inside the communitarian Israeli society, seek to play the role of educators by providing alternative information and analysis on the conflict. They challenge the ideological consensus and, as such, aim to change the existing power structure. The establishment of Zochrot, the enthusiasm of the Anarchists, and a possible development in the work of the refuseniks and New Profile, could be seen as a sign of hope for real change.

Compared with the case of white protest in apartheid South Africa, it can be argued that the latter's politics and roles were more advanced in terms of accepting universal principles and international law, and in understanding and supporting the demands of the oppressed side. The white South Africans, by contributing to the dismantling of the exclusive ideology in power and supporting an inclusive alternative, were effective in altering the dominant consensus in a peace-enabling direction that made a difference when conditions and the balance of power became conducive. This has not been the case in the Israeli case, as this chapter proves and the next chapter concludes.

John Dugard, Knox and Quirk, and Bangani Ngeleza reached a similar conclusion. They argue that Israeli protest is far behind that of the white South Africans. According to Dugard, Israeli opposition is non-existent in comparison with the white South Africans.[242] Others who did not compare the two cases, but who have been involved in one or another of them, by a majority stress the limited role or impact, the secondary role or even the failure, of protest groups in both cases in affecting the course of events in order to reach a settlement. The author, as mentioned earlier in the research argument, challenges this conclusion. Only a very few stress that there is a substantial role for protest groups, and not necessarily for similar reasons, e.g. Ron Pundak in Israel and Heribert Adam in South Africa. These points are discussed further in the concluding chapter, where a comparison on the macro and micro levels will be drawn out, along with the patterns that exist/ed in and across the two cases. The book's argument will also be revisited and examined.

5 Conclusion based on comparative analysis

Introduction

The previous four chapters and the Introduction of this book examined and compared the politics, political platforms and roles of protest groups among the dominant communities in apartheid South Africa and Zionist Israel, doing so through the theoretical framework of state–civil society relations. This framework differs from that used by the few previous studies which investigated processes of peace building or mobilization for peace in the two conflict areas. Here, the state–civil society framework provided the structure for studying the political systems that emerged and developed in both cases of settler societies, and for examining both civil societies and the relation between them. Through this, protest groups in the civil-society field could be located and studied, after which a detailed examination, using qualitative research and empirical data, could be made of the two sets of protest groups. In the process, it was also possible to locate the intermediate variables as a second dimension or level between the independent variable (political system) and the dependant variable (politics and roles of protest groups). Eventually, the influence of the intermediate variables could be inferred by determining variations in the outcomes of the two cases.

As well as adopting a different theoretical framework, the study also developed a new classification for both sets of protest groups, by categorizing them according to their politics and political platforms, and in relation to the ideology in power. This classification was intended to tie in with answering the research question, since it would assist in understanding both the details of the political positions and, later, the variety of roles played by the different categories. In terms of analysing these roles, the study's contribution is discussed at the end of this chapter.

Chapter 5 clarifies the results of the whole book since it summarizes the work done in the four previous chapters and in the Introduction. In this way, the new insights added in each chapter while the study's overall topic was being examined are accumulated and presented here in an organized manner. However, before the layout of this final chapter is described, it is important to restate the research question, research hypothesis and methodology used to examine it, as well as the findings arrived at in the individual chapters.

The question to be answered in this research was: with regard to peace building, what are the politics, political platforms and roles of protest groups from the dominant community in two settler ethnic-national states? The two cases of protest groups are derived from areas that have been/are in conflict, i.e. apartheid South Africa and Zionist Israel. As to the research hypothesis, it examines whether or not protest groups make a difference in peace building, and whether they promote an inclusive (just) peace or a partial settlement benefiting the status quo. It also verifies whether intermediate variables between the system and outcomes affect the different pathways that can be taken by a protest group. The research argued that the role of protest groups as a component of civil society in the processes of peace building in the two ethnic-national states is limited, but can in certain circumstances become significant. In contrast to the views of a majority of scholars and activists/practitioners, this study suggests that although limited, their roles are at the same time quite significant since, along with their small roles, they play an important role in developing political discourse/s and elements of compromise that shape settlements when conditions and the balance of power are conducive to this. By the end of this chapter, the hypothesis and research argument will have been revisited, proved or refuted, totally or partially.

As discussed in the Introduction, a comparative qualitative methodology with an inductive approach was used in examining the research question. The theoretical framework of the research, which is state–civil society relations, distinguishes between the focal independent variable and other contextual/intermediate variables. The focal independent variable, i.e. the causal variable, is the political system in the ethnic-national state. In both cases the politics and roles of protest groups are the dependent variables, and these are studied as a component of both civil societies. The intermediate variables, e.g. the visions and strategies of the dominated sides' resistance, along with the balance of power at the international level that creates the subject's environment, are mentioned only when necessary.

Accordingly, this research has two levels of analysis. The first examines the political systems in both cases at the macro level. The second examines the two civil societies and the politics and roles of protest groups at the micro level. The influence of the macro level on the micro level is then addressed. Based on this, the present chapter compares the two case studies at both the macro and micro levels by exploring the similarities, the differences and the patterns that exist in each case, and the shared patterns across the two cases. In this context, 'pattern' means a form of relation that exists between a number of variables or issues over a period of time, while 'similarity' describes a point or issue of resemblance between the two cases. Thus a similarity can exist within a shared pattern between the two cases.

As qualitative research, the study sought evidence in kind, not in numbers, and used semi-structured interviews as a major research tool. It also utilized other primary data, including statements, brochures and reports from the protest groups, as well as secondary sources. The periods researched have in both cases been described as periods of transition. In the case of apartheid South Africa,

174 Conclusion

this was the period from the early 1980s until the first non-racial elections in 1994, when apartheid as a system was formally dismantled. In the case of Zionist Israel, it is the period from the first Intifada up to the signing of the Geneva Initiative, three years after the second Intifada had erupted. The Geneva Initiative was negotiated and signed by semi-officials and grassroots leaders on both sides of the Palestinian–Israeli divide, at a time when a resolution to the conflict seemed highly unlikely.

According to the research methodology, the study was designed to include five chapters, in addition to an introduction. Each chapter contributed to answering the research question by accomplishing certain tasks that are briefly recapitulated here. The results and connections between them are aggregated by the author in the following sections. The Introduction presented the idea of the research, its added value, and the methodology adopted, and briefly addressed such concepts as equality, justice, racism, truth and peace, in accordance with their respective literature and how they were used in the two case studies. This was an important task since it showed how these concepts, which are vital to understanding the politics, political platforms and roles of protest groups in the peace-building process, were utilized. In the general literature, where different scholars stress different issues, they are regarded as elusive terms. In the two case studies, they were perceived and used differently in many aspects.

Chapter 1 compared the political situations of apartheid South Africa and Zionist Israel by referring to each country's historical development. It also analysed the kind of relations that developed between the dominant and the oppressed sides as a result of their respective exclusive ideologies and political systems, and showed the similarities, the differences and the significance of both in the two cases. Chapter 2 scrutinized the political systems and civil societies in the dominant communities of the two ethnic national states, and then examined the relations between the two political systems and their respective civil societies. Doing this enabled the theoretical framework of the study to be opened up and explored.

Chapter 3 discussed the politics, political platforms and roles of protest groups in apartheid South Africa, while Chapter 4 discussed the politics and roles of protest groups in Zionist Israel. Both chapters were based mainly on the empirical data collected through the interviews, and both evaluated certain contextual aspects that included descriptions of the political right, centre, liberal and left in each case, and of the membership of the protest groups and their protest models (where available). In addition the author developed new categorizations for the different protest groups. Both chapters also showed the political positions and roles of the different categories along the political spectrum of exclusivity versus inclusivity for peace (different visions and meanings), from mainstream liberal to radical leftist. Chapter 5, as the final chapter, draws out the research results further by assembling the conclusions reached throughout the study. It develops an overall analysis that shows the relation between the different variables while drawing comparisons and establishing patterns in and across the two cases.

In order to collect up and organize the research results and present them in the best possible form, this concluding chapter is arranged as follows: after this introductory section, it is divided into further sections. The first two of these are divided into two sub-sections, which respectively sum up the similarities and the differences at the macro level and the micro level across the two cases. The next two sections then draw out the individual patterns in each case and the shared patterns across the two cases, while the final section provides further insights into the overall findings. It briefly answers the question of what the Palestinians can learn from the case of South Africa, and revisits the basic research argument which it discusses again in light of the accumulated findings of the study.

Similarities and differences at the macro level across the two cases

Grouping of similarities at the macro level across the two cases

In examining the similarities and differences at the macro level it can be seen that both cases have had similar political systems. Both were founded on colonial and exclusive ethnic foundations, and both developed exclusive ethnonational political systems. On the political continuum of inclusivity and civic nationalism versus exclusivity and communitarian nationalism, both cases exercised exclusive 'democracy' or restricted 'democracy' for the ethnic group in power. Thus they were neither democracies nor authoritarian regimes but represent 'Herrenvolk' democracy[1] for the dominant master race or ethnicity. Though concluding that such a system is not democratic, the author is nevertheless aware that it has certain democratic characteristics that distinguish it from totally authoritarian regimes. For instance, in both cases limited space for civil society continued to exist, and thus allowed a few to challenge the politics of consensus.

To maintain their systems of privilege and exclusivity, both states continuously regenerated their respective ideologies – apartheid and Zionism. It is important to note that the ideology of Afrikaner nationalism, which manifested itself in the apartheid idea, shared a number of basic tenets with the ideology of Zionism. These include the fact that: membership in them is based on belonging to the exclusive ethnicity of the Volk, or on being a Jew; claiming rights to land is based on settlement, biblical texts and historical connections; there is a felt need to have power and control over their own destiny; both developed national identities in light of past trauma; and both held convictions and/or feelings of superiority, e.g. by being God's chosen people, and being culturally superior.

Both political systems developed to become highly centralized, i.e. strong states vis-à-vis their respective societies. As centralized political systems, they built interlocking relations with the different societal spheres, civil society, the market or private sector, and the political society. The state has/had the upper hand in deciding the parameters for the work of the different spheres, leaving the latter with limited independent space. All spheres were part-and-parcel of the national effort of nation and state building and later of state protection. As a result of this interlocking relationship, lines between the political system, the political society, the elite of the business sector and the majority of the civil-society elite (have) blurred. This blurring provided a sophisticated system of political socialization, where society voluntarily accepts/ed state hegemony. Both cases fit with Gramsci's argument on state–society and state–civil society relations, where the hegemony of the political elite is achieved in a sophisticated manner, leading to voluntary consent.

In line with the above point, both systems continue/d to exert almost total control over the moral order of their respective societies. This was done through corporatist regimes, where the system and main party in power penetrated all societal spheres, horizontally and vertically. Corporatist regimes manifested themselves in the politics of national consensus and a *laager* mentality developed in both societies, where fear of the Other prevailed. Thus, both political systems contributed to shaping ethnically based, mainly exclusive, limited and weak civil societies. In both cases, civil society was left with small margins or societal space in which to function, and acquired certain characteristics that are similar to those of the ideology in power, as is discussed in the next subsection.

In terms of relations with the Other, the two political systems developed similar strategies towards the dominated side, adopting policies of discrimination and oppression. The ramifications of both policies covered many areas. For example, discrimination by law has been widely used. In Israel, discriminatory laws included the ethnic-based citizenship or naturalization law (1952), the law of return (1950) and the state's arrangements for land distribution (early 1950s). There are many more examples in the South African case, including the Native Act of 1913 for land distribution and the Population Registration Act of 1950. Policies of discrimination against the indigenous people were also translated by enforcing the settler society's ethnic-national symbols while diminishing those of the natives. Such policies were founded on racial grounds in the case of South Africa and on national grounds in the Palestinian–Israeli case. To stay in control while keeping policies of discrimination intact meant that oppression became part of the norm that shaped their relations with the local populations. Resistance groups which negated the legitimacy of the system and acted against it were subject to banning, imprisonment, torture and killing. Both systems developed into authoritarian ones vis-à-vis the dominated side.

Both political systems which represent/ed ethnic-national ideologies (have) also developed into highly militarized ones. In both, the role of the armed forces became/has become visible and influential beyond the confines of the military establishment, acting in the realm of civil life as well. In addition to developing sophisticated armies and military industries, in the two cases a militarized culture characterized both regime and society. The military's roles included educational, economic and integrative tasks, the latter being associated with playing the role of an agent promoting a moral order that continuously legitimizes the state's ideology and promotes exclusive unity against the Other. Eventually, the military establishments not only produced 'nations in arms', but also became powerful enough to influence decision-making in both political establishments.

The two political systems developed indoctrinated societies as part of the processes of nation building and political consolidation around the ideology in power, both before and after they had come to power in 1948. Education policies and the media contributed heavily to this task. They promoted the national ideological aims of the state, stressed the rightness of self-ethnic goals, prioritized security, de-legitimized the opponent, and projected a positive image and perception of themselves as being simultaneously heroes and victims.

Both political systems also adopted the vision of 'separation' as the prime option for reaching a settlement of the existing conflicts with the Other. They (have) held to this vision in defending the 'rightful' exclusive ideology in power, the political system, and the privileges enjoyed by the dominant side, and out of arrogance and fear. However, the success of this vision differed in the two cases.

Based on the comparison in Chapter 1 between the two political situations of apartheid South Africa and Zionist Israel and on the discussion here, the author concludes that Zionist Israel represents another form of apartheid. However, this form is more sophisticated, more subtle in some aspects, and more vicious. It should be noted that this issue is quite controversial among scholars and activists who have been engaged in researching the two cases. While Israeli scholars like Ilan Pappé, Uri Davis, Tanya Reinhat and Michael Warschawski argue that Israel is an apartheid state, most Israeli academics strongly contest this view. Ronnie Kasrils, a current ANC cabinet minister in the South African government and a Jew who was a leading member of the ANC during the years of struggle, claims that it is an apartheid case, while Professor John Dugard, the UN Special Rapporteur to the OPT, argues that a number of elements of the Israeli occupation constitute forms of colonialism and of apartheid. On the basis of the evidence of scholars and activists that the comparison is accurate, campaigns in different parts of the world calling for a boycott of apartheid Israel have been initiated and some are gaining momentum.

Grouping of differences at the macro level across the two cases

The policy of separation adopted by both political systems failed in the case of apartheid South Africa, but has so far been accepted as the best vision for settling the Palestinian–Israeli conflict. The policy of separate development and Bantustans failed as a framed vision for a new South Africa, but in the case of the Israeli–Palestinian conflict, separation as part of the framed vision of a two-state solution has prevailed over the united secular state envisioned by the PLO during the late 1960s and early 1970s. It is important to note that this vision of separation in the form of a two-state formula (Palestinian and Israeli), which is the declared official policy of the Israeli political system, was first advocated by the Israeli Communist Party and leftist protest groups, and later adopted by the Israeli liberal protest groups. A decade or so ago, the Israeli political establishment avoided using the two-state vision as a clear policy, but now does so, as part of a security based approach. It has moved from negating the existence of a Palestinian nation to supporting a form of Palestinian autonomy and finally to accepting the notion of a Palestinian state.

While the apartheid political system of South Africa was condemned throughout the world, the Zionist system of Israel has not received the same international condemnation. Most states boycotted the apartheid system and imposed sanctions on it, but the Israeli system is perceived as legitimate by major powers in the international community and beyond, and it enjoys unparalleled support compared with what the South Africans received at that time. Apartheid, the ideology in power in the South African case, was undermined both locally and internationally, and by the mid- to late 1980s had lost much of its credibility, even within the white community. In the case of Zionism, the ideology in power in Israel, it remains strong and is perceived as legitimate and credible, locally and internationally. This point highlights a related intermediate variable, the substantial advantage enjoyed by the Zionists at the international level, and especially their relation with the world hegemonic powers. This makes it hard to impose sanctions on Israel in the way that was done in the case of South Africa.

Religious institutional support for the ideology in power differs. The Dutch Reformed Church supported Afrikaner nationalism and justified apartheid before and after the 1948 change in power. The case of Israel is different. At the beginning of the twentieth century the ideologues of Zionism were secular, but used the biblical texts to justify and give legitimacy to the Zionist political project in Palestine. No specific rabbinical group or synagogue has ever played the role of the official religious institution for the Zionist movement. The support of the religious groups for the state was negotiated a year before the state was established, and was focused on preserving a Jewish identity and culture in the new state, rather than supporting Zionism per se. However, the support of these groups for Zionism became increasingly evident during subsequent years.

In terms of their nature, causes and resolution the two conflicts have been framed differently. In apartheid South Africa, the nature of the conflict was framed around race and class. In the Israeli–Palestinian case, it was mainly framed around nationality and rights to the land. In terms of causes, historical narratives picked up different echoes across the two cases. In the case of South Africa, historical narrative did not develop as a strong issue. This was related to the development of an alternative discourse that perceived the conflict not as a black–white conflict but rather as a non-racial one. In the second case, the existence of two conflicting national narratives prevailed. In terms of resolution, they were framed differently, as noted earlier.

In terms of intermediate variables, it should be emphasized that the premise and nature of the interim political agreements signed between the leaderships of the two sides does differ. While the ANC managed to negotiate an interim agreement that did not undermine its political end goal or the leverage needed to enforce it, the Palestinian side has not been able to do this. The South African agreements did not impede the goal of having a united non-racial democratic South Africa. However, the Oslo Accords and subsequent agreements hinder the establishment of a viable sovereign state.

It is also important to note that the similarities and differences noted above exist in two contexts in which a number of other intermediate variables differ. These variables include the size of the area of each state,[2] the demography of the conflicting parties, the scope for granting citizenship to the dominated side, the visions and strategies of the resistance movements (the ANC and the PLO), the support given by neighbouring states to the resistance movements, the level and kind of international support (beyond the regional) for the resistance movements, the substantial advantage for the Zionists of being able to shape the policies of the hegemonic powers (the UK and the US), the economic relations between the dominant and dominated sides, and the role of religion. All these add to the complexity of the two cases and have also affected the pathways of protest groups.

Similarities and differences at the micro level across the two cases

Grouping of similarities at the micro level across the two cases

Both civil societies are/were ethnically based, mainly exclusive, limited and weak. Both are/were ethnic, having been formed in line with the definition of the state being white or Jewish. They are/were exclusive because both states are/were defined on the basis of ethnicity, and promote/d a communitarian, 'tribal' culture for the group in power. Thus, most components making up the two civil societies failed to hold the values of universal civic rights for all as equal citizens, and universalism continued to be overcome by exclusivity and particularism. Both also (have) enjoyed limited space because both states developed strong centralized systems in which relations between the different societal spheres became interlocked under state hegemony. Consequently, both civil societies developed into weak spheres vis-à-vis the state. In this context, it could be argued that both civil societies continue/d to reflect the level of development of the existing political system. They have been far from being representative of the genuine civil society of a liberal democracy. The civil-society space continued to be activated in line with the hegemonic political discourse of the political and military establishments, which perpetuated exclusive ethno-national culture.

Used by both political systems as part-and-parcel of the national effort of nation and state building and later for power consolidation around their respective exclusive ideologies, both civil societies were left with a limited margin of independence. The widely socialized political culture and the system's financial relations with most actors in civil society (have) had a strong influence, and this translated itself in the political views and modes of action of most civil-society actors. In this context, one should not forget that in the case of apartheid South Africa, a majority of civil-society organizations were affiliated with the National Party, the Broederbond and its branches, the Dutch Reformed Church, and the white trade unions. In the case of Israel, most civil organizations have been affiliated to, or worked closely with, the Labour Party and its branches e.g. the Histadrut, and nowadays, a majority still functions as arms suppliers for the government or sub-contractors to the state. Others, on the whole, represent/ed the interests of exclusive ethnic and religious groups. In both cases, protest groups constitute/d a small percentage within the civil-society sphere.

Thus, issues of inclusivity, independence, equality and subsequently citizenship constitute/d challenges for both civil societies. Inclusivity and independence have been/were concerned with the reasons outlined above, while equality and citizenship are/were involved with the political culture and the laws generated by the ideology in power. The notion and applicability of civil universal rights (have) continued to be either absent or addressed on a selective and/or conditional basis by organizations in both civil societies. Also, a majority among them (have) continued to be exclusive in their membership and decision-making.

The issues discussed above fit with a point discussed in the introduction of Chapter 2, where a number of notions relevant to the study of civil society were proposed. The author argued that there are examples where civil society can be uncivil, ethnically based, tribal or even racist, and that these fit with standards that are less value-charged for defining civil society. In both the cases researched, the majority of actors in both civil societies do/did not question militarism, are/were ethnically based, and can/could justify double standards in the application of civic universal rights. Consequently, it could be argued that regarding the inequalities and injustices existing in the two cases, both civil societies have/had contributed to, and even prolonged, them.

A component present in both civil societies is/was the protest groups that include/d liberals and leftist organizations. Most groups belong/ed to the liberal section. The liberals sought change from within the system and have/had different degrees of respect towards their respective national consensuses. The liberals tended to be more gradualistic, pragmatic and opportunistic, compared to the leftists who tended to be more uncompromising. However, changes have occurred over the years across the political spectrum of protest, thereby producing blurred lines between some of the liberals and some of the leftists. For example, the progressive liberals found much common ground with mainstream leftists in the case of South Africa. In the case of Israel, liberal critical Zionists have many points of agreement with non-Zionist leftists, mainly with those belonging to the Israeli communist party. It is worth noting that, in both cases, the political platforms of the liberal protest groups initially advocated change that would preserve the ideology in power but later found a compromise that granted more rights to the dominated side. Over the years, however, this position changed dramatically in the case of South Africa, compared with the case of Zionist Israel, a point discussed in the following section.

In terms of functions, the liberals in both cases played a number of similar roles towards their own community and the Other. On the one hand they work/ed on sensitizing the dominant side to the suffering of the dominated side by disseminating information on human rights violations. They also play/ed an advocacy role, justifying and calling for compromise and for a non-violent settlement of the existing conflicts. In addition, they attempted to sensitize their publics to the effects of apartheid and occupation on their own societies and, over the years, managed to promote a discourse of pragmatism, compromise and non-violence. However, the various sections of the liberals differ/ed over the nature of proposed compromise/s. On the other hand, protest groups in both cases send/sent messages to the dominated side that not all whites or all Jewish Israelis are/were 'bad'.[3] The progressive liberals in South Africa, working closely with the UDF and at the grassroots level, communicated this to the black people. Earlier, those whites who had joined the ANC, the SACP and their military wings, sent the same message, but more powerfully since they were ready to sacrifice their lives. They planted the seeds for a possible joint struggle and a possible joint future. In the case of Israeli protest groups, critical Zionist groups working with the leftists at the grassroots level in protest against house demolition, settlement building and Wall construction, have also made it known that not all Israelis support the occupation or the policies of their governments.

Across the two cases, the mainstream liberal protest groups in South Africa and the mainstream liberals in Israel continued to preach for a compromise that made no commitment to a clear end result. Other liberals (the progressives in South Africa and critical Zionists in Israel) held/hold clearer positions, though very different in content, as discussed in the next section. However, all accept/ed the notion of constructive ambiguity and often use/d it. As such, some have view/ed the liberal approaches and roles as important and necessary for finding a bargaining point and not simply leaving all efforts to reach a settlement in the hands of the extremists. Others have been more sceptical and critical of the ambiguous positions and roles of the liberals, arguing that they have promoted discourses of compromise that first and foremost meet/met the interests of the powerful side. Those who hold this view see the liberals as perpetuators of the status quo of oppression, whether it is apartheid, economic apartheid after 1994, occupation, or the unremitting Palestinian *Nakba*, the Catastrophe.

Protest groups in both cases have been involved in second-track diplomacy meetings. Since many of their leading members reached the conclusion that neither side could win over the other, they joined such meetings to develop the alternative(s). To a great extent, the parameters for both settlements were drawn up in these meetings, which also served the objectives of legitimizing the Other, promoting a compromise discourse, and creating a cadre of future leaders. They produced new elites, out of which some of their members became involved in the formal negotiations. However, the period of time during which these meetings took place differed, as did the content and nature of the compromise that was agreed upon in the two cases, a point discussed in the next section.

In terms of representation, size, membership and motivation, protest groups share significant similarities. In both cases, they represented a small section in both civil societies, and continued to represent a minority in both societies. While their numbers flourished during both the transition periods, they continued to be a minority representing a minority, even at their peak. As to membership, in both cases most members have been well educated and from the middle class. In South Africa they were mainly English-speaking, and in Israel are mainly Ashkenazi, with most being liberals who can afford to oppose the system. In both cases, too, members of protest groups have been similarly motivated; they fall into three categories, prompted mainly by self- and national interest, ideological conviction and morality.

Being a minority representing a minority has to a degree resulted from the kind of relations that existed between the state and civil society, the kind of civil society that developed in both cases, and the *laager* mentality that developed in both societies. Those who challenged the system or the national consensus were usually ostracized according to the extent of their challenge to the political or ideological consensus. This limited the number of those who would join protest groups, and also placed constraints on the politics of protest, especially if implemented from within the system. Even so, it is important to note that while the number of leftists in both cases was limited, it was larger in the case of South Africa, as discussed in the next section. As for the radical leftist groups and individuals in the two cases, numerically they continued to be a mere handful as well as marginal in their respective communities, and their ability to recruit and mobilize has continued to be limited. In both cases, too, they negated the legitimacy of the existing political systems and sought structural change. By a majority, both communities viewed them as suicidal and/or self-hating.

Grouping of differences at the micro level across the two cases

The models of protest across the two cases differ. The South African protest groups defined themselves as anti-apartheid groups. For them, dismantling the ideology in power and its system was an acceptable principle, although they differed over what the new system would look like and the strategies to be used to get rid of apartheid. All agreed that apartheid was bad, as well as politically and morally bankrupt. As to who was part of the anti-apartheid movement, human rights organizations, many research centres, and many churches and church-based organizations saw themselves as part of it, and considered that shaming the apartheid system was one of their roles. Also, a majority challenged the system using strategies that fitted with the overall strategies of the UDF.

The Israeli protest groups, on the other hand, defined themselves as peace groups, where 'peace' meant different things for different groups. For the majority, as Zionists, the option of an anti-Zionism definition was inconceivable. Being Zionist and holding different perspectives about the occupation of 1967 made the option of an anti-occupation definition problematic as well. In this context, one should not forget that the Israeli Zionist ethos refers to the Occupied Territories as part of 'Eretz Israel'. Thus, it could be argued that the Israeli naming of 'peace groups', 'peace camps' or 'peace movements' has been perceived as more appropriate because it has good connotations and is sufficiently vague. As to who is included in the 'camp', human rights organizations and research centres have not regarded themselves as part of it. They do not take political positions as many South Africans did, but see themselves as professional national organizations which are apolitical. Their work is helpful to that of the protest groups but is not part of it. Israeli inter-faith groups also define themselves as apolitical.

There is no equivalent to the South African Council of Churches in the Israeli case. The two conflicts have been framed differently in terms of vision, and agreement between religious organizations on an agreed-upon religious–political vision is lacking. It is therefore difficult to imagine the example of the SACC in the Israeli case. Nor is there in Israel a counterpart to South Africa's United Democratic Front, a cross-cutting civil-society umbrella organization; a majority of black and white progressive groups adopted its platform and organized strategies to achieve its aims. One should remember that the UDF was the public arm of the mainly black-run ANC.

Whilst the labelling of protest groups as liberal or leftist in apartheid South Africa reflected the way the terms are used in political science, this has not been the case in Zionist Israel. The leftist group in South Africa adopted socialist political and economic views, while the majority of liberals, to a significant extent, advocated liberal political and economic policies. In Zionist Israel, the liberals are labelled as leftists or the left, for which there are two main reasons. First, stressing issues of human rights is associated, for the Israeli public, with being leftist or being critical towards Israel; nor are international law and human rights topics popular among the Israeli public. Second, on the political continuum, the liberals are located at the other end of the Zionist political spectrum vis-à-vis the extreme rightist groups. Thus they are seen as the left contrasting with the right, while both are Zionist and Jewish. In this context, one could argue that the socialist left, which is either non-Zionist or anti-Zionist, is considered very marginal or irrelevant.

The political platforms of the liberals evolved differently across the two cases. By the late 1970s and during the 1980s, a rift had occurred between the liberal groups in South Africa as the majority moved towards the inclusive universal platform of the UDF/ANC. This study labels them 'progressive liberals', while those who rejected the UDF platform and many of its strategies and maintained their earlier positions are labelled 'mainstream liberals'. Mainstream liberals stressed certain principles: e.g. by opposing what the government was doing and organizing against it in such fields as trade unions and forced removals; being defensive against violence and the violent overthrow of the state; being exploratory and co-operative with the reform initiatives of the government; and being innovative in putting forward new policies, especially in the fields of unemployment, housing and education. The progressives, however, moved far ahead of these principles by accepting notions of inclusivity and equal citizenship and giving up on the government.

While committed to the ideology of Zionism, the mainstream Israeli liberal groups continue to stress a security based two-state settlement that guarantees maximum gains for the state of Israel. The critical Zionist groups stress security, though less than the mainstream groups do, and are more vocal in criticizing governmental policies. They campaign for a better offer to be given to the Palestinians as part of a two-state settlement, describing it as a 'just peace'. It is important to note that disagreement over issues like borders, Jerusalem and right of return, is common among and between the two categories.

184 *Conclusion*

While the South African progressive liberals and the liberal critical Zionists (have) held clearer positions about the future peace settlement than have the mainstream liberals, the content of both positions is quite different. The progressive liberals spoke clearly about the need to dismantle the ideology and system of apartheid, and supported a 'one-person-one-vote' majority rule in a new united democratic and non-racial South Africa. They worked together and/or closely with the black-run UDF to achieve this goal. The critical Zionist groups in Israel do not question Zionism, the ideology in power, or the existing structure of power, but support a two-state settlement. They work on an ad hoc basis with Palestinian organizations when they agree on the aims behind a specific event, and on the strategies to be used in implementing it.

As such, South African protest developed into an inclusive form where, in the main, black and most white protest groups worked closely together to dismantle the apartheid system. There was no separate white lobby or movement. In the case of the Palestinian–Israeli conflict, protest is carried out along national lines. Nevertheless, joint actions are organized on an ad hoc basis, as noted earlier. Another way of putting it is that the political notion of inclusivity produced the strategy of joint struggle in South Africa. However, the notion of separation in the Israeli case has produced the tendency towards working separately. It has been generally agreed that each side will work with its own public and will work together when possible.

Besides the lack of a joint protest umbrella, an umbrella body for the Israeli protest groups themselves is also lacking. As discussed in Chapter 4, there are a number of reasons for this. First, the conflict has been addressed piecemeal. Second, there is lack of agreement as to what constitutes an acceptable end result. Third, there is considerable personal rivalry among leading figures. Even so, one could argue that there are two protest movements in Israel; one that is led by Peace Now on a sporadic basis, and the other an ad hoc movement that organizes critical Zionist groups and the leftists together whenever it is seen as necessary and possible.

In South Africa, the white liberal organizations, particularly the progressive ones, moved away from the political culture of the existing exclusive civil society at the time, and, to varying degrees, shifted towards the mainstream leftist politics led by the South African-resisting civil society. They were turning towards inclusivity and political equality, and away from the political values of the communitarian Volk. As discussed earlier, this shift was due to intermediate variables, and was different in content from that of Israeli liberal groups who left the loop of mainstream liberalism. The liberal critical Zionists remain entrenched within the values of the ideological communitarian consensus. However, they try to make changes in the political consensus by adopting more daring positions compared with the mainstream liberals; they do this out of national patriotism.

In both cases, the leftist groups and individuals differed in their positions over two substantive issues. Most leftists in apartheid South Africa adopted the position of the South African Communist Party, which believes in a united South

Africa that belongs to all equally, both black and white. In Zionist Israel, a big section of the Israeli left adopted the position of the Israeli Communist Party (ICP) which embraces the notion of separation, i.e. a two-state solution. The ICP was the first Israeli party to take up such a position. The South African leftists negated the legitimacy of the apartheid system altogether, whereas the Israeli left that was associated with the ICP did not question the legitimacy of the state upon establishment or later, although it eventually defined itself as non-Zionist.

The white South African leftists who joined the ANC, the SACP and their military wings, were greater in number (hundreds) than those in the case of Israel (a mere handful). It could be argued that this had a lot to do with how the two conflicts were framed in terms of their vision for a future settlement. In the South African case, the vision of the ANC succeeded over that of the National Party government, and the vision of a united non-racial and democratic South Africa won over the vision of the Bantustans. In the case of the Palestinian–Israeli conflict, the vision of the Israeli leftists[4] and liberals that was later adopted by the political centre, prevailed over that of the PLO. The two-state vision won over the vision of a secular democratic Palestine state.

In the Israeli case, the majority of Israeli groups that are liberal still see the Israeli government as the proper focus for their lobby for change, since it is regarded as the legitimate channel through which change can come. Only a very few non-Zionist groups, such as ICAHD and those on its left, have given up on lobbying the government. Some of them seek change through advocacy at the international level, hoping that pressure from outside might create a force for change. In the case of South Africa, by the mid-1980s the progressive liberals had abandoned the government and the whole political system, and instead sought change through working with the UDF. Even members of parliament, such as Drs Slabbert and Boraine from the Progressive Party, withdrew from the parliament and spoke publicly to the effect that opposition from within had no effect on producing change in South Africa. They found refuge instead in the civil-society sphere by establishing the Institute for a Democratic Alternative for South Africa (IDASA), and opening direct and public contact with the ANC. Both these and many other grassroots leaders and professional activists devised initiatives aimed at building an alternative means of addressing the existing power relations and presenting a new joint vision.

While the progressive liberals in South Africa stood firmly for non-violence, they were much more vocal in showing their understanding of why the blacks had resorted to violence. They blamed their own government for leaving the blacks without feasible options. This has not been the case among the liberals in Israel, whether mainstream or critical Zionist. Furthermore, both categories stressed security as a determining issue, but in different degrees. In South Africa, the progressive liberals perceived security as one of the results of an agreed-upon settlement.

Compared with the Israeli groups, the anti-militarism protest and the call for ending conscription in apartheid South Africa took daring and clearer positions and actions. The End Conscription Campaign, supported by many leading organizations and figures, led the campaign while working closely with the UDF. The Israeli groups that have worked on this issue have been divided by many initiatives and by various positions as to what to refuse, why, and for how long. In addition, their actions have been rather sporadic, while the South African campaign was constant until it was banned.

Issues of equality, justice, racism and truth, which are intrinsic components in processes of peace building have, to a large extent, been differently addressed in the two cases. For example, protest groups in apartheid South Africa admitted the existence of inequalities and called for equality, without delving into the nature of that proposed equality beyond the one-person-one-vote which, by the mid-1980s, had been accepted by the majority. In the case of Zionist Israel, the issue of equality has been used in relation to the rights of Palestinian citizens of Israel, but not in relation to those in the Occupied Palestinian Territories. Concerning the latter, mainstream Zionist groups avoid addressing the issue while a few critical Zionist groups mention it mainly on the slogan level but without discussing its details. The tiny anti-Zionist groups which adopt the principles of universal human rights and accept international law as a term of reference, believe in the inclusion of the principle of equality and consider it a prerequisite to achieving a just peace. Based on that they support the Palestinian right of return and a one-state solution.

Concerning the issue of justice, the mainstream and the progressive liberals agreed that the apartheid system was not just and should be dismantled. The progressives were more ready to discuss the details than were the mainstream groups who preferred not to do so. In the case of Israel, both liberal Zionist groups stress the just cause of Zionism and the state. The mainstream groups argue that an attainable justice can be agreed upon through a two-state settlement. They do not dig into the past before the 1967 war. However, in recent years, a few critical Zionist groups have started to make a link between the *Nakba* of 1948 and the 1967 war, and to discuss it. The majority avoids taking positions, while a few speak about the need to recognize a kind of responsibility for the refugee problem. As for the leftist anti-Zionist groups, they accept the Palestinian demand for justice in accordance with international law. Differences are also obvious concerning issues of racism and truth. For example, while apartheid was seen as a racist ideology by all South African protest groups, Zionism has been seen as such only by the anti-Zionists. Thus, the issue of racism is not discussed by most Israeli protest groups. As to truth, the Israelis preach two valid historical narratives or truths; something that was not the case in South Africa. More details are given in the Introduction of the book.

Second-track diplomacy meetings that were held in the case of South Africa had different content and outcomes from those of the Palestinian–Israeli meetings. In the former case, after five years of covert and public second-track diplomacy meetings, direct public negotiations between the formal leaderships took place in 1990. The agreements reached in the following four years, whether interim or final, were very similar to those that had been discussed and agreed upon in the informal meetings. Those meetings brought together members from the ANC's coalition, progressive liberals, and representatives of the business sector. The political framework for a new South Africa had by then been agreed upon – a united non-racial and democratic South Africa. Issues of how to achieve that goal, the future economic policies, the future policies on education, the rule of law, the whites' request for a bill of rights, and so on, were put up for discussion. The most difficult issue facing them at that point was the new South Africa's economic policy. During these meetings the whites argued against the nationalization of private property while the ANC watered down its socialist agenda. Eventually, the basic parameters were laid down for a power-sharing agreement, whereby the blacks would lead a majority rule political system and the whites would retain economic power.

In the case of the Palestinian–Israeli conflict, second-track diplomacy meetings were started in the mid-1970s by the leftists, and flourished over the years with the liberals. Though secret in the 1970s and most of the 1980s, they later became more open. From the beginning, both sides had different aims. Meetings did not start with a political phase in which a clear grand goal or framework was agreed upon, as was the case in South Africa. The conflict was addressed in piecemeal form, and in the process the asymmetry of power was reflected in the outcomes of these meetings, which produced the parameters of the Oslo Accords. They represented existing power relations and thus did not prepare the ground for a resolution capable of addressing past injustices and for moving ahead as separate but equal entities. The Oslo Accords aimed to produce peace by power,[5] by giving up international law as the term of reference.

The outcome parameters in the respective cases of second-track diplomacy reflect different processes and different power relations. The South African case reflects a shift in power[6] that did not occur in the Palestinian–Israeli case. This shift allowed for a structural change which made an inclusive political settlement possible. However, after almost thirty years no such shift has occurred in the Palestinian–Israeli case. One of the latest schemes, the 2003 Geneva Initiative which, for the first time, developed an almost detailed peace plan, again sought change by political compromise that would preserve the existing power structure. Peace Now members and others who were actively involved in negotiating the Geneva Initiative, used the old tactics of Oslo, which required the Palestinians to prove once again that they were partners for peace. As part of the outcome, the Palestinian participants publicly gave up the right of return and most of the land of occupied East Jerusalem, and accepted limited control over borders and air space. They also recognized the state of Israel as a Jewish state. As such, not only was the political product of Zionism recognized, but also Zionism itself.

Second-track diplomacy meetings have been looked at differently across the two divides and beyond. The radical leftists view/ed the parameters of the settlement in South Africa negatively, accusing the ANC leadership and its new elite of being misled by the articulate and well-educated white liberals. According to them, being 'misled' meant that they had sold out on the aims of the revolution by giving up socialism and popular democracy for a liberal procedural democracy. Based on this, they also accused them of perpetuating the status quo by replacing racial apartheid with economic apartheid. The white liberals and the mainstream left read the parameters differently, seeing them as providing the best possible scenarios and leading to the best possible settlement. In the case of the Palestinian–Israeli conflict, different meetings over the years produced a variety of results on similar and different agendas. The critics of these meetings argue that the Israeli participants, who are Peace Now political types, have promoted ideas that perpetuate the status quo or have bought time for the Israeli governments to protect Zionism, protect existing political structures, and continue with policies of expansion. Those who hold positive views about these encounters argue that they have promoted realistic compromises which are a necessity. For them, realpolitik means accepting Israel as it is and not challenging the asymmetry of power, as well as finding a compromise that will not endanger the long-term interests of Israel as a Jewish state.

While protest groups in both cases shared similar roles (as discussed in the previous sub-section), they also had different ones. To differing degrees, all white protest groups played a role in undermining the ideology of apartheid, thereby opening the door to addressing the existing power structure, and becoming part of the search for the alternative. It was an alternative that recognized existing racism, inequalities and injustices, and attempted to address them. As such, while they contributed on the one hand to the creation of a political rift within the white society, on the other, they contributed to the creation of a political environment where eventually a majority from both societies, white and black, accepted the deal agreed upon by both leaderships. Accepting the principle of universal rights, and coming closer to the inclusive platform of the oppressed, sent a significant message that future co-existence was possible. It shifted the political discourse from being based on white against black to being both against racialism and the system.

This has not been the case of the Israeli protest groups. Only the tiny radical leftists have tried to undermine the ideology of Zionism and have sought an inclusive settlement based on the principle of equal universal rights, arguing the need for radical change in the existing power structures. However, the majority, represented by mainstream and critical Zionists groups, has played a major role in keeping the ideology in power intact, and in preserving the unity of Israeli (Jewish) people around the idea of an exclusive Jewish state. Consequently, the conflict continues to be seen as Palestinian versus Israeli, and starting from 1967 has been addressed piecemeal and on a selective basis. Additionally, the ramifications that arose from the state being defined as Jewish, including existing 'legal' discrimination, denial for decades of the national right of the Palestinians, and the denial of, and/or the responsibility for, the right of return, were either ignored or justified. The asymmetry of power between the Israelis and the Palestinians was not discussed, and the aimed-for alternative was framed in line with the existing power structures and the long-term interests of the Jewish state. Ironically, the liberals and their roles have not been well received by the majority of Israeli Jewish society.

Compared with Israeli-Jewish protest groups, the South African groups represented wider sectors. For example, many universities, university teachers, writers, intellectuals, theatre groups and NUSAS (the main white student movement), were integral elements in the protest against apartheid. The role of NUSAS has no equivalent in the Israeli case. Also, while a number of universities stood publicly against apartheid and the system, none of the Israeli universities have yet stood formally and publicly against the occupation.

The Zochrot organization, too, has no equivalent in the South African case. As discussed earlier, the issue of historical narratives was not a core factor in the South African conflict, as it has been in the Israeli case. The establishment of Zochrot in 2003 reflects a newly realized awareness among a tiny number of Jewish–Israeli activists of the need to address past injustices inflicted on the Palestinian society in order to find a better future for both. As discussed earlier, Zochrot opens the file of Palestinian history before the 1948 war and the Palestinian *Nakba*, and makes it accessible to the Israeli society. It is a mission that is seen as very radical in the context of the Israeli political culture.

There is also no equivalent to the Israeli organization Peace Now as a supporter of war. In 2006, Peace Now gave unconditional backing to the war on Lebanon. Even some of its best-known members, who had become members of the Israeli cabinet representing the Labour Party, were either leaders in, or gave absolute support to the war, e.g. the defence and education ministers.

Many liberal Israeli protest groups have sought normalization with the Palestinian side and the Arab states before a settlement is reached and without committing themselves to a specific peace or end result. They argue that co-operation between both sides will eventually contribute to peace building. The case of South Africa represents a majority of liberals who worked together with the black majority towards achieving a clearly agreed-upon result that included dismantling the existing political system. By the 1980s, most liberals no longer sought to normalize the abnormal relations with the existing system.

Finally, political protest in apartheid South Africa reflected and polarized the existing ethnically based division of English-speaking versus Afrikaner. Most of those who joined and led from within the white protest realm were English-speaking. In the case of Zionist Israel, the (mainly) Ashkenazi members stressed the unity of the nation by preserving the ideological consensus. The author did not encounter any views that considered the Ashkenazi protest as a source for further polarization of Jewish ethnic divisions, e.g. Mizrahi Jews, Russian Jews, Ashkenazi Jews.

As well as the similarities and the differences between the two cases at the macro and micro levels, discussed in the previous section, this concluding comparative analysis sheds light on existing patterns. Examining existing patterns provides further insight into the analysis of the outcomes of this study. As noted earlier, a pattern is a form of relation that exists between a number of variables or issues over a period of time. It changes when change occurs in the balance of forces between the different variables involved. The two following sections present patterns that exist in each case and the shared patterns across the two cases.

Patterns specific to each case

The loss of legitimacy of the ideology in power created a new pattern of relations with the South African political system. As it happened, protest groups and other forces such as business sector initiatives, used the space of civil society in a more proactive manner to create change, which included changing the political system itself. Most protest groups developed more daring positions and roles that contributed to the idea of structural regime change. They contributed to the promotion of a political compromise that gives up the political system but protects other interests that the dominant side may have. This change in the pattern of relations was not possible without the effects of many of the intermediate variables, such as the strategies used by the ANC which produced a shift in power in its favour. The ANC's strategies undermined apartheid ideology internationally, made the country ungovernable, and led to economic sanctions that weakened the economy.

However, in the case of Israel, the pattern of relations between the political system and other societal spheres, including civil society, is still dominated by the hegemony of the political system and its ideology. The state is still the legitimate address for civil-society actors, including most protest groups. In addition, Zionism remains the backbone of the national Jewish consensus that unites the political right, centre and liberals (left as named by Israelis). The historic pattern is still solid.

Israeli protest groups have developed a sporadic or seasonal pattern of activism over the years. The size and visibility of protest activities has traditionally been associated with specific political developments or turning points, e.g. eruption of an Intifada, a war, or a military operation in which many Palestinians are killed. At times of relative calmness, some groups disappear for a while until an event sets the wheel of protest turning again, others minimize their activities and tone down their voices, while the rest might disappear forever. Along this seasonal pattern, many of the same strategies and tactics are constantly repeated.

The pattern of seasonal activism is quite noticeably linked to another pattern of relations. For more than two decades, liberal critical Zionists, and leftist non-Zionist and anti-Zionist protest groups, have developed a pattern for their joint work. They cluster on an ad hoc basis, without an ideological banner, to address issues of human rights and to perform solidarity activities with the Palestinians. They develop common grounds on a case-by-case basis.

Existing political divisions among the different Israeli protest groups have also produced another pattern that involves addressing the conflict in a vague and piecemeal way, or with what has been called 'constructive ambiguity'. Most groups developed into issue-oriented organizations where each believes that it contributes to peace but without defining the peace that all are striving for. This is why fragmentation of efforts has been one of the features of Israeli protest activism.

In contrast to the Israeli case, most white South African protest groups were, by the mid-1980s, acting in a pattern that addressed the conflict in a way that fed into the grand vision of the UDF/ANC – a united, non-racial and democratic South Africa. They planned their activities and strategies in a collective manner to meet this goal. In other words, the 1980s witnessed a change in the pattern of relations between white and black organizations. While most had initially worked separately, with the undermining of the ideology in power and the consequent political shift, more and more white protest groups moved closer to the politics of the oppressed and worked closely with the black majority towards a new agreed-upon vision. White–black antagonism was replaced by white and black antagonism to racialism.

Finally, the leftists in South Africa developed a pattern of relations with the state that was confrontational. They repudiated the system altogether and fought against it. The South African Communist Party was the leading power of the left and had very close connections with the ANC. Most leftists accommodated a white–black power-sharing compromise only as part of a final settlement. In the case of Israel, the pattern has been different. Most leftists in Zionist Israel have developed a pattern of relations with the state that is accommodating. They have run their opposition from within the system and have avoided the question of state legitimacy. This has mainly been because of the political positions of the Israeli Communist Party, which first signed the declaration of Israel's independence and then started to lean towards being a non-Zionist force.

Shared patterns across the two cases

Both ethnic-national states developed a relationship of hegemony with other societal spheres. This pattern has served the existence of the political system by providing ideological socialization and a consensus that fits with building and maintaining such ethnic-national projects. The interlocking relations between the different spheres since 1948, constituted in both cases a pattern that survived very well for decades. As noted earlier, in the case of apartheid South Africa it was weakened and later wrecked, but this has not been the case in Zionist Israel.

Because of this interlocking relationship, both civil societies and societies developed a pattern of relations with the state where both ended up feeding into each other in perpetuating the values of their exclusive ethnicities. While the state exercised hegemony in shaping the political culture or the moral order in the first place, it eventually became difficult for both to escape from the mindset of communitarianism and consensus of the 'tribe'. It became difficult for the state to manage a peace process without being afraid of domestic disapproval or even of disunity, e.g. the split in the national party over the reform policy in South Africa in the 1980s, the assassination of Rabin in 1996. As discussed earlier, a number of intermediate variables led to the weakening of this pattern of relations in the case of apartheid South Africa in the 1980s. This has not occurred in the Israeli case where domestic legitimacy has continued to be sought from within the moral order that evolved around Zionism.

As both conflicts became protracted and their impact became more obvious in terms of loss of lives, economic deterioration, and moral and image decline

192 *Conclusion*

(self-image and image to the outside world), more liberals (have) made shifts in their political positions and proposed more progressive political views that offer better compromise to the dominated side. In the case of the apartheid South Africa pattern, they took many steps towards an inclusive and universal rights-based settlement. In the case of Zionist Israel, they have moved towards admitting more Palestinian rights and offering a better deal in the framework of a two-state solution formula. As such, each case of protest stood/stands on a different side in the inclusivity versus exclusivity political continuum.

Relations between exclusive ideologies, protest activism and universal principles (such as equality, justice and anti-racism), make a certain pattern too. As long as exclusive ethnic ideologies are powerful and hegemonic, these principles are generally ignored, marginalized or addressed in a way that stresses or justifies a right to ethnic-national particularism and exclusivity. However, once the exclusive ideology is questioned, weakens, and gradually starts to lose its legitimacy, these principles become more present and meaningful in the political discourse of protest. Both cases fit with the first section of this pattern. However, over the years, the case of apartheid South Africa evolved in the direction of the second section of the pattern. To a great extent the old pattern still prevails in the case of Zionist Israel, but it is important to note that limited progress is occurring in the direction of the new pattern. This is because new organizations have begun to give up working according to the historic pattern, e.g. Zochrot and the Anarchists.

In both cases, the mainstream liberals set a pattern of relations with the state that is/was not confrontational but accommodating. Being pragmatic, gradualist and opportunistic, their opposition is carried out from within the system and the existing moral order, and they maintain this pattern to a point where they are often accused of perpetuating existing oppression and its structures.

Finally, this limited number of shared patterns raises the question of why they are so few. The main reason stems from the influence of the intermediate variables which change/d the pathways of protest in the two cases. As previously discussed, the nature of the two political systems at the macro level, and their relationship with their respective civil societies and the dominated side, has been very similar. However, the shift in power that occurred in apartheid South Africa over the years, as a result of the intermediate variables, created more differences between the two cases at the micro-level of protest. Consequently, different patterns evolved in each case, which is why the shared patterns are so few.

Further insights and lessons from these findings

The nature and number of similarities and difference at the macro and micro levels indicates that the two cases share substantive similarities in terms of exclusive ethnic ideologies, type of political system and civil societies. Both civil societies have been part-and-parcel of the national project and its survival. Their space functioned under the hegemony of the state, which constantly regenerated the ideology in power and its national moral order. Concerning the protest groups, the component of civil society examined in this book, the liberals constituted a majority in both cases. While a substantive shift occurred in the political platforms and roles of the liberals in apartheid South Africa during the 1980s, the change in views among the liberals in Israel has been limited. The South African liberals sought a joint future away from the apartheid ideology. The Israeli liberal groups continue to be tied to the national ideological consensus. Nonetheless, the mainstream and the critical Zionist groups differ over the degree to which the political consensus is to be challenged. As to the leftist protest groups, the majority in both cases differed in their political platforms and in many of their roles. This was due to the fact that in South Africa the leftists denied the system and developed a confrontational relationship with the political system, while most of the Israeli leftists have accommodated the political system and its ideology.

As mentioned earlier, many intermediate variables affected the development of politics, political platforms, and roles of protest groups in both cases. This is obvious in the patterns specific to each case (see pp. 190–191). For instance, the visions and strategies of both resistance movements, the ANC and the PLO, contributed to how both conflicts were eventually framed in terms of causes, nature and resolution. The ANC worked together with leftist and liberal whites, and at the international level,[7] to de-legitimize apartheid and was successful. The PLO failed to galvanize international forces and the Israeli liberals into de-legitimizing Zionism. Once this element of power was weakened in the case of apartheid South Africa, along with others, it was possible to find common ground on the causes, nature and vision for a solution. Most of the liberals and the leftists worked with the UDF/ANC for an inclusive settlement, and for a united non-racial democratic South Africa.

In the Israeli case, the Israeli framing succeeded, and a two-state formula that protects Israel's ideology and security has become dominant. This frame was originally initiated by the leftists, and later by the liberals, at times when the existence of a Palestinian nation was denied by the Israeli governments and the public. Based on this frame, most Israeli protest efforts have continued to be based on separate national lines, which can only be overcome on an ad hoc basis, and as deemed necessary at certain political moments. Different groups have had different views about the details of the best foreseeable settlement. Most have addressed the conflict bit by bit, and their efforts continue to be fragmented. In addition, most protest groups have failed to address the existing asymmetry of power for the last thirty years.

Being for a peace (in its different meanings and versions) based on exclusive Zionism made it inconceivable for most Israeli groups to include the universal principles of equality, justice and anti-racism as part of their political discourse for peace beyond the slogan level. The perceived particularism and uniqueness of the Israeli case prevailed over a self-critique of state history and the contradictory nature of the ideology in power. This made peace by territorial compromise the best and only option. The historical injustices inflicted on the Palestinians were either ignored and/or addressed superficially because they undermine the foundations of the state itself, its legitimacy, ideology, nature and future. Along the same line of thought, Israeli protest groups, by a vast majority, do not question the exclusivity of the state and the contradiction between being Jewish and democratic, and wanting peace with the indigenous population, the Palestinians. Most stress that the problem is only – or mainly – with the occupation of 1967, and that a two-state solution is the only workable and even just settlement. The latter requires the Palestinians to compromise over the land occupied in 1967 (which accounts for 22 per cent of mandatory Palestine), water, the right of return, Jerusalem and the sovereignty of a future Palestinian 'state' if it is to be established.

Thus, if one compares the two cases of protest groups in terms of using the space of civil society to create an alternative political discourse, to build a new pattern of relations with the state, build a new pattern of relations with civil-society groups on the other side of the divide, and send a new message to the dominated side, one can surely conclude that the white South African groups were many steps ahead. This concerned the content, the model of protest and subsequently the roles they played, which were substantive and daring in raising domestic and external consciousness about the ideology of apartheid and the existing political system. By building a new pattern of relations with the political system, they sent a message for a possible shared future. Eventually, they contributed to the dismantling of apartheid and to setting the parameters for the future settlement which, despite all its uncertainties, is far more progressive than any proposed by the Israeli liberal protest groups.[8] On the other hand, the author believes that white protest groups have not been fully credited for the roles they have played.

In the case of Israeli protest groups, the majority has been moving very slowly in making limited and sometimes merely cosmetic changes to the political national consensus. They have not altered the pattern of relations with the existing political system, and most groups, uncritically entrenched in Zionism, have continued to base their relations with the other side along separate national lines. Also, since they have addressed the conflict in a piecemeal fashion and sporadically, they have transmitted different messages to the Other. For many, co-existence and normalization within the existing asymmetry of powers has been perceived as possible. Based on the above, the author argues that most Israeli groups have had a significant role which involves protecting the ideology in power and the existing political system, and setting the parameters for political settlement/s that will constitute a 'cheap' peace for Israel. Such parameters do not include critiques of the exclusive and racist components of the state. On the contrary, they are stressed as correct and legitimate, as containing almost no recognition of responsibility for the eviction of Palestinian refugees, and offering no assessment of the ramifications of these two parameters on the past, present and future of the Palestinians inside the Green Line, in the OPT, and beyond.

If I am asked what the Palestinians could learn from the South African case, I would argue that they should ask themselves if their rights can be achieved as part of a deal with Zionism – an ideology that inevitably contradicts their rights as full citizens and as a free nation in its land. They should also ask if a two-state settlement can achieve equality and justice for the Palestinians in their different locations according to international law. As discussed above, a two-state solution will entail many compromises, and produce an autonomous administration rather than an independently viable state. If the Palestinians choose it as the 'realistic' option, they will most probably receive a settlement based on the parameters of the proposal/s of the liberal protest groups – if indeed there is a future Israeli government ready to apply a two-state vision. If they decide to revoke the two-state formula because it fails seriously to address their rights, then the one-state vision, as has been the case in South Africa, will be the option. To achieve this goal, they would then need to establish their strategies, one of which would deal with how to build alliances with Israeli protest groups.

Finally, the concluding analysis above answers the research hypothesis, and if the research argument is revisited, this study concludes that it is valid. In both cases, protest groups continue/d to constitute a limited section in both civil societies and represent/ed a small element in both societies. During the periods studied, the population of both ethnic states voted increasingly for right-wing parties. This led many commentators to argue that protest groups had failed to influence public opinion and to play a key role in peace building. The majority of scholars and activists encountered in this research have referred to the role of protest groups as limited, marginal, on the fringe, secondary, tiny, or a failure. Others, who do not agree with such conclusions, have two points of view. First, some of the roles played by both protest groups should not be underestimated even though criticisms can be made. Second, a handful would argue that the roles of protest groups have been substantial. This study reaches the same conclusion as this 'very few', but not necessarily for the same reasons.

It is important to note that those from the majority who describe the roles of protest groups as 'limited' or 'marginal', often represent an ambivalent analysis of the roles of protest groups. On one hand they mention that their role is tiny, but on the other they often speak of very important tasks performed by protest groups. For example, protest groups provide space for debate in which perspectives on reframing issues and solutions are shared across the divides. Protest groups also provide space to make personal contacts between influentials on both sides who, as noted, (have) managed to find various common political grounds across the two political divides.

In both cases, new elites associated with the 'peace industry' ended up filling half the cabinet posts in the new South African dispensation, and part of the PLO negotiating team and the PNA cabinet. In South Africa, many mentioned that white protest groups contributed to the development of a non-racial discourse and the dismantling of apartheid as an idea and as a system. In addition, their educational and awareness-raising programmes further undermined apartheid, locally and internationally, and contributed to shifting the political discourse towards unity and equality. In the case of Israeli protest groups, similar roles have been played but to achieve a different peace – one of power politics, not of the universal principles of human rights. The majority of Israeli protest groups have worked on making a shift in the Israeli political discourse, but from within the ideology in power. Their educational and awareness-raising programmes show the violations of human rights in the OPT on one hand, while advocating separation on the other. In their quest for peace, the principle of equality is either absent or marginal.

This study accepts the belief that apartheid did not collapse because of protest activism; it also believes that peace will not be achieved by the work of Israeli protest groups. However, it differs from the majority who consider the role of protest work as limited or marginal. Examining the politics, political platforms and roles of protest groups in apartheid South Africa, and the political settlement achieved there, proves that white protest activism was one of the few fundamental factors that brought about change. Even though a political settlement has not been achieved in the case of the Palestinian–Israeli conflict, a similar conclusion can be drawn there too. The findings of this comparative research prove that the 'limited' role/s of the protest groups have been significant in shaping the process[9] and the outcomes of both quests for peace.

When the domestic and external political conditions in South Africa became ripe for a settlement, the accumulated political developments in the protest space provided substantive contributions. They included an alternative political discourse and an agreed set of parameters for a future settlement. During the 1980s, most protest groups used their space in civil society to battle against the apartheid ideology and build alliances with the other side on the basis of a new moral order. They worked on shaping the end result and preparing the political environment for it. The necessary work was done, and when the 'magic moment'[10] or the 'tipping point' occurred, the environment was ready to take onboard the ideas agreed by both the progressive liberals and the mainstream left. In that moment, the perceived 'tiny' role or factor became just as significant as other fundamental factors. Hence, this study argues that such a role should not be ignored, underestimated or considered marginal.

In the case of Zionist Israel, the conditions or intermediate variables for reaching a settlement, domestic and external, have not so far matured. However, were a settlement to be reached now, with an Israeli government that would seriously adopt the two-state vision, political analysts argue that most probably it would be based on the political principles of the Geneva Initiative. It would entail normalization with Zionism and the obtaining of guarantees for Israel's security. These two conditions are not disputed by the liberal Zionist groups. On the contrary, both have been advocated for decades. Both mainstream and critical Zionist groups agree about them; they have Palestinian partners who are influential and who also accept them. If this is to be the case, the research argument is valid, since it concludes that their role is quite significant.

Contrary to the case of protest groups in apartheid South Africa, Israeli protest groups have, by a majority, fought the battle for changing peoples' ideas and convictions from within the ideology in power – Zionism and its moral order. They therefore continued to stand on the 'exclusivity' side of the political

Conclusion 197

continuum of exclusivity versus inclusivity. A new lexicon of compromise and a two-state idea entered the Israeli political discourse of consensus, and promoted a set of general parameters for a perceived peace. This protects the existing political system and power structure, and thus fails to provide an alternative moral order, similar to that seen in the South African case, where universal principles and rights were adopted as part of the peace-building discourse and process.

Hence, this political reality provides room to argue that the liberal Israeli protest groups, which constitute a majority, perpetuate the status quo of oppression and injustice; even though many of them report, and demonstrate against, violations of human rights in the Occupied Palestinian Territories. While they refuse or steer clear of addressing the existing structure of power that causes extensive violations of human rights, they continue to highlight the latter. This contradiction exists widely among Israeli liberals. It is based on, and similar to, the conviction that the state of Israel can be Jewish and democratic at the same time.

Appendices

1 South African interviewees

1. **Luckyboy Loyd Pitswane**, a black ANC activist in the struggle, currently the general secretary of YWCA in Garankuwa in South Africa. During 2005–2006 he went to Palestine for six months, as part of a YMCA joint programme. Interviewed in Beit Sahur – Bethlehem, 3 October 2005.
2. **Dr Richard Ballard**, Centre for Civil Society, School of Development Studies, University of KwaZulu-Natal, Durban, 27 February 2006.
3. **Dr Keith Gottschalk**, Head of Department, Political Studies, University of Western Cape, a white (Jewish) progressive liberal activist in the 1980s, Cape Town, 8 March 2006.
4. **Phyllis Naidoo**, an Indian veteran member of the South African Communist Party, Durban, 2 March 2006.
5. **Jeremy Routledge**, a veteran Quaker and member of the Quaker Peace Centre, Cape Town, 5 March 2006. A previous interview was conducted with him in Jerusalem on 19 September 2004 when he was a participant in the Ecumenical Accompaniment Programme in Palestine and Israel.
6. **Nozizwe Madlala-Routledge**, a black member of the ANC, the SACP, a Quaker and at the time a deputy defence minister. Interviewed briefly in Cape Town on 5 March 2006.
7. **Dr Salim Vally**, Senior Researcher in the School of Education, University of Witwartersrand, Johannesburg, a coloured activist associated with the Black Consciousness Movement and at present with the Socialist Movement, 22 February 2006.
8. **Makgane Thobejane**, a black ANC member, Director of the Strategic Support Unit, Office of the City Manager, City of Johannesburg, 20 February 2006.
9. **Erika Wessels**, an Afrikaner staff member of Black Sash in Cape Town, 7 March 2006.
10. **Bangani Ngeleza**, a black member of the ANC and an active member of the UDF in the 1980s. At present he co-operates with the Palestinian groups campaigning for boycotting Israel. He is the managing director of Bangi and Associates in Johannesburg, 24 February 2006.

11 **Yazir Henri** (coloured), ex-member of the MK, the military wing of the ANC and a member of the SACP, Cape Town, 6 March 2006.
12 **Dr Caroline White**, an English-speaking activist in the United Women organization and Black Sash in the 1980s, a lecturer in the University of Natal from 1997–2000. At present lives in London, 29 January 2006.
13 **Frans Cronje**, Researcher, South African Institute of Race Relations, Johannesburg, 23 February 2006.
14 **Dr Heribert Adam**, a political sociologist at Simon Fraser University in Vancouver who also teaches at the University of Cape Town, interviewed in Cape Town on 7 March 2006.
15 **Professor Hermann Giliomee**, Afrikaner political scientist, former lecturer at the University of Cape Town, and member of board at the SAIRR from 1995–1997, lives in Stellenbosch, 10 March 2006.
16 **Heidi Grunebaum**, a Jewish activist for peace and social justice, Cape Town, 6 March 2006.
17 **Na'eem Jeenah**, head of the anti-censorship programme at the Freedom of Expression Institute, Johannesburg, a coloured ex-activist in the Black Consciousness Movement and at present associated with the Socialist Movement, Johannesburg, 23 February 2006.
18 **Dr John Greene**, member of the Cape Town Democrats in the 1980s, lecturer at the University of Cape Town University, Cape Town, 7 March 2006.
19 **Gilad Stern**, activist in NUSAS in the 1970s, Jewish liberal who worked for the Progressive Party, at present a businessman, Cape Town, 10 March 2006.
20 **Sarah Carneson**, a white (Jewish) member of the Communist Party, Cape Town, 5 March 2006.
21 **Dr Jon Hyslop**, University of the Witwatersrand, Johannesburg, 20 February 2006.
22 **Helen Suzman**, a prominent (Jewish) leader of the Progressive Party for many years. She is famous for challenging apartheid policies inside the Parliament, Sandton, Johannesburg, 21 February 2006.
23 **Sheena Dunkan**, President of Black Sash during the 1980s and current member of Black Sash Board of Trustees, interviewed by the researcher in Johannesburg on 24 February 2006.
24 **Patrick Craven**, a white member and magazine editor at the Congress of South African Trade Unions (COSATU), Johannesburg, 21 February 2006.
25 **Stephen Boshoff**, an Afrikaner who joined the ANC in the 1980s, at present the Executive Director of Strategy and Development in the City of Cape Town, interviewed in Cape Town, 7 March 2006.
26 **Brett Davidson**, (white) manager of all media groups in IDASA since 2000, Cape Town, 10 March 2006.
27 **Mark Sweet**, a white member of the ANC since 1977. At present, he is head of the ANC research unit, Cape Town, 8 March 2006.

28 **Professor John Dugard**, UN Special Rapporteur to the Occupied Palestinian Territories. Interviewed in Jerusalem, 29 June 2005.
29 **Roland Hunter**, a white member of the ANC who spied for the ANC on SADF military operations in the early 1980s. Jailed for five years (1983–1989) and is now Director of Revenue for the City of Johannesburg; interviewed by the researcher in Johannesburg on 22 February 2006.
30 **Razia Saleh**, Coordinator of the ANC Archives, Johannesburg, 21 February 2006.
31 **Eddie Makue**, Director of Justice Ministries at the South African Council of Churches (SACC), Johannesburg, 24 February 2006.
32 **Bernard Sponge**, retired veteran member of the SACC, Johannesburg, 24 February 2006.
33 **David Schmidt**, a white member of the ANC, UDF, ECC and former staff member of IDASA (1990–1996), interviewed by the researcher in Cape Town on 9 March 2006.
34 **Sue Briton**, a founding member of the End Conscription Campaign, Durban, 28 February 2006.
35 **Pascal P. Moloi**, a black member of the ANC, former member of NUSAS and at present City Manager of Johannesburg, 20 February 2006.
36 **Judge Albie Sachs** of the Constitutional Court, Johannesburg, interviewed in London on 27 April 2006.
37 **Rashid Seedat**, (colored) member of the ANC, Director of the Corporate Planning Unit, City of Johannesburg, 21 February 2006.
38 **Farid Esack**, a South African Muslim theologian and ex-activist, Toronto, 28 October 2005.
39 **Bhabha Muhamed**, an Indian South African, teacher development adviser at Oxfam Quebec, and anti-apartheid activist. Interviewed in Jerusalem, 24 September 2004.
40 **Sisa Ncwana**, Representative of South Africa in Palestine, Jerusalem, 19 October 2005.
41 **Joan McGregor**, (white South African) Trainer and Learning Co-ordinator, RTC (Responding to Conflict), Birmingham, UK. She was an activist in the SACC and the UDF during the 1980s, interviewed in Jerusalem on 3 October 2005.
42 **Dr Frene Ginwala**, Trustee, Nelson Mandela Foundation, leading ANC member in exile and Speaker of the Parliament after the 1994 elections, interviewed in Istanbul on 26 July 2005.
43 **Dr John Lloyd**, lecturer in Law Department at University of Exeter, UK, member of banned Liberal Party, left South Africa in the 1960s and since then lives in England, interviewed by the researcher on 19 December 2005.
44 **Gillian Slovo**, a writer, daughter of the late Joe Slovo, leader of the SACP for decades and later a minister in the Mandela cabinet. Interviewed by phone by the researcher on 14 November 2005.

2 Israeli interviewees

1. **Reuven Kaminer**, ex-member of the Israeli Communist Party, member of the New Left (Siah) in 1968, a Marxist who is active in Peace Now, interviewed twice in Jerusalem, 27 September 2005 and 6 October 2005.
2. **Gila Svirsky**, a veteran Women in Black activist, member of the Coalition of Women for Peace, former director of Bat Shalom and active board member of B'tselem, Jerusalem, 18 February 2005.
3. **Judy Blanc**, an Israeli veteran peace activist who is currently active in Women in Black, Bat Shalom, Coalition of Women for Peace, Jerusalem, August 2004.
4. **Professor Moshe Machover**, an anti-Zionist Israeli, academic at Kings College London, interviewed by email on 23 July 2006 and in person in London on 23 August 2006.
5. **Khulood Badawi**, a leading activist in Ta'aush, a Palestinian citizen of Israel, field researcher in ACRI (the Association for Civil Rights in Israel), Jerusalem, 1 March 2005.
6. **Molly Maleker**, director of Bat Shalom, Jerusalem, 26 September 2004.
7. **Debby Lerman**, a member of Matzpen, Bat Shalom, Coalition of Women for Peace and Women in Black, Jerusalem, 4 September 2004.
8. **Neta Rotem**, a member of New Profile who used to be a member of the Sheministem, interviewed in Jerusalem on 3 March 2005.
9. **Yehudith Harel**, a veteran activist who moved from Peace Now to Gush Shalom and at present supports a one-state solution, Jerusalem, 8 August 2005.
10. **Galia Golan**, a member of the decision-making core group in Peace Now, and member of the board of Bat Shalom, Jerusalem, 6 July 2005.
11. **Amit Leshem**, a member of Peace Now since 1982, left Labour Party for Yahad party in 2000, at present works at Van Leer Jerusalem Institute as an initiator for joint Palestinian–Israeli projects, Jerusalem, 29 August 2004.
12. **Rabbi Arik Asherman**, the executive director of Rabbis for Human Rights, Jerusalem, 5 September 2004.
13. **Wafa Srur** and **Rabah Halabi**, School of Peace at Neve Shalom, Jerusalem, (joint interview), 10 October 2005.
14. **Uri Avnery**, the leader of Gush Shalom, Tel Aviv, 28 September 2005.
15. **Hussam Abu Baker**, Director of programmes and initiatives at the Abraham Fund Initiatives, 5 October 2005.
16. **Jaber 'Asaqleh**, the director of Palestinian projects in Shatil – a programme of the New Israel Fund, Jerusalem, 21 June 2005 and 26 June 2005.
17. **Jeff Halper**, Co-ordinator of the Israeli Committee Against House Demolitions, Jerusalem, 30 August 2004 and 25 February 2005.
18. **Angela Godfrey-Goldstein**, the Israeli Committee against House Demolitions, involved in planning and guiding political tours in the OPT, Jerusalem, 1 September 2004.
19. **Shimon Tzabar**, ex-member of the Israeli Communist Party, an anti-Zionist who left Israel in 1967, London, 5 August 2006.

202 *Appendices*

20 **Ilan Pappé**, Senior Lecturer in the Department of Political Science in Haifa University, Jerusalem, 28 August 2005.
21 **Dror Etkes**, Co-ordinator of Settlements Watch in Peace Now, Jerusalem, 20 June 2005.
22 **Michael Warschawski**, Co-chair of the Alternative Information Centre, Jerusalem, 1 March 2005 and 22 July 2005.
23 **Dr Ron Pundak**, Director General of the Peres Centre for Peace, Tel Aviv, 10 October 2005.
24 **Mossi Raz**, General Secretary of Peace Now from 1994–2000. Recently Deputy Executive director of Givat Haviva, Givat Haviva, 18 September 2005.
25 **Shiri Iram**, ex-employee of Peace Now, Jerusalem, 28 September 2004.
26 **Dr Uri Davis**, an anti-Zionist political scientist, a member of Fateh movement and a member of Palestine National Council (interviewed by phone), 20 August 2006.
27 **Yitzhak Frankintile**, Chairman of Arik Institute, Jerusalem, 19 October 2005.
28 **Stav Adivi**, board member of ICAHD in Jerusalem and staff member of ICAHD in the US, interviewed in Toronto, 30 October 2005.
29 **Hanna Aviram**, a leading member of New Profile, Jerusalem, 14 July 2005.
30 **Eitan Bronstein**, director of Zochrot, Tel-Aviv, 1 September 2005.
31 **Eitan Reich**, Resources Co-ordinator in Zochrot, Tel-Aviv, 1 September 2005.
32 **Eli Fabrikant**, a member of the Anarchists Against the Wall, Jerusalem, September 2005.
33 **Ilan Halavi**, an Israeli Jew who is a member of Fateh, Palestinian ministry for foreign affairs, Ramallah, 17 September 2005.
34 **Dr Naomi Chazan**, political scientist, member of Meretz Party and ex-member of Knesset for Meretz Party, member of board of Bat Shalom, Jerusalem, 9 August 2005.
35 **Dr Benjamin Gidron**, Director of the Israeli Centre for Third Sector Research, Ben Gurion University of the Negev, Be'er Al Sabe', 9 October 2005.
36 **Binjamin Bugrund**, a Jewish South African who was an anti-apartheid activist and journalist. Moved to Israel in 1997 and initiated the Centre for Social Concern, of which he is the director, Jerusalem, 9 June 2004.
37 **Imad Ya'qup Shaqur**, an adviser to Yasser Arafat on Israeli Affairs from 1981–2004, a Palestinian citizen of Israel, 5 September 2004.
38 **Arabiyah Mansour**, a Palestinian citizen of Israel, ex-member of Hadash, ex-member of the National Coalition party (Tajamu'), member of Bat Shalom, Jerusalem, 1 August 2005.
39 **Teddy Katz**, leading member of Gush Shalom, Barcelona, 23 June 2004 (he and the researcher were speakers at the Barcelona Social Forum).

3 Palestinian interviewees who are/were involved in joint initiatives

1. **Nassar Ibrahim**, co-ordinator of *Ru'ya Ukhra* and co-editor of *News from Within*, both published by the Alternative Information Centre which is an Israeli Palestinian anti-Zionist organization, 11 June 2005.
2. **Dr Sami Udwan**, staff member in the Department of Education, Bethlehem University, Co-Director of the Peace Research Institute in the Middle East (PRIME), a joint Palestinian–Israeli research centre focusing on education. Interviewed in Bethlehem on 12 September 2005.
3. **Dr Salim Tamari**, Director of Institute of Jerusalem Studies, Ramallah, 15 September 2004.
4. **Afif Safiah**, Head of the Palestinian Representative Office in London, 25 April 2005.

4 International interviewees

1. **Dr Mushtaq Husain Khan**, Senior Lecturer at SOAS, University of London, interviewed in Jerusalem, 7 February 2005 and on 23 April 2005 in London. He has researched Palestinian development versus Israeli strategies.
2. **Professor Herbert Kelman**, an American Jew, director of the International Conflict Analysis and Resolution Program in Harvard University, Jerusalem, 9 June 2004.
3. **Paul Usiskin**, an English Jew, leading member of Peace Now branch in London, London, 24 April 2005 .
4. **Dr Raphael Ezekiel**, a Jewish American, Senior Research Scientist at Harvard Injury Control Research Centre, member of Brit Tzedek organization in the US, Jerusalem, 12 September 2004.

5 Two versions of the officers' letter (referred to in Chapter 5) that led to the establishment of the Peace Now protest group

Below are two texts of the same letter: one version is presented in Reuven Kaminer's book *The Politics of Protest*, and the second is the version that appears on the website of Peace Now. Kaminer refers to a Peace Now pamphlet issued in 1979 where he compares the Hebrew version with his English one.

The first is Kaminer's authorized version:

> This letter is sent by citizens of Israel who serve as reserve officers and soldiers.
>
> It is with a *heavy heart* that we write these words to you. In these days – when for the first *time new vistas are opening* up the state of Israel, for a life of peace and cooperation in the region – we feel duty bound to call upon you to refrain from action which *might become a source of grief for generations to come, for our people and our state.*

204 *Appendices*

> A sense of deep anxiety prompts us to address you. *A government which would prefer Israel with the borders of a "Greater Israel" over Israel's peaceful existence* on the basis of good relations with its neighbors arouses in us severe apprehension. A government which would prefer the establishment of settlements across the "green line" to achieving an end to the historic conflict and the establishment of normal relations, **would disseminate doubt about the justice of our cause**. Government policy leading to the **domination** over one million Arabs would probably impair the Jewish democratic character of the state and would make it difficult for us to *identify with the fundamental path* of the state of Israel.
>
> We are fully aware of the state's security needs and of the difficulties on the path of peace. Nonetheless, we know that *genuine security is possible only with the advent of peace.* The strength of the Israel Defense forces is in the identification of its soldiers *with the fundamental path* of the State of Israel.
>
> ***We call upon you to choose the path of peace, and by this choice, to reinforce our faith in the justice of our cause.***[1]

The second text appears on the website of Peace Now (as accessed on 18 April 2005):

> Citizens that also serve as soldiers and officers in the reserve forces are sending this letter to you. The following words are *not written with a light heart.* However at this time when *new horizons* of peace and cooperation are for the first time being *proposed* to the State of Israel, we feel obliged to call upon you to prevent taking any steps that could *cause endless problems to our people and our state.*
>
> We are writing this with deep anxiety, as a *government that prefers the existence of the State of Israel within the borders of "Greater Israel" to its existence in peace* with good neighborliness, will be difficult for us to accept. A government that prefers existence of settlements beyond the Green Line to elimination of this historic conflict with creation of normalization of relationships in our region **will evoke questions regarding our path we are taking**. A government policy that will cause a continuation of **control** over million Arabs will hurt the Jewish-democratic character of the state, and will make it difficult for us to *identify with the path* of the State of Israel.
>
> We are aware of the security needs of the State of Israel and the difficulties facing the path to peace. But we know that *true security will only be reached with the arrival of peace.* The power of the IDF is in the identification of its soldiers *with the path* of the State of Israel. 348 signatures. March, 1978.

A quick comparison between the two texts, show how different the translations are. Today, Peace Now would not accept any public political discussion on the legitimacy of the cause of Zionism. It would not challenge the fundamental path of the state. It would not argue that Israel could be blamed for the continued conflict. Peace Now has become more cautious with its wording.

6 The different categories for South African white protest groups and individual activism and lists of organizations/groups that belong to each (as developed in this study)

Table A.1 The different categories for South African white protest groups and individual activism and lists of organizations/groups that belong to each (as developed in this study)

1 Liberal groups	2 White individuals in leftist resistance groups (black run):
	2 They joined in their personal capacities the:
	African National Congress
	South African Communist Party
	United Democratic Front
	Congress of South African Trade Unions
	Socialist groups on the left of the SACP, e.g. Trotskyist

1A Mainstream liberal groups
South African Institute of Race Relations (SAIRR)
The Urban Foundation
Association of South African Champers of Commerce, (Assocom)
The South Africa Foundation
The Steel and Engineering Industries Federation of South Africa

1B Progressive liberal groups
The National Union of South African Students (NUSAS)
Black Sash (BS)
The End Conscription Campaign (ECC)
The Five Freedom Forum (FFF)
The Institute of Democratic Alternative for South Africa (IDASA)
The Christian Institute for Southern Africa (CISA)
The Centre for Inter-group Studies or Centre for Conflict Resolution (CCR)
The Cape Town Democrats
Youth Christian Workers
The Civil Rights League
The Conscientious Objector Support Groups
The Christian Institute for Southern Africa
Johannesburg Democratic Action Committee (JODAC)
The Youth Congresses

7 The different categories of Israeli (Jewish) protest groups and individual activism and lists of organizations that belong to each (as developed in this study)

Table A.2 The different categories of Israeli (Jewish) protest groups and individual activism and list organizations that belong to each (as developed in this study)

1 Liberal Zionist groups	2 Leftist protest organizations/groups	3 Israeli individuals who joined the PLO
	Alternative Information Centre	A dozen over the years
	The Anarchists	
	Zochrot	
	Movement Against Apartheid in Palestine	
	Matzpen (not active as a group at present)	
	Shararah (not active as a group at present)	
	Neturei Karta (anti-Zionist religious group)	
	A few academics and journalists	
1A Mainstream Zionist groups		
Peace Now		
The Economic Co-operation Foundation		
The Peres Peace Centre		
The Israeli side of the Geneva Initiative		
The Four Mothers		
The Council for Peace and Security		
Arik Institute		
The Israeli side of Ayalon–Nesseibeh plan		
1B Critical Zionist groups		
Gush Shalom		
Bat Shalom		
Women in Black		
New Profile		
Yesh Gvul		
The Refusniks		
The Israeli side of the Palestinian–Israeli Joint Action Committee		
The Israeli Committee Against House Demolishing		
Ta'aush		
Coalition of Women for Peace		
Courage to Refuse		
Machsom Watch		
Committee for Israeli–Palestinian dialogue		
Campus LoShotek		

8 The different lists of categories of South African protest groups as classified by Knox and Quirk

Table A.3 Peace organizations in 1980s South Africa

Peace as 'absence of war'	*Exposing facts*	*Peace with justice*
Centre for Conflict Resolution Quaker Peace Centre Independent Mediation Service of South Africa	South Africa Institute for Race Relations Centre for Policy Studies	UDF Affiliates Christian Institute South Africa Catholic Bishops Conference South Africa Council of Churches National Union of South Africa Students National Education Crises Centre National Medical and Dental Association Legal Resources Centre Black Sash Five Freedoms Forum Institute for a Democratic Alternative For South Africa

Source: Knox and Quirk (2000: 165).

9 The different lists of categories of South African protest groups as classified by Gidron *et al.*

Table A.4 The leading peace and conflict-resolution organizations in apartheid South Africa

Organization	Acronym	Dates of existence
South African Institute of Race Relations	SAIRR	1929–
Black Sash		1955–
Justice and Peace Commission, SACBC	J&P	1967–
Centre for Intergroup Studies	CIS	1968–
End Conscription Campaign	ECC	1983–1994
Independent Mediation Service of South Africa	IMSSA	1984–2000
Institute for a Democratic Alternative for South Africa	Idasa	1986–
Koinonia Southern Africa	KSA	1986–1992
Project for the Study of Violence	PSV	1988–
Quaker Peace Centre	QPC	1988–

Source: Gidron *et al.* (2002: 72).

Table A.5 The leading anti-apartheid non-governmental organizations in apartheid South Africa

Organization	Acronym	Date formed
National Union of South African Students	Nusas	1924
SA Council on Higher Education	Sached	1959
South African Council of Churches	SACC	1968
Centre for Applied Legal Studies	CALS	1978
Lawyers for Human Rights	LHR	1979
Legal Resources Centre	LRC	1979
National Medical and Dental Association	Namda	1981
Organization for Alternative Social Services for SA	Oasssa	1981
Transvaal Rural Action Committee	TRAC	1983
Five Freedoms Forum	FFF	1986
National Education Crisis Committee	NECC	1986
Human Rights Commission	HRC	1988

Source: Gidron *et al.* (2002: 78).

10 The ECC's launching declaration and its list of supporters

TOWARDS A JUST PEACE IN OUR LAND

A Declaration to End Conscription

We live in an unjust society where basic human rights are denied to the majority of the people.

We live in an unequal society where the land and wealth are owned by the minority.

We live in a society in a state of civil war, where brother is called on to fight brother.

We call for an end to conscription.

Young men are conscripted to maintain the illegal occupation of Namibia, and to wage unjust war against foreign countries.

Young men are conscripted to assist in the implementation and defence of apartheid policies.

Young men who refuse to serve are faced with the choice of a life of exile or a possible six years in prison.

We call for an end to conscription.

We believe that the financial cost of the war increases the poverty of our country, and that money should rather be used in the interests of peace.

We believe that the extension of conscription to coloured and Indian youth will increase conflict and further divide our country.

WE BELIEVE THAT IT IS THE MORAL RIGHT OF SOUTH AFRICANS TO EXERCISE FREEDOM OF CONSCIENCE AND TO CHOOSE NOT TO SERVE IN THE SADF.

WE CALL FOR AN END TO CONSCRIPTION

WE CALL FOR A JUST PEACE IN OUR LAND

Figure A.1 The ECC's launching declaration.

ECC MEMBER ORGANIZATIONS
Anglican Board of Social Responsibility
Black Sash
Catholic Justice and Peace
Catholic War and Peace
Civil Rights League
Conscientious Objectors Support Group
Methodist Christian Citizenship Department
National Union of South African Students
The Ecumenical Action Movement (TEAM)
United Democratic Front – Claremont, Gardens and Observatory area committees
University of Cape Town Students Representative Council
Western Province Council of Churches
Women's Movement for Peace
Detention Action Committee (observer)
United Women's Organization (observer)

Over forty organizations have endorsed the declaration. Besides the above these include:

South African Institute of Race Relations (Western Cape)
South African Council of Churches
Evangelical Lutheran Church
United Congregational Church of South Africa
Quaker Church
National Catholic Federation of Students
Congress of South African Students
Cape Areas Housing Action Committee
Cape Youth Congress
Organisation of Appropriate Social Services in South Africa

A range of prominent individuals have also endorsed the ECC declaration. Besides those appearing at the press conference, these include:

Revd Alan Boesak
Sir Richard Luyt
Bishop Orsmond
Dr Margaret Nash
Prof. David Welsh
Prof. Francis Wilson
Dr Oscar Wollheim
Revd David Russell
Mr Peter Moll
Mrs Noel Robb
Mrs Di Bishop, MPC
Mr Brian Bishop
Mr Keith Gottschalk

Figure A.2 A list of the ECC's supporting member organizations.

Notes

Introduction

1 "I am Prepared to Die", Nelson Mandela's statement from the dock at the opening of the defence case in the Rivonia Trial, Pretoria Supreme Court, 20 April 1964. Online, available at: www.anc.org.za/ancdocs/history/rivonia (accessed 28 May 2007).
2 Lederach (2005: 33).
3 Knox and Quirk (2000: 24–28). It should be noted that Knox and Quirk have applied the Lederach peace-building model; they conclude that the case of the Israeli peace-building process has been far behind the South African case, and that it has not reached the transition phase (pp. 210–215). In the case of South Africa, they maintain that the reconciliation process has not been successful.
4 Azar and Burton (1986: 92–97).
5 Bell (2002: 15).
6 Smith (2000: 15–20).
7 Vickery (1974: 309–328). Vickery argues that 'Masters' democracy' is that of Herrenvolk democracy. It is a regime "democratic for the master race but tyrannical for the subordinate groups". It is authoritarian vis-à-vis the Other but can be very egalitarian towards its own group. It enforces race and class markings.
8 Pennings *et al.* (2006: 35).
9 Burnham *et al.* (2004: 35–36).
10 Ibid., pp. 45–46.
11 Silbergh (2001: 16–17).
12 A 'magical moment' is a point in time when conditions become ripe for enforcing change that can culminate in a peace agreement. This happens when change in domestic power relations meets with change at the international level, e.g. the fall of the Berlin Wall. This term was used by Knox and Quirk (2000: 166), who refer to Habib and his analysis of the change in the internal balance of power in South Africa that allowed for a settlement to be achieved. The same idea of ripeness of conditions is also discussed by Yaacove Bar-Siman-Tov in "Peace Policy as Domestic and Foreign Policy: the Israeli Case" (in Sofer, 2001: 27–28). Paul R. Pillar also discusses the issue of ripeness but from another angle – the timing factor vis-à-vis readiness to negotiate (1983: 53–57).
13 The elite referred to in this context includes persons who have had leading roles in churches and influential NGOs, ex-leading members of the ANC who nowadays hold prominent positions in the public sphere, prominent academics, and (ex) members of parliament. They are influentials in shaping public discourse and are sometimes able to influence government policies. Because of their influence, some have recognized status at the international level.
14 The concept of civil society is briefly explored in Chapter 2.

15 Rossi *et al.* (1979). Comprehensive evaluation of social programmes includes: programme planning questions, programme monitoring questions, impact assessment questions and economic efficiency questions (p. 33).
16 Silbergh (2001: 31–32).
17 Landman (2003: 55).
18 Ibid., p. 53.
19 With regard to the role of morality, the realist stands at the other end from the idealist. The idealist emphasizes morality as a major determining factor in deciding what is equal and just, a position that the realists consider illusionary. Raymond Aron argues that there are two reasons behind the realists' viewpoint: first, the reality of international politics is that of power politics, where the main role of statesmen is to protect a state's national interest and to consider whatever relative morality a state is capable of. Second, if idealism takes the path of deciding good and evil, it falls into the trap of power politics since it takes the role of punishing evil and supporting good, during which it might go to extremes. See Aron (2003: 584, 585).
20 In this context, the meaning of power exceeds that of political, military and economic power to that of ideas, arguments, morality and national pride. For the Israeli side the struggle for power included protecting the ideology of the Zionist claim to the moral high ground, control of land and imposing its political hegemony. For the Palestinians, it meant recognition of injustices inflicted on them, claim to a higher moral ground and recognition of being a nation with its right to self-determination.
21 Sparks (1995: 9).
22 The researcher has divided white South African protest groups into mainstream liberals and progressive liberals. She also highlights the role of white activists in leftist black-run groups. A detailed account of their politics, political platforms and roles is examined in Chapter 3.
23 The researcher has divided Israeli (Jewish) protest groups into mainstream Zionist, critical Zionist and leftist. The latter are non-Zionists or anti-Zionist. A detailed account of their politics, political platforms and roles is examined in Chapter 4.
24 Based on interviews with Mossi Raz, Galia Golan and Ron Pundak
25 "Equality", *Stanford Encyclopedia of Philosophy*. Online, available at: www.plato.stanford.edu/entries/equality (accessed 27 September 2006).
26 Ibid.
27 Ibid.
28 Ibid.
29 "Against Equality", from *Philosophy*, Vol. 40, 1965, pp. 296–307, reprinted in H. Bedau, ed., *Justice and Equality*, Prentice-Hall, 1971, pp. 138–151. Online, available at: www.users.ox.ac.uk/-jrlucas/libeqsor/equality (accessed 27 September 2006).
30 Michelle Maiese, "Type of Justice". Online, available at: www.beyondintractability.org/essay/types_of_justice (accessed 16 May 2007).
31 Ibid.
32 Rawls (1999: 52–53).
33 'Fair' or 'fairness' is associated with impartiality. The word 'fair' is perceived as less demanding (legally and politically) than the word 'justice'.
34 McLean and McMillan (2003: 287).
35 Based on an interview, held in Jerusalem, 12 September 2004, with Dr Raphael Ezekiel, an American psychologist and member of the Brit Tzedek organization, He was referring to an African-American definition of racism.
36 Blackburn (1996: 317).
37 McLean and McMillan (2003: 453).
38 The United Nation International Convention on the Elimination of all Forms of Racial Discrimination, article 1. Online, available at: www.ohchr.org/english/law (accessed 10 October 2006).
39 Bishara (2001: 132).

Notes 213

40 A number of members of ICAHD and New Profile would hold such a position.
41 Theories of Truth. Online, available at: www.thymos.com/science/truth (accessed 25 September 2006).
42 Coherence theory is based on the premise that one's proposition has to be in coherence with the system of beliefs that exists.
43 Pragmatism theory argues that truth depends on its own effectiveness and that agreed-upon truths reflect agreement among humans, not agreement with reality.
44 Semantic truth theory argues that truth can be achieved in language by defining a true statement in relation to that in another language.
45 For the idealist, truth is inside us.
46 Heidegger maintains that truth is freedom that means attunement with the world.
47 Functionalist theory argues that truth is based on common sense where different statements can all be true without being true in the same way, producing plurality of truth.
48 *Stanford Encyclopedia of Philosophy*. Online, available at: www.plato.stanford.edu/entries/truth-correspondence (accessed 31 May 2007). Correspondence theory explicitly embraces the idea that truth consists of a relation to reality or portion of reality.
49 "Constructivist Epistemology". Online, available at: www.stemnet.nf.ca/~elmurphy/emurphy (accessed 2 May 2007). For the constructivists, truth is accorded only to those constructions on which most people of a social group agree. In the words of other sources, truth is constructed in social processes through power struggles within a community.
50 "What is the Truth of Simulation". Online, available at: www.jasss.soc.surrey.ac.uk (accessed 2 May 2007). Consensus theory discusses communicative agreements in assessing the value of truth. For this, truth simulation relies fundamentally on its structure and its output being acceptable for rationally thinking people. Other sources put it in simpler words: "whatever is agreed upon".
51 "The Deflationary Theory of Truth", *Stanford Encyclopedia of Philosophy*. Online, available at: www.plato.stanford.edu/entries/truth-deflationary (accessed 22 May 2007). According to the deflationary theory of truth, to assert that a statement is true is just to assert the statement itself. Truth has no nature for the deflationist, beyond what is captured in ordinary claims such as that 'snow is white' is true just in case snow is white.
52 Kenneth Barton and Ingrid Scheibler, "Saving Isaac: Nietzsche and Kierkegaard on Religion". Online, available at: www.kennethbarton.com/fun/religion (accessed 31 May 2007).
53 "Michel Foucault: Truth and Power", Writings. Online, available at: www.wdog.com/rider/writings/foucault.htm (accessed 20 May 2007).
54 Terry Greenblatt, "Civil Society as a Partner in Promoting Peace in the Middle East", paper at a United Nations conference on The Role of Civil Society in Promoting a Just and Lasting Peace in the Middle East, China, 16–17 June 2004.
55 Violence means to "hurt and harm, insulting basic human needs". This meaning is given by Johan Galtung, Director of Transcend (a Peace and Development Network) in "Peace Studies: A Ten Points Primer". Online, available at: www.transcend.org/t_database/articles, p. 4 (accessed 2 October 2006).
56 Ibid., p. 4. 'Conflict' means a state of incompatible goals, within and between persons, societies, regions, the world. Another word is 'contradiction'.
57 R.J. Rummel, "Understanding Conflict and War, 'Alternative Concepts of Peace'". Online, available at: www.hawaii.edu/powerkills/TJP.CHAP3.HTM, Chapter 3, p. 13 (accessed 21 September 2006). The writer refers to Galtung's perspective of a positive peace.
58 Ibid., p. 14.
59 Aron (2003: 151).
60 Ibid., p. 152.
61 Ibid., p. 151.

214 *Notes*

62 R.J. Rummel, op. cit., p. 10.
63 Wight (1978: 28).
64 R.J. Rummel, op. cit., p. 11.
65 Based on an interview with Dr Ron Pundak in Tel Aviv on 10 October 2005.
66 Adam (2002).
67 Adam and Kogila (2005).
68 Bishara (2001).
69 Mitchell (2000).
70 Davis (2003).
71 Glaser (2003).
72 Greenstein (1995).
73 Younis (2000).

1 Historical backgrounds and political developments in both conflicts

1 Mitchell (2000: 7).
2 Frederikse (1986: 7).
3 Knox and Quirk (2000: 144).
4 Ibid., p. 144.
5 Ibid., p. 145.
6 "South Africa: Religion and Apartheid – Dutch Reformed Churches". Online, available at: www.memory.loc.gov/cgi-bin/query/rfrd/cstdy (accessed summer 2004).
7 Mitchell (2000: 20).
8 Rodinson (1973: 12).
9 Shlomo Avineri (1981: 97–99).
10 Binyamin Neuberger, "Zionism – An Introduction". Online, available at: www.mfa.gov.il/MFA/history/modern+history/centenary+of+Zionism (accessed 5 May 2005).
11 Rodinson (1973: 56–58).
12 *Good News Bible* (1994: 27–53).
13 Knox and Quirk (2000: 89).
14 Ibid., p. 89.
15 Zaru (2004: 6).
16 Rose (2004: 7).
17 Jewish Virtual Library, "Myths and Facts on line". Online, available at: www.Us-israel.org/isource/Zionism/political _Zionism (accessed August 2004).
18 Rose (2004: 80–81).
19 Pappé (2006: 11).
20 Ibid., p. 11.
21 Ibid.
22 Rodinson (1973: 68).
23 Ibid., p. 78.
24 Davis (2003: 162), quoting Golda Meir in *The Sunday Times*, 15 June 1969.
25 The Palestinian Preparatory Group (2001: 5).
26 Sayegh (1976: 9).
27 Khalidi (1992: xv–xxxiii).
28 Ibid., pp. xxxi–xxxiv.
29 Ari Shavit, "Survival of the Fittest", interview with Benny Morris where he explains Zionism, *Ha'aretz*, 9 January 2004. Online, available at: www.indybay.org./news/2004/01/1667397.php.hide (accessed 27 January 2004).
30 Pappé (2006: 38–198).
31 Buheiry (1985: 77).
32 Ibid., p. 77.
33 Ibid., p. 82.

Notes 215

34 Ibid., p. 79.
35 "South Africa, Education under Apartheid–The Bantu Education Act". Online, available at: http://memory.loc.gov/cgi-bin/query/rfrd/cstdy:@field (accessed April 2004).
36 Lehn and Davis (1988: 132–133).
37 Ibid., p. 131.
38 Ibid.
39 "ILA cancels tenders pending court ruling on Jewish-only land sales", *Ha'aretz*, 14 May 2007, accessed from www.haaretz.com.
40 Palestinian Academic Society for the Study of International Affairs (2004: 6).
41 Lehn and Davis (1988). The authors quote Granott who wrote in 1954 that the Palestinian right of return was seen as a threat to the nature of the state being Jewish and to its security; in addition it questioned the state's legitimacy and its narrative of the 1948 war.
42 Ghanem (1998: 434).
43 Amos Schocken, "Does Israel Want Peace?", *Ha'aretz*. Online, available at: www.haaretz.com (accessed 6 May 2005).
44 Rouhana (1997: 83).
45 Ibid.
46 Lustick (1980: 82, 150, 198).
47 Paul Lansu, Statement by Pax Christi International, Brussels, on "Status of Palestinian Citizens in Israel", 12 February 2004, p. 1.
48 Tovah Lazaroff, "UN Anti-racism Panel to Examine Israel", *Jerusalem Post*. Online, available at: www.jpost.com/servlet (accessed 20 February 2007).
49 Ibid.
50 "South Africa, Separate and Unequal". Online, available at: http://memory.loc.gov/cgi-bin/query/rfrd/cstdy:@field, p.1 (accessed August 2005).
51 Cainkar (1985: 17).
52 Ibid., p. 17.
53 Ibid., p. 58.
54 Jiris (1976: 16).
55 Ibid., p. 18.
56 Matar (1984: 120).
57 Ibid., pp. 123–124. The Allon Plan concentrated on Jerusalem and the cultivable lands of the Jordan Valley, while the Sharon Plan concetrated on building another settlement belt that extends from Jenin in the north of the West Bank to Bethlehem in the South.
58 Ibid., pp. 124–126.
59 Palestinian Academic Society for the Study of International Affairs (2004: 10).
60 Etkes and Friedman (2005).
61 Mitchell (2000: 145).
62 Ibid., p. 143.
63 Ibid., p. 145.
64 Ibid., p. 145.
65 Dugard (2007: 2).
66 Ibid.
67 Ibid.
68 Ibid.
69 War on Want, "Fighting Palestinian Poverty, A Survey of the Economic and Social Impact of the Israel Occupation on the Palestinian in the West Bank and Gaza Strip", 16 June 2003. Online, available at: www.waronwant.org, p. 14 (accessed 28 February 2007). The percentage of poverty in the West Bank is that before the imposition of sanctions.
70 Frederikse (1986: 68).

216 *Notes*

71 Ibid., p. 81
72 Lissak and Horowvitz (1995: 44 and 48).
73 Ibid., p. 49.
74 Manna and Bishara (1995: 14).
75 Based on an interview with Stav Adivi, staff and board member of ICAHD, Toronto, 30 October 2005.
76 Ibid., interview with Stav Adivi.
77 Mitchell (2000: 141–142).
78 Cainkar (1985: 88).
79 Mitchell (2000: 142).
80 Sharabi (1962: 177–178).
81 Halper (2005: 64).
82 Dugard (2007: 2).
83 Hilal and Khan (2004: 113–115).
84 Frederikse (1986: 7).
85 Ibid., pp. 8–9.
86 Ibid., p. 67.
87 Benjamin Pogrund is a Jewish South African, a former anti-apartheid journalist who moved to Israel in 1997 and is currently director of the Yakar Centre for Social Concern in West Jerusalem. He was interviewed by the researcher in Jerusalem on 9 June 2004.
88 Ibid., interview with Benjamin Pogrund.
89 Pedahzur (2001: 418).
90 Ibid.
91 Ibid. (here Ami Pedahzur is referring to Smooha).
92 Ibid., p. 419.
93 Ibid.
94 Lomsky-Feder (2004: 295).
95 Ibid., p. 304.
96 Ibid., p. 293.
97 Michael Warcshawski in an interveiw with the researcher on 1 March 2005.
98 Peri (1999: 323–352).
99 Mitchell (2000: 2).
100 Ibid.
101 "A lion has roared, Who can but fear?" (Amos 3:8); cited in "The Lions", a description of *The Jerusalem Haggadah*. Online, available at: www.webstazy.com/haggada/lions.html (accessed 11 June 2007).
102 "Ha Tikva", the Israeli national anthem – Hatikva mentions Zion or its equivalents four times. See Israel Science and Technology homepage. Online, available at: www.science.co.il/Israel-Anthem.asp (accessed 11 June 2007).
103 Flag of Israel, Israel Science and Technology homepage. Online, available at: www.science.co.il/Israel-flag.asp (accessed 11 June 2007).
104 Shahar Ilan, "Meet me on the Corner of Ze'evi and Kahane". Online, available at: www.haaretz.com (accessed 27 February 2007).
105 Knox and Quirk (2000: 143), referring to a South Africa survey of 1998.
106 CUPE, International Solidarity Committee, "The Wall Must Fall: End the Occupation and the Violence in Israel-Palestine: The History of the Conflict" (educational booklet produced by Canadian Union of Public Employees (CUPE), International Solidarity), British Colombia, Canada, p. 2.
107 Ibid., p. 2.
108 Ibid.
109 Ibid.
110 Friedman (2002).
111 Luckyboy Loyd Pipswane, general secretary of the YWCA in Garankuwa, South Africa; the researcher met him in Beit Sahur, Palestine in his capacity as an

international volunteer in a joint advocacy initiative of the international YMCA with the YWCA branch in Palestine. The interview took place on 3 October 2005.
112 Ibid., interview with Pipswane.
113 Younis (2000: 172–180).
114 Ebrahim Ebrahim is Senior Advisor (political and economic) to the current Deputy President (June 2004) of South Africa. He spoke at the Jericho International Conference on The Palestinian–Israeli Conflict: Future Prospects for an Agreed Upon Solution, 3–4 June 2004. The researcher refers to his presentation and to a personal interview with him.
115 Said (2004: 36).
116 The Palestinian Preparatory Group (2001: 7).
117 Haidar (1995: 265).
118 Ibid., p. 265.
119 Sagi (2003: 4).
120 The Palestinian Preparatory Group (2001: 7).
121 Sagi (2003: 2).
122 Ibid.
123 Ibid.
124 Halper (2005: 64).
125 Halper (2004: 20).
126 Mushtaq Khan, Senior Lecturer in Economics at the School of Oriental and African Studies, University of London, interviewed by the researcher on 23 April 2005.
127 Frene Ginwala is a trustee of the Nelson Mandela Foundation and was a leading figure in the ANC during the struggle for liberation and afterwards. She was interviewed by the researcher at a conference held in Istanbul on 26–27 July 2005.
128 Israeli non-governmental organizations (NGOs) of a religious nature, such as Rabbis for Human Rights or the inter-faith dialogue groups, have defined themselves as apolitical. Rather than taking a political stance they address the conflict from a human rights angle, or provide venues for contact on a personal level by bringing together Muslims, Christians and Jews.
129 Dugard (2007: 3).
130 Davis (1987: 4–26). Others who hold this view include Ilan Pappé and Michael Warschawski; also Andy Clarno (2007); and Donald S. Will (2000).
131 This position is held by those who are pro-Israel and by the vast majority of Israelis, including the liberal Zionists. Among the latter are Uri Avnery, Meron Benvenisti and Benjamin Pogrund.
132 Dugard (2007: 19–20).

2 Political systems and civil society in apartheid South Africa and Zionist Israel

1 In this context, when the writer mentions the politics of protest groups, their political platforms are included.
2 In this context, the terms 'state' and 'political system' are used interchangeably. The researcher is aware of the meanings associated with the concept of state, especially in international relations, e.g. the realist theory. Here, however, the term 'state' is used as it is often used in discussions on civil society, and the meaning emphasized in the text is equivalent to the 'state political system', the shortened version of which is 'political system'.
3 The functions of civil society include: defence against the authoritarianism of governments; preserving liberty, order and the state system; acting as agent of the state, elite or bourgeoisie; lobbying for a group interest; provision of services; and contributing to political culture and moral order. Other functions like the integration and legitimization of a political system fit within the latter.

4 In addition to non-governmental organizations, civil society includes social movements such as organized labour/trade unions, and religiously based organizations such as the church and church-based organizations, or Islamist groups. It also includes peasant groups, community based groups, charitable societies, clubs, informal groups, activist groups and/or dissidents' groups. It should also be noted that civil society includes private media and education (which Cohen and Arato refer to as 'publicity institutions'). These two are instrumental in implementing the role of opinion formation that is integral to legitimization and integration functions. Cohen and Arato also refer to two other components: privacy and legality. The first signifies the domain of individual self-development and moral choice; the second includes the structures of the general laws and basic rights recognized by the state, which are needed to demarcate plurality (including families, informal groups and voluntary associations), privacy, and publicity from state and the economy. See Cohen and Arato (1992: 346).

5 This research adopts the model that sees four power spheres, including civil society, within a society. These are: the state, the market/private sector, the political society (political parties with their affiliated organizations and state-affiliated organizations), and the civil society. The four spheres have dialectical relations with each other. Each affects the other in many and variable ways. For example, a change in the nature of a political system will cause a dramatic change in the other spheres. A powerful political society with a socialist agenda in a democratic system will most probably influence economic policies in favour of more social, justice-oriented policies. A civil society that enjoys a wide space for freedom of expression and association will probably have a role that is complementary to that of the state, and exerts substantive influence on the state, the political society and public opinion. It might also have a confrontational relation with the state and will thus use its lobbying capacities to change controversial policies. If it manages to capture public opinion in favour of its views, civil society can become a force for change. In an authoritarian system, civil society (usually small) will most probably seek change by organizing the public and disseminating information to shape public opinion in favour of liberties and political rights. In such cases, some civil societies can be more confrontational than others. If it evolves in terms of representation and influence, civil society can change the power relations in a society and contribute significantly to dramatic political change, as happened in many countries in Eastern Europe where the contribution of civil society was one of many significant influencing factors. In this regard, it is important to note that the case of Eastern Europe, where dissident groups acted independently from the ideology in power, is an example of a developing force for change. In the two case studies in this research, much of one case moved away from the ideology of the political system (most South African white protest groups), whereas in the second case most abide by the state ideology – Zionism (the Israeli protest groups); this point is discussed further in Chapters 3 and 4.

6 This point is of specific importance in understanding civil society in both the case studies, and consequently in examining the politics and roles of protest groups, especially Zionist protest groups (Chapters 3 and 4).

7 It should be noted that the Jewish Israeli and white South African protest groups stressed the value of non-violence. However, most Israeli protest groups disregard the values of non- or anti-militarism and anti-racism in their message vis-à-vis their own society. The South Africans stressed non-racism, and the End Conscription Campaign, supported by many, including prominent organizations, also had an anti-militarism platform.

8 Here it referred to the ideologies in power: Zionism and apartheid.

9 Guelke (2005: 22).

10 Ibid., p. 23.

11 Ibid.

12 John Lloyd, a lecturer in the Department of Law at Exeter University, and former anti-apartheid campaigner, interviewed by the researcher on 19 December 2005.

13 Ibid.
14 Giliomee and Schlemmer (1989: 166). The NP developed the view of 'a nation of minorities' when it saw the whites not as a minority within a majority, but as a minority alongside other ethnic minorities that were constituted on a tribal and linguistic basis.
15 Omond (1985: 12).
16 Kiloh (1997: 295–296).
17 Ibid., p. 295.
18 Ibid., p. 296.
19 Giliomee and Schlemmer (1989: v).
20 Waddy (2004: 63, 65).
21 Waddy (2004: 68).
22 Ibid.
23 Jo Duffy, a specialist in South African history, in a presentation in the History Department at Exeter University, November 2005. Dr Duffy is a lecturer at Bristol University.
24 Adam and Giliomee (1979: 109–117).
25 Giliomee and Schlemmer (1989: 58–59).
26 Cohen (1986: 3).
27 Giliomee and Schlemmer (1989: 41).
28 Ibid., pp. 44, 49, 53, 55.
29 Cornevin (1980: 33). She was referring to the Afrikaans daily newspaper, *Die Burger* in 1976.
30 Orkin (1995: 526). Other scholars include: Patrick Fitzgerald, Robert Fine, Wilmot James, Patrick Bond, Margaret Kiloh, Richard Ballard and Daria Caliguire.
31 Wiarda (2003: 56).
32 Adam and Giliomee (1979: 247–250).
33 Ibid.
34 FAK stands for Federasie van Afrikaanse Kultuurverenigings.
35 Adam and Giliomee (1979: 247–250).
36 Cornevin (1980: 37).
37 Ibid., p. 39.
38 Malan became the state prime minister.
39 Cornevin (1980: 41).
40 Wiarda (2003: 54).
41 Giliomee and Schlemmer (1989: 165).
42 Lemon (1987: 105).
43 Centre for Policy Studies (1989: 117).
44 Ibid., pp. 116, 117, 140, 141.
45 Adam and Giliomee (1979: 248).
46 Cornevin (1980: 42).
47 Ross (2000: 469–470).
48 Slabbert (1989: 13).
49 Gramsci brought another approach to understanding civil society by focusing on the struggle for cultural hegemony, and differentiating between the consent of society in a fascist system and in a liberal democracy, where consent is based on a far more elaborate form of hegemony. He saw the cultural elements that make up civil society as being part of the state hegemonic dominance, where the state works to obtain society's acceptance of a particular set of ideas supporting it. In such a context, the cultural elements or the moral order will be exchanged with the state or become complementary to it, and the state continues to be the proper place to make most of the rules. Gramsci argued that civil society and the state are one and the same. Driven by economic and self-assertion factors, the social strata that lead the civil and military bureaucracies stress that the three state powers – legislative, judiciary and executive – are organs of political hegemony but in different degrees. (Gramsci 1971).

50 Adam and Giliomee (1979: 247–252).
51 Adam and Giliomee (1979: 247–252).
52 Interview with Dr Frene Ginwala, Trustee of the Nelson Mandela Foundation, 26 and 27 July 2005.
53 Slabbert (1989: 10).
54 Ibid., pp. 13–14.
55 *Laager* mentality reflects a mindset where a people sees itself as a tribe against all the others. The Other is seen as the enemy who seeks to wipe them out. As such, they form a 'circle' or a beseiged mentality as part of a defensive mechanism.
56 James (2004: 149).
57 Adam and Giliomee (1979: 243).
58 Ibid., p. 244.
59 Ibid., p. 246.
60 Orkin (1995: 533).
61 Interview with John Lloyd (see n. 12 above).
62 Fine (1992: 71–72).
63 Based on an interview with Dr Adam Heribert, Cape Town, 7 March 2006.
64 Based on an interview with Dr Jon Hyslop, University of the Witwatersrand, Johannesburg, 20 February 2006.
65 Helen Suzman was the leader of the Progressive Party and for many years stood as the only opposition voice in the South African Parliament. She used her membership in the parliament to shame apartheid and call for liberal policies.
66 Based on an interview with Helen Suzman, former leader of the Progressive Party, Johannesburg, 21 February 2006.
67 Dumper (1997: 378).
68 Ghanem (1998: 431).
69 Ibid.
70 Ghanem (1998: 429–448).
71 Yishai (1998: 153–176).
72 Pedahzur (2001: 413).
73 Bishara (1997: 92).
74 Said (1980: 12–47).
75 Michael Warschawski, co-chair of the AIC in an interview with the researcher in Al-Quds/Jerusalem on 1 March 2005.
76 Rodinson (1973: 9–91).
77 Ghanem (1998: 431).
78 Ibid.
79 Ibid.
80 Pedahzur (2001: 417).
81 Ghanem (1998: 431).
82 Pedahzur (2001: 417).
83 Ibid., p. 419.
84 Bishara (1997: 92).
85 Ibid., pp. 92–93.
86 Shafir and Peled (1998: 414).
87 Ibid., p. 414.
88 See Introduction, n. 7.
89 Henry Siegman, "Hurricane Carter", *The Nation*. Online, available at: www.arab-worldbooks.com/Literature/review9.htm (accessed 22 January 2007).
90 Jewish Virtual Library. Online, available at: www.US-Israel.org/isource/Zionism/political_Zionism (accessed August 2004).
91 Ibid.
92 Binyamin Neuberger, "Zionism – An Introduction". Online, available at: www.mfa.gov.il/MFA/history/modern+history/centenary+of+Zionism (accessed 5 May 2005).

93 Ibid.
94 Rose (2004: 7).
95 Ghanem (2005: 116–117).
96 Ibid., p. 117.
97 Avineri (1981: 3).
98 Ibid., p. 13.
99 Ibid., pp. 97–99.
100 Rodinson (1973: 10).
101 Ram (2005: 36–37).
102 Hertzberg (1997: 210–212).
103 Avineri (1981: 198–206).
104 Many scholars stress this point, e.g. Joel S. Migdal (1988), Shlomo Avineri (1981), Ben Halpern and Jehuda Reinhartz (1998), and others.
105 Nur Masalha (2000: 1).
106 Ibid., p. 6.
107 Ibid., p. 2.
108 "Delaration of Israel's Independence 1948". Online, available at: www.yale.edu/lawweb/avalon/mideast/Israel (accessed 22 January 2007).
109 Al-Jazeera net. Online, available at: www.aljazeera,net/News/aspx/print/htm (accessed 24 January 2007).
110 Different factions of the labour movement were unified under the Mapai Party in 1929.
111 Different scholars, such as Reuven Kaminer, Ben Halpen, Jehuda Reinharz, Yoav Peled and Joel Migdal referred to this hegemonic power.
112 Halpern and Reinhartz (1998: 227); also Migdal (1988: 154–157).
113 Halpern and Reinhartz (1998: 228).
114 Migdal (1988: 156).
115 Peled (2005: 20).
116 Ibid., p. 21.
117 Kaminer (1996: 1).
118 Timm (2002: 85).
119 Migdal (2001: 112).
120 Ibid., p. 112.
121 Peled (2005: 24).
122 Kaminer (1996: 21).
123 Yishai (1998: 153–176).
124 Shafir and Peled (1998: 409).
125 For the politics associated with the concept of national consensus see later in this chapter and further in Chapter 4.
126 Migdal (2001: 118).
127 Yishai (1998: 164).
128 Ibid., p. 160.
129 Ibid., p. 172.
130 In this context, statism means the control of state bureaucracies and institutions over nearly all spheres of life. Quoted from Ben Eliezer (2005: 50).
131 Shafir and Peled (1998: 412).
132 Ibid.
133 Ibid., pp. 409–427.
134 Ram (2005: 36).
135 www.geography-site.co.uk/pages/countries/atlas/israel.htm (accessed 6 February 2007).
136 www.jewishvirtuallibrary.org/jsource/Politics/knesset06.html (accessed 6 February 2007).
137 www.jewishvirtuallibrary.org/jsource/Politics/mktoc.htm (accessed 6 February 2007).
138 Michael Warschawski, co-chair of the Alternative Information Centre, in an interview with the researcher on 1 March 2005 in Jerusalem.

139 An Indian South African who has been active against apartheid and currently works as a Teacher Development Advisor at Oxfam Quebec. Interviewed by the researcher in Jerusalem, 24 September 2004.
140 Ibid.
141 Based on an interview with Jeff Halper, Director of the Israeli Committee Against House Demolition, Jerusalem, 25 February 2005.
142 Based on an interview with Judy Blanc, a veteran Israeli peace activist, August 2004.
143 Interview with Jeff Halper (see n. 141).
144 Based on an interview with Jaber 'Asaqleh, Director of the Palestinian projects in Shatil, a programme of the New Israel Fund, Jerusalem 26 June 2005.
145 Shimon Tzabar, "Just the Word Peace is not Enough", article published at KK-Forum: Ein stat I Palestina. Online, available at: www.itk.ntnu.no/ansatte (accessed 3 August 2006). Shimon Tzabar is an anti-Zionist Israeli activist based in London.
146 Warschawski (1994: 4–5).
147 Kaufman-Nun (1993: 45).
148 Hermann (2002: 106).
149 Ibid., pp. 106–107.
150 Ben Eliezer (2005: 50).
151 Timm (2002: 88).
152 Ibid.
153 Gidron et al. (2004: 22, 24).
154 Ibid., p. 18.
155 Ibid., p. 14.
156 Timm (2002: 90).
157 Migdal (2001: 113–118).
158 Gidron et al. (2004: 6).
159 Ibid., p. 5.
160 Ibid.
161 Ibid., p. 6.
162 Timm (2002: 99–102).
163 Ram (2005: 33).
164 Silberstein (1999: 2).
165 Ibid., p. 7.
166 This view is held by activists such as Uri Avneri of Gush Shalom and Gila Svirsky of Women in Black. Their views are referred to in Chapter 5.
167 Silberstein (1999: 8).
168 Ibid., p. 3.
169 Ibid.
170 Erlich (1998: 21–30).
171 For some, a racist group can be a settler group which colonized Palestinian land occupied in 1967 and denied the Palestinians their basic rights there. For others, any Zionist group is a racist one because it adopts exclusive and expansionist ideology which denies the Palestinian their rights in their homeland.
172 Ben Eliezer (2005: 51).
173 Migdal (2001: 120).

3 The politics and roles of white protest groups in apartheid South Africa

1 The difference between protest groups' politics and platforms and what is meant by protest groups' roles is explained in the Introduction on p. 7.
2 Bachrach (1969: 47–53).
3 Centre for Inter-group Studies (1990a: 3).

Notes 223

4 The 'competitive circle' refers to representative actors of leading interests, e.g. the political establishment and its bureaucracy, the military establishment, the business sector, the church etc. They compete to influence the direction of state policy.
5 Bachrach (1969: 8–48). Elite consensus is what is agreed on by representatives of the competitive circle.
6 Ibid., pp. 8–50.
7 Based on an interview with Dr Caroline White, an English-speaking activist in the United Women's Organization and Black Sash during the 1980s, and a former lecturer in the University of Natal, 1997–2000. She currently lives in London.
8 Lemon (1987: 85).
9 Dr John Lloyd, a white English activist, interviewed by the researcher in Exeter, 19 December 2005. He teaches in the Department of Law at Exeter University.
10 Lemon (1987: 88).
11 Ibid., p. 103.
12 Ibid.
13 The website of the Helen Suzman Foundation. Online, available at: www.hsf.org.za/_mizsion.asp (accessed 9 May 2006).
14 Helen Suzman is famous as the leader of the Progressive Party. For many years, she was the sole voice to criticize apartheid from within the parliament.
15 Gillian Slovo, who was interviewed by the researcher by telephone on 14 November 2005. She is the daughter of the late Joe Slovo, President of the South African Communist Party for decades and later a minister in the Mandela cabinet.
16 Adam and Giliomee (1979: 279).
17 Taylor (2002: 31).
18 Lemon (1987: 93).
19 Based on an interview with Sheena Dunkan, former president of Black Sash in the 1980s, and a current member of the Black Sash Board of Trustees, Johannesburg, 24 February 2006.
20 Gidron *et al.* (2002: 72).
21 Ibid.
22 Ibid.
23 Roland Hunter, a white member of the ANC, who spied for and shared information about planned operations of the South African Defence Forces in neighbouring countries, and spent five years in prison (1983–1989). He was interviewed by the author in Johannesburg on 22 February 2006.
24 Knox and Quirk (2000: 162).
25 It is important to note that whites who joined the struggle against apartheid in their personal capacities by joining the ANC and/or the SACP have not been given sufficient attention in scholarly studies. They have either been neglected or mentioned briefly in a way that has not shown their role in the struggle.
26 Lists of the organizations in each category are found in the book's Appendix.
27 Gidron *et al.* (2002: 72–78).
28 Based on an interview with Professor John Dugard, Jerusalem, 29 June 2005.
29 Gidron *et al.* (2002: 72–78).
30 Gidron *et al.* (2002: 71).
31 Ibid., p. 83.
32 Ibid., p. 71.
33 Knox and Quirk (2000: 165). The lists of categories and their organizations are included in the Appendix.
34 Interview with Sheena Dunkan (see n. 19).
35 Based on an interview with Makgane Thobejane in Johannesburg on 20 February 2006. At present he is the Director of the Strategic Support Unit in the office of the City Manager of Johannesburg City.
36 Kane-Berman (1985) (article written in his capacity as a director of the SAIRR).

224   Notes

37 In a press statement on political violence issued by the SAIRR to the South African Press Association on 11 July 1985.
38 Based on an interview with Jeremy Routledge, a veteran Quaker member, Cape Town, 5 March 2006.
39 Interview with Jeremy Routledge.
40 Ibid.
41 The website of the Helen Suzman Foundation, Mission Statement (see n. 13).
42 Ibid.
43 Wentzel (1995: vii).
44 Knox and Quirk (2000: 167).
45 Wentzel (1995: 287).
46 Interview with Sheena Dunkan (n. 19).
47 Based on an interview with David Schmidt, a former staff member of IDASA, Cape Town, 9 March 2006.
48 Raymond Louw, ed., *Four Days in Lusaka: Whites in a Changing Society June 29-July 2, 1989*, Five Freedom Forum, South Africa, pp. 39–54.
49 Based on an interview with Sue Briton, a founder member of the End Conscription Campaign, Durban 28 February 2006.
50 Based on an interview with Dr Jon Hyslop at the University of the Witwatersrand, Johannesburg, 20 February 2006.
51 Based on an interview with Frans Cronje, a researcher at the SAIRR, Johannesburg, 23 February 2006.
52 Based on an interview with Na'eem Jeenah, head of the anti-censorship programme at the Freedom of Expression Institute, Johannesburg, 23 February 2006.
53 Interview with Frans Cronje (see n. 51).
54 Centre for Policy Studies (1989: 116).
55 Ibid.
56 Interview with Dr Caroline White (see n. 7).
57 The Charterist politics referred to are those of the Freedom Charter of the Congresses in 1955.
58 Interview with Professor John Dugard (see n. 28).
59 Interview with Dr Jon Hyslop (see n. 50).
60 Based on interviews with Na'eem Jeenah (n. 52), Makgane Thobejane (n. 35), Drs Jon Hyslop (n. 50) and Caroline White (n. 7).
61 Omond (1985: 46).
62 Karis (1986: 128).
63 "What is the African National Congress". Online, available at: www.anc.org.za/anc.html (accessed summer 2004).
64 Karis (1986: 127).
65 UDF papers, "Call to Whites", historical papers at the University of the Witwatersrand, p. 1 (file: AG1977/H1-H2).
66 Based on an interview with Dr John Greene, member of the Cape Town Democrats and lecturer at the University of Cape Town University, Cape Town, 7 March 2006.
67 Interview with Sheena Dunkan (n. 19).
68 *Black Sash 1955–2005: The Golden Jubilee Report*, published by Black Sash, Cape Town, 2005, pp. 1–8.
69 Ibid., p. 7.
70 Louw (1989: back cover).
71 Interview with Sheena Dunkan (n. 19).
72 Press release issued by Black Sash, 15 December 1982. The records of the Black Sash 1955–1995 are held at the library of the University of the Witwatersrand, Johannesburg, and are compiled by Carol Archibald as Historical and Literary Papers.
73 Press release issued by Black Sash, 23 February 1983 which was sent as a letter to the *Cape Times*. The records of the Black Sash 1955–1995 are held at the library of

Notes 225

the University of the Witwatersrand, Johannesburg, and are compiled by Carol Archibald as Historical and Literary Papers.
74 Press Release signed by Sheena Dunkan in July 1987. The records of the Black Sash 1955–1995 are held at the library of the University of the Witwatersrand, Johannesburg, and are compiled by Carol Archibald as Historical and Literary Papers.
75 Numbers are based on an interview with Sheena Dunkan (n. 462).
76 Based on an interview with Erika Wessels, Afrikaner member of staff of Black Sash, Cape Town, 7 March 2006.
77 "Introduction: Background Notes on the Students' Resource Centre", University of the Witwatersrand library, Historical Papers, pp. v–vi (approximate date mid-1990s).
78 Based on a discussion with Pascal P. Moloi, leading member of NUSAS, currently the City Manager of Johannesburg, Johannesburg, 20 February 2006.
79 Interview with Makgane Thobejane (n. 35).
80 Interview with Makgane Thobejane (n. 35).
81 NUSAS papers, Historical Papers, the University of the Witwatersrand, file: AG177/H1-H2 (approximate date late 1980s)
82 NUSAS papers, Joint NUSAS-SANSCO statement, Historical Papers, the University of the Witwatersrand, file: AG177/H1-H2 (approximate date 1987–1988).
83 Ibid.
84 Ibid.
85 "Introduction: Background Notes on the Students' Resource Centre", Historical Papers, Library, University of the Witwatersrand.
86 NUSAS papers, op. cit.
87 NUSAS papers, "Introduction: Government Attack on the Universities", approximate date 1986–1987.
88 "Bibliographical Sketch, The Helen Joseph Papers", compiled by Michele Pickover, Historical Papers, the library of the University of the Witwatersrand, Johannesburg, 1993.
89 "A Brief History of SASCO and the Student Movement: An ABC of the Organization". Online, available at: www.sasco.org.za/contents/history (accessed 25 June 2007).
90 Background on the Campaign, ECC Papers, Historical Papers at the University of the Witwatersrand.
91 Interview with Na'eem Jeenah (n. 52).
92 Interview with Sue Britton, a founding member of the End Conscription Campaign, Durban, 28 February 2006.
93 Ibid.
94 Based on interview with Eddie Makue and Bernard Spong of the SACC, 24 February 2006.
95 "Press Statement by End Conscription Campaign (WITS)", ECC papers, Historical Paper at the library of the University of the Witwatersrand, file: AG1977, issued on 17 August 1987.
96 Interview with Sue Britton (n. 92).
97 Interview with Dr Jon Hyslop (see n. 50).
98 "Background on the Campaign", ECC papers, Historical Papers at the University of the Witwatersrand, file: AG1977, p. 3.
99 Interview with Sue Britton (see n. 92).
100 "Background on the Campaign", ECC papers, op. cit., p. 2.
101 "The ECC Declaration at the Launching Day, November 1983", the ECC papers, Historical Papers at the library of the University of the Witwatersrand, file: AG1977. (The declaration and the list of ECC supporters are attached in the Appendix.)
102 Ibid.
103 Knox and Quirk (2000: 166).

104 Oliver *et al.* (1989: 39–54).
105 Oliver *et al.* (1989: 5).
106 Schlemmer (1989).
107 Oliver *et al.* (1989: 44).
108 Ibid., p. 5.
109 Based on interview with David Schmidt, a white staff member of IDASA from 1990–1996 who was also a member of the ANC, UDF and ECC. Interviewed in Cape Town on 9 March 2006
110 "Dakar Communiqué", Democracy in Action newsletter, IDASA publication, August 1987.
111 Ibid.
112 Interview with Makhane Thobejane (n. 35). According to Thobejane, the two-stage theory is one that assumes that political liberation has to precede economic revolution. It is based on the premise that radical economic change and socialism, in the case of South Africa, were not possible at that moment in time and that political liberation needed to be achieved first, while economic change would be achieved at a later stage. It reflects a pragmatic strategic approach within the ANC high ranks.
113 Based on interview with Brett Davidson, manager of IDASA's all-media group since 2000, Cape Town, 10 March 2006.
114 Interview with David Schmidt (n. 109).
115 "Dakar Communiqué", op. cit.
116 Ibid.
117 Oliver *et al.* (1989: 5–26).
118 Ibid., p. 7.
119 Ibid., p. 25.
120 The expression 'Creative Ambiguity' was used by the constitutional judge, Albie Sachs, when asked about the negotiation process in which he participated (i.e. negotiations for the new constitution) in an interview with the author in London, 27 April 2006.
121 Oliver *et al.* (1989: 81–82). The book does not mention the name of the ANC speaker since several participant organizations and their members were banned by government security legislation (p. 6).
122 Brian Pottinger is assistant editor (politics) of *The Sunday Times*. Peter Hugo is director of Shell (SA) and a past chairperson of the Cape Town Chamber of Commerce (Oliver *et al.* 1989: 12 and 17).
123 Ibid., pp. 82–83.
124 Ibid., p. 83.
125 Dr Ronnie Bethlehem is a group economics consultant at Johannesburg Consolidated Investment Co Ltd., editor of the *Investment Analysts' Journal* and vice chairman of Assocom's Economic Affairs Committee in Johannesburg (Louw 1989: 9).
126 Ibid., Ronnie Bethlehem (Louw 1989: 84).
127 Ibid., Ronnie Bethlehem (Louw 1989: 3–4).
128 Bachrach (1969: 44). He refers to Kornhauser's discussion on the issue of intermediary groups.
129 Knox and Quirk (2000: 25).
130 Mike Oliver (chairperson of FFF), "Overview of the Conference", in Oliver *et al.* (1989: 30–31).
131 Based on the interview with Judge Albie Sachs of the Constitutional Court (see n. 120).
132 Ibid.
133 Ibid.
134 Republic of South Africa, *The Constitution of the Republic of South Africa of 1996*, Act 108, a publication of the Parliament, p. 12.
135 Ibid., p. 11.
136 Oliver *et al.* (1989: 40).

Notes 227

137 Interview with Makgane Thobejane (n. 35).
138 Centre for Inter-group Studies (1990b: 2).
139 Centre for Inter-group Studies (1990a: 4).
140 Centre for Inter-group Studies (1989: 7).
141 Ibid., p. 2.
142 Ibid., p. 5.
143 Centre for Conflict Resolution (1994: 3).
144 Omond (1985: 222).
145 Cornevin (1980: 43).
146 Omond (1985: 222).
147 Based on an interview with Eddie Makue (a black Director – Justice Ministries) and Bernard Spong (a retired white veteran member) of the South African Council of Churches, Johannesburg, 24 February 2006.
148 Interview with Eddie Makue and Bernard Spong (n. 94).
149 Ibid.
150 It is important to note that a number of the Council's members were leaders in the UDF.
151 Interview with Eddie Makue and Bernard Spong (n. 94).
152 Interview with Makgane Thobejane (n. 35).
153 Based on discussion with Razia Saleh, the ANC Archives Coordinator, Johannesburg, 21 February 2006.
154 Based on an interview with Phyllis Naidoo, a veteran Indian member of SACP, Durban, 2 March 2006.
155 Ibid.
156 Based on an interview with Yazir Henri, a coloured member of the SACP and ex-member of the MK, the military wing of the ANC, Cape Town, 6 March 2006.
157 The researcher visited the Apartheid Museum in Johannesburg on 21 February 2006.
158 Based on interview with Salim Vally, senior researcher in the School of Education, University of the Witwatersrand, Johannesburg, a coloured activist who was associated with the Black Consciousness Movement and at present with the Socialist Movement, 22 February 2006.
159 Oliver et al. (1989: 51).
160 Interview with Caroline White (n. 7).
161 Interview with Na'eem Jeenah (n. 52).
162 Based on an interview with Dr Keith Cottschalk, head of Department of Political Studies, University of the Western Cape, 8 March 2006.
163 Ibid.
164 Based on an interview with Roland Hunter, Johannesburg, 22 February 2006. Hunter is at present the Director of Revenue in the Department of Finance and Economic Development in the City of Johannesburg.
165 Ibid.
166 Ibid.
167 Based on an interview with Stephen Boshoff, an Afrikaner member of the ANC who at present is the executive director of Strategy and Development in the City of Cape Town, interviewed in Cape Town on 7 March 2006.
168 Ibid.
169 Based on an interview with Mark Sweet, at present head of the ANC Research Unit, Cape Town, 8 March 2006.
170 Based on an interview with Professor Hermann Giliomee, an Afrikaner political scientist, and former lecturer at the University of Cape Town; a member of board at the SAIRR from 1995 to 1997, Stellenbosch, 10 March 2006.
171 Interview with Mark Sweet (n. 169).
172 Interview with Roland Hunter (n. 164).
173 Interview with Makgane Thobejane (n. 35).

228 *Notes*

174 Interview with Phyllis Naidoo (n. 154).
175 Interviews with Makgane Thobejane (n. 35) and Nozizwe Madlala-Routledge (the latter a black member of the ANC, the SACP, a Quaker and then deputy defence minister). Interviewed briefly in Cape Town on 5 March 2006.
176 Interview with Na'eem Jeenah (n. 52).
177 Ibid.
178 Based on interview with Yazir Henri (n. 156).
179 Pond (2000: esp. the introduction and first two chapters).
180 "Chasing the Rainbow – A Survey of South Africa", *The Economist*, 8 April 2006, p. 8.
181 Ibid., p. 4.
182 Ibid., p. 5.
183 The author witnessed this during her field visit and stay in Durban.
184 A speech by Patrick Bond at a colloquium on Economy, Society and Nature, held at University of Kwazulu-Natal, Durban, 28 February–2 March 2006.
185 The intermediate variables were discussed earlier in the Introduction and Chapter 1. They include: the vision and strategies of the resistance movement and its sucesses locally and internationally, changes at the international level i.e. the fall of the Soviet Union, the economic interdependency between the two sides, the legitimacy of the ideology in power.

4 The politics and roles of Israeli (Jewish) protest groups

1 The same point was discussed in the Introduction to Chapter 4.
2 The concept of national consensus was discussed in Chapter 2, pp. 79–80.
3 Bachrach (1969: 8–48).
4 Bell (2002: 15).
5 Jan Demarest Abu Shakrah, "Israeli Peace Forces: Can they Change Israel's Direction?", photocopied article in author's possession, p. 2. (Abu Shakrah is a researcher and a human rights specialist.)
6 Kaminer (1996: xxi).
7 Kaminer (1996: xxi–xxii).
8 Bell (2002: 187).
9 Based on an interview with Gila Svirsky, a veteran Women in Black activist, Jerusalem, 18 February 2005.
10 Hermann (2002: 106).
11 Warchawski (1994: 7–8).
12 Ibid., pp. 4–5.
13 Based on an interview with Judy Blanc, an Israeli veteran peace activist who is currently active in Women in Black, Bat Shalom, Coalition of Women for Peace, Jerusalem, August 2004.
14 Kaminer (1996: xxii).
15 Based on an interview (by email) with Professor Moshe Machover, an anti-Zionist Israeli academic, Kings College, London, 23 July 2006.
16 Kaminer (1996: xxii).
17 Based on an interview with Nassar Ibrahim, coordinator of *Ru'ya Ukhra* and co-editor of *News from Within*: these two magazines are published by the Alternative Information Centre which is an Israeli–Palestinian anti-Zionist organisation, Beit Sahour, Palestine, 11 June 2005.
18 Interview with Judy Blanc (n. 13).
19 Based on an interview with Khulood Badawi, a leading activist in Ta'aush, Jerusalem, 1 March 2005.
20 Molly Maleker, director of Bat Shalom, speaking at a workshop on What Palestinians Want From Joint Work With Israeli Peace Groups, YMCA, Beit Sahour, 9 July 2004.

Notes 229

21 Membership is this context does not mean formal membership. Most Israeli protest groups are not membership-styled organizations, but have lists of supporters who receive their publications and calls for activities. Each has committed core activists.
22 Interview with Gila Svirsky (see n. 9), a core activist of Women in Black (WIB). According to her, WIB had forty vigils per week in different locations in 1989, but after the signing of Oslo, only three vigils continued to take place (ten women in Tel-Aviv, thirty women in Jerusalem and five in Kibbutz Nahshoun). She noted that before 2000, only fifteen women showed up but when the second Intifada began many more women started to come back to the vigil.
23 Based on an interview with Neta Rotem, a member of New Profile who used to be a member of the Sheministem group (it is important to note that statistics on those who refused to serve in the army show that their number reached 1,000 in the first Intifada and 1,666 in the second).
24 Interview with Khulood Badawi (see n. 19).
25 Based on an interview with Yehudith Harel, Jerusalem, 8 August 2005. Harel is a veteran Israeli peace activist. An ex-member of Peace Now who moved to Gush Shalom, she finally become a supporter of a one-state solution.
26 Interview with Yehudith Harel.
27 Ibid.
28 Gush Shalom press release on 30 July 2006.
29 Peace Now website, www.peacenow.org.il (accessed 7 April 2005).
30 Based on an interview with Galia Golan, a member of the decision-making core group in Peace Now, Jerusalem, 6 June 2005. (The demonstration mentioned above coincided with the destruction of 3,000 homes in Rafah City in the Gaza Strip.)
31 Ibid..
32 Based on an interview with a leading member of Peace Now, who requested anonymity.
33 Hermann (2002: 111).
34 Based on an interview with Debby Lerman, a member of Matzpen, Bat Shalom, Coalition of Women for Peace and Women in Black, Jerusalem, 4 September 2004.
35 Interview with Moshe Machover London, 23 June 2006.
36 Interview with Judy Blanc (see n. 13).
37 David Kimhi of Copenhagen Group peace initiative, in an interview on the BBC's *Hard Talk*, 21 May 2003; and Knox and Quirk (2000: 127).
38 Interview with Gila Svirsky (see n. 9).
39 Based on an interview with Amit Leshem, a member of Peace Now since 1982, who left the Labour Party for Yahad Party in 2000, and at present works at Van Leer Jerusalem Institute as an initiator for joint Palestinian–Israeli projects, Jerusalem, 29 August 2004.
40 Based on an interview with Rabbi Arik Asherman, the executive director of Rabbis for Human Rights, in Jerusalem, 5 September 2004.
41 In religious terms, B'tselem means "in the image of God" but in Modern Hebrew it means human dignity. See B'tselem brochure entitled: *Documenting the Facts, Fostering Debate*, Jerusalem, 2003.
42 Ibid.
43 Hermann (2002: 98).
44 Ibid.
45 Leibowitz (1995: III).
46 Jan Demarest Abu Shakrah, op. cit., p. 15.
47 Ibid.
48 Ibid., pp. 24 and 25.
49 Hermann (2002: 100). (According to Hermann both failed to win support. The Movement for Peace and Security was badly stigmatized and isolated by the Mapai

Party while Oz ve Shalom failed to win the support of rabbis with significant religious authority.)
50 A number of reasons made the destiny of Peace Now different: the Likud was in power then and defeated Labour was keen to create opposition to it; the visit of Sadat, president of Egypt, the biggest and at the time most influential Arab state, to Jerusalem and his willingness to negotiate separately from the other Arab states and the PLO; the fact that Peace Now was established as a product of military officers' initiative and finally the strategies it has adopted. These fit with Labour's historical political line of pragmatism, opportunism and gradualism, characteristics reflected by Janet Aviad's description of the perceived role of Peace Now:

> We cannot create an environment. The environment is the reality and we have to work within it. I cannot create a public agenda any more than I can do it in Peace Now. We respond to what happens... and we plan and we will be ready when the right moment comes but we don't create moments. We can't.
> (Jan Demarest Abu Shakrah, op. cit., p. 15)

51 Jan Demarest Abu Shakrah, op. cit., p. 15. (This group chose to oppose Zionism on its own. Most of the time it was not heard.)
52 Ibid., pp. 33–34.
53 Ibid., p. 32.
54 Ibid., p. 34.
55 Hermann (2002: 102).
56 Interview with Judy Blanc (see n. 13).
57 Jan Demarest Abu Shakrah, op. cit., p. 10.
58 Knox and Quirk (2000: 110–111).
59 In an interview with Wafa Srur and Rabah Halabi of the School of Peace at Neve Shalom (Jerusalem, 10 October 2005), both argued that the Peace School chose to move away from mainstream Givat Haviva and the Van Leer Institute's traditional style of co-existence work. It runs open encounters to discuss the conflict, raise the political awareness of the participants and subsequently their understanding of their identity. As described by both planners, such meetings are not facilitated to address stereotypes and seek co-existence according the political reality that exists, but rather to allow participants to dig into their values and recognize the existing colonial mindset that justifies lack of respect for equality and justice – being raised on Zionist exclusive values, not humanist universal ones.
60 Based on interview with Hussam Abu Baker, Director of Programmes and Initiatives at the Abraham Fund Initiatives, Jerusalem, 5 October 2005.
61 About the Abraham Fund, www.abrahamfund.org/main/siteNew (accessed 16 August 2006).
62 New Israel Fund, www.nif.org/printer,cfm (accessed 16 August 2006).
63 Based on interviews with Jaber 'Asaqleh (Shateel) and Hussam Abu Baker (Abraham Fund), Jerusalem, 21 June 2005 and 5 October 2005 respectively.
64 Based on an interview with Jaber 'Asaqleh, Jerusalem, 26 June 2005 (more details in n. 59).
65 Ameer Makhoul, "Do Arab Institutions and Local Government Pay a Price for the Donations of American Jews", and "We are not Waiting for the Zionist Jewish Lobby: Arab Societies in Front of a Test of Credibility": both these articles, written in Arabic, were disseminated through email and hard copies and are in the researcher's possession, 18 October 2004.
66 Aluf Ben, "Sharon and the Israeli Consensus Map", a translation in *Al-Ayyam* newspaper, 3 August 2005.
67 Based on interviews with Michael Warschawski, a leading member of the Alternative Information Center and Jeff Halper, co-ordinator of the Israeli Committee Against House Demolition.

Notes 231

68 Tanya Reinhart, "Why Academic Boycott: a Reply to an Israeli Comrade", published on the website of the Movement Against Israeli Apartheid in Palestine (MAIAP). Online, available at: www.maiap.org/maiap/movement (accessed 27 June 2006).
69 Hermann (2002: 106, 107, 108, 109).
70 Knox and Quirk (2000: 124).
71 Ibid., pp. 124–125.
72 Ibid., p. 127.
73 Naomi Chazan, "Peace Action and Conflict Resolution: An Israeli-Palestinian Exploration"; photocopy of the draft paper is in the possession of the researcher, pp. 301–302.
74 Ibid., p. 301.
75 Ibid., p. 302.
76 Based on an interview with Dr Ilan Pappé, Senior Lecturer in the Department of Political Science at Haifa University, Jerusalem, 28 August 2005.
77 Based on an interview with Jeff Halper, the coordinator of ICAHD, Jerusalem, 30 August 2004.
78 Based on interviews with Dror Etkes (Co-ordinator of Settlements Watch at Peace Now) and Uri Avnery of Gush Shalom, 20 June 2005 and 28 September 2005, respectively.
79 Interview with Jeff Halper (see n. 77).
80 Warschawski (1994). He is quoting Jamal Zahalka in Maxine Kaufman-Nun's edited book (1993: 100).
81 Ibid. p. 100.
82 Kaminer (1996: 98).
83 Interview with Galia Golan (see n. 30)
84 Jan Demarest Abu Shakrah, op. cit., p. 26.
85 Kaminer (1996: 113).
86 Ibid., p. 112.
87 Based on an interview with Professor Moshe Machover, who was involved in such meetings, in London, 23 August 2006.
88 Interview with Galia Golan (see n. 30)
89 Kaminer (1996: 112).
90 Jan Demarest Abu Shakrah, op. cit., p. 27.
91 Kaminer (1996: 193).
92 Ibid., p. 190.
93 Knox and Quirk (2000: 125, quoting Dan Leon).
94 Interview with Yehudith Harel (see n. 25)
95 Interview with Rabbi Arik Asherman of Rabbis for Human Rights (see n. 40), who referred to Sarid's view on human rights in the mid-1990s.
96 Avnery (1995: 27).
97 The short-lived tunnel uprising occurred in September 1996.
98 Reference is made to those cases that took place in 1996 and 1997.
99 Second interview with Michael Warschawski, Jerusalem, 22 July 2005.
100 Second interview with Warschawski.
101 Mahmoud Muhareb, "About the Zionist Left", two-part article in *Al-Quds* newspaper, 16 June and 1 July 2005.
102 Interview with Dror Etkes (see n. 78)
103 Based on an interview with Mossi Raz, General Secretary of Peace Now from 1994–2000, and recently Deputy Executive Director of Givat Haviva, 18 September 2005.
104 Based on interview with Molly Moleker, Director of Bat Shalom, Jerusalem, 26 September 2004.
105 Interview with Molly Moleker.
106 Interview with Mossi Raz (see n. 103).

232 *Notes*

107 Interview with Galia Golan (see n. 30).
108 Interview with Galia Golan (see n. 30).
109 'Oslo minus' means proposing or imposing a deal on the Palestinians that falls below what was offered to them in the Camp David talks in 2000 (extract from the interview with Ilan Pappé – see note 76).
110 Interview with Dr Ilan Pappé (n. 76).
111 Interview with Michael Warschawski in which he quotes Ghassan Andoni, the latter is a founding member of the Rapprochement Centre in Beit Sahour – Bethlehem (see n. 99).
112 Interview with Yehudith Harel (n. 25).
113 Interview with Galia Golan (see n. 30).
114 The word 'occupation' started to appear after an absence of almost ten years.
115 Sharon was projected as the one responsible for government policies in the OPT, even though the Labour Party was in the unity government.
116 It is important to note that Peace Now publications do not treat East Jerusalem as part of the West Bank. For example in the population map that it published for the West Bank, there is no sign of any Palestinian population in Jerusalem compared with other cities in the West Bank. When counting Israeli settlers in the West Bank, those living in the East Jerusalem settlement are not included with the rest of the settlers. See, Peace Now's Settlement Watch Team, 'the West Bank population map', October 2005.
117 Interview with Dror Etkes (see n. 78).
118 Interview with Dror Etkes (n. 78).
119 See Peace Now website, www.peacenow.org.il/site/en/peace.asp (accessed 7 July 2005).
120 Interviews with Yehudith Harel (n. 25) and Shiri Iram, ex-employee of Peace Now, interviewed in Jerusalem on 18 September 2004.
121 Based on interview with Dr Uri Davis (by telephone), 20 August 2006.
122 Burston (2006).
123 Sarid (2006).
124 Based on an interview with Yitzhak Frankintile, Chairman of Arik Institute, Jerusalem, 19 October 2005.
125 Based on an interview with Dr Ron Pundak, Director General of the Peres Centre for Peace, 10 October 2005.
126 About the Peres Centre for Peace, see www.Peres-center.org/pages/aboutus (accessed 8 October 2005).
127 Interview with Ron Pundak (n. 125)
128 Interview with Ron Pundak (n. 125)
129 Interview with Ron Pundak.
130 In 2004, Nadia Nasser Najjab, a PhD graduate of Exeter University examined 'People-to-People' programmes and concluded that they had not had positive results because of an absence of common goals and the kind of relations between the two conflicting parties at the macro level. The latter represented an unequal structure of power where one group dominated the other. See Nadia Najjab, "Palestinian-Israeli People to People Contact Experience: 1993–2004; An Evaluation", unpublished PhD thesis, University of Exeter, pp. 236–243.
131 Interview with Ron Pundak (n. 125)
132 Interview with Yithak Frankintile (n. 124)
133 Introductory brochure of the Arik Institute.
134 Ibid.
135 Interview with Yithak Frankintile (n. 124)
136 Yitzhak Frankenthal, "Reconciliation?", a one-page handout definition, 19 October 2005.
137 Interview with Yithak Frankintile (n. 124)

138 See the website of the Economic Cooperation Foundation, www.encyclopedia.thefreedictionary.com/Economic+Cooperation+Foundation (accessed 31 August 2006).
139 Ibid.
140 Based on an interview with Uri Avnery, leader of Gush Shalom, Tel Aviv, 28 September 2005.
141 ICAHD is located on the edge of the left in this sub-category.
142 This was founded by Israelis of oriental origin.
143 This group is similar to the campus-based student organizations established in the first Intifada and that later disappeared.
144 Introduction to Gush Shalom, http://gush-shalom.org/english/intro.html (accessed 8 September 2005).
145 Interview with Uri Avnery (see n. 140)
146 Schwartz (2004: 23).
147 Avnery (1995: 30).
148 "Our Jerusalem" handout, and the interview with Uri Avnery (n. 140).
149 Interview with Avnery.
150 This point was expressed by many interviewees.
151 Interview with Uri Avnery (n. 140)
152 A pamphlet by Gush Shalom entitled: "Truth Against Truth – A Completely Different Look at the Israeli–Palestinian Conflict", published in 2003, p. 28.
153 Interview with Uri Avnery.
154 Historical compromise means in this context, the Palestinian acceptance of having a Palestinian state on the land occupied in 1967, which consists of 22 per cent of mandatory Palestine. The remaining 78 per cent is already under the control of Israel.
155 Gush Shalom pamphlet: "Truth Against Truth", op. cit., p. 27.
156 Women in Black activists differ in their positions on the issue of boycott.
157 Uri Avnery, in a press release entitled: "The Sharon's New Clothes", 30 January 2003.
158 Avnery (1995: 27).
159 Gush Shalom advertisement in *Ha'aretz* newspaper, 5 December 2003.
160 Interview with Uri Avnery (see n. 140). He defines a post-Zionist as a person who thinks that Zionism belongs to the past and should have come to an end with the establishment of Israel.
161 Interview with Moshe Machover (see n. 15).
162 Ibid.
163 Interview with Yehudith Harel (see n. 25).
164 Ibid.
165 Interview with Uri Davis (see n. 121).
166 Davis (2003: 148).
167 Interview with Uri Avnery (n. 140).
168 The Arabic word 'ta'aush' means 'co-existence'.
169 Dai Lakibush (translated into English: 'stop the occupation') brought together members of socialist leftists groups and unaffiliated activists. It adopted the political platform of the Israeli communist party of a two-state solution by negotiation with the PLO, the correct partner. Its aim was actively to oppose the occupation and support Palestinian demands for independence, using strategies that Ta'aush adopts today, e.g. house meetings, solidarity visits, demonstrations.
170 The website of Ta'aush uses the word 'Arab' to refer to the Palestinian citizens of Israel. This usage is part of the Israeli political lexicon which avoids using the word 'Palestinian'.
171 Ta'aush: Arab Jewish Partnership website, www.taayush.tripod.com/new/we (accessed 4 April 2005).
172 Interview with Khulood Badawi of Ta'aush (see n. 19).
173 Interview with Khulood Badawai (n. 19).
174 Interview with Molly Maleker (see n. 104).

175 Interview with Khulood Badawi (n. 19).
176 Machsom Watch means observing checkpoints.
177 See Machsom Watch's website, www.machsomwatch.org/eng/aboutus (accessed 8 April 2005).
178 Hass (2004).
179 Interview with Gila Svirsky (see n. 9).
180 Ibid.
181 According to Gila Svirsky, a post-Zionist is one who believes that the mission of Zionism was to find a state for the Jewish people. This mission is finished; therefore we do not need Zionism any more. Gila adds that many Israelis understand Zionism as: "control of Eretz Israel by the Jewish state".
182 Interview with Gila Svirsky (see n. 9).
183 "Women in Black: An International Movement of Women for Peace", a descriptive paper on the International WIB movement published as part of the annual WIB conference held in Jerusalem in August 2005.
184 Interview with Gila Svirsky (n. 9).
185 Mushtaq Husain Khan, of SOAS, University of London, interviewed in Jerusalem on 7 February 2005. He has researched development in Palestine vis-à-vis Israeli strategies of control.
186 The website of Yesh Gvul, www.yeshgvul.org/english/about (accessed 30 August 2006).
187 Ibid.
188 Interview with Neta Rotem (see n. 23).
189 "We Want Peace, Don't We? After All Nobody Wants War", New Profile brochure, approximate date 2002, p. 2.
190 Refusenik Watch is produced and maintained by the Oznik.com news service. See their website at www.oznik.com/about_oznik.html (accessed 7 September 2006).
191 Kaufman-Nun (1993: 57).
192 ICAHD's homepage, www.icahd.org/eng (accessed 8 September 2006).
193 Based on interview with Stav Adivi, board member of ICAHD Jerusalem and staff member of ICAHD in the US, Toronto, 30 October 2005.
194 Based on second interview with Jeff Halper, Jerusalem, 25 February 2005.
195 ICAHD press release entitled "Sanctions Against the Israeli Occupation: It's Time", 28 January 2005, p. 3.
196 Ibid., pp. 3–5.
197 For instance, ICAHD accepts the right of return in principle, although it considers it a negotiable issue.
198 Jeff Halper, on the ICAHD website (n. 192) (accessed 8 September 2006).
199 Shararah, the Spark, is no longer active as a group. In the 1980s it had close ties with the Democratic Front for the Liberation of Palestine, and was harassed by the Israeli government which imprisoned a number of its members.
200 The researcher acknowledges that the Neturei Karta religious group is not by any means leftist but it shares one leftist political position by being anti-Zionist. There is no other case like it, so rather than leaving it out, the researcher chose to mention it in this category.
201 The Movement against Israeli Apartheid in Palestine is not yet active but it has a website. It is registered in England and expects to start working in two/three years when financial resources are available and the political environment is conducive. Based on an interview with Uri Davis (see n. 121).
202 Interview with Moshe Machover (see n. 15)
203 Interview with Michael Warschawski, Jerusalem, 22 July 2005.
204 Ibid.
205 Interview with Michael Warschawski, Jerusalem, 1 March 2005.
206 Ibid.

207 Interview with Nassar Ibraheem (see n. 644).
208 The Alternative Information Centre, www.alternativenews.org/p.1 (accessed 18 December 2005).
209 Interview with Michael Warschawski, 1 March 2005.
210 Zochrot website, www.nakbainhebrew.org/index (accessed 10 September 2006).
211 Based on an interview with Eitan Bronstein, Director of Zochrot, Tel-Aviv, 1 September 2005.
212 Interview with Eitan Bronstein.
213 Interview with Eitan Bronstein (n. 211).
214 Interview with Eli Fabrikant, member of Anarchists Against the Fence, Jerusalem, September 2005.
215 Ibid.
216 Ibid.
217 The Emil Touma Institute is an institute for Palestinian and Israeli Studies, located in Haifa. It seeks to sustain and improve the Israeli–Palestinian academic and cultural dialogue. It publishes, in Hebrew, articles, reports, poems and novels from the Palestinian communities wherever they are, and from the Arab world. It also holds annual symposia and workshops for the same purpose. Established in 1986, the institute focuses its activities around the status and conditions of the Palestinian minority inside Israel. During the second Intifada, a new management stepped in and expanded its activities, bringing a broader vision to this much-needed dialogue. See www.shimur.org.il (accessed on 10 September 2006).
218 *Occupation Magazine* is a web magazine that aims to provide information and alternative commentary on the region, and on developments in the Occupied Territories, in Hebrew, English and Russian, since information presented by Israel and the American media misrepresent the devastation of Palestinian lands and people. Its editors believe that a viable solution must be based on the *unconditional* end to the Israeli military occupation and on principles of equality, justice and mutual respect. It provides space for voices that represent (in differing degrees) a range of opinions that step outside the political discourse of the liberal Zionists. See www.kibush.co.il (accessed 10 September 2006).
219 Israel Shamir is an Israeli journalist based in Jaffa. He is of Russian origin and he calls for a one-state solution.
220 For instance, a section of the AIC compromised over their principles as the Oslo Accords were signed.
221 Interview with Uri Davis (see n. 121).
222 Based on an interview with Ilan Halavi, an Israeli Jewish member of the Fateh movement, Ramallah, 17 September 2005.
223 Interview with Ilan Halavi (see n. 222).
224 Ibid.
225 The 'influentials' are usually parliamentarians, members of political organizations/movements/parties, religious leaders, academics, journalists, editors, formal officials – political and military, community leaders, representatives of the market sphere, and so on.
226 Based on an interview with Professor Herbert Kelman, director of the programme on international conflict analysis and resolution at Harvard University, Jerusalem, 9 June 2004.
227 Budeiri (1994: 19).
228 Hermann (2002: 101).
229 Ibid.
230 Uri Avnery, press release entitled "Don't Envy Abu-Mazen", 26 April 2003.
231 This is how such meetings were referred to in the 1970s and early 1980s. During the Oslo period, the word 'dialogue' became associated with the people-to-people programmes.

232 Said (1994: 42–43).
233 Interview with Moshe Machover (see n. 15).
234 Kelman (2004: 1–2).
235 Interview with Herbert Kelman (see n. 226).
236 Kelman (2004: 2).
237 Interview with Judy Blanc (see n. 13).
238 Interview with Debby Lerman (see n. 34).
239 The Geneva Document, supplement in *Al-Ayyam* newspaper, 1 November 2003, p. 15 (in Arabic).
240 Based on an interview with Dr Naomi Chazan, political scientist, member of Meretz Party and ex-member of Knesset for Meretz Party, and member of the board of Bat Shalom, Jerusalem, 9 August 2005.
241 In this case, reference is made to leading members of mainstream groups, Peace Now in particular. Many of whom are members or ex-members of Knesset, members of Labour or Meretz parties or ex-army high-ranking personnel.
242 Based on an interview with John Dugard, UN Special Rapporteur to the Occupied Palestinian Territories, Jerusalem, 29 June 2005.

5 Conclusion based on comparative analysis

1 The type of democracy is referred to earlier, in the Introduction and Chapter 2.
2 The state of Israel has no defined borders.
3 The meaning of 'bad' in this context is to be in favour of the policies of the respective governments towards the dominated side. In the South African case, favouring the political system itself was also considered bad.
4 The leftists who are referred to here are those who adopt/ed the position of the Israeli Communist Party.
5 The concept of peace by power is discussed in the Introduction.
6 The shift in power that occurred in the case of apartheid South Africa is related to a number of intermediate variables between the political system and protest activism. They include changes at the international level and the success of the ANC's strategies: e.g. managing to undermine the ideology of apartheid, making the country ungovernable, causing the imposition of economic and cultural sanctions, and building alliances with progressive liberals against the existing political system.
7 At the level of the global balance of power, the Zionists have a bigger advantage which makes pressure and sanctions on Israel almost non-existent compared to the South African case.
8 It is more progressive in many ways but particularly in the adoption of a human rights-based approach to reaching a settlement.
9 A process of peace making has been more obvious in the case of Israeli protest groups.
10 The 'magic moment' concerns changes at the international and domestic levels. In this case it was concerned with the fall of the Berlin Wall, the election of De Klerk, the undermining of the ideology of apartheid, the growing deterioration of the economy, and the increasing ungovernability of the state (see note 12 in the Introduction).

Appendices

1 Kaminer (1996: 23).

Bibliography

Adam, Heribert, *Peace Making in Divided Societies: the Israel–South Africa Analogy*, HSRC, South Africa, 2002.
Adam, Heribert and Hermann Giliomee, *The Rise and Crises of Afrikaner Power*, David Philip, Cape Town, 1979.
Adam, Heribert and Moodley Kogila, *Seeking Mandela: Peace Making between Israelis and Palestinians*, Wits University, Johannesburg, 2005.
Aluf, Ben, "Sharon and the Israeli Consensus Map", a translation in *Al-Ayyam* newspaper, 3 August 2005.
Anheier, Helmut, "Civil Society in the United States of America: Prototype or Exception? An Essay on Cultural Self-understanding", in Marlies Glasius, David Lewis and Hakan Seckinelgin, eds, *Exploring Civil Society: Political and Cultural Contexts*, Routledge, London, 2004.
Aron, Raymond, *Peace and War: a Theory of International Relations*, Transaction Publishers, New Jersey, 2003.
Asef, Bayat, *Social Movements, Activism and Social Developments in the Middle East*, Programme paper no. 3, United Nations Research Institute for Social Development, New York, 2000.
Avineri, Shlomo, *The Making of Modern Zionism: the Intellectual Origin of the Jewish State*, Basic Books, New York, 1981.
Avnery, Uri, "Is Oslo Dead", *Palestine-Israel Journal*, No. 5, winter 1995.
Avritzer, Leonardo, "Civil Society in Latin America: Uncivil, Liberal and Participatory Models", in Marlies Glasius, David Lewis and Hakan Seckinelgin, eds, *Exploring Civil Society: Political and Cultural Contexts*, Routledge, London, 2004.
Azar, E. Edward and Burton W. John, eds, *International Conflict Resolution: Theory and Practice*, Wheatsheaf Books, Sussex, 1986.
Bachrach, Peter, *The Theory of Democratic Elitism: A Critique*, University of London Press, London, 1969.
Barton, Kenneth and Ingrid Scheibler, "Saving Isaac: Nietzsche and Kierkegaard on Religion". Online, available at: www.kennethbarton.com/fun/religion (accessed 31 May 2007).
Becker, Marvin B., *The Emergence of Civil Society in the Eighteenth Century*, Indiana University Press, Indiana, 1994.
Bell, Christine, *Peace Agreements and Human Rights*, Oxford University Press, Oxford, 2002.
Ben Eliezer, Uri, "The Civil Society and the Military Society of Israel", *Palestine–Israel Journal*, Vol. 12, No. 1, 2005.

Bethlehem, Ronnie, "Socialism, Nationalism and Free Enterprise", paper presented in Four Days in Lusaka, edited by Raymond Louw, Five Freedom Forum, 1989.
Bishara, Azmi, "Israeli Democracy Exposed", Voices for Vanunu, The Campaign to Free Vanunu, UK, 1997.
Bishara, Marwan, *Palestine/Israel: Peace or Apartheid*, Zed Books, London, 2001.
Blackburn, Simon, ed., *Oxford Dictionary of Philosophy*, Oxford University Press, Oxford, 1996.
The Blackwell Encyclopaedia of Political Thought, edited by David Miller, Basil Blackwell, Oxford, 1987.
Brice, Robert M., "Apartheid and White Supremacy: Apartheid as Ends and Means". Online, available at: www.geocities.com/~anntothill/demo/text.htm (accessed 12 October 2004).
Budeiri, Musa, "Al huar al filistini – al israeeli mina al intifada ila al mufawadat" [Palestinian-Israeli Dialogue from the Intifada to Negotiations], in Edward Said, Michael Warschawski and Musa Budeiri, eds, *Critical views on Israeli Peace Camp and Palestinian – Israeli Dialogue*, Educational Project of the Alternative Information Centre, Bethlehem, 1994 (in Arabic).
Buheiry, Marwan, "A Historic Relationship", in Louise Cainkar, ed., *Separate and Unequal: The Dynamics of South African and Israeli Rule*, Palestine Human Rights Campaign, Chicago, 1985.
Burnham, Peter, Karin Gilland, Wyn Grant and Zig Layton-Henry, *Research Methods in Politics*, Palgrave Macmillan, New York, 2004.
Burston, Bradly, "Lebanon II: the First War Run by Peace Now", *Ha'aretz*, 2 August 2006.
Cainkar, Louise, ed., "South African Apartheid: An Overview", *Separate and Unequal: The Dynamics of South African and Israeli Rule*, Palestine Human Rights Campaign, Chicago, 1985.
Canadian Union of Public Employees (CUPE), "The Wall Must Fall: End the Occupation and the Violence in Israel-Palestine: the History of the Conflict", an educational booklet produced by CUPE's International Solidarity Committee, British Colombia, Canada, June 2005.
Carnegie Commission on Preventing Deadly Conflict, *Preventing Deadly Conflict*, final report of the Commission, Carnegie Corporation of New York, December 1997.
Carter, Jimmy, *Palestine Peace Not Apartheid*, Simon and Schuster, New York, 2006.
Centre for Conflict Resolution, *Annual Report*, Cape Town, 1994.
Centre for Inter-group Studies, *Twenty-one Years of Building Bridges 1968–1989*, Cape Town, 1989.
Centre for Inter-group Studies, *The 21st Anniversary Review*, Cape Town, 1990a.
Centre for Inter-group Studies, *Twenty Third Annual Report*, Cape Town, 1990b.
Centre for Policy Studies, *South Africa at the End of the Eighties: Policy Perspectives 1989*, University of the Witwatersrand, Johannesburg, 1989.
Clarno, Andy, "Neo-Liberal Apartheid: Lessons from the Crises in South African Liberation", paper presented at the Palestine Centre, Washington, DC, 27 February 2007.
Cohen Jean L. and Andrew Arato, *Civil Society and Political Theory*, MIT Press, Boston, 1992.
Cohen, Robin, *Endgame in South Africa*, UNESCO, Paris, 1986.
Cornevin, Marianne, *Apartheid Power and Historical Falsification*, UNESCO, Paris, 1980.
Davis Uri, *Israel: An Apartheid State*, Zed Books, London, 1987.
Davis, Uri, *Apartheid Israel: Possibilities for the Struggle Within*, Zed Books, London, 2003.

Dugard, John, *Report of the Special Rapporteur on the Situation of Human Rights in the Palestinian Territories Occupied since 1967*, Fourth Session of the UN Human Rights Council, 29 January 2007.

Dumper, Michael, "Israel: Constraints on Consolidation", in David Potter, David Goldblatt, Margaret Kiloh and Paul Lewis, eds, *Democratization*, Blackwell, Malden, 1997.

Ebrahim, Ebrahim, "The Palestinian–Israeli Conflict: Future Prospects for an Agreed Upon Solution", speech at Jericho International Conference, 3–4 June 2004.

Erlich, Avishai, "Fikrat ma ba'da al-suhuniah wa naqduha" [The Idea of Post Zionism and its Criticism], in The Alternative Information Centre, *The Ideology and Economy in Israel*, Bethlehem, 1998 (in Arabic).

Etkes, Dror and Lara Friedman, *Bypass Roads in the West Bank*, a report of Peace Now, August 2005.

Fine, Robert, "Civil Society Theory and the Politics of Transition in South Africa", *Review of African Political Economy*, No. 55, November 1992.

Fitzgerald, Patrick, "Democracy and Civil Society in South Africa: A Response to Daryl Glaser", *Review of African Political Economy*, No. 49, winter 1990.

Fowler, H.W. and F.G. Fowler, eds, *Concise Oxford Dictionary of Current English*, Oxford University Press, Oxford, 1964.

Frederikse, Julie, *South Africa a Different Kind of War: From Soweto to Pretoria*, Mambo Rress, Johannesburg, 1986.

Friedman, Thomas, "History and Demographics are Ganging up on Israel", 2 July 2002. Online, available at: www.theage.com.au/articles/2002/07/01/1023864712219.html (accessed 8 June 2006).

Galtung, Johan, "Peace Studies: A Ten Points Primer". Online, available at: www.transcend.org/t_database/articles/ (accessed 2 October 2006).

Gellner, Ernest, *The Importance of Being Modular, Civil Society: Theory, History, Comparison*, John A. Hall, ed., Polity Press, Cambridge, 1995.

Ghanem, As'ad, "State and Minority in Israel: the Case of Ethnic State and the Predicament of its Minority", *Ethnic and Racial Studies*, Vol. 21, No. 3, May 1998.

Ghanem, As'ad, *Marginalized Groups in Israel: A Challenge to Ashkenazi Dominance*, Madar, Ramallah, Palestine, 2005.

Gidron, Benjamin, Michal Bar and Hagai Katz, eds, *The Israeli Third Sector: Between Welfare State and Civil Society*, Kluwer Academic/Plenum Publishers, New York, 2004.

Gidron, Benjamin, Stanley N. Katz and Yeheskel Hasenfeld, eds, *Mobilizing for Peace: Conflict Resolution in Northern Ireland, Israel/Palestine and South Africa*, Oxford University Press, Oxford, 2002.

Giliomee, Hermann and Schlemmer Lawrence, *From Apartheid to Nation Building*, Oxford University Press, Oxford, 1989.

Glaser, Daryl J., "Zionism and Apartheid: a Moral Comparison", *Ethnic and Racial Studies*, Vol. 26, No. 3, May 2003.

Gramsci, Antonio, *Selections from Prison Notebooks*, Quintin Hoare and Geoffrey Nowell Smith, eds, Lawrence and Wishart, London, 1971.

Greenblatt, Terry, "Civil Society as a Partner in Promoting Peace in the Middle East", paper at a United Nations conference on The Role of Civil Society in Promoting a Just and Lasting Peace in the Middle East, China, 16–17 June 2004.

Greenstein, Ran, *Genealogies of Conflict: Class, Identity, and State in Palestine/Israel and South Africa*, University Press of New England, Hanover, 1995.

Guelke, Adrian, *Rethinking the Rise and Fall of Apartheid*, Palgrave Macmillan, Basingstoke, 2005.

Haidar, Aziz, "Al-nitham al-iqtisadi fi Israee" [The Economic System in Israel], in Adel Manna and Azmi Bishara, eds, *Studies on the Israeli Society*, The Institute for Israeli Arab Studies, Israel, 1995 (in Arabic).

Halper, Jeff, "Nishul (displacement): Israel's Form of Apartheid", paper at a seminar organized by Yakar Center for Social Concern, West Jerusalem, 7 September 2004.

Halper, Jeff, "Paralysis Over Palestine: Questions of Strategy", *Journal of Palestine Studies*, Vol. xxxiv, No. 2, winter 2005.

Halpern, Ben and Jehuda Reinhartz, *Zionism and the Creation of a New Society*, Oxford University Press, Oxford, 1998.

Hass, Amira, "Checkpoint Behaviour", *Ha'aretz*, 2 September 2004.

Havel, Vaclav, *Living in Truth*, Jan Vladislav, ed., Faber and Faber, London, 1987.

Hermann, Tamar "The Sour Taste of Success: The Israeli Peace Movement, 1967–1998", in Benjamin Gidron, Stanley N Katz and Yeheskel Hasenfeld, eds, *Mobilizing for Peace: Conflict Resolution in Northern Ireland, Israel/Palestine and South Africa*, Oxford University Press, Oxford, 2002.

Hertzberg, Arthur, ed., *The Zionist Idea: a Historical Analysis and Reader*, Philadelphia and Jerusalem, the Jewish Publication, 1997.

Hilal, Jamil and Mushtaq Khan, "State Formation under the PNA: Potential Outcomes and their Viability", in Mushtaq Khan, George Giacaman and Inge Amundsen, eds, *State Formation in Palestine: Viability and Governance during a Social Transformation*, Routledge, London, 2004.

Hinnebusch, Raymond A., 'State, Civil Society, and Political Change in Syria', in Augustus Norton, ed., *Civil Society in the Middle East*, E.J. Brill, Netherlands, 1995.

Howell, Jude, "Seizing Spaces, Challenging Marginalization and Claiming Voice: New Trends in Civil Society in China", in Marlies Glasius, David Lewis and Hakan Seckinelgin, eds, *Exploring Civil Society: Political and Cultural Contexts*, Routledge, London, 2004.

Hytham, Manna', "Of Which Civil Society do They Talk?", *Al-Jazeera* net, www.aljazeera.net, 20 November 2006.

James, Deborah, "Civil Society in South Africa", in Marlies Glasius, David Lewis and Hakan Seckinelgin, eds, *Exploring Civil Society; Political and Cultural Contexts*, Routledge, London, 2004.

Janoski, Thomas, *Citizenship and Civil Society*, Cambridge University Press, Cambridge, 1998.

Jiris, Sabri, *The Arabs in Israel*, Monthly Review Press, New York, 1976.

Kaminer, Reuven, *The Politics of Protest: The Israeli Peace Movement and the Palestinian Intifada*, Academic Press, Sussex, 1996.

Kane-Berman, John, "Ten-point Peace Package", *The Financial Mail*, 26 July 1985.

Karis, Thomas G., "Apartheid in Crisis", in Mark A. Uhlig, ed., *Black Politics: The Road to Revolution*, Penguin, Harmondsworth, 1986.

Kaufman-Nun, Maxine, ed., "Bucking and Shifting the Consensus", in Alternative Information Centre, ed., *Creative Resistance: Anecdotes of Non-violent Action by Israeli Based Groups*, Jerusalem, 1993.

Kelman, Herbert, "Talking Peace – the Impact of a Private Initiative on the Public", paper at conference of the Swiss Foundation for World Affairs on The Geneva Initiative: A Possible Solution to the Israeli-Palestinian Conflict?, Jericho, 10 February 2004.

Khalidi, Walid, ed., *All That Remains: The Palestinian Villages Occupied and Depopulated by Israel in 1948*, The Institute of Palestine Studies, Beirut, 1992, pp. xv–xxxiii.

Kiloh, Margaret, "South Africa: Democracy Delayed", in David Potter, David Goldblatt, Margaret Kiloh and Paul Lewis, eds, *Democratisation*, Polity Press, Cambridge, 1997.

Knox, Colin and Padraic Quirk, *Peace Building in Northern Ireland, Israel and South Africa: Transition, Transformation and Reconciliation*, Macmillan, London, 2000.

Landman, Todd, *Issues and Methods in Comparative Politics: An Introduction*, 2nd edn, Routledge, London, 2003.

Lazaroff, Tovah, "UN Anti-racism Panel to Examine Israel", *Jerusalem Post*. Online, available at: www.jpost.com/servlet (accessed 20 February 2007).

Lederach, John Paul, *The Moral Imagination: the Art and Soul of Building Peace*, Oxford University Press, Oxford, 2005.

Lehn, Walter and Uri Davis, *The Jewish National Fund*, Kegan Paul International, London, 1988.

Leibowitz, Yeshaayahu, *Al-'Ilm w'al-qiam* [Science and Values], Adel Mana', Centre for Studies of Arab Society in Israel, ed., 1995 (Translated to Arabic by Salman Natur).

Lemon, Anthony, *Apartheid in Transition*, Gower, London, 1987.

Lissak, M., "The Israel Defence Forces as an Agent of Socialization and Education: a Research in Role-Expansion in a Democratic Society", in M.R. Van Gils, ed., *The Perceived Role of the Military*, Rotterdam University Press, Belgium, 1971.

Lissak, Moshe and Dan Horowvitz, "Al-dimuqratiyya wa amn fi sira' mustamer" [Democracy and Security in Continuous Conflict], in Adel Manna and Azmi Bishara, eds, *Studies on Israeli Society*, The Institute for Israeli Arab Studies, Israel, 1995 (in Arabic).

Lomsky-Feder, Edna, "The Memorial Ceremony in Israeli Schools: between the State and Civil Society", *British Journal of Sociology of Education*, Vol. 25, No. 3, July 2004.

Louw, Raymond, "Whites from 'Home' in talks with the ANC", paper presented at the Four Days in Lusaka conference, in Raymond Louw, ed., *Four Days in Lusaka*, Five Freedoms Forum, South Africa, 1989.

Lustick, Ian, *Arabs in the Jewish State: Israel's Control of a National Minority*, University of Texas Press, Austin, 1980.

McLean, Iain and Alistair McMillan, eds, *Concise Oxford Dictionary of Politics*, Oxford University Press, Oxford, 2003.

Maiese, Michelle, "Types of Justice". Online, available at: www.beyondintractability.org/essay/types_of_justice (accessed 16 May 2007).

Manna, Adel and Azmi Bishara, eds, "Introduction", in *Studies on Israeli Society*, Institute for Israeli Arab Studies, Israel, 1995 (in Arabic).

Maroshek-Klarman Uki, *Education for Peace among Equals: Without Compromises and Without Concessions*, The Adam Institute for Democracy and Peace, Jerusalem, November 1995.

Masalha, Nur, *Imperial Israel and the Palestinians: the Politics of Expansion*, Pluto Press, London, 2000.

Matar, Ibrahim, "Israeli Settlements and Palestinian Rights", in Naseer Aruri, ed., *Occupation: Israel Over Palestine*, Zed Books, London, 1984.

Migdal, Joel, *Strong Societies and Weak States*, Princeton University Press, Princeton, 1988.

Migdal, Joel, *Through the Lens of Israel: Explorations in State and Society*, State University of New York Press, New York, 2001.

Mitchell, Thomas G., *Native versus Settler; Ethnic Conflict in Israel/Palestine, Northern Ireland, and South Africa*, Greenwood Press, Westport, 2000.

Muhareb, Mahmoud, "About the Zionist Left", *Al-Quds*, 16 June 2005 and 1 July 2005.

242 Bibliography

Muller, Karel B., "The Civil Society–State Relationship in Contemporary Discourse: A Complementary Account from Giddens' Perspective", *The British Journal of Politics and International Relations*, Vol. 8, No. 2, May 2006.

Nagy, Rosemary, "The Ambiguities of Reconciliation and Responsibility in South Africa", *Political Studies*, Vol. 52, 2004.

Najjab, Nadia N., "Palestinian–Israeli People to People Contact Experience: 1993–2004; An Evaluation", unpublished PhD thesis, University of Exeter, UK.

Nathan, Susan, *The Other Side of Israel: My Journey Across the Jewish–Arab Divide*, Harper, London, 2006.

Neuberger, Binyamin, "Zionism; an Introduction". Online, available at: www.mfa.gov.il/MFA/history/modern+history/centenary+of+Zionism (accessed 5 May 2005).

Norton, Augustus, "Introduction", in Augustus Norton, ed., *Civil Society in the Middle East*, Vol. I, E.J. Brill, the Netherlands, 1995.

Oliver, Mike, "Overview of the Conference", in Raymond Louw, ed., *Four Days in Lusaka*, Five Freedom Forum, 1989.

Oliver, Mike, Cavin Evans and Gael Neke, "The Role of Whites in a Changing Society", paper presented at the Four Days in Lusaka conference, in Raymond Louw, ed., *Four Days in Lusaka*, Five Freedom Forum, 1989.

Omond, Roger, *The Apartheid Handbook: A Guide to South Africa's Everyday Racial Policies*, Penguin, Harmondsworth, 1985.

Orkin, Mark, "Building Democracy in the New South Africa: Civil Society, Citizenship and Political Ideology", *Review of African Political Economy*, No. 66, 1995.

Palestinian Academic Society for the Study of International Affairs (PASSIA), *Settlements and the Wall: Pre-empting the Two-state Solution*, PASSIA, Jerusalem, 2004.

Palestinian Preparatory Group for the World Conference Against Racism, "Palestinian NGO Position Paper for the World Conference Against Racism, Racial Discrimination, Xenophobia and other Forms of Intolerance", Durban, South Africa, August–September 2001.

Pappé, Ilan, *The Ethnic Cleansing of Palestine*, Oneworld, Oxford, 2006.

Pareck, Bhikhu, "Putting Civil Society in its Place", in Marlies Glasius, David Lewis and Hakan Seckinelgin, eds, *Exploring Civil Society: Political and Cultural Contexts*, Routledge, London, 2004.

Paya, Ali, "Civil Society in Iran: Past, Present and the Future", in Marlies Glasius, David Lewis and Hakan Seckinelgin, eds, *Exploring Civil Society: Political and Cultural Contexts*, Routledge, London, 2004.

Pedahzur, Ami, "The Paradox of Civic Education in Non-liberal Democracies: the Case of Israel", *Journal of Education Policy*, Vol. 16, No. 5, 2001.

Peled, Yoav, "Civil Society in Israel", *Palestine–Israel Journal*, Vol. 12, No. 1, 2005.

Pennings, Paul, Hans Keman and Jan Kleinnijenhuis, *Doing Research in Political Science: an Introduction to Comparative Methods and Statistics*, 2nd edn, SAGE, London, 2006.

Peri, Yoram, "Media, War and Citizenship", *The Communication Review*, Vol. 3, No. 4, Overseas Publishers Association, Malaysia, 1999.

Pickover, Michele, *Bibliographical Sketch, The Helen Joseph Papers*, compiler M. Pickover, Historical Papers, the library of the University of the Witwatersrand, Johannesburg, 1993.

Pillar, Paul R., *Negotiating Peace: War Termination as a Bargaining Process*, Princeton University Press, Princeton, 1983.

Pogrund, Benjamin, "Is Israel the New Apartheid?" Seminar paper, Yakar Center for Social Concern, Jerusalem, 7 September 2004.

Pond, Patrick, *Elite Transition: From Apartheid to Neo-liberalism in South Africa*, Natal University Press, Durban, 2000.
Ram, Uri, "Four Perspectives on Civil Society and Post Zionism in Israel", *Palestine-Israel Journal*, Jerusalem, Vol. 12, No. 1, 2005.
Rawls, John, *A Theory of Justice*, Oxford University Press, Oxford, 1999.
Reinhart, Tanya, "Why Academic Boycott: a Reply to an Israeli Comrade". Online, available at: www.maiap.org/maiap/movement (accessed 27 July 2006).
Ross, Robert, "Review of Tracy Kuperus: *State, Civil Society and Apartheid in South Africa: an Examination of Dutch Reformed Church-State Relations*", *Canadian Journal of African Studies*, Vol. 34, No. 2, 2000, pp. 469–470.
Rodinson, Maxime, *Israel A Colonial-Settler State?* Monad Press, New York, 1973.
Rose, John, *The Myths of Zionism*, Pluto Press, London, 2004.
Rossi, Peter H., Howard E. Freeman and Sonia R. Wright, *Evaluation: A Systematic Approach*, Sage, Beverly Hills, 1979.
Rouhana, Nadim N., *Palestinian Citizens in an Ethnic Jewish State*, Yale University Press, New Haven, 1997.
Sagi, Eli, "Looking Ahead: Coping Strategies for the Palestinian Economy", paper at the United Nations Seminar on Assistance to the Palestinian People, United Nations Office at Geneva, 15–16 July 2003.
Said, Edward, *The Question of Palestine*, Vintage Books, New York, 1980.
Said, Edward, "Muhadidat al ta'awun bayna al filistineen wal israeleen" [The Limitations of Cooperation between Palestinians and Israelis], in Edward Said, Michael Warschawski and Musa Bedeiri, eds, *Critical Views on Israeli Peace Camp and Palestinian–Israeli Dialogue*, educational project of the Alternative Information Centre, Bethlehem, 1994 (in Arabic).
Said, Edward, *Isra'eel, 'iraq wal wilayat al-mutahida* [Israel, Iraq and the US], 1st edn, Dar Al-Adab, Beirut, 2004 (in Arabic).
Sarid, Yossi, "With Such a Left, Who Needs a Right?" *Ha'aretz*, 15 August 2006.
Sayegh, Fayez A., "Zionism: A Form of Racism and Racial Discrimination", Four Statements made at the UN General Assembly, Office of the Permanent Observer of the Palestine Liberation Organization to the United Nations, 1976. Reprinted by Americans for Middle East Understanding (AMEU), New York.
Schlemmer, Lawrence, "Dialogue with the Resistance: Introductory Comments", *Indicator South Africa*, Vol. 6, Nos. 1–2, Summer/Autumn 1989.
Schnall, David, *Radical Dissent in Contemporary Israeli Politics: Cracks in the Wall*, Praeger, New York, 1979.
Schocken, Amos, "Does Israel want Peace?", *Ha'aretz*. Online, available at: www.haaretz.com (accessed 6 May 2005).
Schwartz, Yossi, "The Israeli Left between the Al-Aqsa Intifada and the Road Map", in Yasser Akawi, Gabriel Angelone and Lisa Nessan, eds, *From Communal Strife to Global Struggle: Justice for the Palestinian People*, Alternative Information Centre, Latin Patriarchate Printing Press, Jerusalem, 2004.
Shafir, Gershon and Yoav Peled, "Citizenship and Stratification in an Ethnic Democracy", *Ethics and Racial Studies*, Vol. 21, No. 3, May 1998.
Shahar, Ilan, "Meet Me on the Corner of Ze'evi and Kahane". Online, available at: www.haaretz.com (accessed 27 February 2007).
Sharabi, Hisham, *Governments and Politics of the Middle East in the Twentieth Century*, D. Van Nostrand Company, New Jersey, 1962.
Shlaim, Avi, "Israel and the Conflict", paper for the international conference on 1990–1991 Gulf Conflict, Keele University, 24–25 September 1992.

Bibliography

Siegman, Henry, "Hurricane Carter", *The Nation*. Online, available at: www.arabworldbooks.com/Literature/review9.htm (accessed 22 January 2007).

Silbergh, David M., *Doing Dissertations in Politics: A Student Guide*, Routledge, London, 2001.

Silberstein, Laurence J., *The Post Zionism Debates*, Routledge, London, 1999.

Slabbert, Frederik van Zyl, *The System and the Struggle: Reform, Revolt, and Reaction in South Africa*, Dene Smuts, ed., Jonathan Ball, Johannesburg, 1989.

Smith, Anthony D. *The Nations in History: Historigraphical Debates about Ethnicity and Nationalism*, Polity Press, Oxford, 2000.

Sofer, Sasson, ed., *Peacemaking in a Divided Society: Israel after Rabin*, Frank Cass, London, 2001.

Sola, Akinrinade, "On the Evolution of Civil Society in Nigeria", in Marlies Glasius, David Lewis and Hakan Seckinelgin, eds, *Exploring Civil Society: Political and Cultural Contexts*, Routledge, London, 2004.

Sparks, Allister, *Tomorrow is Another Country: the Inside Story of South Africa's Negotiated Revolution*, Heinemann, London, 1995.

Tamari, Salim, "Kissing Cousins: A Cautionary Note on People to People Projects", *Palestine-Israel Journal of Politics, Economics and Culture*, Jerusalem, Al-Amal Press, Vol. 12, No. 4, and Vol. 13, No. 1, 2005/2006.

Taylor, Ian, "South Africa's Transition to Democracy and the 'Change Industry': a Case Study of IDASA", *Politikon*, Vol. 29, No. 1, 2002.

The Times English Dictionary, HarperCollins, London, 2000.

Timm, Angelika, "Israeli Civil Society: Historical Development and New Challenges", in Amr Hamzawy, ed., *Civil Society in the Middle East*, Verlag Hans Schiler, Berlin, 2002.

Tirman, John, "Forces of Civility: the NGO Revolution and the Search for Peace", *Boston Review*. Online, available at: www.bostonreview.net./BR23.6/triman.html (accessed March 2005).

Tzabar, Shimon, "Just the Word Peace is Not Enough". Online, available at: www.itk.ntnu.no/ansatte (accessed 3 August 2006).

United Nations Commission on Human Rights, "Violations of Human Rights in Southern Africa", *Report of the Ad hoc Working Group of Experts*, United Nations Economic and Social Council, Forty-first session, Item 6 of the provisional agenda, E/CN.4/1985/14.

Vickery, Kenneth P., "'Herrenvolk' Democracy and Egalitarianism in South Africa and the US South", *Comparative Studies in Society and History*, Vol. 16, No. 3, June 1974.

Voigt, Karsten D., "Power, Sovereignty and Rule of Law", *International Politik*, Vol. 4, winter 2003.

Waddy, Nicholas L., "Certain Destiny: The Presentist Obsession with 'Apartheid' in South African History", *Historia*, Vol. 49, No. 2, November 2004.

Wainwright, Hilary, "Western Europe: Democratic Civil Society versus Neoliberalism", in Marlies Glasius, David Lewis and Hakan Seckinelgin, eds, *Exploring Civil Society: Political and Cultural Contexts*, Routledge, London, 2004.

Warchawski, Michael, "'An al huwar, al tadamun wal mufawadat" (About Dialogue, Solidarity and Negotiations), in Edward Said, Michael Warschawski and Musa Budeiri, eds, *Critical Views on Israeli Peace Camp and Palestinian–Israeli Dialogue*, educational project of the Alternative Information Centre, Bethlehem, 1994 (in Arabic).

Wentzel, Jill, *The Liberal Slideaway*, South African Institute of Race Relations, Johannesburg, 1995.

Wiarda, Howard J., *Civil Society: the American Model and Third World Development*, Westview Press, Boulder, 2003.

Wight, Martin, *Power Politics*, edited by Hedley Bull and Carsten Holbraad, 2nd edn, Penguin, London, 1978.
Will, Donald S., "Non-Racialism Versus Nationalism: Contrasting Solutions to Conflict in South Africa and Israel/Palestine", *Peace and Change*, Vol. 25, No. 2, April 2000.
Wilmot, James and Daria Caliguire, "The New South Africa: Renewing Civil Society", *Journal of Democracy*, Vol. 7, No. 1, January 1996.
Younis, Mona, *Liberation and Democratization: the South African and Palestinian National Movements*, University of Minnesota Press, Minneapolis, 2000.
Yishai, Yael, "The Guardian State: A Comparative Analysis of Interest Group Regulation", *Governance: An International Journal of Policy and Administration*, Vol. 11, No. 2, April 1998.
Zaru, Jean, *A Christian Palestinian Life: Faith and Struggle & Overcoming Direct and Structural Violence, Truth and Peace Making in the Palestinian Experience*, Sabeel Documents, No. 2, Jerusalem, 2004.

Historical papers and other documents

Avnery, Uri, "The Sharon's New Clothes", press release, 30 January 2003.
Avnery, Uri, "Don't Envy Abu-Mazen", press release distributed on Gush Shalom's email list, 26 April 2003.
Avnery, Uri, "One State: Solution or Utopia", an article distributed on Gush Shalom's mailing list, 12 May 2007.
"Background on the Campaign", the ECC papers, Historical Papers at the library of the University of the Witwatersrand, file: AG1977.
Black Sash 1955–2005: the Golden Jubilee Report, published by Black Sash, Cape Town, 2005.
"Call to Whites", the United Democratic Front papers, Historical Papers at the library of the University of the Witwatersrand, file: AG1977/H1-H2.
"Chasing the Rainbow – A Survey of South Africa", *The Economist*, 8 April 2006.
Chazan, Naomi, "Peace Action and Conflict Resolution: An Israeli–Palestinian Exploration", a photocopy of the paper is in the possession of the researcher.
The Constitution of the Republic of South Africa, published by the parliament, 1996.
"Dakar Communiqué", Democracy in Action newsletter, IDASA publication, August 1987.
Demarest-Abu Shakrah, Jan, "Israeli Peace Forces: Can they Change Israel's Direction?", a photocopy of the paper is in the possession of the researcher.
"Documenting the Facts, Fostering Debate", a brochure by B'tselem, 2003.
"The Document of the Geneva Initiative", supplement issued in *Al-Ayyam* newspaper on 1 November 2003 (in Arabic).
"The ECC Declaration at the Launching Day, November 1983", the ECC papers, Historical Papers, library of the University of the Witwatersrand, file: AG1977.
Frankenthal, Yitzhak, "Reconciliation?", a one-page handout definition, Arik Institute, 19 October 2005.
Good News Bible, Bath Press, Bath, 1996.
Gush Shalom advertisement in *Ha'aretz* newspaper in support of the Geneva Initiative, 5 December 2003.
"Introduction: Background Notes on the Students' Resource Centre", library of the University of the Witwatersrand, Historical Papers, pp. v–vi (approximate date mid-1990s).
"Introduction: Government Attack on the Universities", NUSAS Papers, Historical Papers, library of the University of the Witwatersrand, file: AG177/H1-H2.

246 *Bibliography*

Al-Kenneset yusadiq 'ala qanun yamna' zawaj al-'arab min al-filistineen w'al-sureen wal-lubnaneen wal-iraqeen wal-iraneen' [The Knesset Ratifies a Law that Forbids Israeli Arabs from Marrying Palestinian, Syrians, Lebanese, Iraqis and Iranians], *Al-Quds Al-'Arabi*, 22 March 2007.

Kimhi, David, of Copenhagen Group peace initiative, in an interview on *Hard Talk*, BBC, 21 May 2003.

Lansu, Paul, "Statement", Pax Christi International on *Status of Palestinian Citizens in Israel*, Brussels, 12 February 2004.

Makhoul, Ameer, "Do Arab Institutions and Local Government Pay a Price for the Donations of American Jews", and "We are Not Waiting for Zionist Jewish Lobby: Arab Societies in Front of a Test of Credibility", both articles, written in Arabic, were disseminated through email and hard copies are in the researcher's possession, 18 October 2004.

NUSAS papers, Historical Papers, library of the University of the Witwatersrand, file: AG177/ H1-H2 (approximate date late 1980s).

NUSAS papers, Joint NUSAS – SANSCO statement, Historical Papers, library of the University of the Witwatersrand, file: AG177/H1-H2 (approximate date 1987–1988).

"Our Jerusalem", a Gush Shalom handout, 1998.

Peace Now: the Settlement Watch Team, "West Bank Population Map", October 2005.

Press release issued by Black Sash on 15 December 1982. Records of the Black Sash 1955–1995 compiled by Carol Archibald, Historical and Literary Papers, the library of the University of the Witwatersrand, Johannesburg.

Press release issued by Black Sash on 23 February 1983, sent as a letter to the *Cape Times*, Records of the Black Sash 1955–1995 compiled by Carol Archibald, Historical and Literary Papers, the library of the University of the Witwatersrand, Johannesburg.

Press release signed by Sheena Dunkan in July 1987, Records of the Black Sash 1955–1995 compiled by Carol Archibald, Historical and Literary Papers, the library of the University of the Witwatersrand, Johannesburg.

Press statement on political violence issued by the SAIRR to the South African Press Association on 11 July 1985.

Press statement by End Conscription Campaign (WITS), ECC papers, Historical Papers at the library of the University of the Witwatersrand, file: AG1977, issued on 17 August 1987.

"Sanctions Against the Israeli Occupation: It's Time", ICAHD press release, 28 January 2005.

"Truth against Truth: A Completely Different Look at the Israeli–Palestinian Conflict", a pamphlet by Gush Shalom, 2003.

"We Want Peace, Don't We? After All Nobody Wants War", brochure by New Profile, approximate date 2002.

"Women in Black: An International Movement of Women for Peace", a descriptive paper for International Women in Black movement, published as part of the annual WIB conference, Jerusalem, August 2005.

Sources from the Internet

About the Abraham Fund, www.abrahamfund.org/main/siteNew (accessed 16 August 2006).

A brief history of SASCO and the student movement: An ABC of the organisation, www.sasco.org.za/contents/history, accessed on 25/6/2007

Bibliography

"Against Equality", from *Philosophy*, 40, 1965, pp. 296–307, reprinted in H. Bedau, ed., *Justice and Equality*, Prentice-Hall, 1971, pp. 138–151, www.users.ox.ac.uk/-jrlucas/libeqsor/equality (accessed on 27/9/2006).

African National Congress, "Negotiations: A Strategic Perspective" as adopted by the National Working Committee on 18 November 1992, www.anc.org.za/ancdocs/history/transition/perspect (accessed 12 October 2004).

The Alternative Information Centre, www.alternativenews.org/p.1 (accessed 18 December 2005).

"Colonialism of a Special Type", www.anc.org.az/ancdocs/history/special (accessed 12 October 2004).

"Constructivist Epistemology", www.stemnet.nf.ca/~elmurphy/emurphy (accessed 2 May 2007).

Declaration of Israel's Independence 1948, www.yale.edu/lawweb/avalon/mideast/Israel (accessed 22 January 2007).

"The Deflationary Theory of Truth", *Stanford Encyclopedia of Philosophy*, www.plato.stanford.edu/entries/truth-deflationary (accessed 22 May 2007)

Economic Cooperation Foundation website, www.encyclopedia.thefreedictionary.com/Economic+Cooperation+Foundation (accessed 31 August 2006).

Emil Touma Institute in Haifa, www.shimur.org.il (accessed 10 September 2006).

"Equality", *Stanford Encyclopaedia of Philosophy*, www.plato.stanford.edu/entries/equality (accessed 27 September 2006).

Flag of Israel, Israel Science and Technology homepage, www.science.co.il/Israel-flag.asp (accessed 11 June 2007).

The Helen Suzman Foundation, "Mission Statement", www.hsf.org.za/_mission.asp (accessed 9 May 2006).

"I am Prepared to Die", Nelson Mandela's statement from the dock at the opening of the defence case in the Rivonia Trial, Pretoria Supreme Court, 20 April 1964, www.anc.org.za/ancdocs/history/rivonia/ (accessed 28 May 2007).

ICAHD homepage, www.icahd.org/eng (accessed 8 September 2006).

"ILA Cancels Tenders Pending Court Ruling on Jewish-only Land Sales", *Ha'aretz* www.haaretz.com (accessed 14 May 2007).

Introduction to Gush Shalom, http://gush-shalom.org/english/intro.html (accessed 8 September 2005).

Jewish Virtual Library, www.jewishvirtuallibrary.org/jsource/Politics/knesset06.html (accessed 6 February 2007).

Jewish Virtual Library, Myths and Facts online, www.us-israel.org/isource/Zionism/political_Zionism (accessed July 2004).

"John Rawls' Theory of Justice: An Introduction", www.faithnet.org.uk/A2%20Subjects/Ethics/rawlsjustice (accessed 15 May 2007).

The Lions, Welcome to the Jerusalem Haggadah-Aryeh Editions, www.webstazy.com/haggada/lions.html (accessed 11 June 2007).

Machsom Watch website, www.machsomwatch.org/eng/aboutus (accessed 8 April 2005).

Michel Foucault: Truth and Power, Writings, www.wdog.com/rider/writings/foucault.htm (accessed 20 May 2007).

National Anthem of Israel: Ha Tikva, Israel Science and Technology homepage, www.science.co.il/Israel-Anthem.asp (accessed 11 June 2007).

New Israel Fund, www.nif.org/printer,cfm (accessed 16 August 2006).

Occupation Magazine, www.kibush.co.il (accessed 10 September 2006).

Oznik.com news service, produces and maintains Refusenik Watch, www.oznik.com/about_oznik.html (accessed 7 September 2006).

248 Bibliography

Peace Now's website, www.peacenow.org.il/site/en/peace.asp (accessed 7 July 2005).
Peres Centre for Peace, www.peres-center.org/pages (accessed 8 October 2005).
Rummel, R.J., "Understanding Conflict and War, Alternative Concepts of Peace", www.hawaii.edu/powerkills/TJP.CHAP3.HTM (accessed 21 September 2006).
Shavit, Ari, interview with Benny Morris where he explains Zionism, "Survival of the Fittest", *Ha'aretz*, 9 January 2004. Online, available at: www.indybay.org./news/2004/01/1667397.php.hide (accessed 27 January 2004).
South Africa, Education under Apartheid – The Bantu Education Act, http://memory.loc.gov/cgi-bin/query/rfrd/cstdy:@field (accessed April 2004).
South Africa: Religion and Apartheid – Dutch Reformed Churches, www.memory.loc.gov/cgi-bin/query/rfrd/cstdy (accessed summer 2004).
Stanford Encyclopaedia of Philosophy, www.plato.stanford.edu/entries/truth-correspondence (accessed 31 May 2007).
Stephen James Mintorn, "Kierkegaard and Truth as Subjectivity", *Practical Philosophy*, www.practical-philosophy.org.uk/Volume3Articles/Minton (accessed 26 May 2007).
Ta'aush: Arab Jewish Partnership website, www.taayush.tripod.com/new/we (accessed 4 April 2005).
"Theories of Truth", www.thymos.com/science/truth (accessed 25 September 2006).
United Nations International Convention on the Elimination of all Forms of Racial Discrimination, article 1, www.ohchr.org/english/law (accessed 10 October 2006).
War on Want, "Fighting Palestinian Poverty", A Survey of the Economic and Social Impact of the Israel Occupation on the Palestinian in the West Bank and Gaza Strip, 16 June 2003, www.waronwant.org (accessed 28 February 2007).
What is the African National Congress, www.anc.org.za/anc.html (accessed summer 2004 and February 2006).
"What is the Truth of Simulation", www.jasss.soc.surrey.ac.uk (accessed 2 May 2007).
Yesh Gvul website, www.yeshgvul.org/english/about (accessed 30 August 2006).
Zochrot website, www.nakbainhebrew.org/index (accessed 10 September 2006).

Index

Abraham Fund 82, 135
Adam, Heribert 171
Adoni, Ghassan 146
African National Congress (ANC): Declaration of Lusaka 108–11; exiled members 113–14; membership 115–19, 181, 185; and NUSAS 105; support for 45–6, 96; visions and strategies 41–3, 47, 95, 101, 102–3, 106, 107, 119, 190, 191, 193
Afrikaner Freedom Foundation 113
Afrikaner nationalism 55–60
Afrikaner Studentbond 113
Afrikaners' organized civil initiatives 61–2
Agudat Israel 71
Al Ard 77
Aloni, Sholamit 77
Alternative Information Centre (AIC) 128, 129, 138, 153, 160–1, 169
Anarchists 153, 160, 161–2, 169, 170
Anarchists Against the Wall 162
Andoni, Ghassan 165
Angola 36
anti-apartheid organizations 94–5, 182
anti-Zionist groups 133–4
apartheid: civil society under 62–5; legitimacy of 45–6
apartheid system 55–60
Arab League 44
Arafat, Yasser 142, 143, 144, 153, 154, 164
Arik Institute 140, 148, 149–50
Aristotle 14
Arnon, Ya'acov 164
Aron, Raymond 20
Asherman, Rabbi Arik 131
Ashkenazi Jews 45, 74, 75–6, 78, 128, 140, 181–2, 189
Assocom 100

authoritarian systems 4–5, 53, 57, 66, 86, 161, 176
Averini, Shlomo 27, 71
Aviad, Janet 144–5
Avnery, Uri 144, 152–5, 164
Ayalon, Ami 148
Ayalon-Nusseibeh plan 140, 146, 147, 148, 166
Azanian Student Union (AZASU) 104

Badawi, Khulood 128, 155
Balfour Declaration (1917) 28, 30
Bantu Authorities Act (1951) 30
Bantustans 30–1, 32, 41, 46, 90
Barak, Ehud 146, 147, 152–3, 168
Bat Shalom 104, 138, 151, 154, 155
Begin, Menachem 141
Beilin-Abu Mazen Understanding 150
Beit Sahour Rapprochement Centre 146
Bell, Christine 126
Ben-Gurion, David 27–8, 38, 71, 72
Bethlehem, Ronnie 110
Bible 28, 46, 70–1
Biko, Steve 104, 112–13
Bir Zeit University 134
Bishara, Azmi 35–6, 59, 68, 69, 160
black civil society 65
Black Consciousness Movement 104, 112–13
Black Sash (BS) 92, 94–5, 100–1, 103–4, 106, 112, 157
Blanc, Judy 130
book overview 1–4
Boshof, Carel 113
Boshoff, Stephen 117
Britain 27, 28, 29, 71, 72
Britton, Sue 107
Broederbond (Band of Brothers) 61, 62, 63–4, 179
Burger's Daughter (Gordimer) 101

Camp David agreement (1978) 37, 146, 147, 152–3, 168
Campus LoShotek 151
Cape Town Democrats 101, 116
Cape Town University 101
Centre for Conflict Resolution (CCR) 96, 101, 112
Centre for Inter-Group Studies 89, 96, 101, 112–13
centre parties, Israel 125–6
Chazan, Naomi 129, 138
Christian Institute for Southern Africa (CISA) 101, 113–14
Christian National Education 37–8
Christian Organization for Southern Africa 106
Christian Youth Workers 101
citizens versus non-citizens 46
citizenship 31–2, 54, 78–9
civil initiatives: Israel 74–6; similarities 179–82; South Africa 61–2
Civil Rights League 101
civil society: comparison of 85–7; definitions of 65–7, 83–5; Israel 73–85; South Africa 60–7; under apartheid 62–5; Zionist Israel 76–83
civil society organizations: examination of 80–3
Coalition of Women for Peace 129, 138, 151
co-existence programmes 96, 134–5, 148–9
Cohen, Robin 59
colonialism 26–30, 57, 58–9
Coloured People's Congress 101
Committee Against the War in Lebanon 134
Committee for Israeli–Palestinian Dialogue 151
communitarianism 64, 79, 191, 193, 205
comparative analysis: case-specific patterns 190–1; insights/lessons from 192–7; macro level similarities/differences 175–9; micro level similarities/differences 179–89; shared patterns 191–2
conceptual discussion 12–22
conflict resolution, framing of 47–8, 49, 61–2, 178, 193, 207
conflicts: differences between 41–8; similarities between 26–40
Congress of Democrats 101
Congress of South African Trade Unions (COSATU) 44, 117

Conscientious Objector Support Groups (COSG) 106
conscription 35–6, 106–7, 185–6, 209
Conservative Party (CP) 90
consociational democracy 68–70
Constitution, South Africa 56–7, 61, 73, 111–12
constructive ambiguity 125, 190
Consultative Business Movement 63, 113
control, use of oppression 34–5
Cornevin, Marianne 59
corporatism 79, 93, 176
Council for Peace and Security 138, 140, 148
Courage to Refuse 129, 151, 158
Criminal Law Amendment Acts (1953) 30
critical liberal Zionist groups 151–9, 188
Cronje, Frans 99
cultural sphere 101
"Custodian of Absentee Property" 30

Dai Lakibush 138, 142, 163
Davis, Uri 147–8, 154–5, 163, 177
Declaration of Lusaka 108–11
democracy 68–70; two-stage theory 109–10
Democratic Front for the Liberation of Palestine 130, 163
Democratic Party 113
demographics 5, 41, 42
Development Authority 30
discrimination, by law and policy 30–2
distributive justice 15–16
dominant states and indoctrination 37–40
Dugard, John 171, 177
Dumper, Mick 67
Dunkan, Sheena 92, 95–6, 102–3
Dutch Reformed Church 26–7, 46, 58–9, 61, 62, 63, 86, 90, 113, 178, 179

East for Peace 134
Ebrahim, Ebrahim 44
Economic Cooperation Foundation (ECF) 138, 140, 148, 150, 165
economic dependency/interdependency 6, 44–5
economic revolution 109–10
economic sanctions 100, 153–4, 157, 178
economic systems 34–5, 48–9
education 37–9
Election Law (1985) 69
Emil Touma Institute 163

empire, peace by 20
employment 44–5
End Conscription Campaign (ECC):
  effectiveness 158–9, 185–6; launching declaration 209; membership 96, 105, 210; politics of 95; Towards a Just Peace in Our Land Declaration 107; vision/strategies 100–1, 106–7
equality, concept of 12–15
equilibrium, peace by 20
Eretz Israel 46, 70, 71, 73, 125, 166
ethnic cleansing 29
ethnic democracy 68–70
ethnic symbols 40
ethno-national democracy 68–70
European Jews 27
'exposing facts' 95–6

Fateh 142, 147, 163, 164, 169
Fine, Robert 65
'First Day Syndrome' 140, 146, 151
First Intifada (1987) 23–4, 58, 90, 95–6, 128–30, 135–6, 141–3, 145–7, 155–8, 160–1
Five Freedom Forum (FFF) 100–1, 103, 108, 112
Foucault, Michel 19
Four Mothers 133, 140
Frankintile, Yitzhak 149
Frederickse, Julie 35
Freedom Charter (1955) 98, 101–2, 107, 115
freedom of association 77–8

Gandhi, Mahatma 20
Gaza Strip 29, 31, 33–4, 43
General Labour Federation *see* Histadrut
Geneva Initiative 129, 140, 146, 147, 150, 154, 158, 163, 166–7, 187
Ghanem, As'ad 68
Gidron, Benjamin 23, 82, 92, 94, 95, 137, 208
Giliomee, Hermann 57, 59, 117–18
Golan, Galia 129, 141, 146
Gordimer, Nadine 101
Gramsci, Antonio 63, 66, 75, 78, 176
Green Line 81, 136, 147, 153
Greenblatt, Terry 19
Group Area Act (1957) 30
Guelke, Adrian 56
Gush Emunim (Bloc of the Faithful) 133
Gush Shalom 129, 138, 151–5, 163

Ha'aretz 124, 153, 156

Hadash *see* Israeli Communist Party
Halavi, Ilan 163, 165
Halper, Jeff 79, 138, 165
Haredi Jews 74
Harel, Yehudith 129, 154, 163
Harvard University 165
Hasenfeld, Yeheskel 23, 82, 92, 94, 95, 137, 208
Hass, Amira 156
Hebrew language 72, 162
hegemony 36–7, 66, 175–6; peace by 20
Helen Suzman Foundation 97
Hermann, Tamar 130, 137–8
Herrenvolk regime 70, 175
Herzliya group 73
Hirschfeld, Yair 148, 150
Histadrut 72, 74–5, 76, 77, 179–80
historical background: Afrikaners' organized civil initiatives 61–2; differences between conflicts 41–8; Israeli activism 132–5; Jewish civil organized civil initiatives 74–6; similarities between conflicts 26–40
Holocaust 72
House of Assembly 56
Houses of Delegates 101
Hugo, Peter 110
Hunter, Roland 92, 117, 118

ideological consensus 80
ideology 3, 19, 28, 45–6, 57–9, 175, 192
inclusivity 54, 70, 150
Indian National Congress 101
individual activism: categorizing 93–7, 137–9; differences 184–5; similarities 182
indoctrination 37–40, 177
inductive research approach 7
Inkatha 112–13
Institute for a Democratic Alternative for South Africa (IDASA) 95, 98, 112
Institute of Democratic Alternative for South Africa (IDASA) 100–1, 108–9, 185
Integrated within the Welfare State System organizations (IWSSs) 82
International Convention on the Elimination of all Forms of Racial Discrimination 17, 49
International Convention on the Suppression and Punishment of the Crime of Apartheid (1973) 49
interviews/interviewees 8, 198–203
Ir Shalem 145

252 Index

Israel: categorizing protest groups/ individual activism 137–9, 206; civil society 73–85; definition of civil society 83–5; individuals joining PLO 163–7; leftist protest organizations/groups 159–63; liberal Zionist protest groups 139–59; period of study 10; political system 67–73; protest groups in context 124–37
Israel Lands Administration (ILA) 31
Israeli Committee Against House Demolitions (ICAHD) 129, 138, 151, 159, 185
Israeli Committee of Solidarity 134
Israeli Communist Party (ICP) 127–8, 133, 151, 160, 163, 164, 177, 185
Israeli Council for Israeli–Palestinian Peace 134, 164
Israeli Education Act (1953) 38
Israeli Information Centre for Human Rights in the Occupied Territories (B'tselem) 131
Israeli Law of Return 13, 136, 153
issue-oriented organizations 133, 156–7

Jerusalem 153
Jerusalem Centre for Women 8
Jewish Agency 71
Jewish civil organized initiatives 74–6
Jewish National Fund (JNF) 30–1
Johannesburg Democratic Action Committee (JODAC) 116
Jordan 36–7, 141, 143
Joseph, Helen 106
justice, concept of 15–16

Kach Party 69
Kadima Party 126
Kahane, Meir 40, 69
Kaminer, Reuven 75, 76, 125, 126, 127, 203–4
Kane-Berman, John 96, 99
Kasrils, Ronnie 177
Katz, Stanley N. 23, 82, 92, 94, 95, 137, 208
Keller, Adam 154
Kiloh, Margaret 57
Kimerling, Baruch 35–6, 68
King, Martin Luther 20
Knox, Colin 23, 27–8, 93, 94, 95, 96, 110–11, 134–5, 137–8, 171, 207
Kuwait, invasion of 143

Labour Party 72, 76–7, 84, 125–6, 140, 147–8, 179–80

land acquisition 30–1
law: discrimination by 30–2; equality by 14
Law of Association (1980) 77–8
Law of Return (1950) 31
Lebanon, war on 37, 189
Lederach, John Paul 2–3, 110
leftist groups: differences 183, 184–5; Israel 159–63; similarities 180–1, 182; South Africa 115–19
leftist parties, Israel 127–8
Leibowitz, Yeshaayahu 132–3
Lemon, Anthony 90, 92
Lerman, Debby 165
liberal groups/organizations: differences 183, 184, 185, 188, 189; Israel 82, 126–7; similarities 180–1; South Africa 97–115
liberal Zionist groups, Israel 139–59
liberation movements: support from neighbouring states 44; visions and strategies 41–3
Likud Party 78, 126, 141
literature review 22–4
Lloyd, John 56
Lomsky-Feder, Edna 39
Lustick, Ian 31, 68

Machover, Moshe 165
Machsom Watch 129, 138, 151, 155–6
macro analysis 9, 175–9
mainstream leftist groups 116–18, 188
mainstream liberal organizations 99–100, 181, 183, 186, 188
Makhoul, Ameer 135
Maleker, Molly 128–9, 155
Mandela, Nelson 1, 11, 103, 108–9, 113
Manna, Adel 35–6
Mapai Party 64, 74, 75, 125–6
Mapam Party 125–6
Marx–Leninists 91
Matzpen 128, 130, 133, 160, 162, 169
media 38, 39–40
Meir, Golda 28–9
Meretz Party 78, 91, 127, 138, 140, 147
meta-conflict 124–5; definition of 3–4
micro analysis 9, 179–89
Migdal, Joel 77, 81
militarization 35–6, 176–7
minority status 28–9
Mitchell, Thomas G. 40
Mizrahi Jews 74, 78, 81, 128, 189
Mobilizing for peace (Gidron/Katz/ Hasenfeld) 23, 94, 137

Mochover, Moshe 160
Moloi, Pascal P. 105
Morris, Benny 29
Movement Against Israeli Apartheid in Palestine 160, 163
Movement for Peace and Security 133
Muhammed, Bhabha 79
Muhareb, Mahmoud 165

Naidoo, Phyllis 118
Nakba 155, 160, 162, 186
Namibia 36
Nathan, Laurie 113
national consensus 78–80, 136–7
National Party (NP) 55–60, 61, 62–3, 66, 90, 113, 179, 185
National Peace Accord 113
National Union of South African Students (NUSAS) 100–1, 103, 104–6, 107, 112–13, 116, 189
nationalism 4–5, 17, 27, 55–60, 63, 65–6, 71–2, 90
Native Act (1913) 26, 30, 176
Natives' Representative Council 58
Naude, Beyers 106, 113–14
Nazi Germany 104
neighbouring states, support from 44
Neturie Karta 133, 160, 162–3
Neuberger, Binyamin 27
New Israel Fund (NIF) 82, 135
New Profile 129, 151, 158, 170
Ngeleza, Bangani 171
non-citizens versus citizens 46
non-liberal democracy 70

objective-driven protest model 92–3
Occupation Magazine 163
Oliver, Mike 112
Oppenheimer, Harry 100
oppression as means of control 34–5
Orient House 152
Ormond, Roger 57
Oslo Accords (1993): aftermath 10; building blocks 165; Declaration of Principles 152, 156; effects of 17–18; failure of 132, 156, 161, 166–7, 178; and PNA 43; support for 22, 126, 143–5, 152, 154
Oz ve Shalom (Strength and Peace) 133

Palestine Liberation Organization (PLO): dialogue with 134, 136, 142–3, 146–7; Israeli individuals in 163–7; National Covenant 166; political agreements 37; strategies/visions 17, 47–8, 160, 185, 193
Palestine National Congress 164
Palestine National Council (PNC) 163
Palestinian National Authority (PNA) 43, 136, 161, 195
Palestinian–Israeli Joint Action Committee 151
Pappé, Ilan 128, 138, 162–3, 177
Parents Against Silence 133
Parents Circle 149
Paton, Alan 101
peace, concept of 19–22
peace and conflict resolution organizations 94–5, 182
'peace as absence of war' 95–6
peace building, definition of 2–3
Peace building in Northern Ireland, Israel and South Africa (Knox/Quirk) 23, 93, 137
Peace Covenant (Brit Shalom) 132
Peace Now (PN): membership 129, 130; officers' letter 204; and Oslo Accords 156, 166; political inconsistency of 154; role of 138, 140–8, 169–70; Settlements Watch programme 170; and war on Lebanon 189
'peace with justice' 95–6
Pedahzur, Ami 38–9, 68, 69
Peled, Matti 68, 76, 77–8, 164
People's Council 73
People's Peace Campaign 129, 140, 146, 148
Peres, Shimon 148
Peres Centre for Peace 13, 22, 138, 140, 148–9
Peretz, Amir 147–8
Peri, Yoram 39
Plato 14, 21
Pogrund, Benjamin 38
policy, discrimination by 30–2
political consensus 80
political equality 12–14
political parties: Israel 125–8; South Africa 90–1
political polarization 66
political positions, inconsistency in 154
political system: comparison of 85–7; differences 177–9; Israel 67–73; similarities 175–7; South Africa 55–60
politics of consensus 64–5
Politics of Protest (Kaminer) 203–4
Popular Front for the Liberation of Palestine 163

254 Index

Population Registration Act (1950) 30, 176
post-Zionists 82–3
Pottinger, Brian 110
power sharing 96
primary data 8
Progressive Federal Party (PFP) 90–1, 97, 106, 107, 113
progressive liberal organizations 98–9, 100–15, 184, 185, 186
Progressive Party (PP) 62, 90–1, 97, 106, 185
property rights 111–12
protest groups/organizations: categorizing 93–7, 137–9, 205–6; in context 90–3, 124–37; definition of 3; membership of 128–30, 181–2; reasons for joining 92, 130–1, 181–2; roles 188
protest model, Israel 131–2
Public Safety Act (1953) 30
Pundak, Ron 22, 148, 165, 171

Quaker Peace Centre 96
Quirk, Padraic 23, 27–8, 93, 94, 95, 96, 110–11, 134–5, 137–8, 171, 207

Rabbis for Human Rights (RHR) 131, 138
Rabin, Yitzhak 154, 191
racism, concept of 16–18
racist notions 26–30
radical leftist groups 118–19, 187–8
Rand Daily Mail 101
Rawls, John 15
Refusniks 129, 151, 157–9
regional superpower status 36–7
Reinhart, Tanya 137, 163, 177
religion, role of 46–7, 70–1
religious organizations 113–15
religious support 178
religious supremacy 26–8
research methodology 4–24
research variables 4–6, 9
Reservation of Separate Amenities Act (1953) 30
Reshef, Tsali 141, 143
retributive justice 15–16
right-wing parties, Israel 125
Rodinson, Maxime 68, 69

Sachs, Albie 117
Said, Edward 44, 68, 69
Sarid, Yossi 143, 144, 148
Schmidt, David 108, 112
seasonal activism 190

Second Intifada (2000) 104, 108, 120–1, 142–3, 146–7, 150, 152–3, 161, 166
second-track diplomacy 134, 164–7, 181, 186–8
security issues 111–12
Separate Amenities Act No 49 (1953) 32
separation 57–8; failure of 177–8; as solution 32–4
Sephardim Jews 45
settler's colonial states 68–70
Shafir, Gershon 68, 76, 77–8
Shamir, Israel 142, 163
Sharabi, Hisham 36
Shararah (Spark) Group 130, 160
Sheministem 129, 158
Shinui Party 140
Sillbergh, David M. 7
Slabbert, Frederik van Zyl 64
Slovo, Joe 118
socio-economic equality 14
South Africa: categorizing white protest groups/individual activism 93–7, 205, 207–8; civil society 60–7; liberal protest groups/organizations 97–115; period of study 10–11; political system 55–60; protest groups in context 90–3; whites in leftist (black-run) resistance groups 115–19
South Africa Act (1909) 56
South Africa Foundation 100
South African Bureau of Racial Affairs 65
South African Communist Party (SACP) 91, 101, 102, 115–16, 118, 121, 122, 160, 181, 184–5, 191
South African Congress of Democrats 106
South African Council of Churches (SACC) 16, 46, 106, 107, 113–15, 117–18, 183
South African Institute of Race Relations (SAIRR) 94–5, 96, 99–100; Operation Hunger 100
South African National Students Congress (SANSCO) 105, 106
South African Student Congress (SASCO) 106
Soweto Civic Association 113
state boundaries 72–3
state–civil society relations: Israel 76–83; similarities 176; South Africa 62–5
state legitimacy 5, 45–6, 59, 151, 191
Steel and Engineering Industries Federation of South Africa 100
strategies, liberation movements 41–3
student unions 104–6

study, period of 9–11
Suzman, Helen 66, 91, 100
Svirsky, Gila 153–4
Sweet, Mark 117–18

Ta'aush 129, 138, 151, 153, 155–6, 163
Taayush 128
Tamir, Yuli 147–8
targeted assassinations 34
Terrorism Act (1967) 34
Thobejane, Makgane 96, 108, 118
Thom, H.B. 64
Timm, Angelika 75
totalitarian systems 4, 53, 57
trade unions 41, 44, 74–5, 116–17
transition period: Israel 128; South Africa 91–2
tribal democracy 68–70
Trotskyites 91
truth, concept of 18–19
Truth and Reconciliation Commission 16
Tzabar, Shimon 160

Umkhonto we Sizwe 113
Union (Ihud) 132
United Democratic Front (UDF): and conscription 106–7; Freedom Charter 101–2; leadership of 10, 43; membership 96, 98; partnerships 147, 193; strategy/visions 93, 94, 112, 115, 120, 182, 191; support for 66, 114, 121; whites in 116–18, 181
United Nations (UN): Committee on the Elimination of Racial Discrimination 32; Conventions 17, 49; Resolution 194 131, 153; Resolution 242 142
United Party (UP) 57–9, 62, 90–1
universities 64–5, 101, 106, 189
University of Natal 101
University of Witwatersrand 89, 101

Urban Foundation 63, 100

van der Merwe, H.W. 112
visions, liberation movements 41–3

Waddy, Nicholas L. 57
Wall 31, 33–4, 35, 136, 147, 153, 162
Warschawski, Michael 68, 69, 79, 80, 144–5, 165, 177
Weizmann, Chaim 29–30, 72
Wentzel, Jill 97–8
Wessels, Erika 104
West Bank 33, 141
wheel model 6
White, Caroline 112
white civil society, definition of 65–7
white protest groups: categorizing 93–7; culture shift 184
whites: in leftist (black-run) groups 115–19, 185; in mainstream leftist groups 116–18; in radical leftist groups 118–19
Wight, Martin 21
Wilner, Meir 127
Women Against the War 134
Women in Black (WIB) 104, 128–9, 138, 151, 154, 156–7
World Council of Churches 63, 114

Yesh Gvul 129, 134, 138, 151, 157–8
Yishai, Yael 68, 76, 77
Younis, Mona 43
Youth Congress 116

Zionism: legitimacy of 45–6; nature of 70–3
Zionist Congress (1897) 27, 70–1
Zionist Israel, civil society under 76–83
Zionist protest groups 139–59
Zochrot 160, 161–2, 163, 169, 170, 189

eBooks – at www.eBookstore.tandf.co.uk

A library at your fingertips!

eBooks are electronic versions of printed books. You can store them on your PC/laptop or browse them online.

They have advantages for anyone needing rapid access to a wide variety of published, copyright information.

eBooks can help your research by enabling you to bookmark chapters, annotate text and use instant searches to find specific words or phrases. Several eBook files would fit on even a small laptop or PDA.

NEW: Save money by eSubscribing: cheap, online access to any eBook for as long as you need it.

Annual subscription packages

We now offer special low-cost bulk subscriptions to packages of eBooks in certain subject areas. These are available to libraries or to individuals.

For more information please contact webmaster.ebooks@tandf.co.uk

We're continually developing the eBook concept, so keep up to date by visiting the website.

www.eBookstore.tandf.co.uk